MW00632617

FASHION DOLL Dream Home™

the Needlecraft Shop™

PUBLISHER • Donna Robertson
DESIGN DIRECTOR • Fran Rohus
PRODUCTION DIRECTOR • Ange Workman

EDITORIAL
Senior Editor • Janet Tipton
Editorial & Graphics Team • Trina Burch, Kristine Kirst, Susan Koellner,
Kim Pierce, Jennifer Simcik, Marianne Telesca

PHOTOGRAPHERS
Tammy Cromer-Campbell, Mary Craft, Renée Agee

PRODUCTION MANAGER
Jean Schrecengost

BOOK DESIGN
Debby Keel

DESIGN COORDINATOR
Brenda Wendling

BUSINESS
C.E.O. • John Robinson
Vice President, Customer Service • Karen Pierce
Vice President, Marketing • Greg Deily
Vice President, M.I.S. • John Trotter

ACKNOWLEGEMENTS
The projects in this book were made using Darice® plastic canvas, Nylon Plus™ yarn, metallic cord, acrylic mirrors, acrylic stones, silver pearl beads and rattail cord, and Spinrite yarn. Sincerest thanks to the manufacturers for supplying these products to our designers. Thanks also to the designers and to the other professionals whose talents and dedication have made this book possible. BARBIE® doll and friends pictured on cover with permission of Mattel, Inc. ©1996 Mattel, Inc. All rights reserved. Special thanks to David Norris of Quebecor Printing Book Group, Kingsport, TN.

Copyright ©1996 *The Needlecraft Shop*, LLC
All rights reserved. No part of this book may be reproduced in any form or by any means without the written permission of the publisher, excepting for brief quotations in connection with reviews written specifically for inclusion in magazines, newspapers and other publications.

Library of Congress Cataloging-in-Publication Data
ISBN: 1-57367-066-9
First Printing: 1996
Library of Congress Catalogue Number: 95-72038
Published and Distributed by *The Needlecraft Shop,* LLC.

Dear Fashion Doll Friends,

The popularity and universal appeal of fashion dolls has been with us for decades now. Who would have guessed that an 11½" doll would be the favorite toy of children of all ages? More adults enjoy collecting dolls than ever before, and those of us who enjoy stitching on plastic canvas are no exception. It was you, our customers, who encouraged us to continue to bring fashion doll projects to life.

When The Needlecraft Shop began to publish plastic canvas designs, a fashion doll carrying case appeared in the very first issue of Plastic Canvas Magazine in the late 1980s. Everyone loved it. Since that time, we have published many fashion doll projects in our magazines and books. Favorites include Fashion Doll Fantasy, a collection of plastic canvas and crochet designs, and Fashion Doll Dream Castle, the ultimate story-time doll house. Both books have found a wide audience and are available from The Needlecraft Shop catalog.

This book is in your hands now because of the many wonderful customers who have called and written to us with their comments about our patterns. When the fashion doll furnishings and camper collections went out of print, Mary Ann Johnson and several other customer service representatives here at The Needlecraft Shop – after hearing from so many of you who still wanted the patterns – suggested that we reprint the collections together in one volume.

Many, many hours have been spent designing, stitching, constructing and finishing these projects, and countless children and grandchildren have been overjoyed to receive gifts made from the patterns in this book. We have received numerous letters from stitchers who have won ribbons at their county fairs with the projects in this book, and one finished pattern was the prize in a raffle, the proceeds going to a charitable cause. What could be more fun and rewarding than spending all afternoon playing with our dolls and making things for them?

This book is dedicated to you – loving folks who enjoy creating handcrafted toys – our fashion doll friends. From our editors, from our design, production and photography departments, and from our very special customer service representatives, we wish you …

Happy Stitching!

Janet

Meet the Designers

Diane T. Ray *Hours of research go into the designs of Diane T. Ray. When she was preparing to design the living room projects in this book, she visited local furniture stores to see how things were made. Her husband, Rick, encourages Diane's love of designing. He cheerfully accompanied her on visits to the stores, where they lent new meaning to the words "just looking," as they peeked under sofas and examined chair construction. Diane, the mother of two teenaged boys, also designed the bedroom, bathroom and laundry room projects in* Fashion Doll Dream Home.

Diane's attention to detail is evident in the sturdy construction of each piece. "I like to design things that actually work," she says. "I don't want to make something that a child will get tired of playing with after only a few minutes." The bathtub is constructed to hold a small aluminum loaf pan so you can actually use water, and the bellows for the living room fireplace actually squeeze together. Her talents have been appreciated by fashion doll fans all over the country since her first design collection was published in 1992. Diane and her family live in Hobbs, New Mexico.

Trudy Bath Smith and Stephen J. Smith *Being parents of a young child who loves outdoor adventures, Stephen J. and Trudy Bath Smith put their heads together to create the camper and camper accessories in* Fashion Doll Dream Home.

Trudy, a member of the Society of Craft Designers, has been designing with plastic canvas since the early 1990s. She has been responsible for some of the most innovative and delightful designs in the crafts industry, and she credits her son, Zachary, for much of her inspiration. Trudy operates a registered day care service in her home and plans to return to college in the near future. She also enjoys bread dough modeling and designing with beads, chenille, feathers, felt, fur and pom-poms.

Stephen's experience as a mechanic helps him plan sturdy and fun projects for children, such as trucks, cars and games. Stephen now works with developmentally disabled children at a public school near his home in Rushville, New York. In his free time he helps Trudy with her day care business and enjoys spending time with his son.

Carolyn Christmas *A member of the Society of Craft Designers since 1985, professional designer and writer Carolyn Christmas is widely known for her many published needlecraft projects, including the patio projects in* Fashion Doll Dream Home. *Her unique talents include blending form, color and texture in the creation of her designs. Carolyn is the mother of three daughters, the youngest of whom are twins. Carolyn, who also designs crochet, quilts, cross stitch and other crafts, enjoys doll making and doll play. She and her daughters live in Tyler, Texas.*

CONTENTS

BARBIE® doll and friends pictured with permission of Mattel, Inc. ©1996 Mattel, Inc. All rights reserved.

Relax beside a roaring fire in your fashion doll living room. Bright floral motifs on upholstery can be accented with bouquets and matching pillows.

BARBIE® doll and friends pictured with permission of Mattel, Inc. ©1996 Mattel, Inc. All rights reserved.

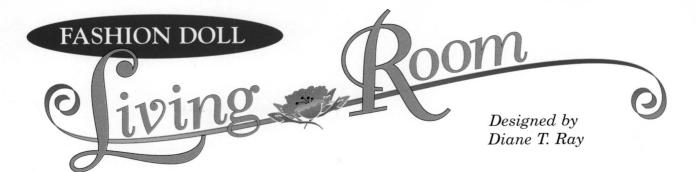

FASHION DOLL Living Room

Designed by
Diane T. Ray

MATERIALS FOR ENTIRE SET:

- ❑ 16 sheets of 7-count plastic canvas
- ❑ ¾ sheet of dusty rose 7-count plastic canvas
- ❑ Scraps of black 7-count plastic canvas
- ❑ Two sheets of 12" x 18" or larger 7-count plastic canvas
- ❑ Two 3" plastic canvas radial circles
- ❑ Four gold 5-mm. beads
- ❑ 90 coordinating color 4-mm. pearl beads
- ❑ 20 gold 4-mm. beads
- ❑ 12 reddish-brown 10 x 12-mm. bell beads
- ❑ Two 9" x 12" sheets of dusty rose felt and matching sewing thread (optional)
- ❑ 4" x 10" aluminum or craft foil
- ❑ 4" x 10" poster board
- ❑ 5" x 6½" black netting or nylon hosiery fabric
- ❑ Two pink ribbon rose and berry sprays (optional)
- ❑ One each pink and rose 9-mm. satin ribbon rose cluster
- ❑ Silk greenery to make 7"-tall plant
- ❑ Spanish moss
- ❑ Sewing needle and off-white thread
- ❑ Polyester fiberfill
- ❑ 1" x 3" x 21" Styrofoam® block
- ❑ 1" square piece of ½"-thick foam rubber
- ❑ Black permanent marker
- ❑ Five ⅝", two ¾" and three 1" metal washers
- ❑ 12" wooden ¼" dowel
- ❑ Craft glue or glue gun
- ❑ Metallic cord:
  - ❑ White/Gold – 142½ yds.
- ❑ Worsted-weight or plastic canvas yarn:

Nylon Plus™	Needloft™ yarn
❑ #02	#00 Black – 74½ yds.
❑ #12	#05 Lavender – 10 oz.
❑ #44	#14 Cinnamon – 16½ yds.
❑ #47	#16 Sandstone – 3 yds.
❑ #32	#29 Forest – 21½ yds.
❑ #24	#39 Eggshell – 11 oz.
❑ #56	#44 Orchid – 15 yds.
❑ #26	#57 Yellow – 5 yds.
❑ #17	#58 Bright Orange – 2 yds.
❑ #55	#59 Plum – 14½ yds.

For materials for individual items, see individual materials lists.

FIREPLACE & SCREEN

SIZE: Fireplace is 6¼" x 9¼" at base x 6⅛" tall; Screen is 4⅝" x 6¼".

MATERIALS:

- ❑ Three sheets of 7-count plastic canvas
- ❑ 5" x 6½" black netting or nylon hosiery fabric
- ❑ Two pink ribbon rose and berry sprays (optional)
- ❑ Craft glue or glue gun
- ❑ Metallic cord; for amount see Color Key on page 9.
- ❑ Worsted-weight or plastic canvas yarn; for amounts see Color Key.

CUTTING INSTRUCTIONS:

NOTE: Graphs on pages 8 & 9.

A: For base, cut one according to graph.

B: For front and back, cut one according to graph for front and one 39 x 47 holes for back.

C: For sides, cut two 19 x 39 holes.

D: For top, cut one 25 x 54 holes.

E: For top long and short rim pieces, cut two each according to graphs.

F: For firebox back wall, cut one 31 x 35 holes (no graph).

G: For firebox side and top walls, cut two 18 x 31 holes and one 18 x 35 holes (no graphs).

H: For screen center panel, cut one according to graph.

I: For screen side panels, cut two according to graph.

STITCHING INSTRUCTIONS:

1: Using colors and stitches indicated, work A, B (leave indicated areas unworked), C, D and E pieces according to graphs. Fill in uncoded areas of back B, C and D pieces using Eggshell and Continental Stitch; Overcast front B as indicated on graph. Using Black and Continental Stitch, work F and G pieces. Using metallic cord and Straight Stitch, embroider detail on front B as indicated; Overcast unfinished edges of A and unfinished cutout edges of H and I pieces.

2: For firebox, holding right sides together, with Black, Whipstitch F and G pieces together according to Firebox Assembly Diagram. With Eggshell, Whipstitch sides and top of firebox to wrong side of front B as indicated.

3: With matching colors, Whipstitch firebox and front to base as indicated. Holding wrong sides together, with Eggshell, Whipstitch back B and C pieces to base as indicated; Whipstitch side edges of front, sides and back together.

4: Holding wrong sides together, with cord, Whipstitch D and E pieces together as indicated. With Eggshell, Overcast unfinished bottom edges of rim; loosely Whipstitch angled edges together. Glue bottom edge of rim to top of fireplace as shown in photo. If desired, twist ends of rose and berry sprays together; pin or glue to top of fireplace.

5: For screen, with cord, Whipstitch one I to each side of H as indicated; Overcast unfinished edges. Stretching nylon or netting slightly, glue to wrong side of screen; trim to fit.

H – Fireplace Screen Center Panel
(cut 1) 20 x 30 holes

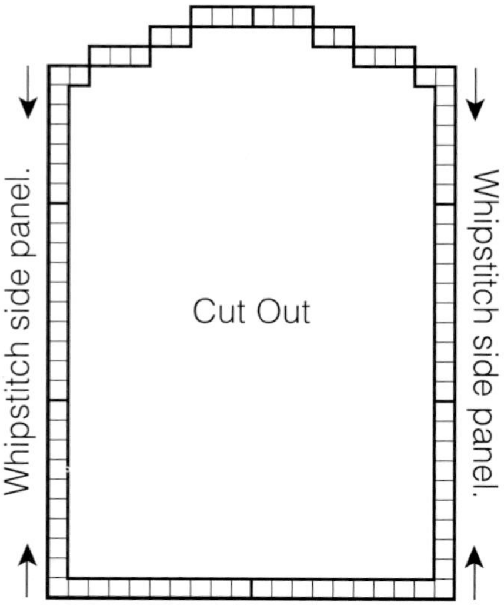

D – Fireplace Top (cut 1) 25 x 54 holes

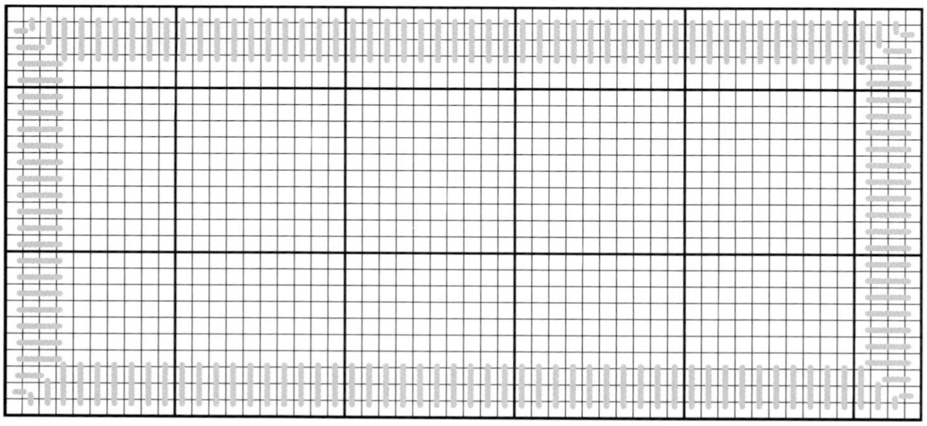

I – Fireplace Screen Side Panel
(cut 2) 9 x 29 holes

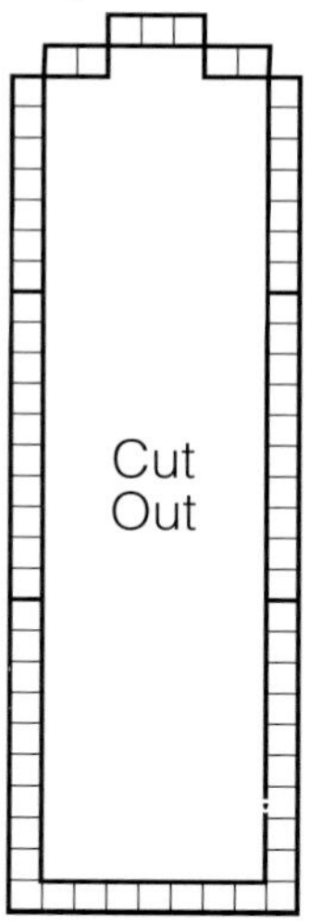

A – Fireplace Base (cut 1) 41 x 61 holes

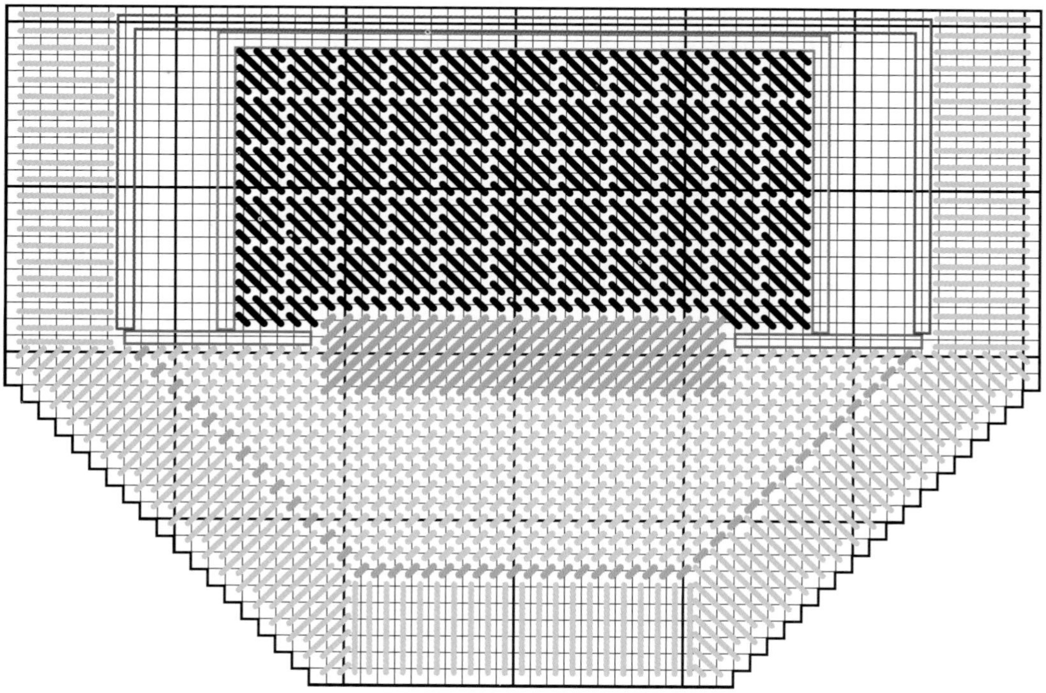

Firebox Assembly Diagram

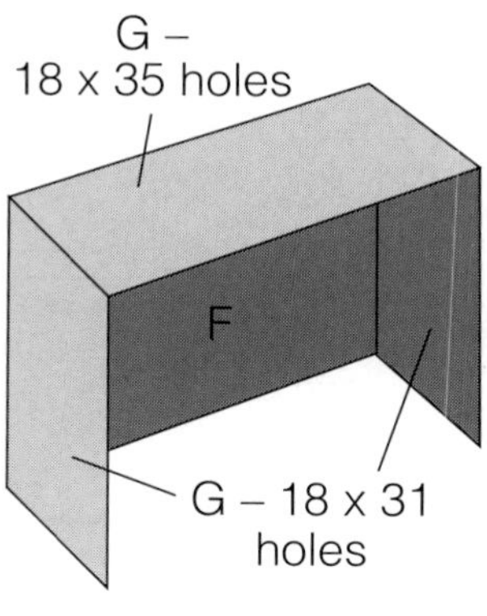

COLOR KEY: Fireplace & Screen

Metallic cord
White/Gold – 12 yds.

Nylon Plus™ Needloft™ yarn
#02 #00 Black – 70 yds.
#24 #39 Eggshell – 4 oz.

STITCH KEY:

- Backstitch/Straight Stitch
- Firebox Attachment
- Front Attachment
- Back & Sides Attachment

B – Fireplace Back (cut 1) 39 x 47 holes

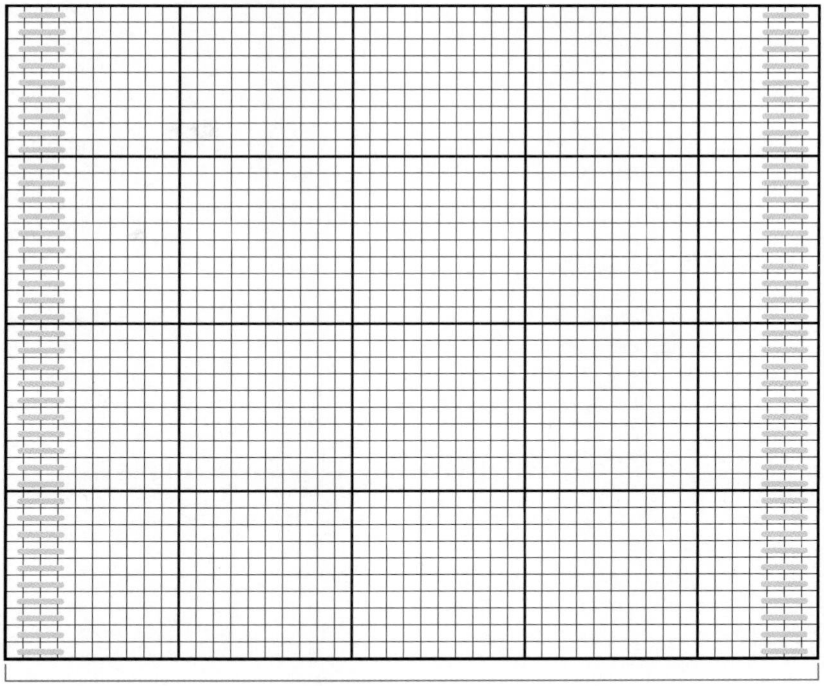

Whipstitch to base.

E – Fireplace Top Short Rim
(cut 2) 4 x 25 holes
Whipstitch to top.

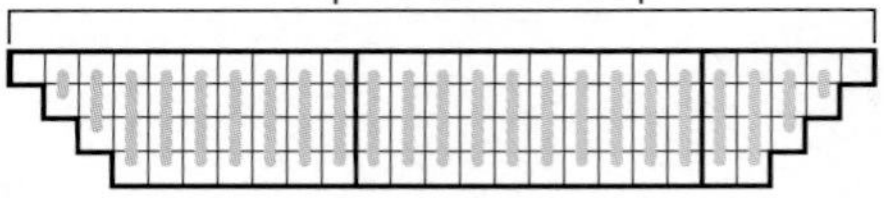

E – Fireplace Top Long Rim (cut 2) 4 x 54 holes
Whipstitch to top.

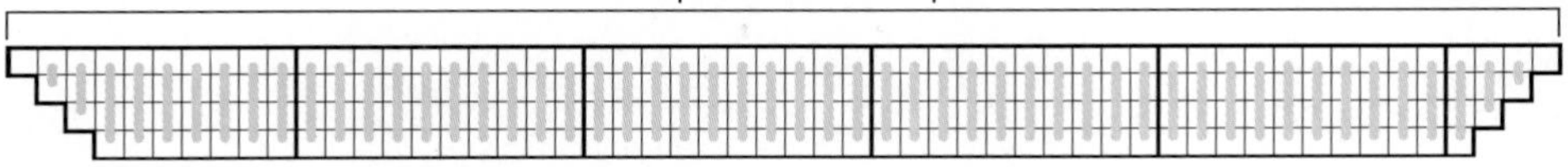

C – Fireplace Side
(cut 2) 19 x 39 holes

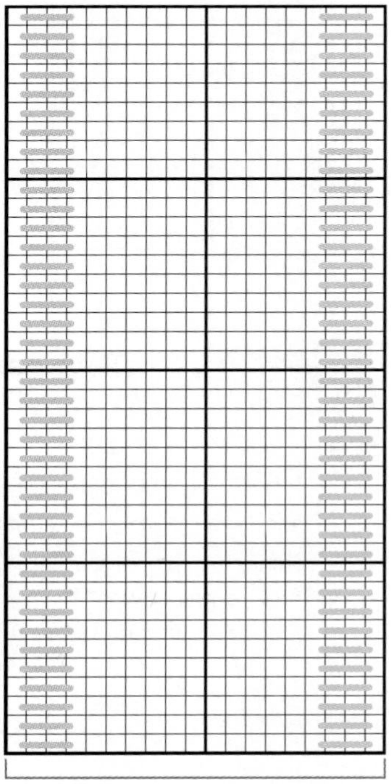

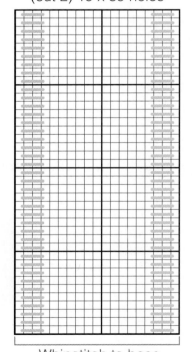

Whipstitch to base.

B – Fireplace Front (cut 1) 39 x 47 holes

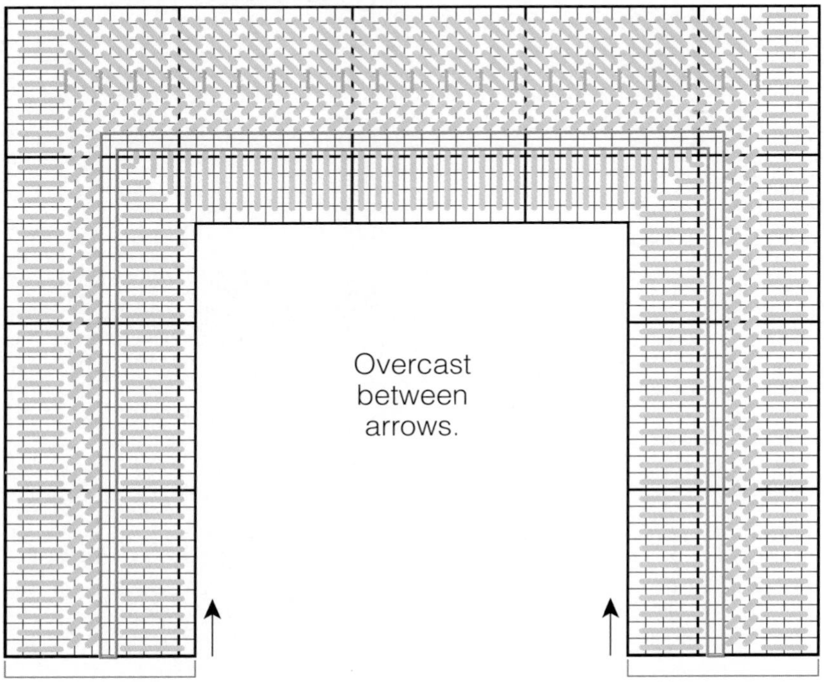

Whipstitch to base.

Whipstitch to base.

LOGS, GRATE & FLAMES

SIZE: Long log is ¾" x 3¼"; short log is ¾" x 2½"; assembled grate with logs and fire is 2" x 3¼" x about 2½" tall and fits inside firebox.

MATERIALS:
- ❏ ¾ sheet of 7-count plastic canvas
- ❏ Scraps of black 7-count plastic canvas
- ❏ Craft glue or glue gun
- ❏ Worsted-weight or plastic canvas yarn; for amounts see Color Key.

CUTTING INSTRUCTIONS:

NOTE: Use black canvas for D and E pieces.

A: For long and short logs, cut three 15 x 20 holes and two 15 x 15 holes.

B: For log ends, cut ten according to graph.

C: For large and small flames, cut two each according to graphs.

D: For grate top, cut one according to graph.

E: For grate base sides and ends, cut two each according to graphs.

STITCHING INSTRUCTIONS:

1: Using colors and stitches indicated, work A (leave uncoded areas unworked), B and C (one each on opposite side of canvas) pieces according to graphs.

2: For each log, overlapping two holes at each edge as indicated on graphs, with Cinnamon, Whipstitch together as indicated. Whipstitch one B to each end of log.

3: For flames, holding matching C pieces wrong sides together, with Yellow for bottom edge and with Bright Orange, Whipstitch together.

4: For grate base, alternating sides and ends, with Black, Whipstitch unworked E pieces together. Whipstitch base and unworked D together as indicated.

5: For fire, glue two long and one short logs to grate top; glue flames to each side of short log as shown in photo. Set remaining logs aside to place in Basket.

B – Log End
(cut 10)
4 x 4 holes

C – Small Flames
(cut 2)
4 x 11 holes

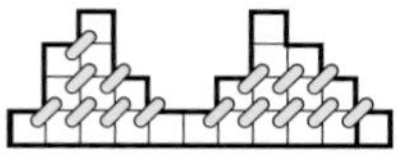

A – Long Log
(cut 3) 15 x 20 holes

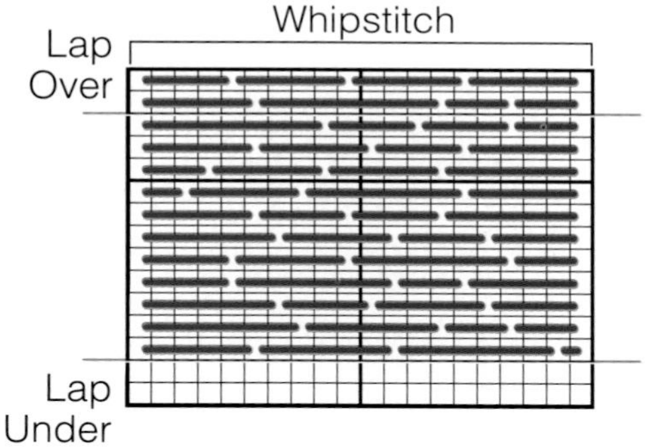

C – Large Flames
(cut 2)
7 x 17 holes

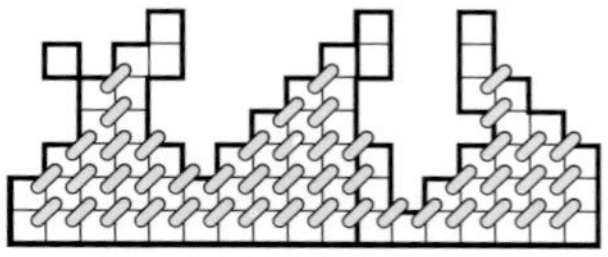

D – Grate Top
(cut 1 from black)
13 x 16 holes

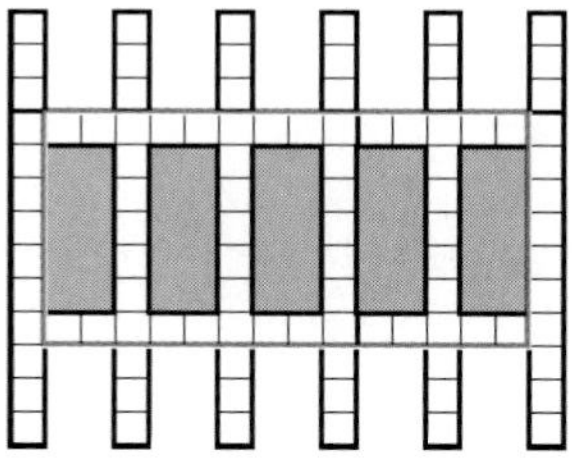

Cut out gray areas.

E – Grate Base Side
(cut 2 from black)
3 x 14 holes

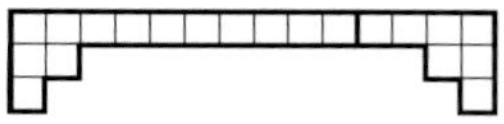

A – Short Log
(cut 2) 15 x 15 holes

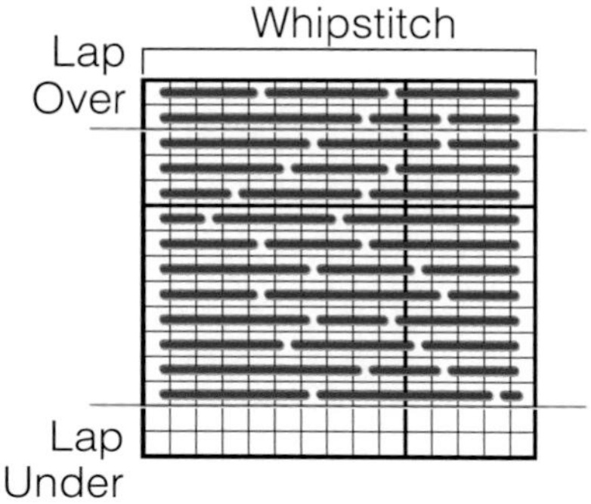

E – Grate Base End
(cut 2 from black)
3 x 7 holes

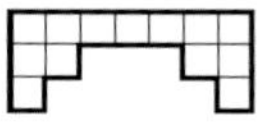

COLOR KEY: Logs, etc.

Nylon Plus™	Needloft™ yarn
☐ #02	#00 Black – 1½ yds.
■ #44	#14 Cinnamon – 14 yds.
▩ #47	#16 Sandstone – 3 yds.
⧄ #26	#57 Yellow – 5 yds.
☐ #17	#58 Bright Orange – 2 yds.

STITCH KEY:
☐ Grate Base Attachment

LOG BASKET & TOOLS

SIZE: Log Basket is 2¼" x 3¼" x 2¾" tall; Tool Stand is 1¼" x 2½" x 3⅜" tall; each Tool is 3¾" long; Bellows is 2¾" long.

MATERIALS:

- ❑ One sheet of 7-count plastic canvas
- ❑ Four gold 5-mm. beads
- ❑ Two gold 4-mm. beads
- ❑ Sewing needle and off-white thread
- ❑ 1" square piece of ½"-thick foam rubber
- ❑ Black permanent marker
- ❑ Craft glue or glue gun
- ❑ Metallic cord; for amount see Color Key.
- ❑ Worsted-weight or plastic canvas yarn; for amounts see Color Key.

CUTTING INSTRUCTIONS:

NOTE: Graphs continued on page 12.

A: For Basket bottom, cut one according to graph.

B: For Basket sides, cut two according to graph.

C: For Basket handle, cut one 1 x 34 holes (no graph).

D: For Stand top and bottom, cut one each according to graphs.

E: For Stand back, cut one according to graph.

F: For Stand sides, cut two according to graph.

G: For Shovel, cut two according to graph.

H: For Shovel lip, cut one 1 x 17 holes (no graph).

I: For Poker, cut two according to graph.

J: For Broom, cut two according to graph.

K: For Bellows, cut two according to graph.

STITCHING INSTRUCTIONS:

1: Using colors and stitches indicated, work A, B, bottom D, G, I (one on opposite side of canvas), J and K pieces according to graphs. With metallic cord, Overcast unfinished edges of C and cutout edges of E and F pieces.

2: For Basket, with cord, Whipstitch one B to each side of A as indicated on graphs; Overcast unfinished edges. Glue ends of handle to sides as indicated. For feet, with thread, sew 5-mm. beads to bottom as indicated. Sew one 4-mm. bead to each end of handle as indicated on B graph.

3: For Stand, with cord, Whipstitch one F to each side of E. With right side of bottom D facing up, Whipstitch D, E and F pieces together as indicated; Overcast unfinished edges.

4: For Shovel, holding G pieces wrong sides together and working through all thicknesses at lip attachment as indicated, with cord for narrow portions of handle and with matching colors, Whipstitch G and H pieces together; with cord, Overcast unfinished edges of lip.

5: For Poker, holding I pieces wrong sides together, with cord for narrow portions of handle and with matching colors as indicated, Whipstitch together.

6: For Broom, with Black, Overcast bristle end of each J piece as indicated. Holding pieces wrong sides together, with cord for narrow portions of handle and with matching colors, Whipstitch unfinished edges together.

NOTE: Trim foam rubber into a circle about the size of a nickel. Color completely with black marker; let dry.

7: For Bellows, with Cinnamon, Overcast bag and handle of each K as indicated. Holding pieces wrong sides together, with cord for unworked tip and with Black, Whipstitch unfinished edges together. Glue foam rubber inside Bellows as indicated.

A – Basket Bottom
(cut 1) 7 x 21 holes

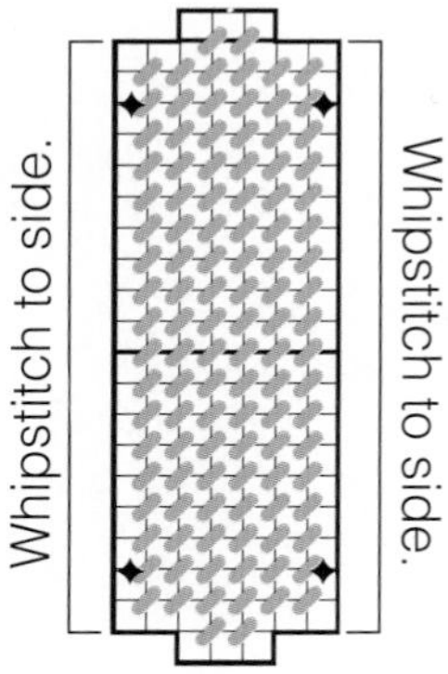

B – Basket Side
(cut 2) 6 x 19 holes

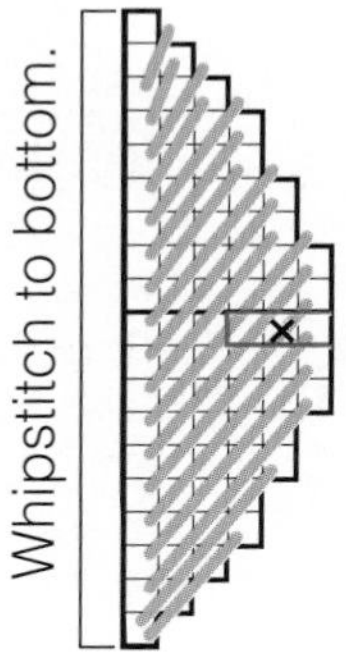

D – Stand Bottom
(cut 1) 11 x 11 holes

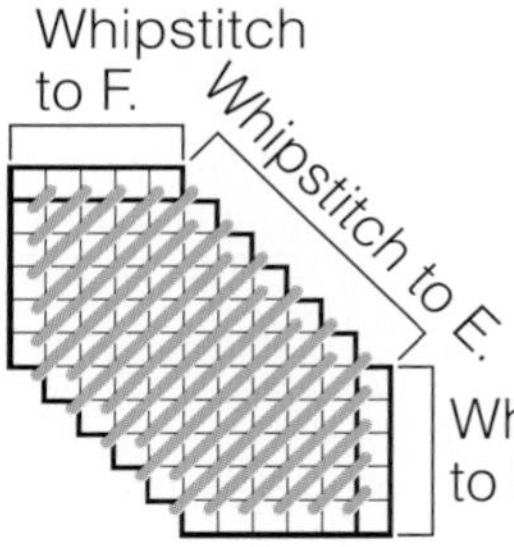

K – Bellows
(cut 2)
7 x 17 holes

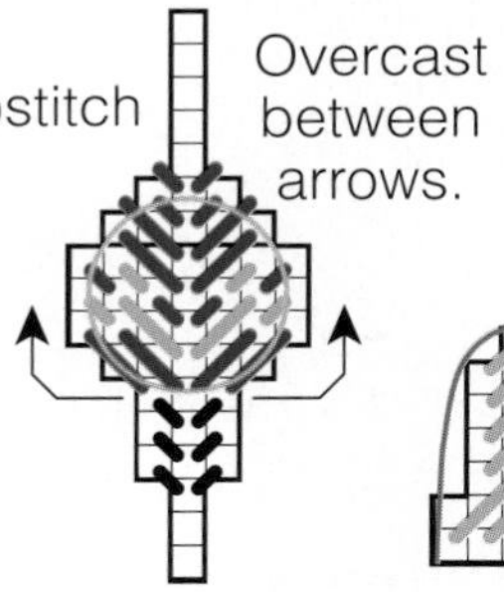

G – Shovel
(cut 2)
7 x 24 holes

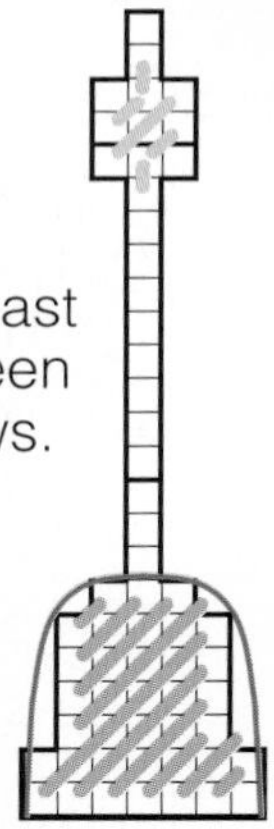

J – Broom
(cut 2)
5 x 24 holes

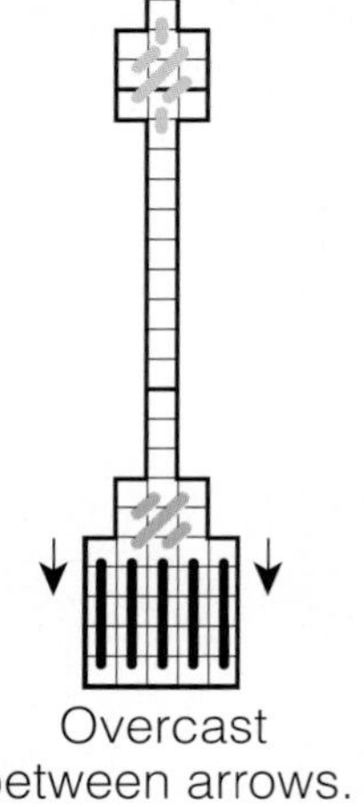

COLOR KEY: Basket & Tools

Metallic cord
- White/Gold – 14 yds.

Nylon Plus™ Needloft™ yarn

Nylon Plus™	Needloft™	
#02	#00 Black	3 yds.
#44	#14 Cinnamon	2½ yds.
#24	#39 Eggshell	1½ yds.

STITCH KEY:
- Handle Placement
- ✦ 5-mm. Bead Attachment
- × 4-mm. Bead Attachment
- Shovel Lip Attachment
- ○ Foam Placement

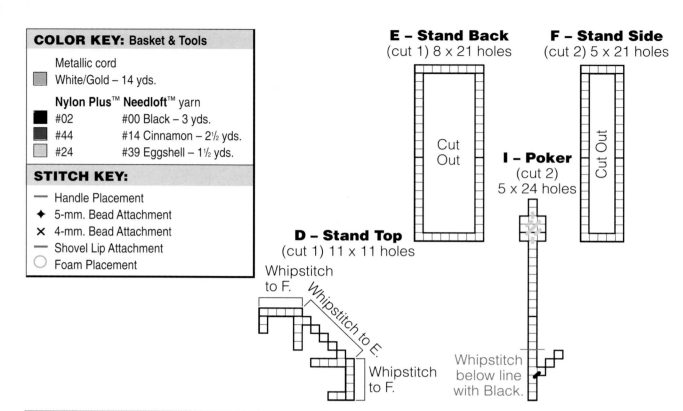

COLOR KEY: Basket & Tools

Metallic cord
- White/Gold – 14 yds.

Nylon Plus™ Needloft™ yarn

#02	#00 Black – 3 yds.
#44	#14 Cinnamon – 2½ yds.
#24	#39 Eggshell – 1½ yds.

STITCH KEY:
- — Handle Placement
- ✦ 5-mm. Bead Attachment
- × 4-mm. Bead Attachment
- — Shovel Lip Attachment
- ○ Foam Placement

E – Stand Back
(cut 1) 8 x 21 holes

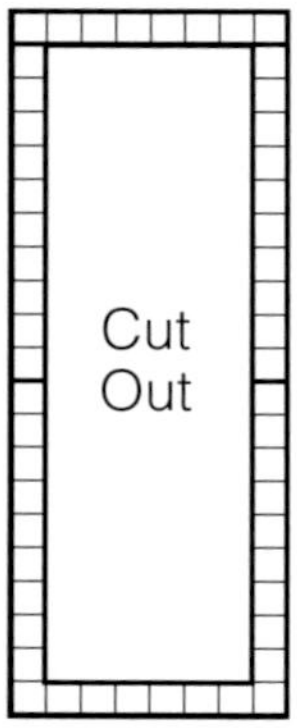

F – Stand Side
(cut 2) 5 x 21 holes

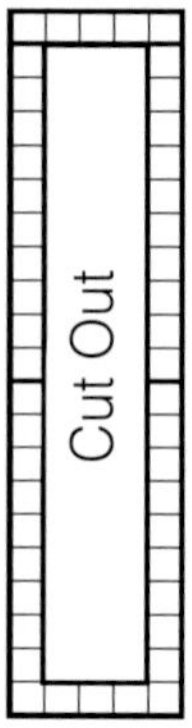

I – Poker
(cut 2)
5 x 24 holes

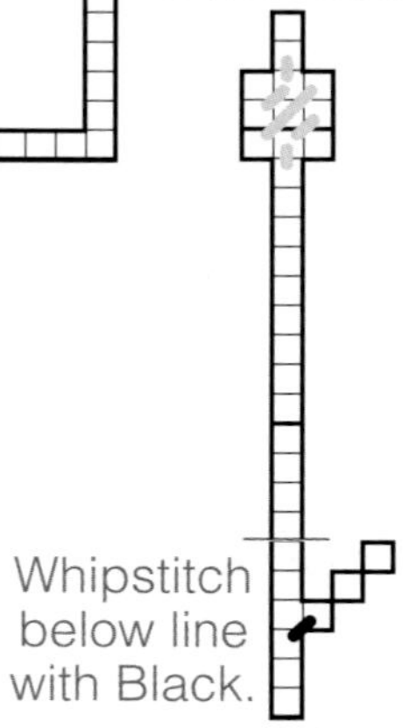

D – Stand Top
(cut 1) 11 x 11 holes

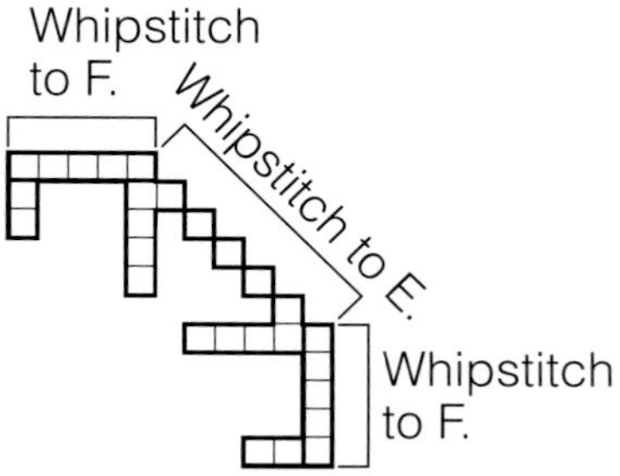

COFFEE TABLE

SIZE: 4½" x 7¼" x 2¾" tall.

MATERIALS:
- ❏ One sheet of 7-count plastic canvas
- ❏ Two 4-mm. gold beads
- ❏ Aluminum foil
- ❏ 4" x 7" poster board
- ❏ Sewing needle and off-white thread
- ❏ Craft glue or glue gun
- ❏ Metallic cord; for amount see Color Key.
- ❏ Worsted-weight or plastic canvas yarn; for amount see Color Key.

CUTTING INSTRUCTIONS:

A: For mirror frame, cut one according to graph.

B: For top, cut one according to graph.

C: For long and short sides, cut two each according to graphs.

D: For mirror, using A as a pattern, cut poster board and foil each ⅛" smaller at outer edges.

COLOR KEY: Coffee Table

Metallic cord
- White/Gold – 13 yds.

Nylon Plus™ Needloft™ yarn

#24	#39 Eggshell – 20 yds.

STITCH KEY:
- o Bead Attachment
- — Sides Attachment
- ☐ Mirror Frame Placement

STITCHING INSTRUCTIONS:

1: Using colors and stitches indicated, work A, B (leave uncoded area unworked) and C pieces according to graphs. With metallic cord, Overcast unfinished edges of A and B pieces.

2: Alternating long and short sides, with cord, Whipstitch C

C – Coffee Table Short Side
(cut 2) 16 x 19 holes

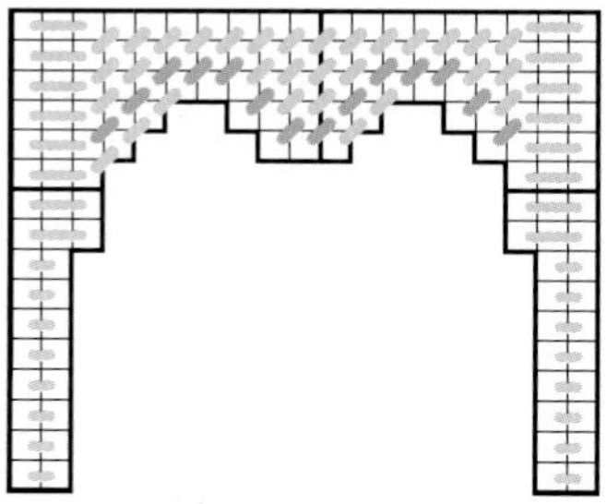

A – Coffee Table Mirror Frame
(cut 1) 25 x 43 holes

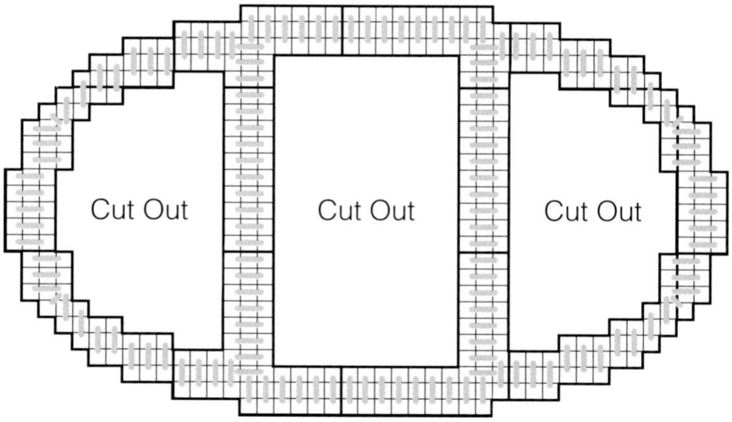

pieces together. With thread, sew one bead to each side as indicated on graph. With Eggshell, Whipstitch sides to wrong side of B as indicated; Overcast unfinished bottom edges.

3: For mirror, glue D pieces together and to wrong side of frame. Glue frame to top as indicated.

B – Coffee Table Top
(cut 1) 29 x 47 holes

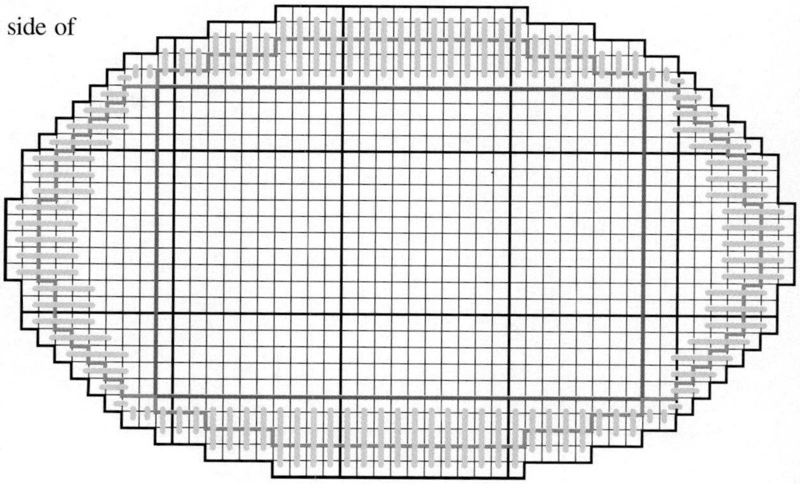

C – Coffee Table Long Side
(cut 2) 16 x 31 holes

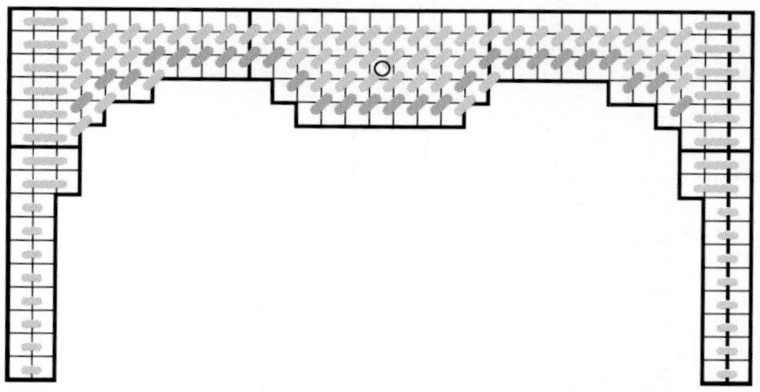

END TABLE

SIZE: 3½" x 4⅜" x 3⅝" tall.

MATERIALS:
- ❏ ½ sheet of 7-count plastic canvas
- ❏ Two 4-mm. gold beads
- ❏ Aluminum foil
- ❏ 3" x 4" poster board
- ❏ Sewing needle and off-white thread
- ❏ Craft glue or glue gun
- ❏ Metallic cord; for amount see Color Key.
- ❏ Worsted-weight or plastic canvas yarn; for amount see Color Key.

CUTTING INSTRUCTIONS:

A: For mirror frame, cut one according to graph.
B: For top, cut one according to graph.
C: For long and short sides, cut two each according to graphs.
D: For mirror, using A as a pattern, cut poster board and foil each ⅛" smaller at outer edges.

STITCHING INSTRUCTIONS:

1: Using End Table pieces in place of Coffee Table pieces, follow Steps 1-3 of Coffee Table on page 12.

A – End Table Mirror Frame
(cut 1) 19 x 24 holes

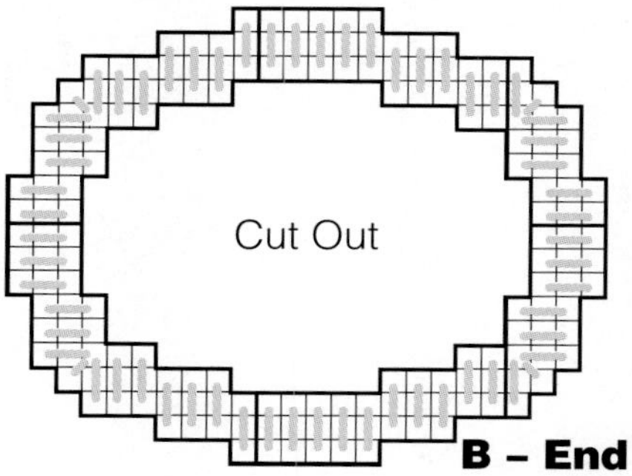

B – End Table Top
(cut 1) 23 x 28 holes

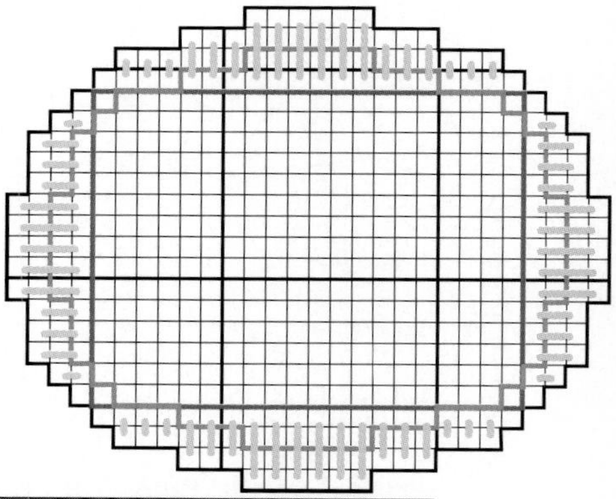

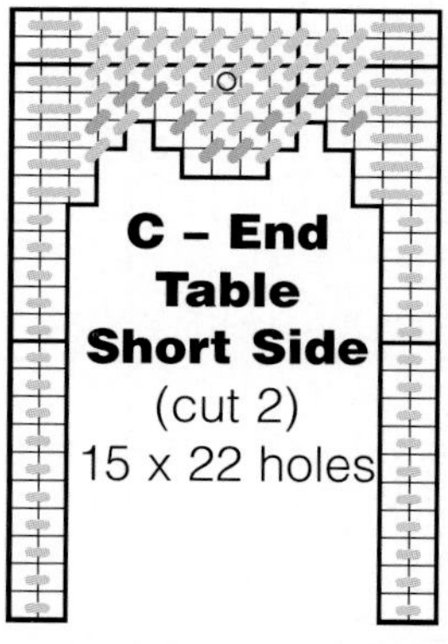

C – End Table Short Side
(cut 2)
15 x 22 holes

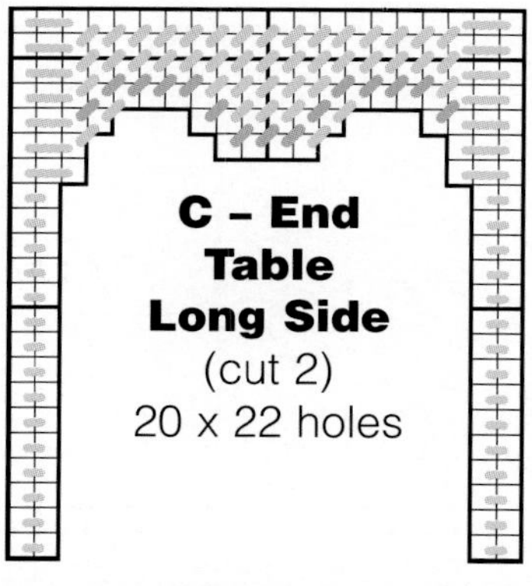

C – End Table Long Side
(cut 2)
20 x 22 holes

COLOR KEY: End Table

Metallic cord		
▩	White/Gold – 7 yds.	
Nylon Plus™ Needloft™ yarn		
▩	#24	#39 Eggshell – 8 yds.

STITCH KEY:
- o Bead Attachment
- — Sides Attachment
- ☐ Mirror Frame Placement

CHAIR

SIZE: 4½" x 7½" x 6⅛" tall.

MATERIALS:

- ❏ Two sheets of 7-count plastic canvas
- ❏ ½ sheet of dusty rose 7-count plastic canvas
- ❏ 12 coordinating color 4-mm. pearl beads
- ❏ Four gold 4-mm. beads
- ❏ Four reddish-brown 10 x 12-mm. bell beads
- ❏ 9" x 12" sheet of dusty rose felt and matching sewing thread (optional)
- ❏ Sewing needle and off-white thread
- ❏ Polyester fiberfill
- ❏ 1" x 3" x 3½" Styrofoam® block
- ❏ Metallic cord; for amount see Color Key.
- ❏ Worsted-weight or plastic canvas yarn; for amounts see Color Key.

CUTTING INSTRUCTIONS:

NOTES: Graphs and diagrams continued on pages 15-17. Use dusty rose canvas for K.

A: For cushion front, cut one according to graph.

B: For top, cut one 7 x 40 holes (no graph).

C: For top ends, cut two 5 x 7 holes (no graph).

D: For top lower ends, cut two 6 x 7 holes (no graph).

E: For seat cushion support, cut one 21 x 24 holes.

F: For right and left armrests, cut two (one for right and one for left) 28 x 41 holes.

G: For armrest bottoms, cut two 3 x 28 holes (no graph).

H: For ends, cut two 16 x 28 holes.

I: For front, cut one according to graph.

J: For back, cut one according to graph.

K: For bottom, cut one from dusty rose 28 x 36 holes (no graph).

L: For optional bottom lining, using K as a pattern, cut one from felt ⅛" smaller at all edges.

M: For seat cushion top and bottom, cut two (one for top and one for bottom) 20 x 22 holes.

N: For seat cushion front and back, cut two (one for front and one for back) 3 x 22 holes (no graph).

O: For seat cushion ends, cut two 3 x 20 holes (no graph).

STITCHING INSTRUCTIONS:

1: Using colors indicated, Continental Stitch and Long Stitch, work A, E, F (leave uncoded areas unworked) and M pieces according to graphs. Using colors indicated, Straight Stitch and Cross Stitch, embroider flowers and leaves on A and one M for top as indicated on graphs. Fill in uncoded areas around embroidery on A (leave lower uncoded area unworked) and top M, and work one N for back using Eggshell and Continental Stitch. Fill in uncoded area of remaining M for bottom and work B, C, D, G, H, I (leave indicated areas unworked), J (leave indicated areas unworked), remaining N for front and O pieces using Lavender and Continental Stitch.

2: With off-white thread, sew coordinating color beads to A and top M as indicated. Using metallic cord and Running Stitch (see Stitch Illustration), embroider F, H, I, J and O pieces as indicated; embroider Lavender N piece according to pattern established on O.

3: With Lavender, Whipstitch B-D pieces together according to Chair/Sofa Assembly Diagram #1. Using cord and Running Stitch and working one stitch over each seam, embroider B and C pieces according to Chair Top Stitch Pattern Guide. Whipstitch A-D pieces together as indicated and according to Chair/Sofa Assembly Diagram #2. (**NOTE:** Back is attached later.)

4: With Eggshell, Whipstitch one long edge of E to right side of A as indicated. Matching bottom edges of armrests and cushion front, with Lavender, Whipstitch each F to A, D and E pieces as indicated and according to Chair/Sofa Assembly Diagram #3. Whipstitch one G to each F and one H to each G

COLOR KEY: Chair

Metallic cord

- ■ White/Gold – 8 yds.

Nylon Plus™ Needloft™ yarn

■	#12	#05 Lavender – 2½ oz.
■	#32	#29 Forest – 3 yds.
■	#24	#39 Eggshell – 18 yds.
■	#56	#44 Orchid – 3 yds.
■	#55	#59 Plum – 2 yds.

STITCH KEY:

- — Backstitch/Straight Stitch
- ✕ Cross Stitch
- ○ Bead Attachment
- ☐ Seat Cushion Support Attachment
- ☐ Cushion Front to Armrest Attachment
- ☐ Top Lower End Attachment
- ☐ Unworked Areas/Armrest to Back Attachment
- — Armrest to Front Attachment (Upper Portion)
- ☐ Unworked Areas/Armrest to Front Attachment (Lower Portion)
- — Armrest Bottom Attachment
- ✦ Leg Attachment

Chair Top Stitch Pattern Guide

H – Chair/Sofa End

(cut 2 each) 16 x 28 holes

Whipstitch to armrest bottom.

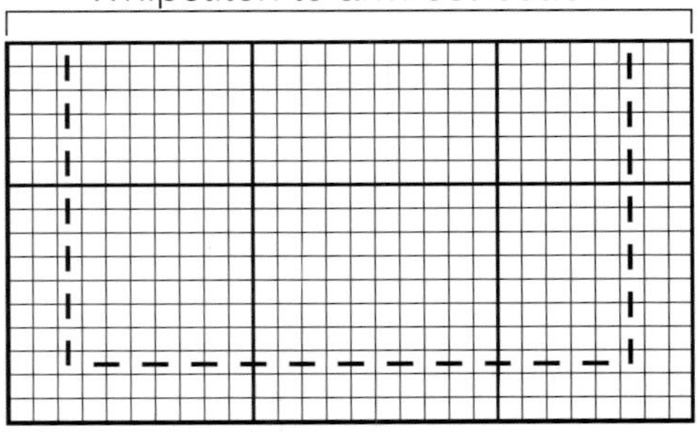

as indicated. Bending F pieces as shown in photo and easing to fit, Whipstitch assembly to I and J pieces as indicated and according to Chair/Sofa Assembly Diagram #4.

NOTE: Separate 1 yd. of Eggshell into 1-ply or worsted-weight into 2-ply.

5: If desired, with rose thread, hand or machine stitch bottom lining to unworked bottom according to Bottom Diagram. (**NOTE:** Felt will be on inside of bottom.) For legs, with 1-ply Eggshell, attach one bell bead to each corner of bottom on side opposite felt as follows (see Leg Assembly Diagram): Insert needle through canvas at one ✦ hole (see Bottom Diagram), go through bell bead, through gold bead, back through bell bead, then back through canvas at neighboring ✦ hole. Pull yarn until gold bead is inside bell bead and bell bead is snug against canvas. Knot yarn to secure; trim excess.

6: Stuff fiberfill between cushion front and back and between armrests and ends. Line seat area with about ½" of fiberfill, place foam block against fiberfill. With Lavender, Whipstitch bottom to chair.

7: For seat cushion, with Lavender, Whipstitch N and O pieces together, forming rectangle. With colors to match top M, Whipstitch front, back and ends to top M. With Lavender, Whipstitch assembly and bottom M together, stuffing lightly with fiberfill before closing.

I – Chair Front
(cut 1) 24 x 48 holes

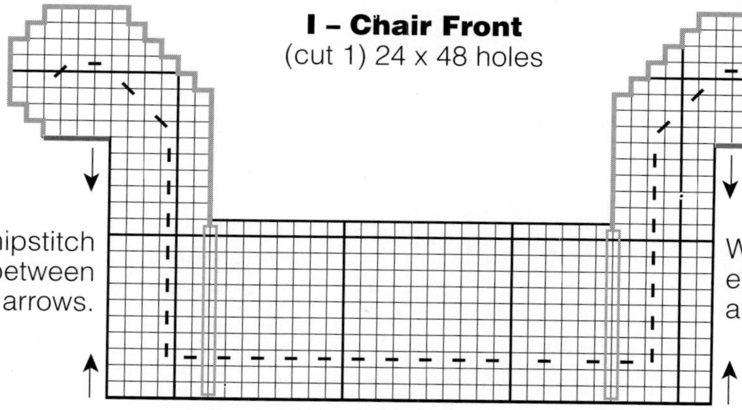

O – Chair/Sofa Seat Cushion End
(cut 2 each) 3 x 20 holes

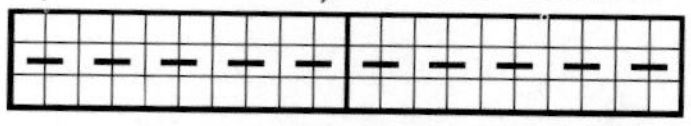

Leg Assembly Diagram

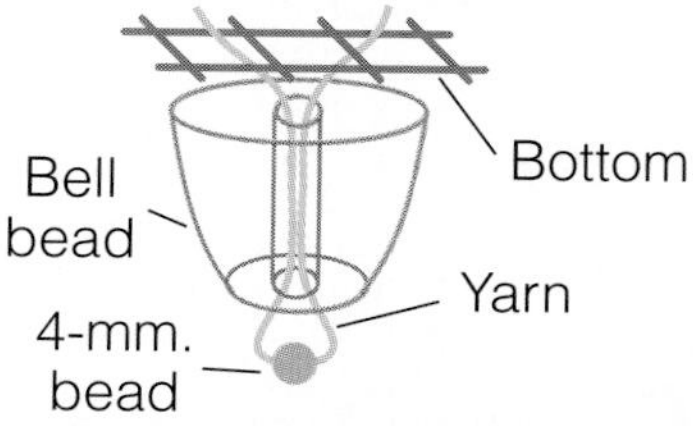

Chair/Sofa Assembly Diagram #1
(center of B not shown)

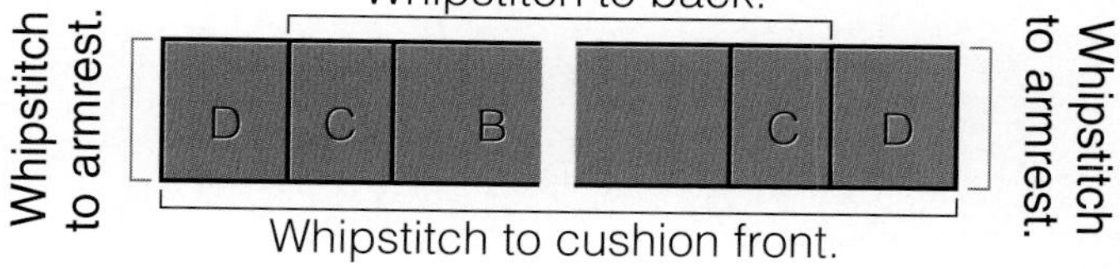

A – Chair Cushion Front (cut 1) 34 x 38 holes
Whipstitch top pieces between blue arrows.

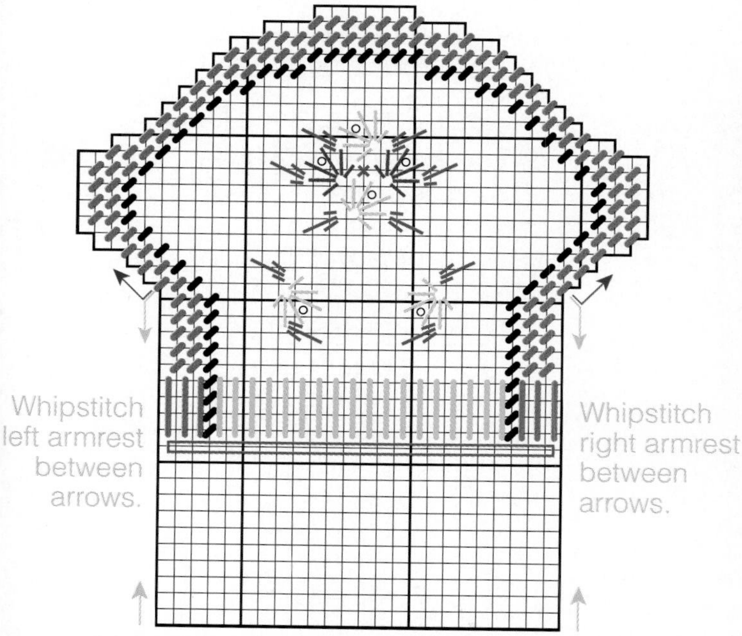

BARBIE® doll and friends pictured with permission of Mattel, Inc. ©1996 Mattel, Inc. All rights reserved.

J – Chair Back
(cut 1)
38 x 48 holes

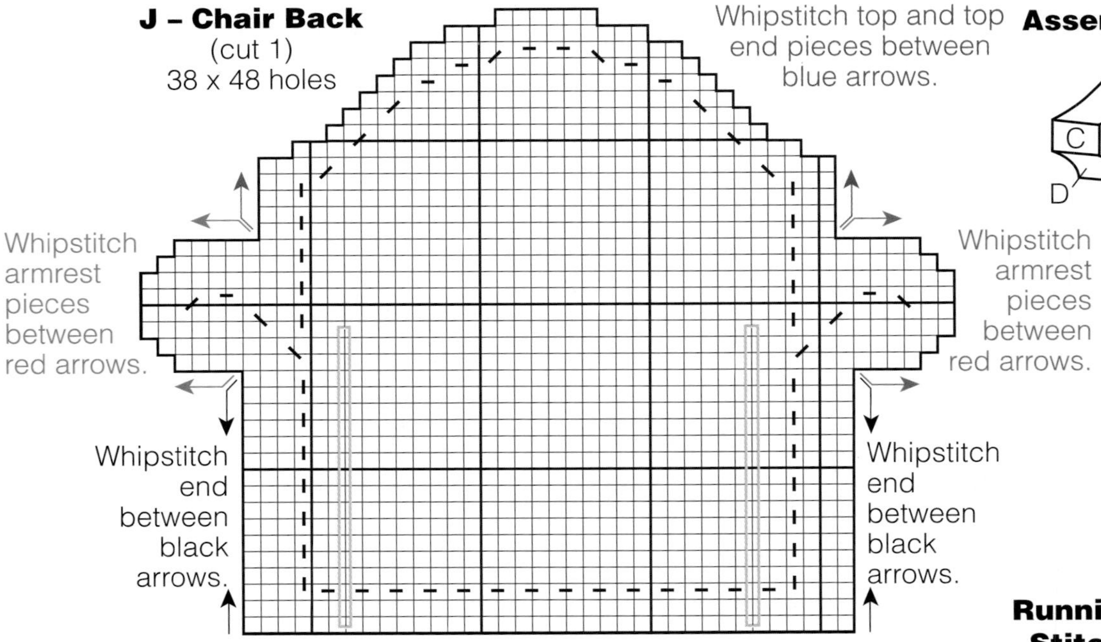

Chair/Sofa Assembly Diagram #2

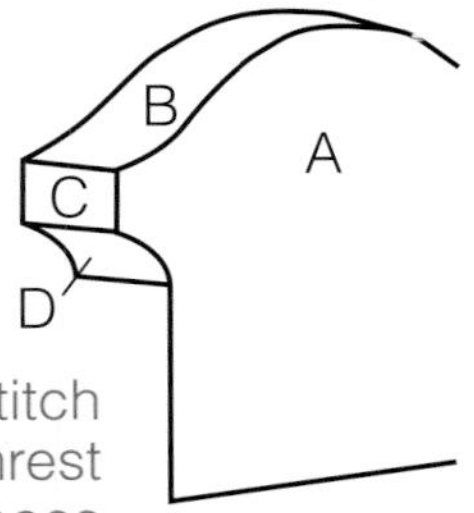

Bottom Diagram

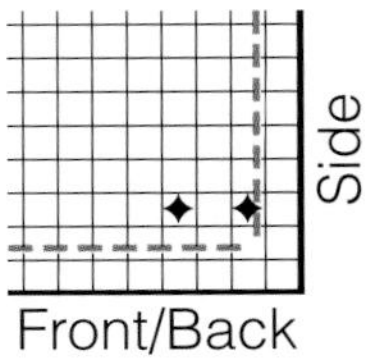

Running Stitch Illustration

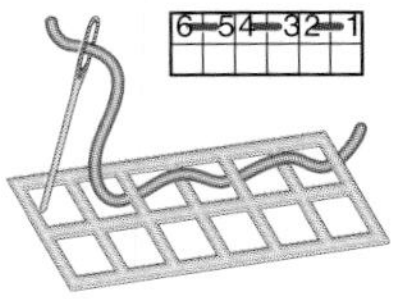

E – Chair Seat Cushion Support
(cut 1) 21 x 24 holes

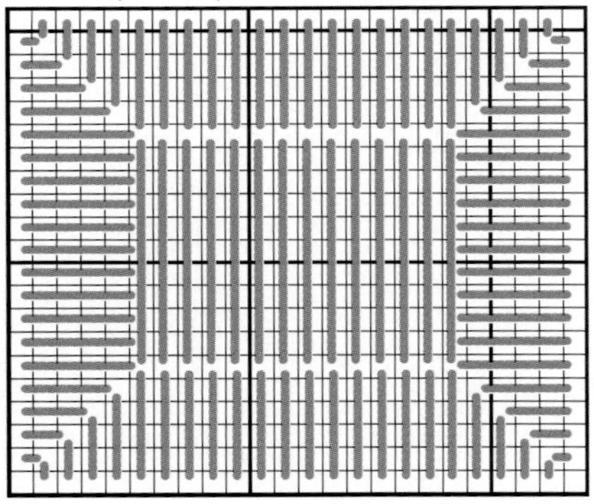

M – Chair Seat Cushion Top & Bottom
(cut 1 each) 20 x 22 holes

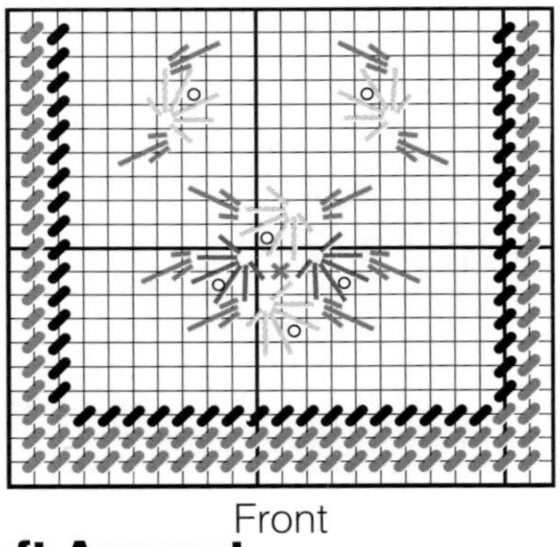

F – Chair/Sofa Left Armrest
(cut 1) 28 x 41 holes

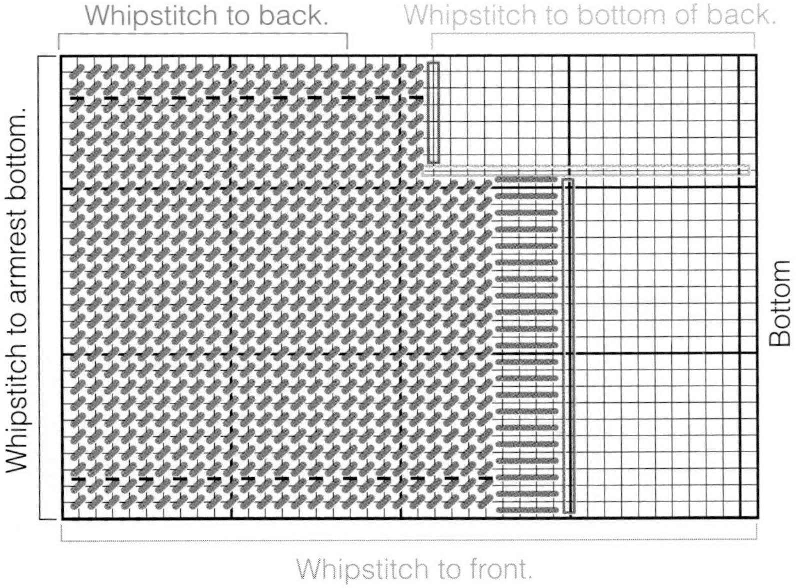

COLOR KEY: Chair

	Metallic cord	
■	White/Gold – 8 yds.	
	Nylon Plus™ Needloft™ yarn	
	#12	#05 Lavender – 2½ oz.
	#32	#29 Forest – 3 yds.
	#24	#39 Eggshell – 18 yds.
	#56	#44 Orchid – 3 yds.
	#55	#59 Plum – 2 yds.

STITCH KEY:

—	Backstitch/Straight Stitch
✕	Cross Stitch
o	Bead Attachment
☐	Seat Cushion Support Attachment
☐	Cushion Front to Armrest Attachment
☐	Top Lower End Attachment
☐	Unworked Areas/Armrest to Back Attachment
—	Armrest to Front Attachment (Upper Portion)
☐	Unworked Areas/Armrest to Front Attachment (Lower Portion)
—	Armrest Bottom Attachment
✦	Leg Attachment

F – Chair/Sofa Right Armrest
(cut 1) 28 x 41 holes

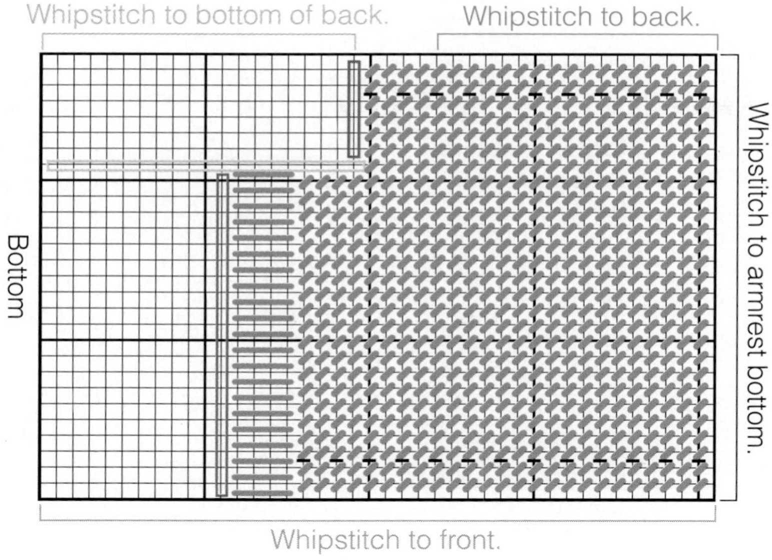

Chair/Sofa Assembly Diagram #3

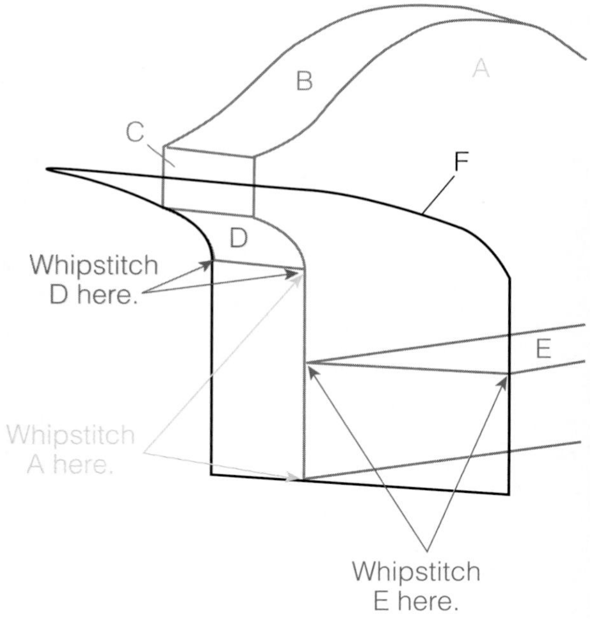

SOFA

SIZE: 4½" x 16" x 6¾" tall.

MATERIALS:
- ❑ One sheet of 7-count plastic canvas
- ❑ Two sheets of 12" x 18" or larger 7-count plastic canvas
- ❑ 39 coordinating color 4-mm. pearl beads
- ❑ Four gold 4-mm. beads
- ❑ Four reddish-brown 10 x 12-mm. bell beads
- ❑ 9" x 12" sheet of dusty rose felt and matching sewing thread (optional)
- ❑ Sewing needle and off-white thread
- ❑ Polyester fiberfill
- ❑ 1" x 3" x 11¾" Styrofoam® block
- ❑ Metallic cord; for amount see Color Key on page 18.
- ❑ Worsted-weight or plastic canvas yarn; for amounts see Color Key.

Chair/Sofa Assembly Diagram #4

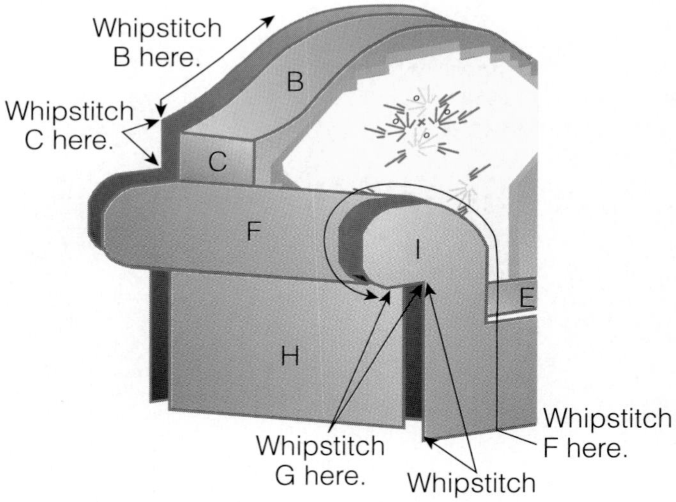

CUTTING INSTRUCTIONS:

NOTE: See Cutting Guides on page 18; graphs on pages 18-20.

A: For cushion front, cut one according to graph.

B: For top, cut one 7 x 101 holes (no graph).

C: For top ends, cut two 5 x 7 holes (no graph).

D: For top lower ends, cut two 6 x 7 holes (no graph).

E: For seat cushion support, cut one 21 x 80 holes.

F: For right and left armrests, cut two (one for right and one for left) 28 x 41 holes.

G: For armrest bottoms, cut two 3 x 28 holes (no graph).

H: For ends, cut two 16 x 28 holes.

I: For front, cut one according to graph.

J: For back, cut one according to graph.

K: For bottom, cut one 28 x 92 holes (no graph).

L: For optional bottom lining, from felt, cut two 5" x 7½" pieces; overlapping short ends ¼", sew together, forming 5" x 14½" piece. Using K as a pattern, cut one from joined piece ⅛" smaller at all edges.

M: For seat cushion top and bottom, cut two (one for top and one for bottom) 20 x 78 holes.

N: For seat cushion front and back, cut two (one for front and one for back) 3 x 78 holes (no graph).

O: For seat cushion ends, cut two 3 x 20 holes (no graph).

STITCHING INSTRUCTIONS:

NOTE: For F, H and O pieces, work according to Chair/Sofa graphs beginning on page 14.

1: Using Sofa pieces in place of Chair pieces and using Sofa Top Stitch Pattern Guide on page 20, follow Steps 1-7 of Chair on pages 14 & 15.

COLOR KEY: Sofa

Metallic cord
- ■ White/Gold – 18 yds.

Nylon Plus™ Needloft™ yarn

■	#12	#05 Lavender – 5 oz.
■	#32	#29 Forest – 7 yds.
■	#24	#39 Eggshell – 60 yds.
■	#56	#44 Orchid – 7 yds.
■	#55	#59 Plum – 7 yds.

STITCH KEY:

- — Backstitch/Straight Stitch
- ✕ Cross Stitch
- o Bead Attachment
- □ Seat Cushion Support Attachment
- □ Cushion Front to Armrest Attachment
- □ Top Lower End Attachment
- □ Unworked Areas/Armrest to Back Attachment
- — Armrest to Front Attachment (Upper Portion)
- □ Unworked Areas/Armrest to Front Attachment (Lower Portion)
- — Armrest Bottom Attachment
- ✦ Leg Attachment

Sofa Cutting Guides

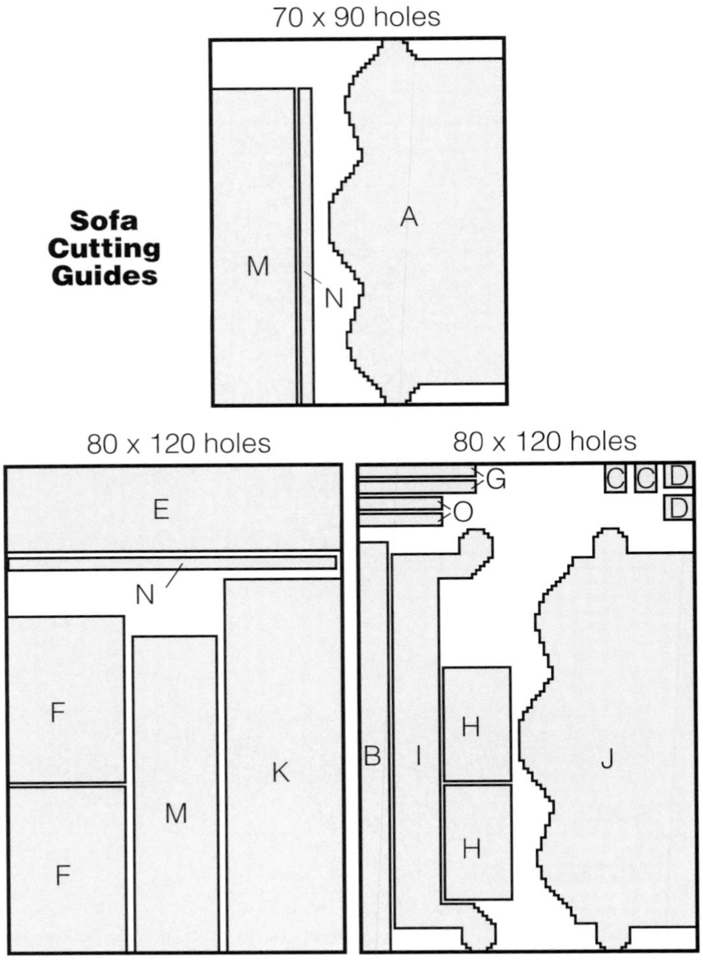

E – Sofa Seat Cushion Support (cut 1) 21 x 80 holes

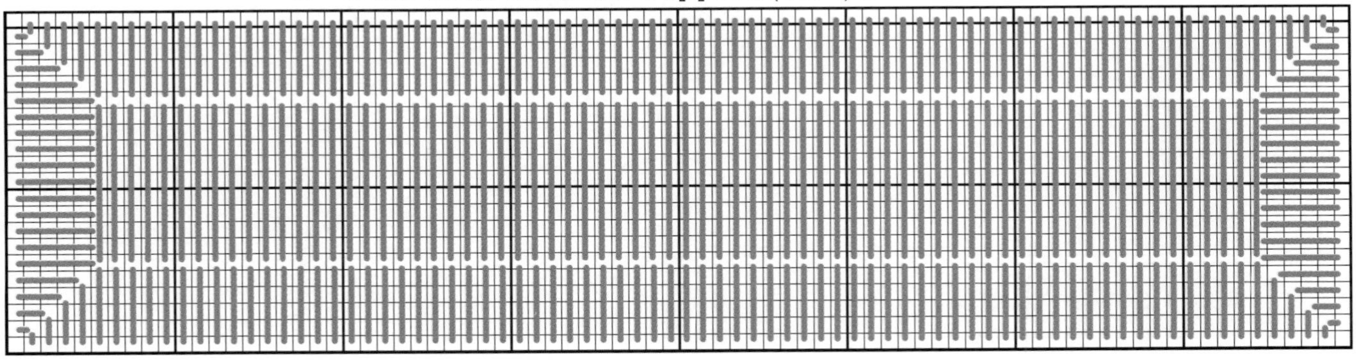

M – Seat Cushion Top & Bottom (cut 1 each) 20 x 78 holes

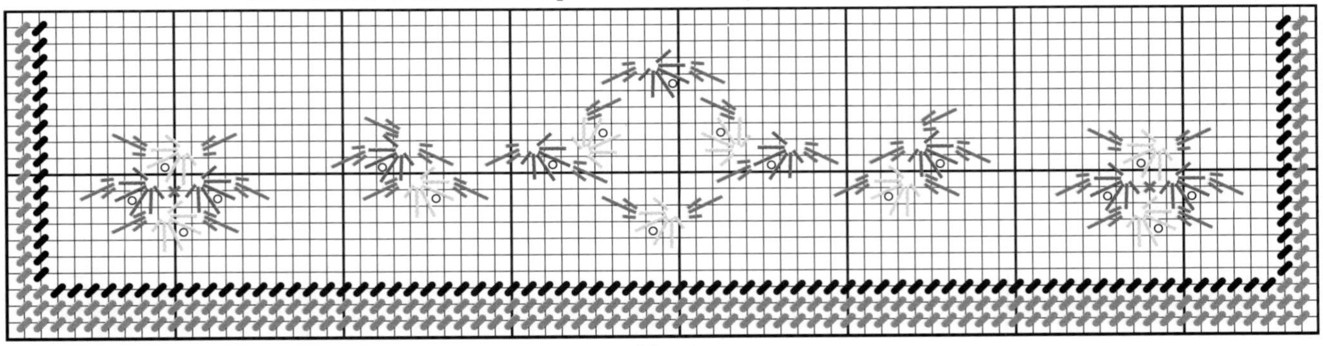

I – Front (cut 1) 24 x 104 holes

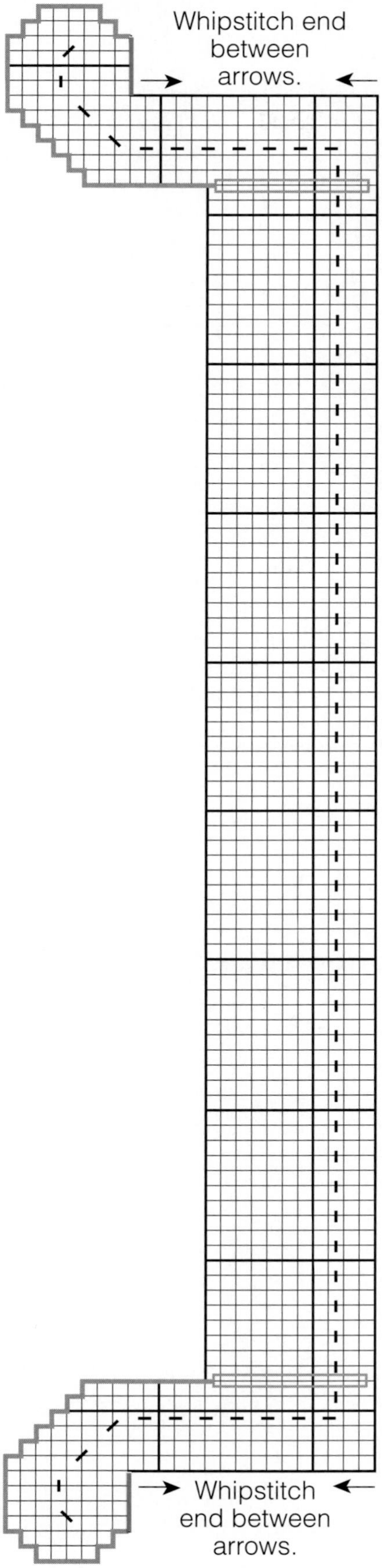

J – Back (cut 1) 42 x 104 holes

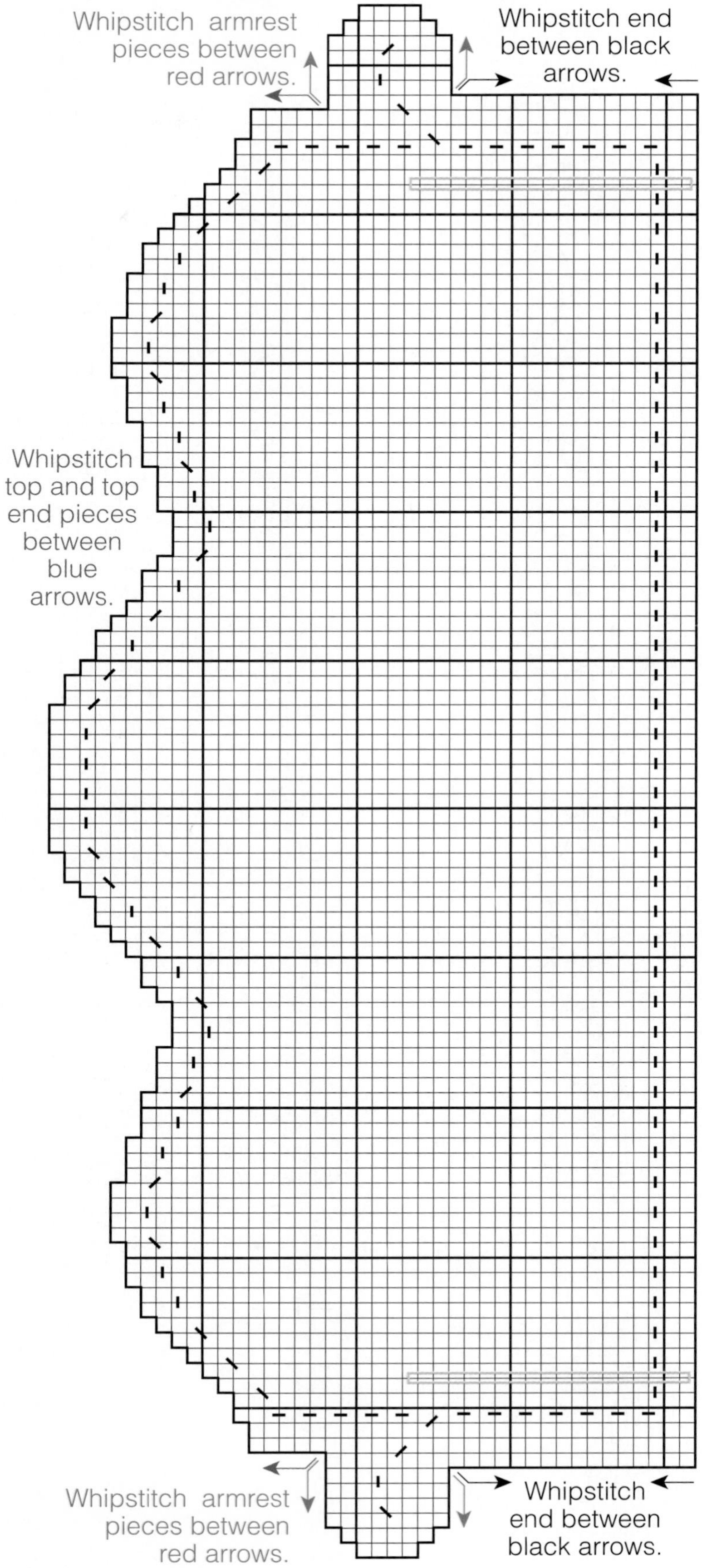

A – Cushion Front (cut 1) 42 x 90 holes

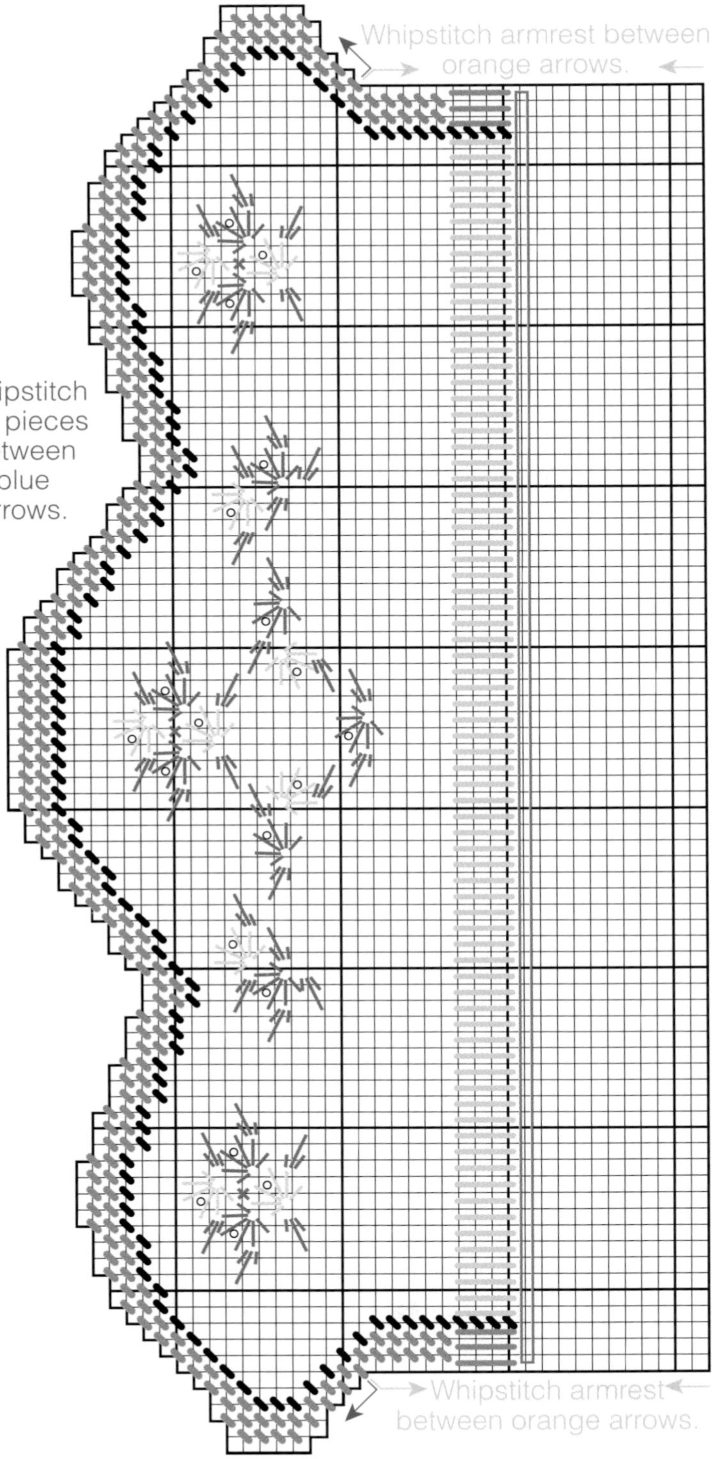

Whipstitch armrest between orange arrows.

Whipstitch armrest between orange arrows.

COLOR KEY: Sofa

Metallic cord
- ■ White/Gold – 18 yds.

Nylon Plus™ Needloft™ yarn

Nylon Plus™	Needloft™
#12	#05 Lavender – 5 oz.
#32	#29 Forest – 7 yds.
#24	#39 Eggshell – 60 yds.
#56	#44 Orchid – 7 yds.
#55	#59 Plum – 7 yds.

STITCH KEY:

- — Backstitch/Straight Stitch
- ✕ Cross Stitch
- ○ Bead Attachment
- ☐ Seat Cushion Support Attachment
- ☐ Cushion Front to Armrest Attachment
- ☐ Top Lower End Attachment
- ☐ Unworked Areas/Armrest to Back Attachment
- — Armrest to Front Attachment (Upper Portion)
- ☐ Unworked Areas/Armrest to Front Attachment (Lower Portion)
- — Armrest Bottom Attachment
- ✦ Leg Attachment

Sofa Top Stitch Pattern Guide

Continue Running Stitch pattern across center of piece.

OTTOMAN

SIZE: 2½" x 4⅜" x 2¼" tall.

MATERIALS:

- ❑ One sheet of 7-count plastic canvas
- ❑ ¼ sheet of dusty rose 7-count plastic canvas
- ❑ Three coordinating color 4-mm. pearl beads
- ❑ Four gold 4-mm. beads
- ❑ Four reddish-brown 10 x 12-mm. bell beads
- ❑ 9" x 12" sheet of dusty rose felt and matching sewing thread (optional)
- ❑ Sewing needle and off-white thread
- ❑ Polyester fiberfill
- ❑ ½" x 2" x 3¾" Styrofoam® block
- ❑ Metallic cord; for amount see Color Key.
- ❑ Worsted-weight or plastic canvas yarn; for amounts see Color Key.

CUTTING INSTRUCTIONS:

NOTE: Use dusty rose canvas for C.

A: For base long and short sides, cut two 8 x 28 holes and two 8 x 16 holes.

B: For cushion support, cut one 16 x 28 holes.

C: For bottom, cut one from dusty rose 16 x 28 holes (no graph).

D: For optional bottom lining, using C as a pattern, cut one from dusty rose felt ⅛" smaller at all edges.

E: For cushion top and bottom, cut two (one for top and one for bottom) 14 x 26 holes.

F: For cushion long and short sides, cut two 5 x 26 holes and two 5 x 14 holes.

STITCHING INSTRUCTIONS:

1: Using colors indicated, Continental Stitch and Long Stitch, work A (leave uncoded areas unworked), B, E and F pieces according to graphs. Using colors indicated, Straight Stitch and Cross Stitch, embroider flowers and leaves on one E for top as indicated on graph. Fill in uncoded areas of top E using Eggshell and bottom E using Lavender and Continental Stitch. With off-white thread, sew coordinating color beads to top E as indicated.

2: For base, with right side of cushion support facing up, with Lavender, Whipstitch B to wrong side of A pieces at unworked areas according to Ottoman Base Assembly Diagram. Whipstitch ends of A pieces together. Overcast unfinished top edges.

3: Using metallic cord and Running Stitch (see Stitch Illustration), embroider detail on base and cushion sides as indicated.

NOTE: Separate 1 yd. of Eggshell into 1-ply or worsted-weight into 2-ply.

4: Follow Step 5 of Chair on page 15.

5: Insert foam block into base below support. With Lavender, Whipstitch bottom to base. For cushion, Whipstitch E and F pieces together, stuffing with fiberfill before closing.

B – Ottoman Cushion Support

(cut 1)
16 x 28 holes

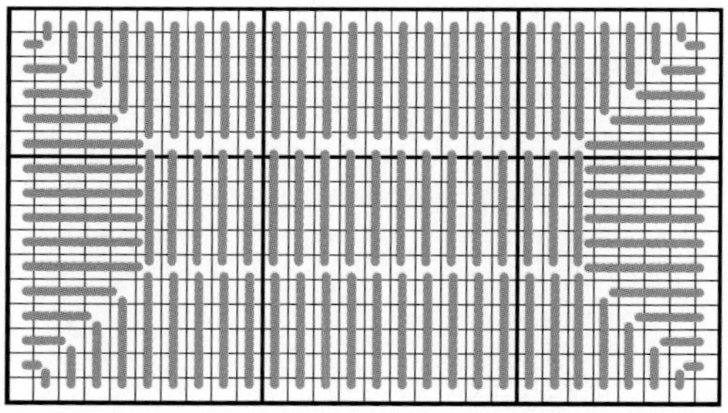

E – Ottoman Cushion Top & Bottom

(cut 1 each)
14 x 26 holes

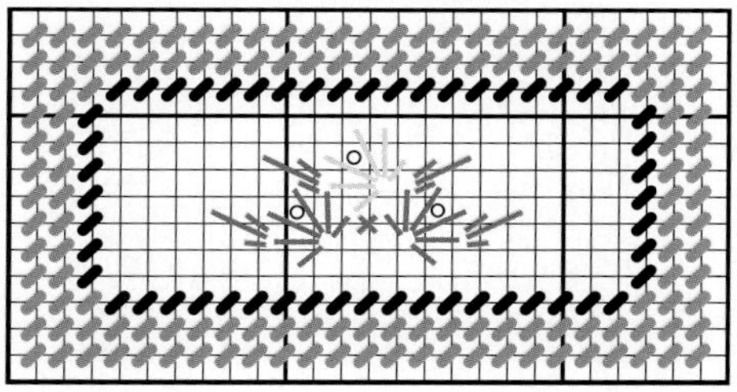

F – Ottoman Cushion Short Side

(cut 2) 5 x 14 holes

F – Ottoman Cushion Long Side

(cut 2) 5 x 26 holes

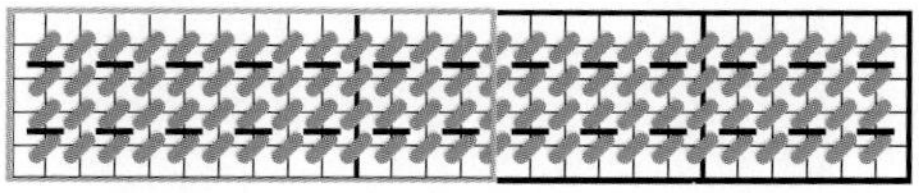

A – Ottoman Base Short Side

(cut 2) 8 x 16 holes

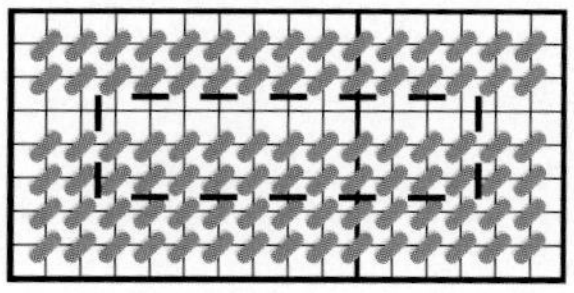

A – Ottoman Base Long Side

(cut 2) 8 x 28 holes

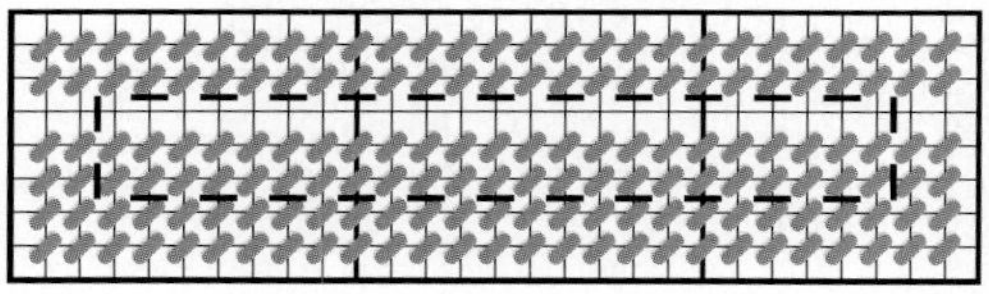

Ottoman Base Assembly Diagram

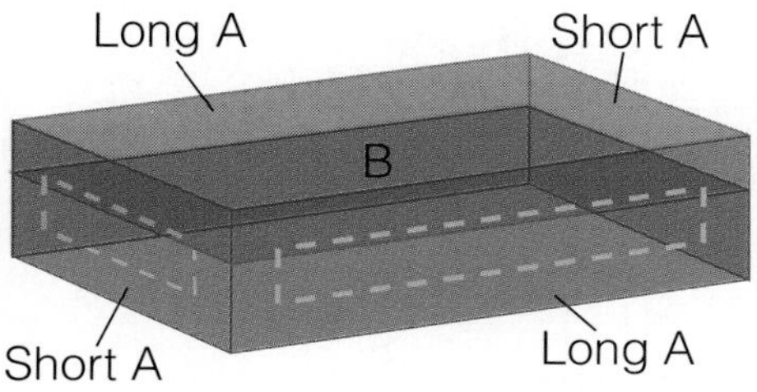

COLOR KEY: Ottoman

Metallic cord
■ White/Gold – 5 yds.

Nylon Plus™ Needloft™ yarn

■	#12	#05 Lavender – 36 yds.
■	#32	#29 Forest – 1 yd.
□	#24	#39 Eggshell – 3 yds.
■	#56	#44 Orchid – ½ yd.
■	#55	#59 Plum – 1 yd.

STITCH KEY:

— Backstitch/Straight Stitch
✕ Cross Stitch
○ Bead Attachment
✦ Leg Attachment

RUG

SIZE: 8⅞" x 13⅝".

MATERIALS:

- ❏ One sheet 7-count plastic canvas
- ❏ 24 coordinating color 4-mm. pearl beads
- ❏ Sewing needle and off-white thread
- ❏ Metallic cord; for amount see Color Key.
- ❏ Worsted-weight or plastic canvas yarn; for amounts see Color Key.

CUTTING INSTRUCTIONS:

A: For rug, cut one according to graph.

STITCHING INSTRUCTIONS:

1: Using colors indicated, Continental Stitch and Long Stitch, work A according to graph. Using colors indicated and Straight Stitch, embroider flowers and leaves as indicated on graph. Holding rug horizontally, fill in uncoded areas using Eggshell and Continental Stitch. With Lavender, Overcast unfinished edges.

2: With thread, sew beads to rug as indicated.

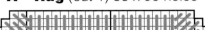

A – Rug (cut 1) 58 x 90 holes

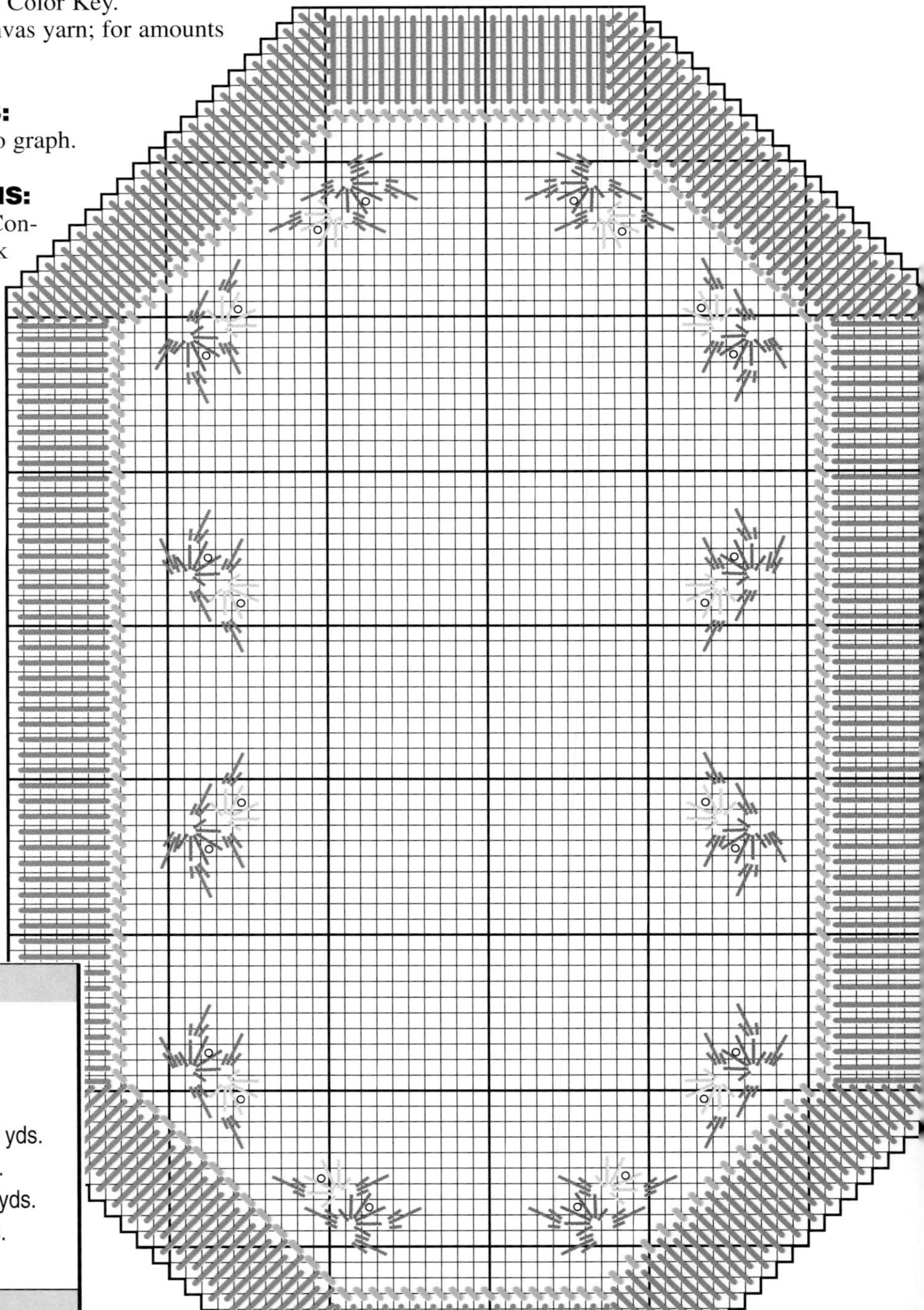

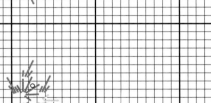

Continue established border pattern over unseen area.

COLOR KEY: Rug

Metallic cord

White/Gold – 5 yds.

Nylon Plus™ Needloft™ yarn

#12	#05 Lavender – 25 yds.
#32	#29 Forest – 8 yds.
#24	#39 Eggshell – 60 yds.
#56	#44 Orchid – 3 yds.
#55	#59 Plum – 3 yds.

STITCH KEY:

— Backstitch/Straight Stitch

o Bead Attachment

POLE LAMP

SIZE: 3¾" x 4⅜" x about 10¼" tall.

MATERIALS:

- ❑ One sheet of 7-count plastic canvas
- ❑ 3" plastic canvas radial circle
- ❑ Aluminum foil
- ❑ 8" wooden ¼" dowel
- ❑ Three 1" metal washers
- ❑ Polyester fiberfill
- ❑ Craft glue or glue gun
- ❑ Metallic cord; for amount see Color Key.
- ❑ Worsted-weight or plastic canvas yarn; for amount see Color Key.

CUTTING INSTRUCTIONS:

A: For table top, cut one according to graph.
B: For mirror frame, cut one according to graph.
C: For upper pole pieces, cut four 2 x 31 holes (no graph).
D: For lower pole pieces, cut four 2 x 19 holes (no graph).
E: For base top, cut one according to graph.
F: For base sides, cut four according to graph.
G: For base bottom, cut one 14 x 14 holes.
H: For shade, cut one according to graph on page 24.
I: For shade brace, cut outer four rows of holes off 3" circle to measure about 1⅞" across (no graph).
J: For mirror, using B as a pattern, cut foil ⅛" smaller at outer edges; using A as guide, cut ½" square from center.

STITCHING INSTRUCTIONS:

1: Using Eggshell and stitches indicated, work A and B pieces according to graphs, leaving uncoded area of A unworked. Using metallic cord and Continental Stitch, work C-F pieces. With cord, Overcast unfinished edges of B and unfinished outer edges of A and unworked G.

2: For shade, overlapping four holes at each end as indicated on graph and working through both thicknesses to join, using Eggshell and Continental Stitch, work H. Whipstitch X edges together as indicated; Overcast unfinished edges. Using cord, Running Stitch (see Stitch Illustration) and Straight Stitch, embroider detail as indicated.

3: Holding C pieces and A right sides together and right side of D pieces to wrong side of A (see Pole Assembly Diagram), with cord and working through all thicknesses, Whipstitch one end of each C and D to each side of cutout on A. Folding pole pieces away from table top (see diagram), Whipstitch side edges of each pole section together. Overcast unfinished top edges of upper pole.

4: With cord, Whipstitch bottom edges of pole to cutout on E. Whipstitch E and F pieces together as indicated; Whipstitch angled edges of F pieces together. Place washers inside base. Whipstitch base sides and G together as indicated, stuffing with fiberfill before closing.

NOTE: Cut one 9" length of metallic cord; tie into a bow and trim ends about 1½" from knot.

5: Place mirror frame over pole with J between; glue frame and table top together as indicated. Glue top of pole to center of I; glue brace inside shade and bow to shade as shown in photo.

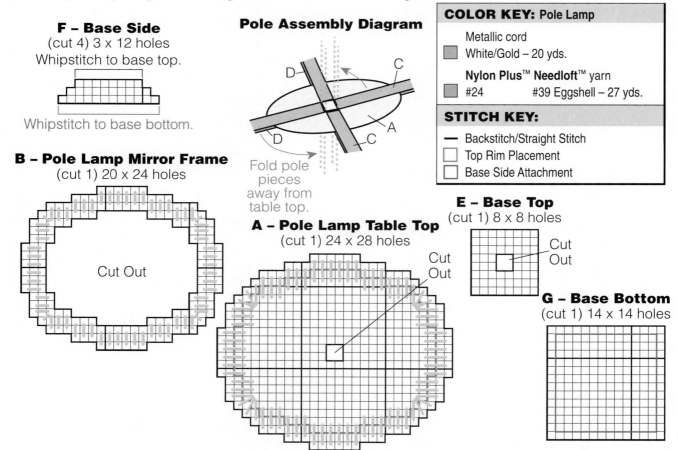

F – Base Side
(cut 4) 3 x 12 holes

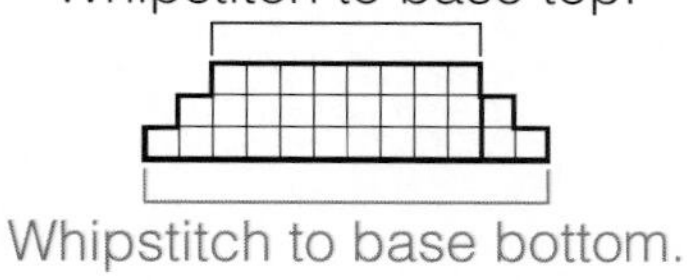

Pole Assembly Diagram

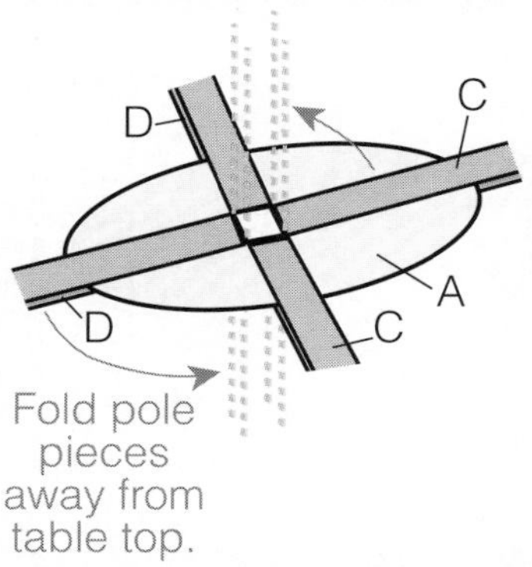

COLOR KEY: Pole Lamp	
Metallic cord	
▪ White/Gold – 20 yds.	
Nylon Plus™ Needloft™ yarn	
▪ #24	#39 Eggshell – 27 yds.

STITCH KEY:

- — Backstitch/Straight Stitch
- ☐ Top Rim Placement
- ☐ Base Side Attachment

B – Pole Lamp Mirror Frame
(cut 1) 20 x 24 holes

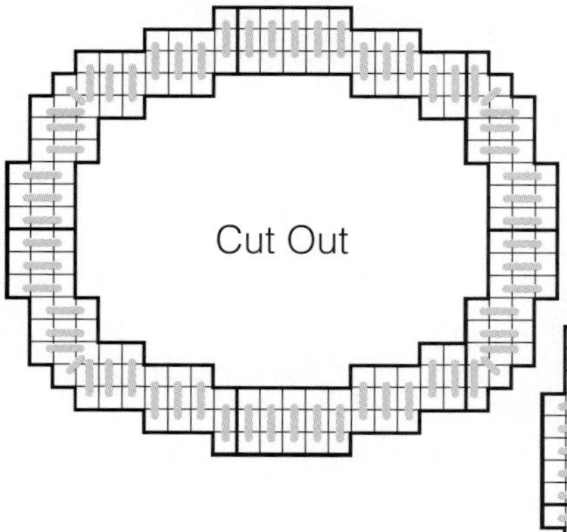

A – Pole Lamp Table Top
(cut 1) 24 x 28 holes

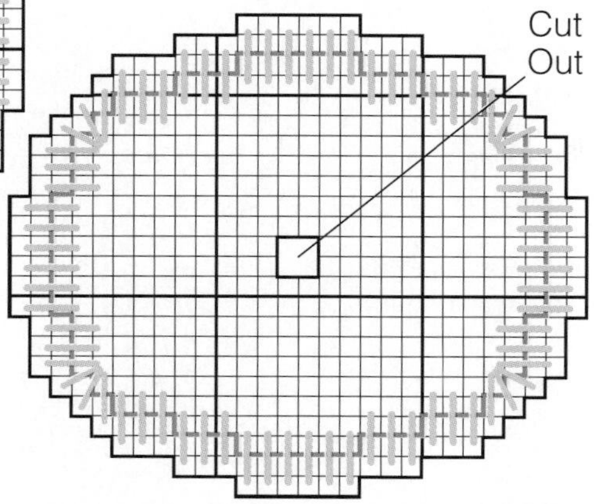

E – Base Top
(cut 1) 8 x 8 holes

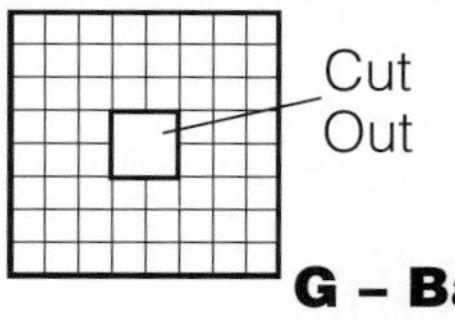

G – Base Bottom
(cut 1) 14 x 14 holes

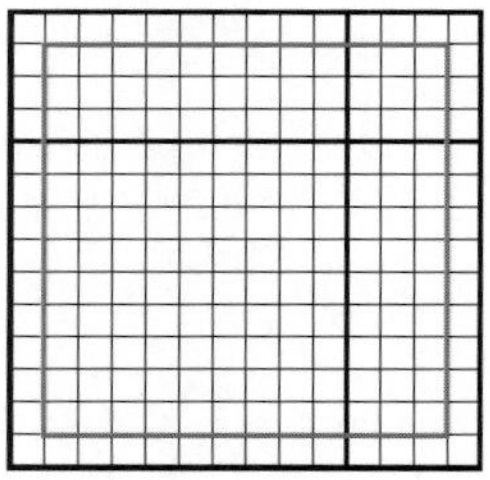

H – Shade (cut 1) 20 x 52 holes

Whipstitch X edges together.

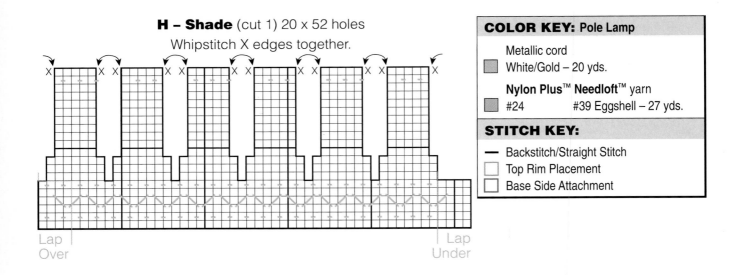

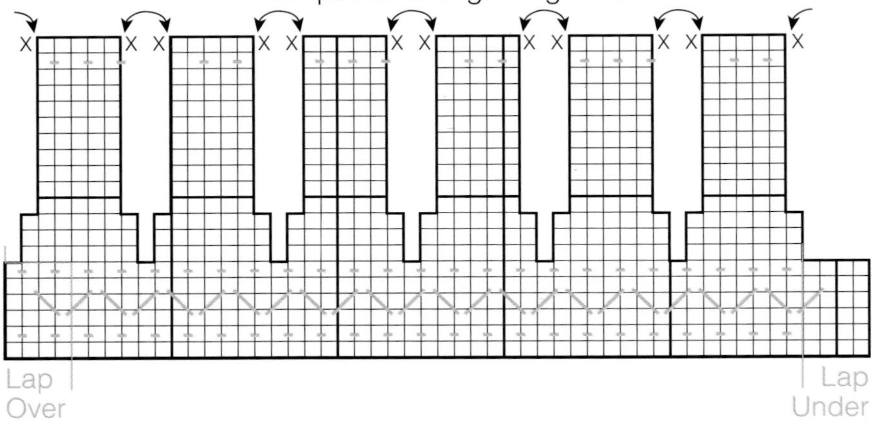

COLOR KEY: Pole Lamp		
	Metallic cord	
▩	White/Gold – 20 yds.	
	Nylon Plus™ Needloft™ yarn	
▩	#24	#39 Eggshell – 27 yds.

STITCH KEY:	
—	Backstitch/Straight Stitch
☐	Top Rim Placement
☐	Base Side Attachment

TABLE LAMP

SIZE: 2⅜" across x about 6¼" tall.

MATERIALS:

- ❑ One sheet of 7-count plastic canvas
- ❑ 3" plastic canvas radial circle
- ❑ 3½" wooden ¼" dowel
- ❑ Two ¾" metal washers
- ❑ Polyester fiberfill
- ❑ Craft glue or glue gun
- ❑ Metallic cord; for amount see Color Key.
- ❑ Worsted-weight or plastic canvas yarn; for amounts see Color Key.

CUTTING INSTRUCTIONS:

A: For body, cut four according to graph.
B: For base top, cut one 5 x 5 holes (no graph).
C: For base sides, cut four according to graph.
D: For base bottom, cut one 9 x 9 holes.
E: For shade, cut one according to Pole Lamp H graph above.
F: For shade brace, cut outer four rows of holes off 3" circle to measure about 1⅞" across (no graph).

STITCHING INSTRUCTIONS:

1: Using Lavender and stitches indicated, work A pieces according to graph. Fill in uncoded areas of A pieces and work C pieces using metallic cord and Continental Stitch.

2: For shade, using E, follow Step 2 of Pole Lamp on page 23.

3: Holding A pieces wrong sides together, with matching colors, Whipstitch together as indicated on graph, stuffing lower portion with fiberfill before closing. With cord, Whipstitch C pieces to unworked B as indicated; Whipstitch angled edges of C pieces together. Whipstitch base sides to unworked D as indicated, placing washers inside base before closing. Overcast unfinished edges of base bottom.

NOTE: Cut one 9" length of metallic cord; tie into a bow, and trim ends about 1½" from knot.

4: Glue bottom of body to center of base top. Insert dowel into body; glue top of body to center of F. Glue brace inside shade and bow to shade as shown in photo.

COLOR KEY: Table Lamp		
	Metallic cord	
▩	White/Gold – 12 yds.	
	Nylon Plus™ Needloft™ yarn	
▩	#12	#05 Lavender – 8 yds.
☐	#24	#39 Eggshell – 20 yds.

STITCH KEY:	
—	Backstitch/Straight Stitch
—	Base Side Attachment

A – Table Lamp Body
(cut 4) 8 x 28 holes

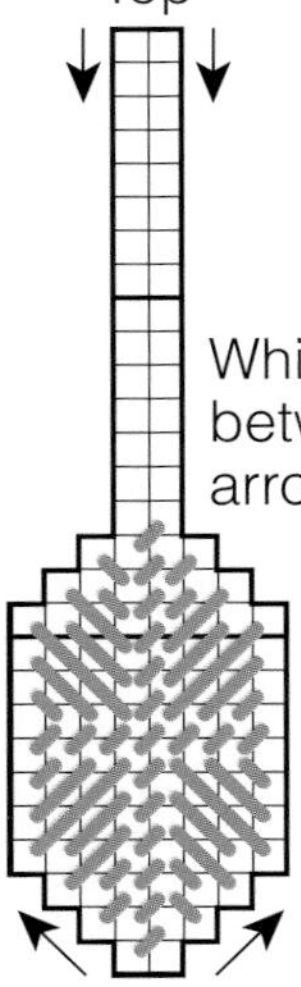

D – Table Lamp Base Bottom
(cut 1)
9 x 9 holes

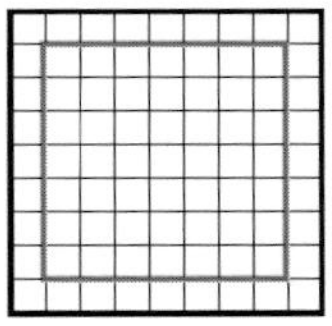

C – Table Lamp Base Side
(cut 4) 2 x 7 holes

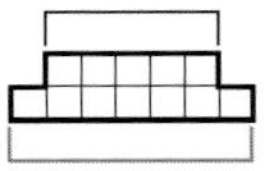

ROCKING CHAIR

Photo on page 26.

SIZE: $4\frac{3}{4}$" x $5\frac{3}{4}$" x $7\frac{1}{4}$" tall.

MATERIALS:

- ❑ Two sheets 7-count plastic canvas
- ❑ Eight coordinating color 4-mm. pearl beads
- ❑ Two gold 4-mm. beads
- ❑ Sewing needle and off-white thread
- ❑ Five $\frac{5}{8}$" metal washers
- ❑ Craft glue or glue gun
- ❑ Metallic cord; for amount see Color Key.
- ❑ Worsted-weight or plastic canvas yarn; for amounts see Color Key.

CUTTING INSTRUCTIONS:

NOTE: Graphs continued on pages 26 & 27.

A: For seat, cut one 22 x 25 holes.

B: For upper front and lower front/armrest pieces, cut one each according to graphs.

C: For back, cut one according to graph.

D: For sides, cut two according to graph.

E: For rocker pieces, cut six according to graph.

F: For top cushion front and back, cut two (one for front and one for back) according to graph.

G: For seat cushion front and back, cut two (one for front and one for back) 18 x 19 holes.

STITCHING INSTRUCTIONS:

1: Using colors indicated, Long Stitch and Continental Stitch, work A-D, four E (two on opposite side of canvas), F and G pieces according to graphs. Using colors indicated, Straight Stitch and Cross Stitch, embroider flowers and leaves on one of each F and G for fronts as indicated on graphs. Fill in uncoded areas of A-D, front F and front G pieces using Eggshell and back F and back G pieces using Lavender and Continental Stitch. With thread, sew coordinating color beads to front F and G pieces as indicated.

2: Holding A and upper B right sides together, with Eggshell, Whipstitch together as indicated. Whipstitch lower B and D pieces to A as indicated and according to Rocking Chair Assembly Diagram on page 27.

3: With metallic cord, Whipstitch lower B and D pieces together as indicated; Overcast unfinished edges of armrests. Holding back and upper front wrong sides together and matching cutouts, with cord, Whipstitch upper B, C and D pieces together as indicated and according to diagram. With Eggshell, Overcast unfinished bottom edges of chair.

4: For each rocker, holding two E pieces wrong sides together with one unworked E between, with cord, Whipstitch together. With Eggshell, tack one gold bead to bottom of each rocker as indicated.

5: Glue ends of armrests to upper front and rockers to sides as indicated and according to diagram. Glue washers together, and glue behind center of lower front and seat for counterweight.

NOTE: Cut four 9" lengths of Lavender.

6: For each cushion, with Lavender, Whipstitch matching front and back pieces wrong sides together. For each tie, thread one 9" strand through each ✦ hole as indicated; pull ends to even. Tie cushions to chair at back cutouts.

COLOR KEY: Rocking Chair

Metallic cord		
■ White/Gold – 25 yds.		
Nylon Plus™ Needloft™ yarn		
■	#12	#05 Lavender – 25 yds.
■	#32	#29 Forest – 2 yds.
■	#24	#39 Eggshell – 60 yds.
■	#56	#44 Orchid – 1 yd.
■	#55	#59 Plum – 1 yd.

STITCH KEY:

- — Backstitch/Straight Stitch
- ✕ Cross Stitch
- o Coordinating Color Bead Attachment
- ☐ Seat Attachment
- ▼ Gold Bead Attachment
- ☐ Armrest Placement
- — Rocker/Side Placement
- ✦ Cushion Tie Attachment

A – Seat (cut 1) 22 x 25 holes

Whipstitch to upper front.

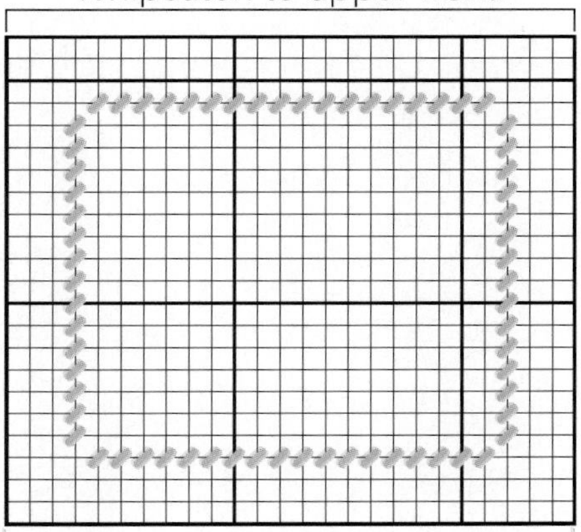

Whipstitch to lower front.

COLOR KEY: Rocking Chair

Metallic cord

▢	White/Gold – 25 yds.	

Nylon Plus™ Needloft™ yarn

▢	#12	#05 Lavender – 25 yds.
▢	#32	#29 Forest – 2 yds.
▢	#24	#39 Eggshell – 60 yds.
▢	#56	#44 Orchid – 1 yd.
▢	#55	#59 Plum – 1 yd.

STITCH KEY:

- — Backstitch/Straight Stitch
- ✕ Cross Stitch
- o Coordinating Color Bead Attachment
- ▢ Seat Attachment
- ▼ Gold Bead Attachment
- ▢ Armrest Placement
- — Rocker/Side Placement
- ✦ Cushion Tie Attachment

D – Side (cut 2) 14 x 22 holes

Whipstitch to seat.

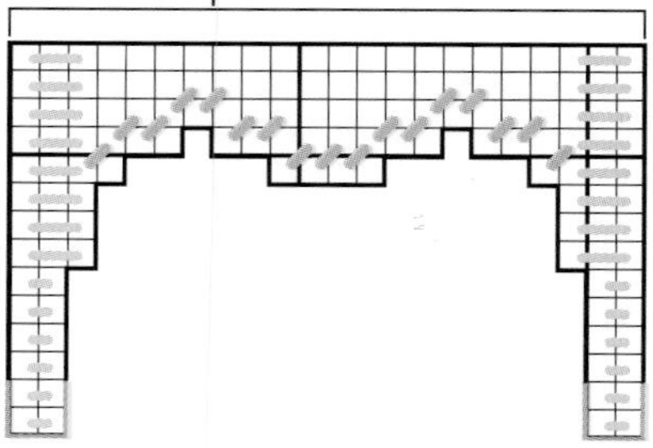

F – Top Cushion Front & Back

(cut 1 each) 18 x 27 holes

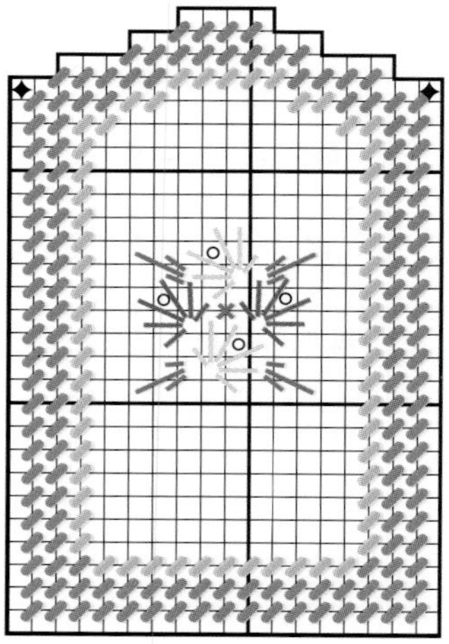

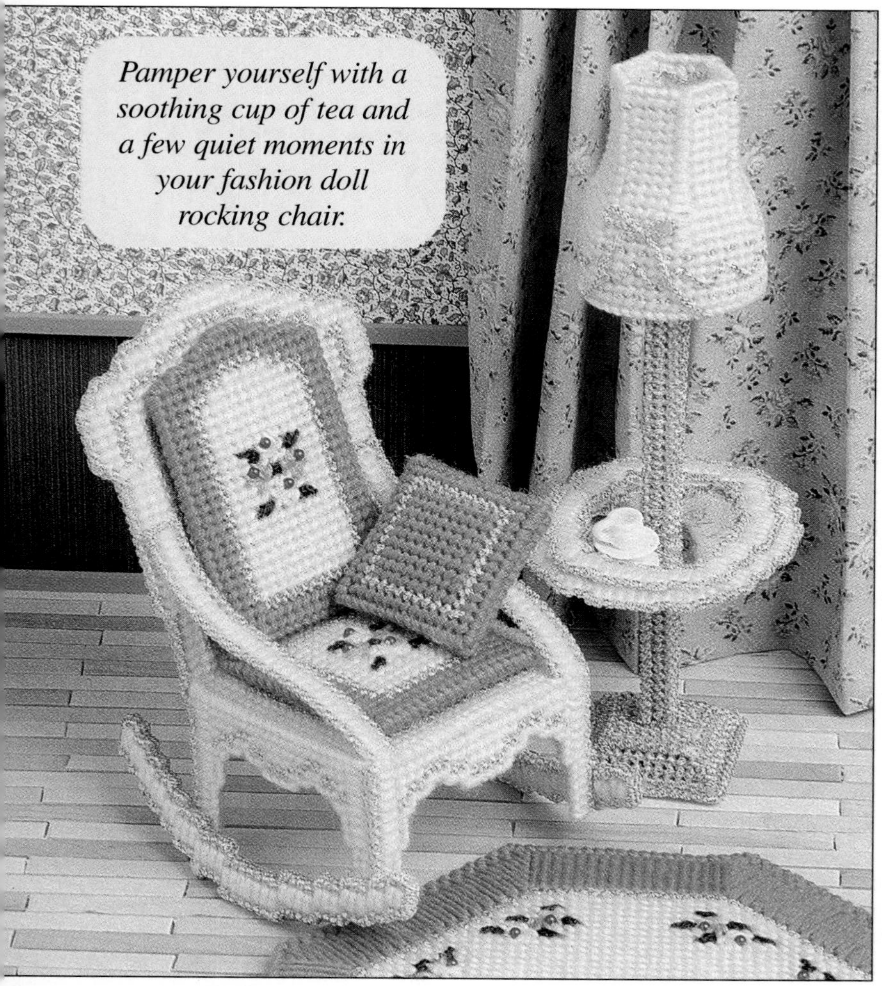

Pamper yourself with a soothing cup of tea and a few quiet moments in your fashion doll rocking chair.

G – Seat Cushion Front & Back

(cut 1 each) 18 x 19 holes

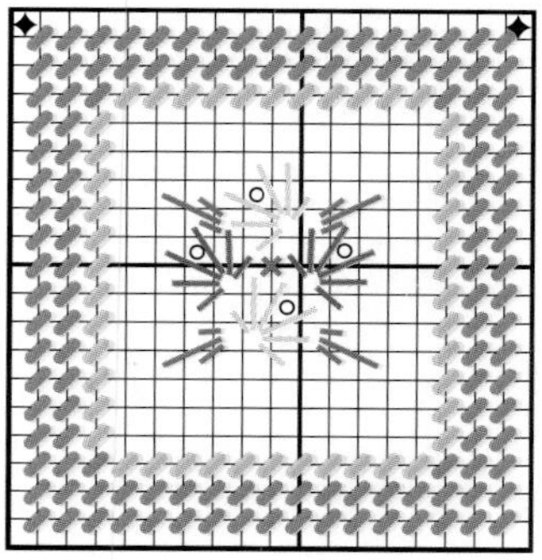

C – Back (cut 1) 31 x 47 holes
Whipstitch between red arrows.

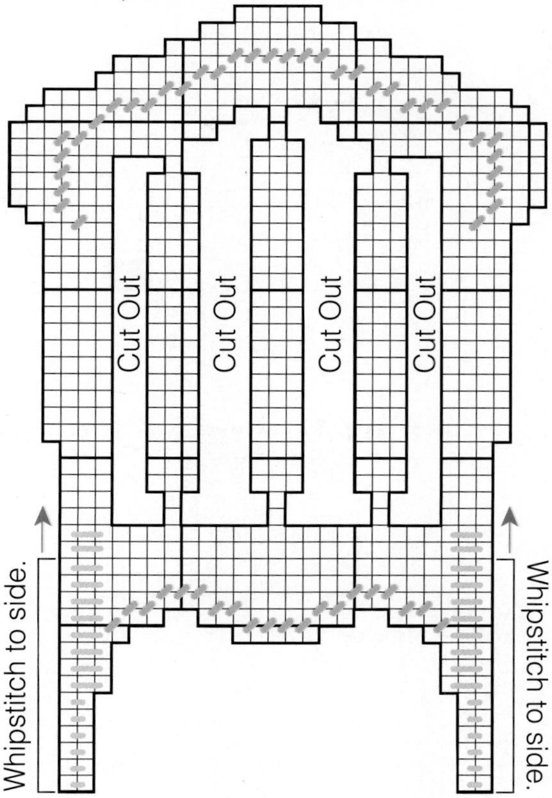

Rocking Chair Assembly Diagram

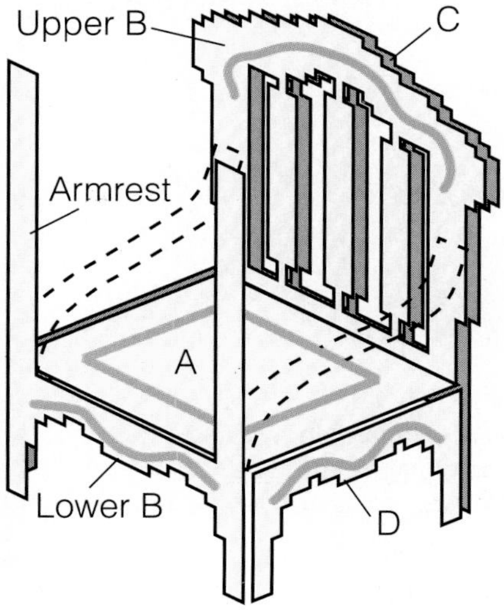

E – Rocker Piece
(cut 6)
10 x 38 holes

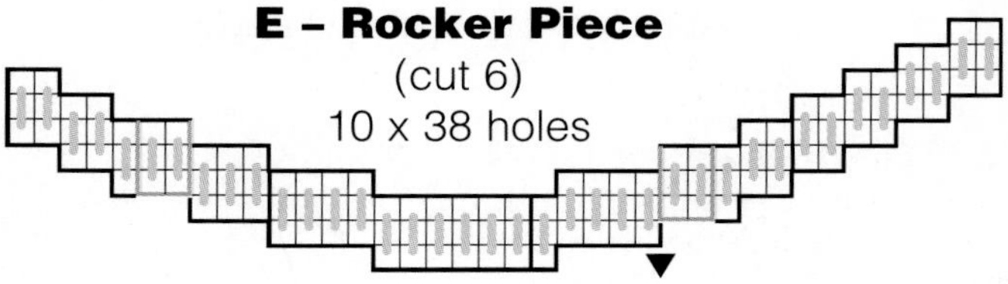

B – Lower Front/Armrests
(cut 1) 25 x 47 holes

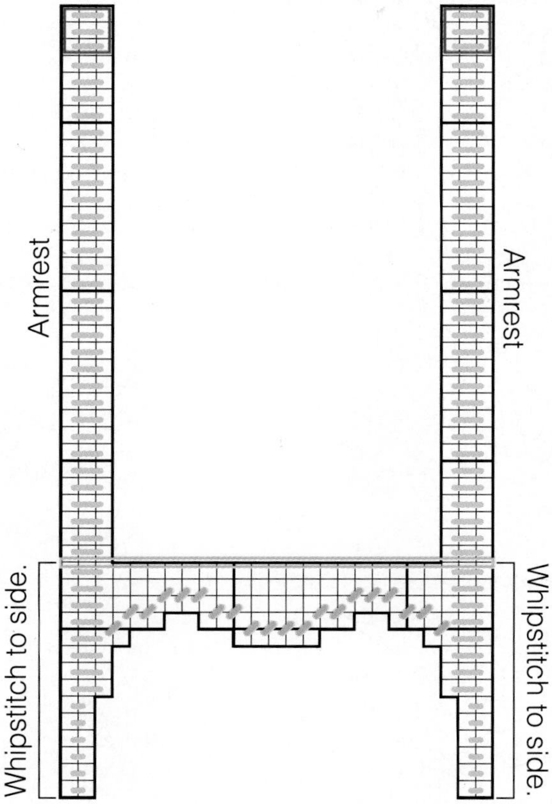

B – Upper Front (cut 1) 31 x 33 holes
Whipstitch between red arrows.

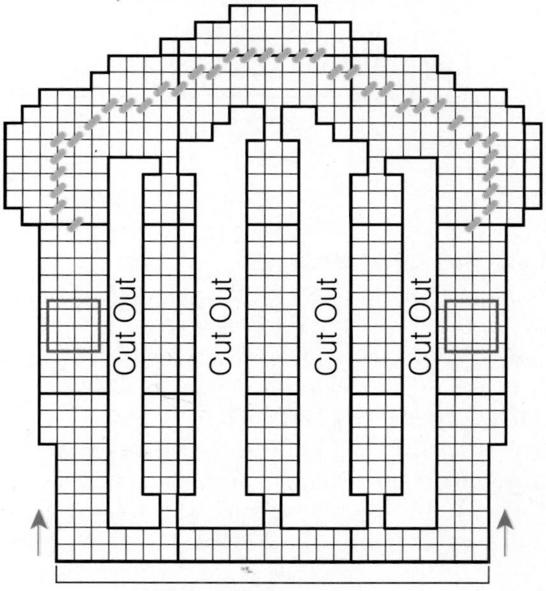

PLANTER & VASE

SIZE: Planter is 2⅛" x 2⅛" x 1¾" tall, not including plant; Vase is 1½" x 1½" x 1⅜" tall, not including flowers.

MATERIALS:
- ❏ ¼ sheet of 7-count plastic canvas
- ❏ One each pink and rose 9-mm. satin ribbon rose cluster
- ❏ Silk greenery to make 7"-tall plant
- ❏ Spanish moss
- ❏ 1" square x 1¼" Styrofoam® block
- ❏ ½ yd. white/gold metallic cord
- ❏ Craft glue or glue gun
- ❏ Worsted-weight or plastic canvas yarn; for amount see Color Key.

CUTTING INSTRUCTIONS:

A: For Planter sides, cut four according to graph.
B: For Planter bottom, cut one 6 x 6 holes.
C: For Vase sides, cut four according to graph.
D: For Vase bottom, cut one 4 x 4 holes.

STITCHING INSTRUCTIONS:

1: Using Eggshell and stitches indicated, work A-D pieces according to graphs.

2: For Planter, with Eggshell, Whipstitch side edges of A pieces together as indicated on graph; Whipstitch sides and B together as indicated. Overcast unfinished top edges of Planter.

NOTES: Cut metallic cord into two 9" lengths; tie each into a bow, and trim ends about 1½" from knot. If desired, from greenery, cut two leaves with stems to use in Vase.

3: Place foam block in planter. Insert greenery into foam; twist together to form plant. Glue Spanish moss to cube around stem. Glue one bow to one side as shown in photo.

4: For Vase, using C and D pieces in place of A and B pieces, follow Step 2. Placing one leaf on each side, if desired, twist rose clusters together; glue arrangement inside Vase. Glue remaining bow to one side as shown in photo.

A – Planter Side
(cut 4)
11 x 14 holes

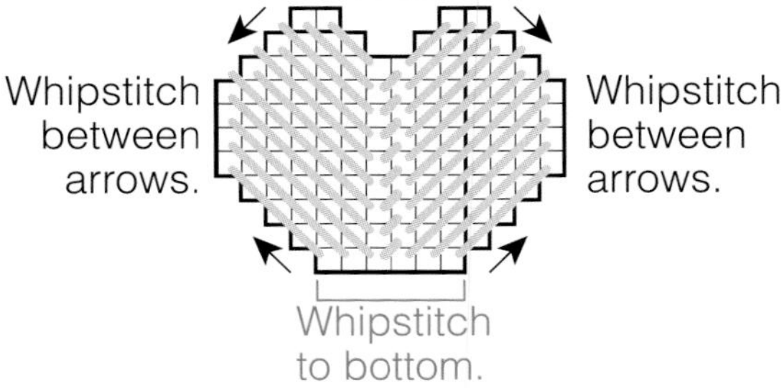

B – Planter Bottom
(cut 1) 6 x 6 holes

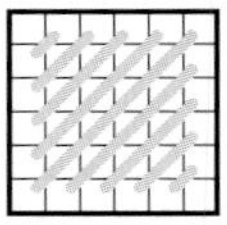

C – Vase Side
(cut 4) 8 x 10 holes

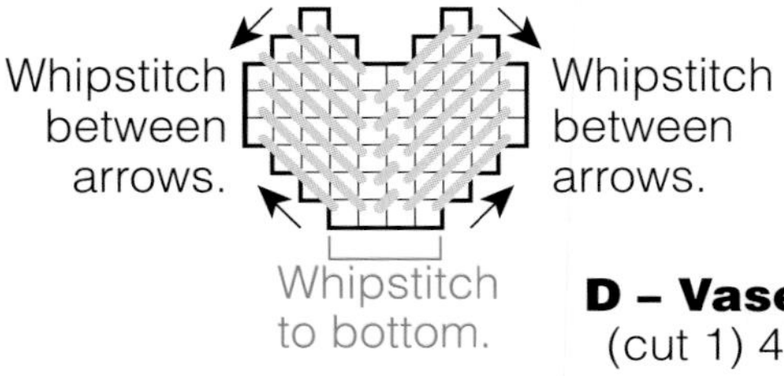

D – Vase Bottom
(cut 1) 4 x 4 holes

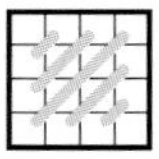

COLOR KEY: Planter & Vase		
	Nylon Plus™	Needloft™ yarn
▩	#24	#39 Eggshell – 17 yds.

THROW PILLOWS

SIZE: Each pillow is 2¼" square.

MATERIALS FOR TWO:
- ❏ ¼ sheet of 7-count plastic canvas
- ❏ Four coordinating color 4-mm. pearl beads
- ❏ Polyester fiberfill
- ❏ Sewing needle and off-white thread
- ❏ Metallic cord; for amount see Color Key.
- ❏ Worsted-weight or plastic canvas yarn; for amounts see Color Key.

CUTTING INSTRUCTIONS:

A: For pillow fronts and backs, cut four (two for fronts and two for backs) 14 x 14 holes.
B: For pillow sides, cut eight 1 x 14 holes (no graph).

STITCHING INSTRUCTIONS:

1: Using colors indicated and Continental Stitch, work A pieces according to graph. Using colors indicated, Straight Stitch and Cross Stitch, embroider flowers and leaves on two pieces for fronts as indicated on graph. Fill in uncoded areas on fronts using Eggshell and backs using Lavender and Continental Stitch.

2: For each pillow, sew two beads to front as indicated. With Lavender, Whipstitch one of each A and four B pieces together, stuffing with fiberfill before closing.

A – Throw Pillow Front & Back
(cut 2 each) 14 x 14 holes

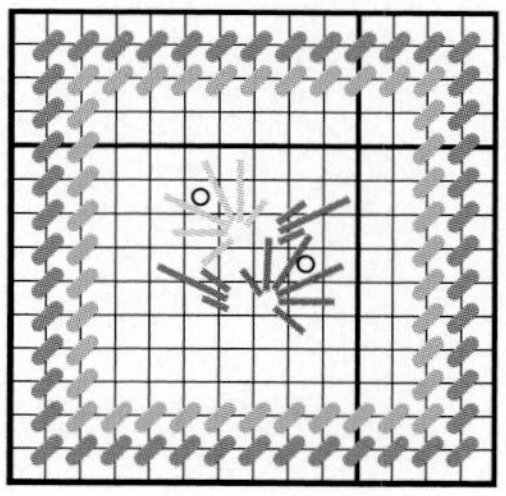

COLOR KEY: Throw Pillows		
	Metallic cord	
■	White/Gold – 2 yds.	
	Nylon Plus™ Needloft™ yarn	
■	#12	#05 Lavender – 12 yds.
■	#32	#29 Forest – ½ yd.
□	#24	#39 Eggshell – 3 yds.
■	#56	#44 Orchid – ½ yd.
■	#55	#59 Plum – ½ yd.

STITCH KEY:
— Backstitch/Straight Stitch
o Bead Attachment

PICTURE FRAME

SIZE: 1¼" x 2"; holds a 1" x 1⅜" picture.

MATERIALS FOR ONE:
- ❑ Scraps of 7-count plastic canvas
- ❑ Metallic cord; for amount see Color Key.
- ❑ Worsted-weight or plastic canvas yarn; for amount see Color Key.

CUTTING INSTRUCTIONS:

A: For front and back, cut one each according to graphs.

B: For stand, cut one according to graph.

STITCHING INSTRUCTIONS:

1: Using colors and stitches indicated, work front A according to graph. Using Eggshell and Continental Stitch, work back A and B pieces; Overcast unfinished edges of B and bottom edges of A pieces as indicated on graphs. With metallic cord, Overcast unfinished cutout edges of front.

2: With Eggshell, tack stand to right side of back as indicated. Holding A pieces wrong sides together, Whipstitch together as indicated.

A – Frame Front
(cut 1) 8 x 12 holes
Whipstitch between arrows.

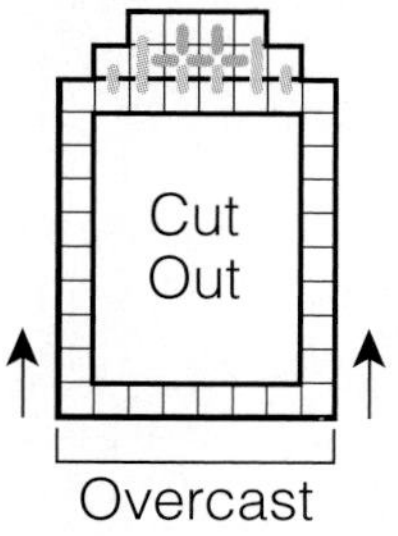

A – Frame Back
(cut 1) 8 x 12 holes
Whipstitch between arrows.

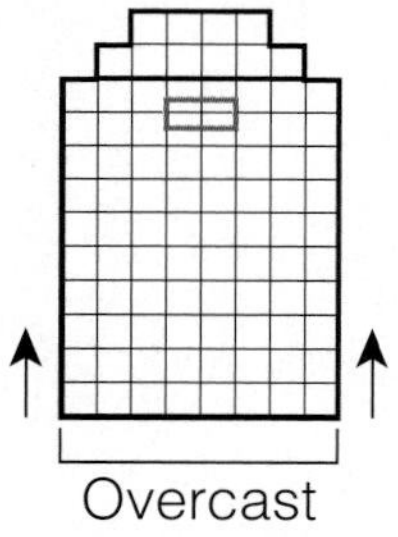

B – Frame Stand
(cut 1)
4 x 9 holes
Tack to back.

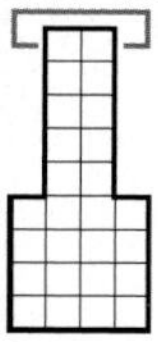

COLOR KEY: Picture Frame		
	Metallic cord	
■	White/Gold – 1 yd.	
	Nylon Plus™ Needloft™ yarn	
■	#24	#39 Eggshell – 4 yds.

STITCH KEY:
— Stand Attachment

Dress up for the palace ball in the privacy of your feminine fashion doll bedroom. Fabulous furnishings keep your jewels and finery fit for a princess.

BARBIE® doll and friends pictured with permission of Mattel, Inc. ©1996 Mattel, Inc. All rights reserved.

FASHION DOLL

Bedroom

Designed by
Diane T. Ray

BASIC INSTRUCTIONS

Fashion Doll Dream Home Bedroom is made using repeating floral motifs. Since the Rose is used throughout the set, instructions for one Rose are given below. For best results, read instructions for each project before you begin to stitch. Materials are given for each individual project; or, if you prefer to make all the projects, see "Materials for Entire Set" below.

Use colors shown, or choose colors to coordinate with a child's bedroom.

MATERIALS FOR ENTIRE SET:

- ❏ 21 sheets of 7-count plastic canvas
- ❏ 37 pearl 5-mm. beads
- ❏ 70 silver 4-mm. beads
- ❏ 3" string of 3-mm. silver beads
- ❏ Two white 9" x 12" sheets of felt (optional)
- ❏ 1½ yds. white 1" pregathered lace
- ❏ 7" white 1¼" pregathered lace
- ❏ ¾ yd. white 2½" pregathered lace
- ❏ 1½ yds. blue 2½" satin ribbon
- ❏ 1½ yds. blue ⅛" satin ribbon
- ❏ ⅔ yd. aluminum foil
- ❏ 2" metal washer
- ❏ 8¼" wooden ⅛" dowel
- ❏ 2" drapery hook
- ❏ 1½" x 2" poster board
- ❏ 5" x 10" poster board
- ❏ Fabric stiffener or spray starch (optional)
- ❏ Polyester fiberfill (optional)
- ❏ Sewing needle and blue thread
- ❏ Three Velcro® closures
- ❏ Craft glue or glue gun
- ❏ Metallic cord:
  - ❏ White/Silver – 121 yds.
- ❏ Worsted-weight or plastic canvas yarn:

Nylon Plus™	Needloft™ yarn
❏ #28	#26 Baby Green – 32 yds.
❏ #31	#27 Holly – 59 yds.
❏ #09	#32 Royal – 4¼ oz.
❏ #01	#41 White – 14¼ oz.

ROSE

SIZE: ¾" across x ½" tall.

MATERIALS FOR ONE:
(**NOTE:** For entire set, make 13 Roses.)

- ❏ Scraps of 7-count plastic canvas
- ❏ One 5-mm. pearl bead
- ❏ Craft glue or glue gun
- ❏ Worsted-weight or plastic canvas yarn; for amount see Color Key.

CUTTING INSTRUCTIONS:

A: For petals, cut four according to graph.
B: For base, cut one according to graph.

STITCHING INSTRUCTIONS:

1: Using Royal and stitches indicated, work A and B pieces according to graphs, leaving uncoded area of B unworked; Overcast unfinished edges.

2: Glue A and B pieces together according to Rose Assembly Diagram; glue bead inside petal opening.

A – Petal
(cut 4)
2 x 2 holes

B – Base
(cut 1)
5 x 5 holes

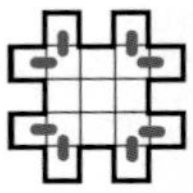

COLOR KEY: Rose	
Nylon Plus™	Needloft™ yarn
■ #09	#32 Royal – 2 yds.

Rose Assembly Diagram

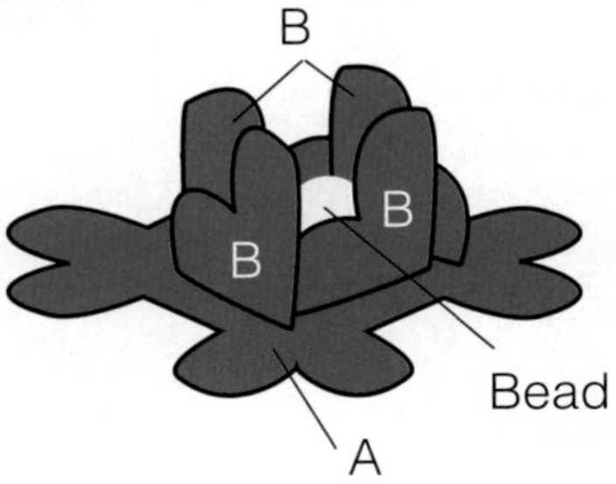

TISSUE CHEST

Photo on page 47.

SIZE: 5¼" square x about 7¼" tall; holds a boutique-style tissue box.

MATERIALS:

❑ 2½ sheets of 7-count plastic canvas
❑ Four 5-mm. pearl beads
❑ 12 silver 4-mm. beads
❑ Velcro® closure
❑ Craft glue or glue gun
❑ Metallic cord; for amount see Color Key.
❑ Worsted-weight or plastic canvas yarn; for amounts see Color Key.
❑ Four Roses; see instructions on page 31.

CUTTING INSTRUCTIONS:

NOTE: Graphs and diagrams continued on page 34.

A: For lid top and base, cut one each according to graphs.

B: For box scallop sides, cut two according to graph.

C: For box solid sides, cut two 30 x 45 holes.

D: For box bottom, cut one 30 x 30 holes (no graph).

E: For bottom support, cut one 6 x 30 holes (no graph).

F: For inner base scallop and solid sides, cut two according to graph for scallop sides and two 5 x 31 holes for solid sides (no solid side graph).

G: For outer base scallop and solid sides, cut two according to graph for scallop sides and two 4 x 32 holes for solid sides (no solid side graph).

H: For lid cutout frame, cut one according to graph.

I: For motif frames, cut two according to graph.

STITCHING INSTRUCTIONS:

1: Using colors and stitches indicated, work base A (work gray areas on wrong side of canvas and leave indicated area unworked), B, C, scallop F and scallop G pieces according to graphs. Fill in uncoded areas of B and C pieces (leave indicated areas unworked) and work lid top A using White and Continental Stitch. Using White and Long Stitch over narrow width, work remaining F and G pieces.

2: With White for outside edges of lid top A, metallic cord for outside edges of base A and inner edges of motif frames, and Royal for outer edges of lid cutout frame and motif frames, Overcast unfinished edges of A, H (leave inner edges unfinished) and I pieces.

NOTE: Separate Baby Green and Holly into 1-ply or worsted-weight into 2-ply.

3: Using 1-ply Holly and Straight Stitch for stems, one 1-ply strand each of Holly and Baby Green and Lazy Daisy Stitch for leaves, and Royal and Straight Stitch for flowers, embroider as indicated on graphs.

4: For each handle, with White, thread needle from back to front through one ◆ hole as indicated on B graph; thread one pearl bead, six silver beads and one pearl bead on yarn. Thread needle from front to back through remaining ◆ hole; pull ends firmly to align beads, and knot ends together on wrong side.

5: To attach lid base, with right side of base A facing wrong side of one scallop side, with White, Whipstitch unworked bar on base A to top edge of one B.

6: Holding lid top and base wrong sides together (outer edge of base will have right side showing) at matching cutout edges, glue together. Holding H to right side of lid top over cutout and working through all thicknesses, with cord, Whipstitch cutout edges together.

7: For box, alternating scallop and solid sides, with White, Whipstitch B and C pieces together. Whipstitch one long edge of unworked E to center bar of unworked D according to Tissue Chest Bottom & Support Assembly Diagram. Whipstitch bottom and bottom support to indicated areas on sides (see diagram). Overcast remaining unfinished top edges of box.

8: Alternating scallop and solid sides, with Royal, Whipstitch F pieces together; Overcast unfinished top edges. Alternating scallop and solid sides, with White, Whipstitch G pieces together; Overcast unfinished top edges. Holding inner base, outer base and box together at matching bottom edges according to Inner & Outer Base Assembly Diagram and working through all thicknesses to join, with Royal, Whipstitch bottom edges together. Glue top edges of base pieces together and to box.

9: Glue motif frames to scallop sides as shown in photo and Roses to sides and lid top as indicated. If desired, glue closure to inside of lid front and top of box.

Tissue Chest Bottom & Support Assembly Diagram
(cutaway view)

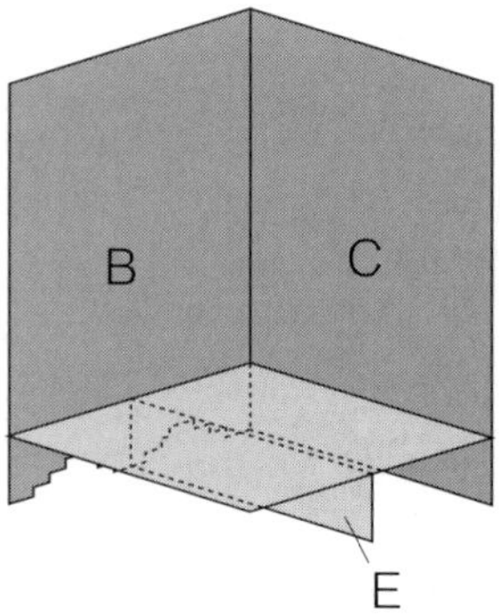

A – Lid Base
(cut 1) 34 x 34 holes

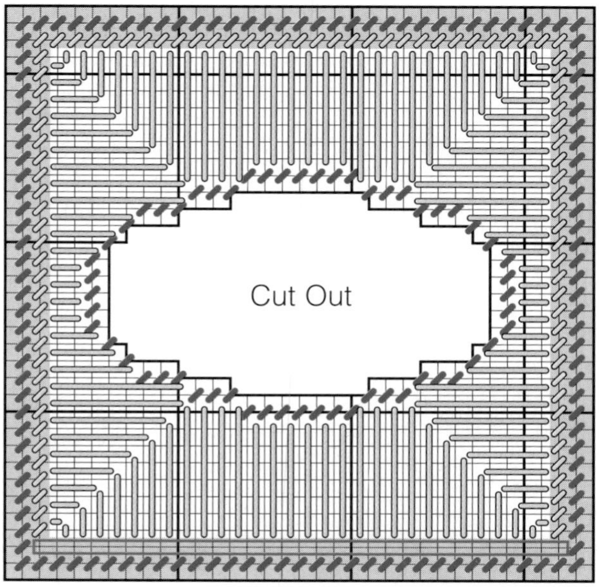

B – Box Scallop Side (cut 2) 30 x 45 holes

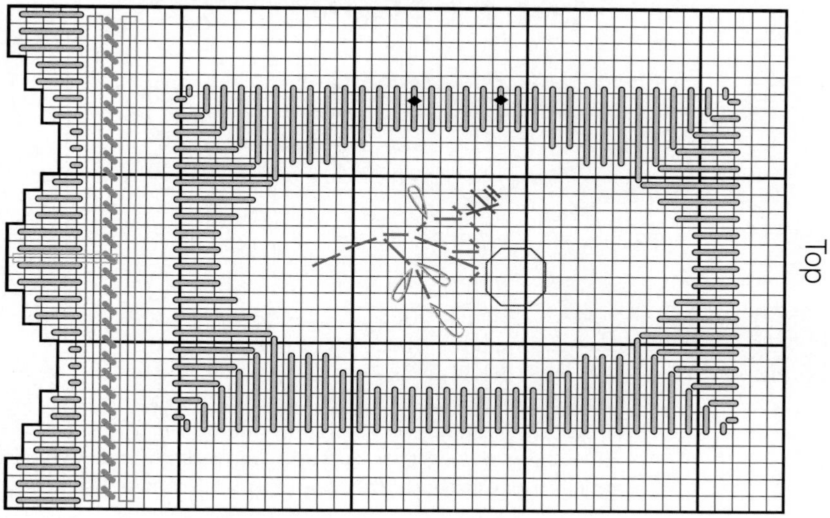

H – Lid Cutout Frame
(cut 1) 14 x 24 holes

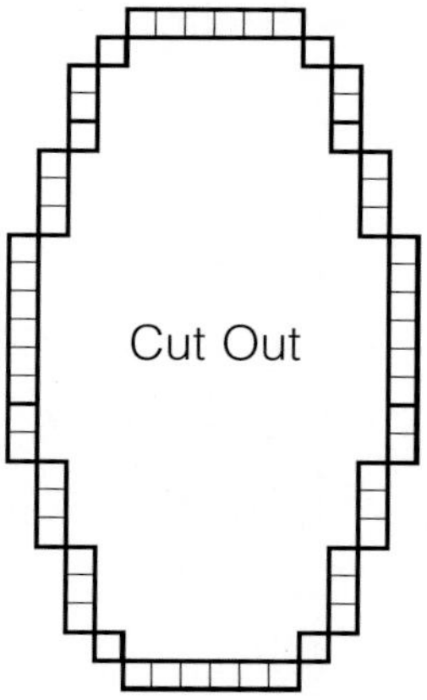

C – Box Solid Side (cut 2) 30 x 45 holes

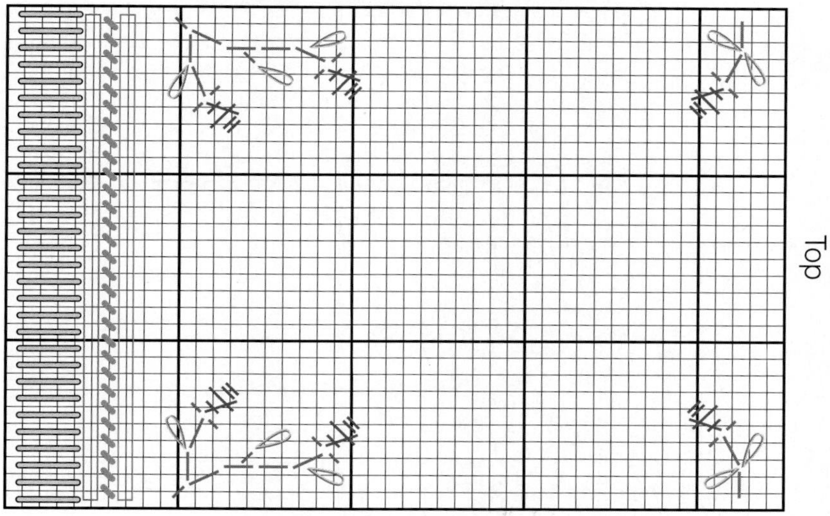

COLOR KEY: **Tissue Chest**

Metallic cord

	White/Silver – 14 yds.	
Nylon Plus™	**Needloft™** yarn	
	#28	#26 Baby Green – 5 yds.
	#31	#27 Holly – 10 yds.
	#09	#32 Royal – 20 yds.
	#01	#41 White – 65 yds.

STITCH KEY:

- Backstitch/Straight Stitch
- Lazy Daisy Stitch
- Unworked Areas
- Unworked Area/Lid Attachment
- Unworked Areas/Bottom Attachment
- Unworked Areas/Bottom Support Attachment
- ♦ Yarn Attachment
- Rosebud Placement

A – Lid Top
(cut 1)
30 x 30 holes

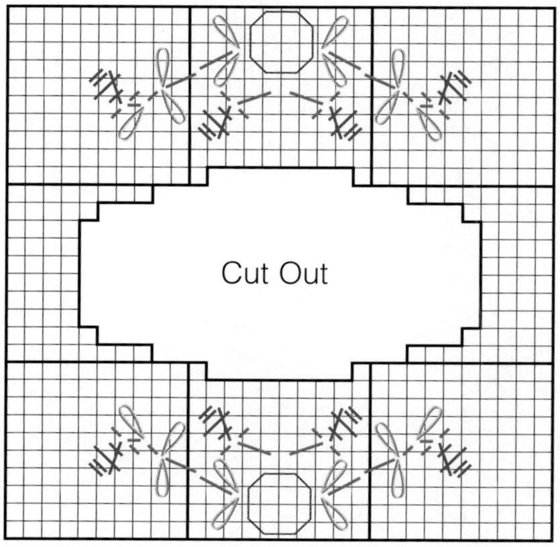

F – Inner Base Scallop Side
(cut 2) 5 x 32 holes

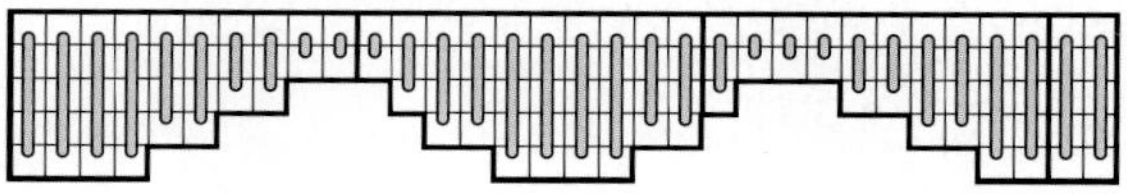

G – Outer Base Scallop Side
(cut 2) 4 x 34 holes

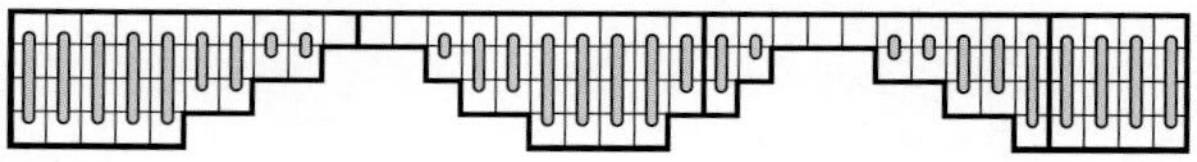

I – Motif Frame

(cut 2) 15 x 28 holes

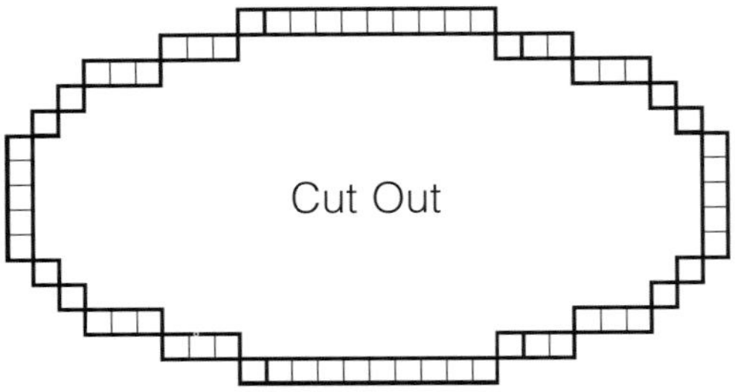

Inner & Outer Base Assembly Diagram

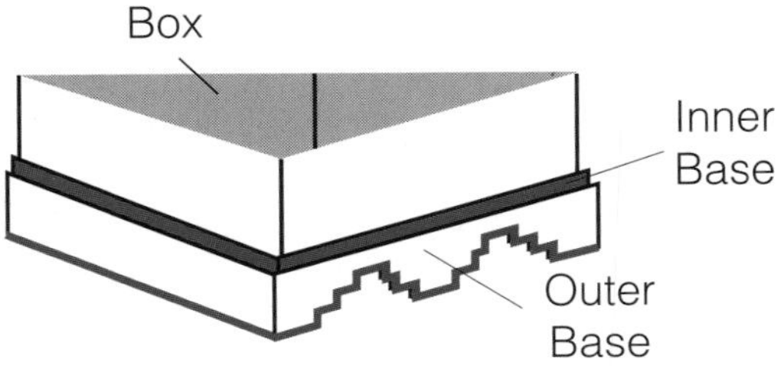

BED CADDY

SIZE: 7" x 12¼" x 8¾" tall.

MATERIALS:

- ❑ 4½ sheets of 7-count plastic canvas
- ❑ Two 4-mm. silver beads
- ❑ 9" x 12" white felt square (optional)
- ❑ ¾ yd. white 1" pregathered lace
- ❑ ¾ yd. white 2½" pregathered lace
- ❑ 1½ yds. blue 2½" satin ribbon
- ❑ 1 yd. blue ⅛" satin ribbon
- ❑ Fabric stiffener or spray starch (optional)
- ❑ Sewing needle and blue thread
- ❑ Craft glue or glue gun
- ❑ Metallic cord; for amount see Color Key.
- ❑ Worsted-weight or plastic canvas yarn; for amounts see Color Key.
- ❑ Two Roses; see instructions on page 31.

CUTTING INSTRUCTIONS:

NOTE: Graphs continued on page 36.

A: For headboard front and back, cut one each according to graphs.

B: For lid top, cut one according to graph.

C: For lid base, cut one according to graph.

D: For box sides, cut two 15 x 77 holes (no graph).

E: For box end and dividers, cut four 15 x 40 holes (no graphs).

F: For box bottom, cut one 40 x 77 holes (no graph).

G: For optional backing, using F as a pattern, cut one from felt ⅛" smaller at all edges.

STITCHING INSTRUCTIONS:

1: Using colors and stitches indicated, work A and B pieces according to graphs. Fill in uncoded areas (leave indicated areas of front A unworked) using White and Continental Stitch. Using Royal and Continental Stitch, work C according to graph, leaving uncoded center area unworked. Using White and Long Stitch over narrow width, work D pieces and one E for box end.

2: See **NOTE** above Step 3, and follow Step 3 of Tissue Chest on page 32.

3: Holding right side of lid base to wrong side of lid top, with White, Whipstitch B and C together as indicated; with metallic cord, Overcast unfinished side and bottom edges of lid base.

4: With White, Whipstitch D, E (dividers are unworked) and unworked F pieces together according to Bed Caddy Assembly Diagram. Whipstitch box and lid to front A as indicated (see diagram). Holding A pieces wrong sides together and working through all thicknesses along bottom of box, with matching colors, Whipstitch together.

NOTE: Cut ⅛" ribbon into four 9" lengths.

5: Tie each 9" ribbon into a bow; trim ends. Apply stiffener or starch to wide ribbon; press in 3" box pleats (see Pleat Illustration). Sew pleats together at top edge. Omitting headboard area, glue top edge of pleated ribbon around outer top edge of box. Glue 1" lace to wrong side of lid base and 2½" lace over 1" lace as shown in photo. Glue Roses to front and back of headboard as indicated, bows to center and bottom corners of lid and to front of headboard and one bead to top of each post as shown. If desired, glue G to bottom of box.

A – Headboard Back

(cut 1) 46 x 57 holes

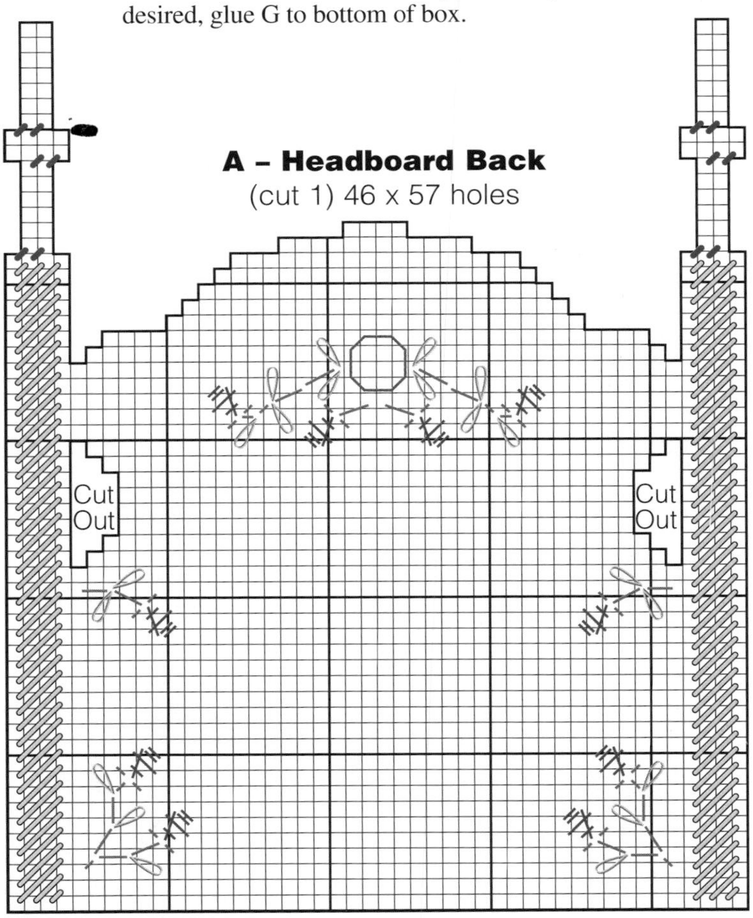

COLOR KEY: Bed Caddy

	Metallic cord	
■	White/Silver – 11 yds.	
	Nylon Plus™ Needloft™ yarn	
■	#28	#26 Baby Green – 6 yds.
■	#31	#27 Holly – 14 yds.
■	#09	#32 Royal – 20 yds.
▨	#01	#41 White – 3 oz.

STITCH KEY:

- Backstitch/Straight Stitch
- Lazy Daisy Stitch
- Unworked Areas/Lid & Box Side Attachment
- Lid Top Attachment
- Rosebud Placement

B – Lid Top (cut 1) 42 x 78 holes

Attach to headboard.

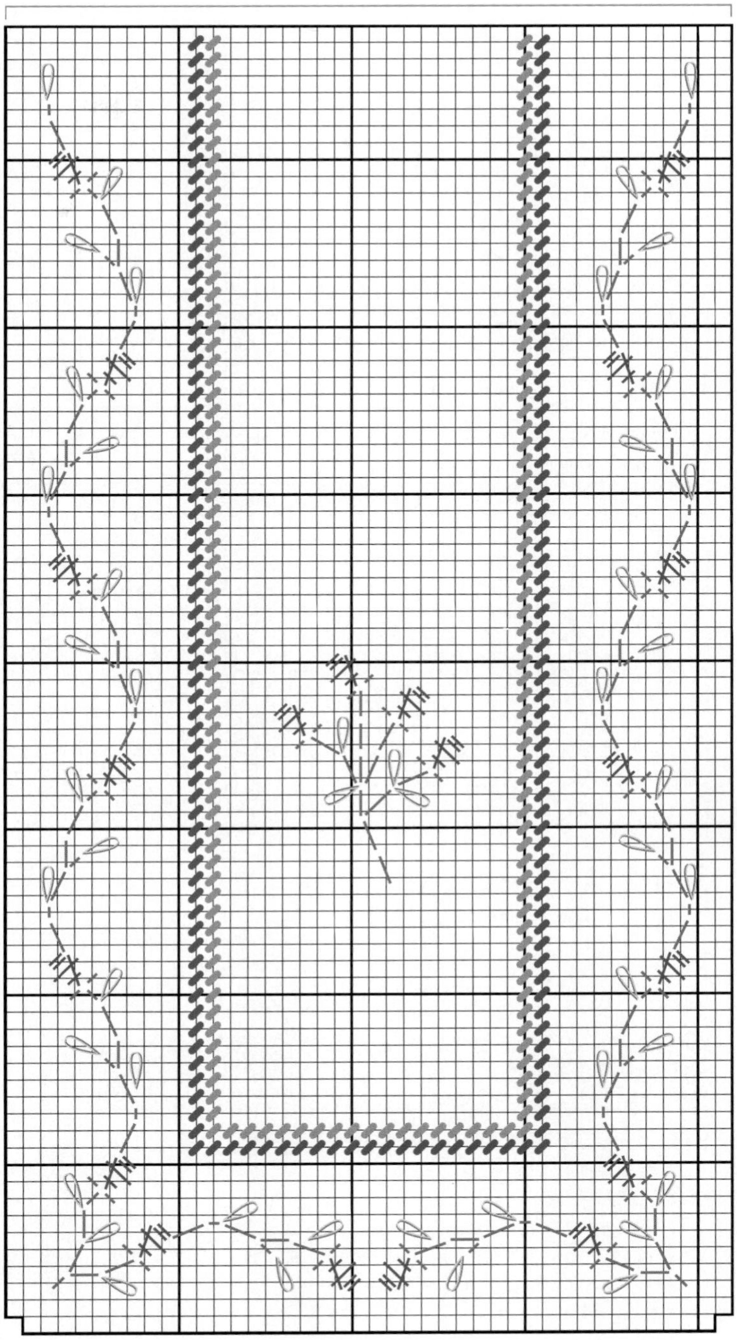

Pleat Illustration

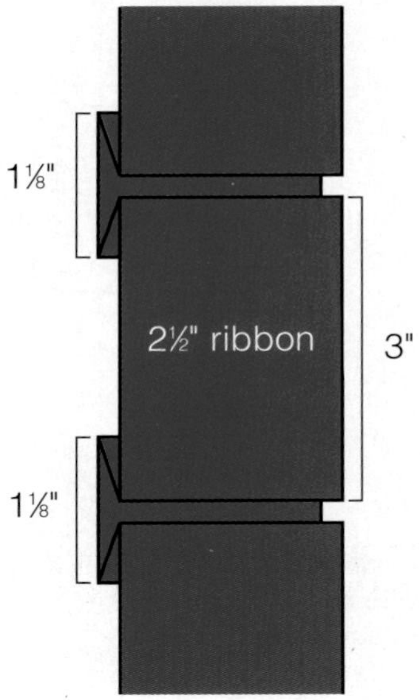

Bed Caddy Assembly Diagram

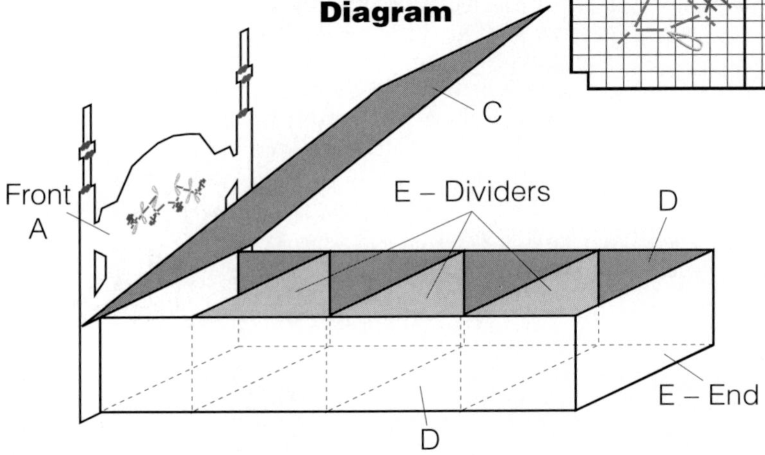

A – Headboard Front

(cut 1) 46 x 57 holes

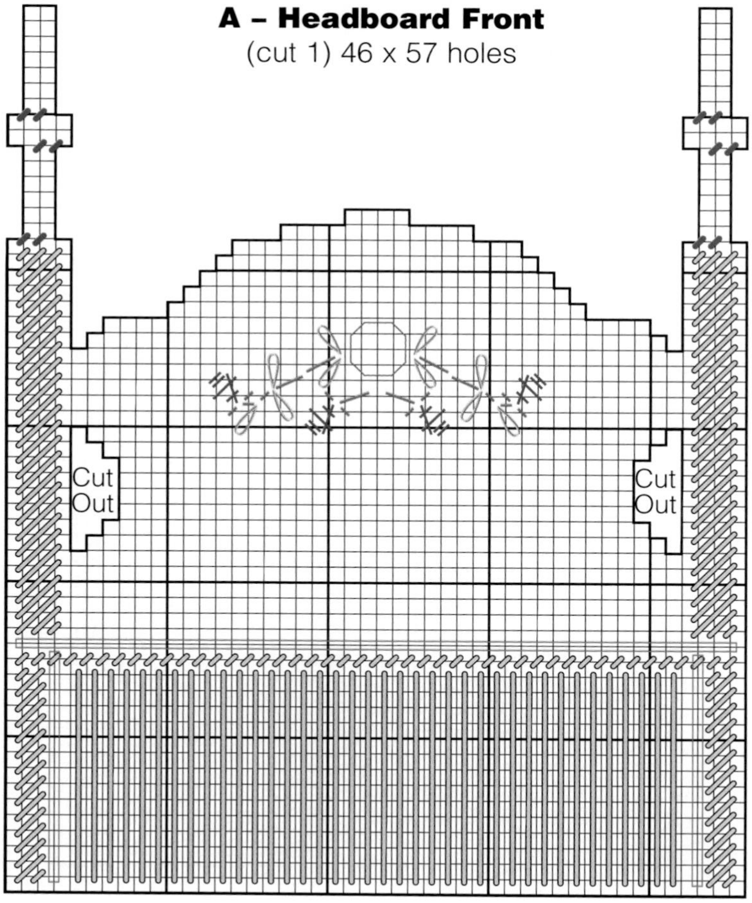

Cut opposite end corners square; continue established border pattern across entire length.

C – Lid Base

(cut 1)
46 x 80 holes

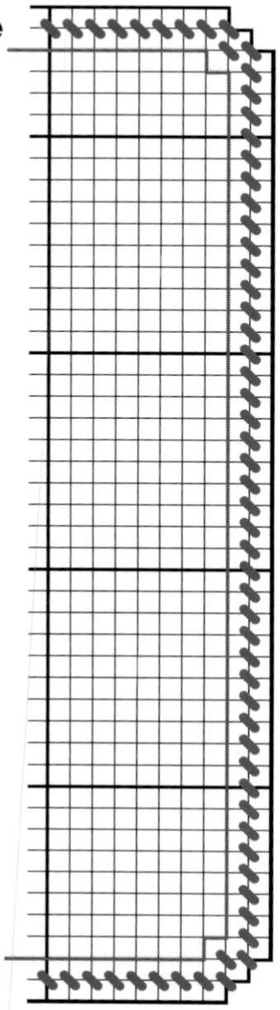

PILLOW

SIZE: 3⅛" x 5⅝" x 1¼" tall, not including lace.

MATERIALS:

- ❏ ½ sheet of 7-count plastic canvas
- ❏ ⅔ yd. white 1" pregathered lace
- ❏ Polyester fiberfill (optional)
- ❏ Craft glue or glue gun
- ❏ Metallic cord; for amount see Color Key.
- ❏ Worsted-weight or plastic canvas yarn; for amounts see Color Key.

CUTTING INSTRUCTIONS:

A: For pillow top, cut one according to graph.

B: For base top and bottom, cut two (one for top and one for bottom) 20 x 37 holes.

C: For motif frame, cut one according to graph.

STITCHING INSTRUCTIONS:

1: Using colors and stitches indicated, work A and top B pieces according to graphs. Fill in uncoded areas of A and work bottom B (leave indicated and uncoded areas of top B unworked) using White and Continental Stitch; Overcast unfinished edges of bottom B.

2: See **NOTE** above Step 3, and follow Step 3 of Tissue Chest on page 32.

3: Holding X edges of A wrong sides together, with White, Whipstitch together as indicated; Whipstitch A and top B together as indicated, stuffing with fiberfill before closing, if desired. With metallic cord for base top and inner edges of frame and Royal for outer edges of frame, Overcast unfinished edges of top B and C pieces.

4: Glue B pieces wrong sides together with lace between. Glue motif frame to pillow as shown in photo.

C – Motif Frame

(cut 1)
9 x 21 holes

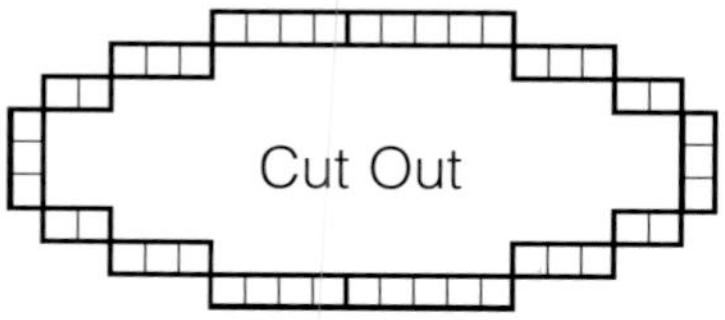

A – Pillow Top
(cut 1) 21 x 39 holes
Whipstitch X edges together.

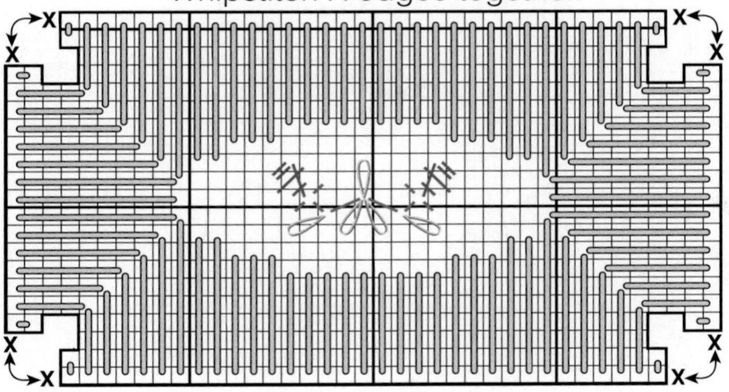

B – Base Top
(cut 1) 20 x 37 holes

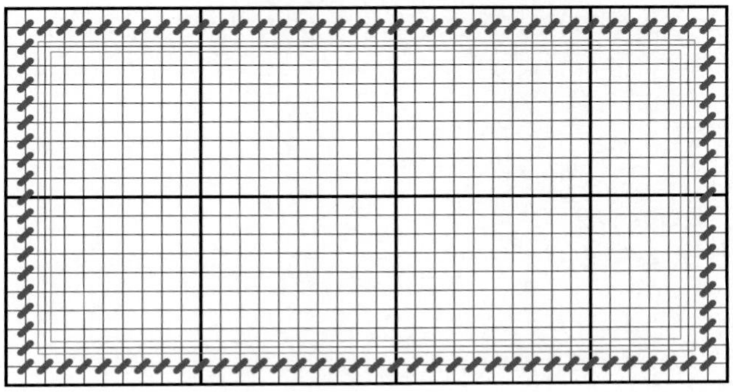

B – Base Bottom (cut 1) 20 x 37 holes

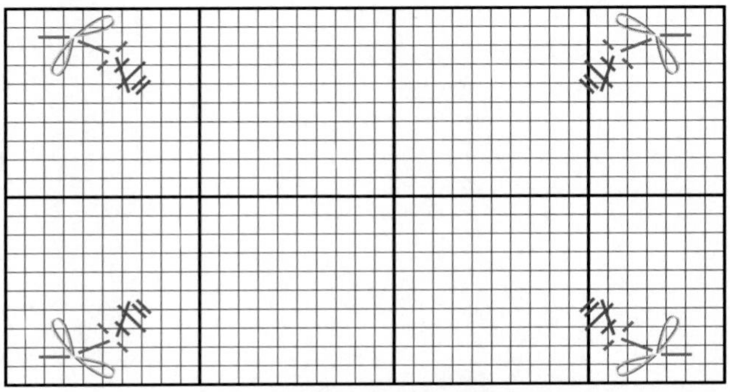

COLOR KEY: Pillow

☐	Metallic cord White/Silver – 3 yds.	
	Nylon Plus™ Needloft™ yarn	
▒	#28	#26 Baby Green – 1 yd.
▒	#31	#27 Holly – 1½ yds.
▒	#09	#32 Royal – 5½ yds.
▨	#01	#41 White – 20 yds.

STITCH KEY:

- — Backstitch/Straight Stitch
- ⊂⊃ Lazy Daisy Stitch
- ☐ Unworked Area/Pillow Top Attachment

NIGHT STAND

SIZE: 3⅞" x 3⅞" x 3⅛" tall.

MATERIALS:

- ❑ ¾ sheet of 7-count plastic canvas
- ❑ Four 5-mm. pearl beads
- ❑ 12 silver 4-mm. beads
- ❑ Craft glue or glue gun
- ❑ Metallic cord; for amount see Color Key on page 38.
- ❑ Worsted-weight or plastic canvas yarn; for amounts see Color Key.

CUTTING INSTRUCTIONS:

NOTE: Diagram and graphs on page 38.

A: For lid top and box bottom, cut two (one for top and one for bottom) 21 x 21 holes.

B: For lid base, cut one 25 x 25 holes.

C: For box scallop and solid sides, cut two according to graph for scallop sides and two 18 x 21 holes for solid sides.

D: For inner base scallop and solid sides, cut two according to graph for scallop sides and two 5 x 22 holes for solid sides (no solid side graph).

E: For outer base scallop and solid sides, cut two according to graph for scallop sides and two 4 x 23 holes for solid sides (no solid side graph).

F: For motif frames, cut three according to graph.

STITCHING INSTRUCTIONS:

1: Using colors and stitches indicated, work A, B (work gray areas on wrong side of canvas and leave indicated area unworked), C, scallop D and scallop E pieces according to graphs. Fill in uncoded areas of A-C pieces (leave indicated areas of C pieces unworked) using White and Continental Stitch. Using White and Long Stitch over narrow width, work remaining D and E pieces.

2: With White for lid top, metallic cord for lid base and inner edges of frames, and Royal for outer edges of frames, Overcast unfinished edges of lid top A, B and F pieces.

3: See **NOTE** above Step 3, and follow Step 3 of Tissue Chest on page 32, omitting embroidery on box bottom.

4: For handles, follow Step 4 of Tissue Chest.

5: To attach lid base, with right side of base facing wrong side of one scallop side, with White, Whipstitch unworked bar on B to top edge of one scallop C.

6: For box, alternating scallop and solid sides and with right side of bottom facing in, with White, Whipstitch C and bottom A pieces together as indicated (see Night Stand Bottom Assembly Diagram); Overcast remaining unfinished top edges of box.

7: For base, using D and E pieces in place of F and G pieces, follow Step 8 of Tissue Chest.

8: Holding wrong sides together, glue lid top to center of lid base (outer edge of base will have right side showing). Glue motif frames to scallop sides and lid top as shown in photo.

A – Lid Top & Box Bottom
(cut 1 each)
21 x 21 holes

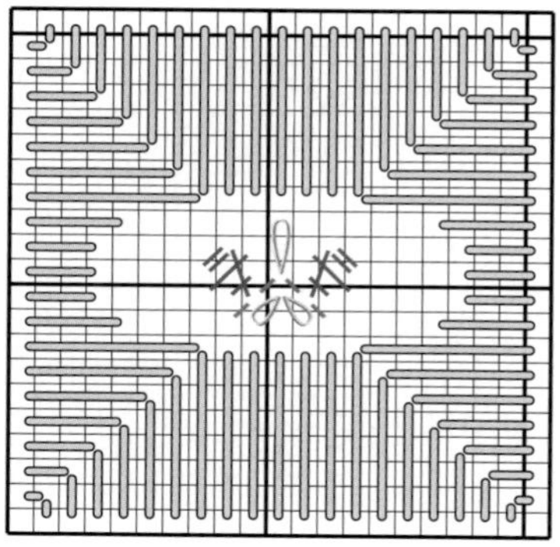

C – Box Solid Side
(cut 2) 18 x 21 holes

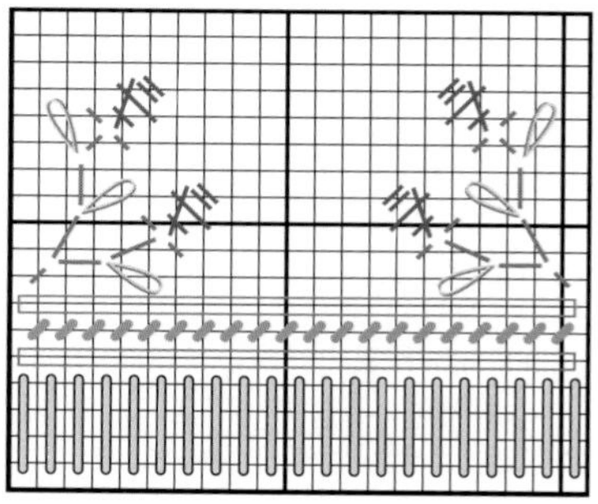

C – Box Scallop Side
(cut 2) 18 x 21 holes

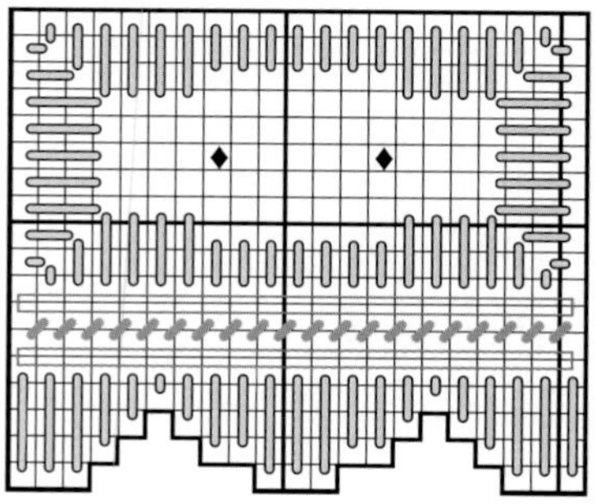

E – Outer Base Scallop Side
(cut 2) 4 x 25 holes

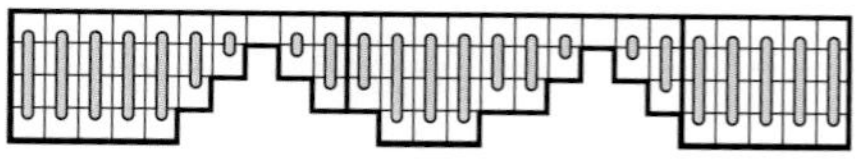

F – Motif Frame
(cut 3) 7 x 15 holes

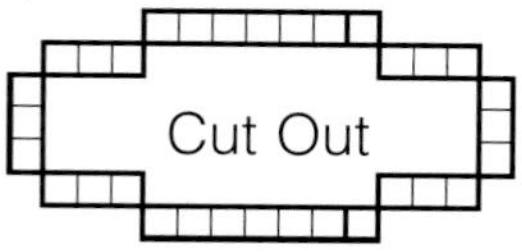

D – Inner Base Scallop Side
(cut 2) 5 x 23 holes

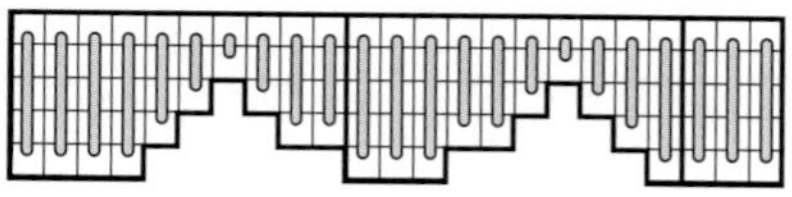

Nightstand Bottom Assembly Diagram
(cutaway view)

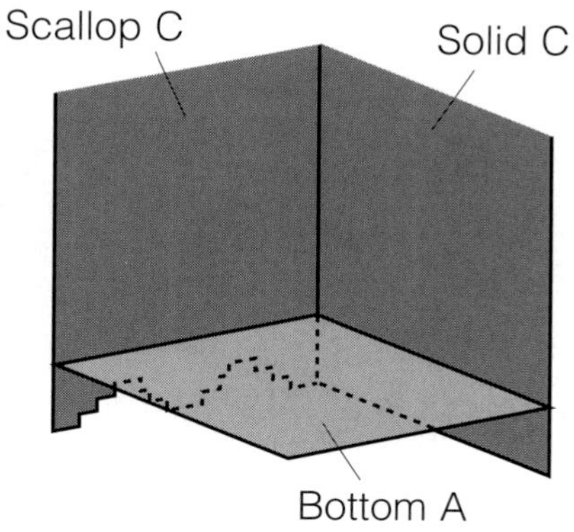

B – Lid Base
(cut 1) 25 x 25 holes

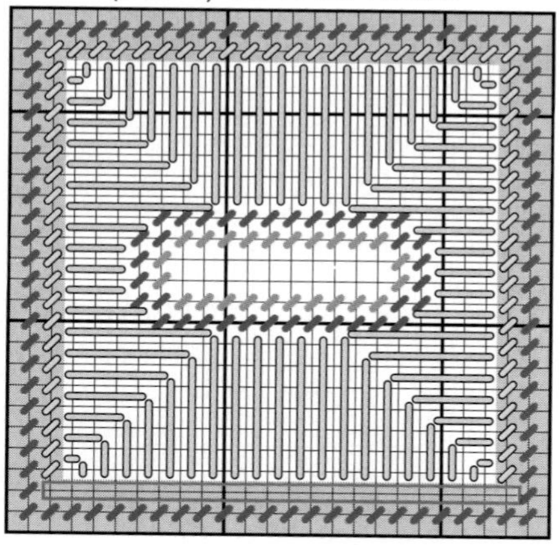

COLOR KEY: Nightstand

Metallic cord		
White/Silver – 8 yds.		
Nylon Plus™ Needloft™ yarn		
#28	#26 Baby Green – 1 yd.	
#31	#27 Holly – 2 yds.	
#09	#32 Royal – 12 yds.	
#01	#41 White – 32 yds.	

STITCH KEY:

- Backstitch/Straight Stitch
- Lazy Daisy Stitch
- Unworked Areas
- Unworked Area/Bottom Attachment
- Unworked Area/ Lid Attachment
- ♦ Yarn Attachment

MIRROR

SIZE: 1⅝" x 3⅛" tall.

MATERIALS:
- ❑ ¼ sheet of 7-count plastic canvas
- ❑ 2" aluminum foil
- ❑ 1½" x 2" poster board
- ❑ Craft glue or glue gun
- ❑ Metallic cord; for amount see Color Key.
- ❑ Worsted-weight or plastic canvas yarn; for amounts see Color Key.

CUTTING INSTRUCTIONS:

A: For frame front and back, cut two (one for front and one for back) according to graph.

B: For stand front and back, cut two (one for front and one for back) according to graph.

C: For stand ends, cut two according to graph.

D: For stand base, cut one 3 x 9 holes (no graph).

E: For mirror, using one A as a pattern, cut one from foil and one from cardboard ⅛" smaller at all edges.

STITCHING INSTRUCTIONS:

1: Using colors and stitches indicated, work A-C pieces according to graphs. Fill in uncoded area of back A using White and Continental Stitch. With metallic cord, Overcast unfinished cutout edges of front A.

2: Holding A pieces wrong sides together, with White, Whipstitch together as indicated on graph; Overcast unfinished bottom edges. Glue E pieces together and slide into frame.

3: Holding B pieces wrong sides together, with matching colors, Whipstitch together as indicated; Whipstitch stand, C and unworked D pieces together according to Mirror Assembly Diagram. Glue stand to back as indicated.

Mirror Assembly Diagram

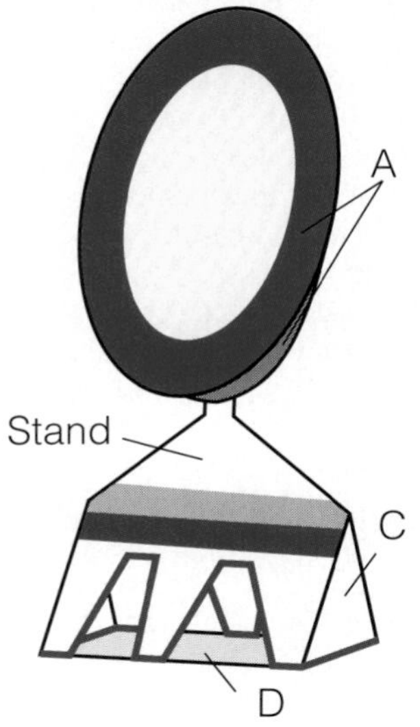

B - Stand Front & Back
(cut 1 each)
9 x 12 holes

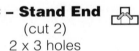

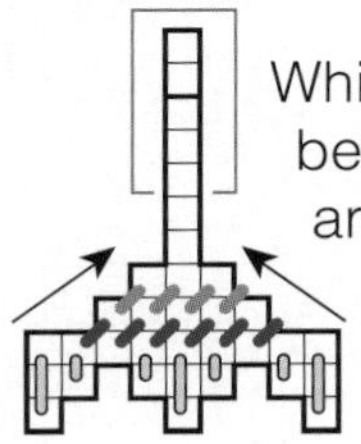

A - Frame Front & Back
(cut 1 each)
10 x 14 holes

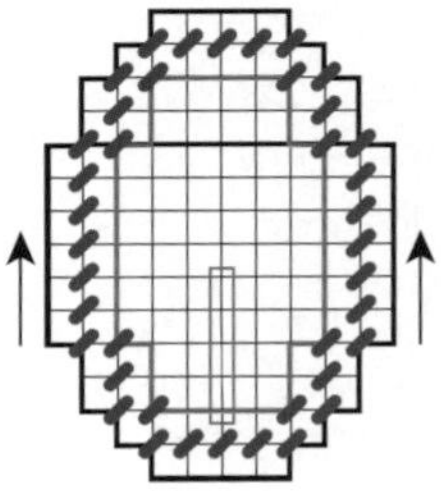

C - Stand End
(cut 2)
2 x 3 holes

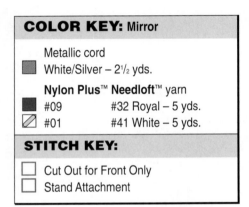

COLOR KEY: Mirror	
Metallic cord	
White/Silver – 2½ yds.	
Nylon Plus™ **Needloft™** yarn	
#09	#32 Royal – 5 yds.
#01	#41 White – 5 yds.
STITCH KEY:	
Cut Out for Front Only	
Stand Attachment	

VANITY

SIZE: 3⅛" x 9¼" x 11¼" tall.

MATERIALS:

- ❑ Four sheets of 7-count plastic canvas
- ❑ Four 5-mm. pearl beads
- ❑ Eight 4-mm. silver beads
- ❑ ½ yd. aluminum foil
- ❑ 5" x 9" poster board
- ❑ Craft glue or glue gun
- ❑ Metallic cord; for amount see Color Key on page 41.
- ❑ Worsted-weight or plastic canvas yarn; for amounts see Color Key.
- ❑ One Rose; see instructions on page 31.

CUTTING INSTRUCTIONS:

NOTE: Graphs and diagrams on pages 40-43.

A: For front and back, cut one each according to graphs.

B: For outer sides, cut two 17 x 30 holes.

C: For inner side pieces, cut two 7 x 17 holes and two 17 x 23 holes (no graphs).

D: For top, cut one 17 x 58 holes.

E: For drawer supports, cut two 17 x 17 holes (no graph).

F: For side lid tops and bases, cut two 14 x 15 holes for tops and two 18 x 19 holes for bases.

G: For round mirror frame, cut one according to graph.

H: For side mirror fronts and backs, cut two each according to graphs.

I: For center mirror, cut one according to graph.

J: For inner base scallop and solid sides, cut four according to graph for scallop sides and four 5 x 18 holes for solid sides (no solid side graph).

K: For outer base scallop and solid sides, cut four according to graph for scallop sides and four 4 x 19 holes for solid sides (no solid side graph).

L: For small drawer facade, cut two 7 x 13 holes.

M: For large drawer fronts, cut two 11 x 13 holes.

N: For large drawer inside pieces, cut four 7 x 16 holes, two 9 x 16 holes and four 7 x 9 holes (no graphs).

O: For small handle frames, cut two according to graph.

P: For large handle frames, cut four according to graph.

Q: For mirrors, using G, H and I pieces as patterns, cut one each from foil and poster board ⅛" smaller at all edges.

STITCHING INSTRUCTIONS:

1: Using colors and stitches indicated, work A, B, D, F (work gray areas on lid base on wrong side of canvas), G, front H (one on opposite side of canvas), I, scallop J, scallop K, L, M and O pieces according to graphs. Fill in uncoded areas of A and B (leave indicated areas unworked), D (omit center area if desired), F, front H, I (leave indicated area unworked), M and work C, back H (one on opposite side of canvas) and N pieces using White and Continental Stitch. Using White and Long Stitch over narrow width, work remaining J and K pieces.

2: With White, Overcast unfinished edges of knee cutouts as indicated and side and top edges of drawer openings on A pieces, bottom edges of H and I as indicated and L and M pieces. With metallic cord, Overcast unfinished edges of F pieces and G as indicated, cutout edges of G, front H, I and P pieces. With Royal, Overcast unfinished edges of O and P pieces.

3: See **NOTE** above Step 3, and follow Step 3 of Tissue Chest on page 32.

4: For handles on large drawer fronts, using two pearl and three silver beads for each handle, follow Step 4 of Tissue Chest.

5: Holding pieces wrong sides together, with cord for round mirror frame and with White, Whipstitch back A, G and I pieces together as indicated and according to Back & Center Mirror Assembly Diagram. Whipstitch D and I together as indicated.

6: With White, Whipstitch C pieces and D together as indicated and according to Vanity Assembly Diagram; Whipstitch C and D pieces to back A as indicated. Whipstitch front A, B and E pieces to assembly as indicated and according to diagram. (**NOTE:** Round mirror frame does not attach to front or inner side pieces.) For each side mirror, holding one of each front and back H pieces wrong sides together, Whipstitch together as indicated. Working through all thicknesses, Whipstitch one side mirror to each side of center mirror and back as indicated (see diagram); Whipstitch remaining unfinished edges of back A and I together.

7: For each mirror, glue matching size Q pieces together. Slide center and side mirrors into corresponding frames, and place round mirror between frame and Vanity top; glue to secure, if desired. To attach each side lid base, holding base with right side facing in (outer edge will have right side showing), with cord, Whipstitch unfinished edge of one F to each side of back A as indicated.

8: For each base, using J and K pieces in place of F and G pieces, follow Step 8 of Tissue Chest.

9: For each drawer, Whipstitch N pieces together according to Large Drawer Assembly Diagram; Overcast unfinished edges. Center and glue one M to one short end of each assembly.

10: Glue Rose to back as indicated, one side lid top to center of each lid base, one silver bead to center of each O, one small handle frame to center of each L, one small drawer facade to front centered above each large drawer cutout and frames to drawer fronts and side lid tops as shown in photo.

A – Back

(cut 1) 58 x 73 holes

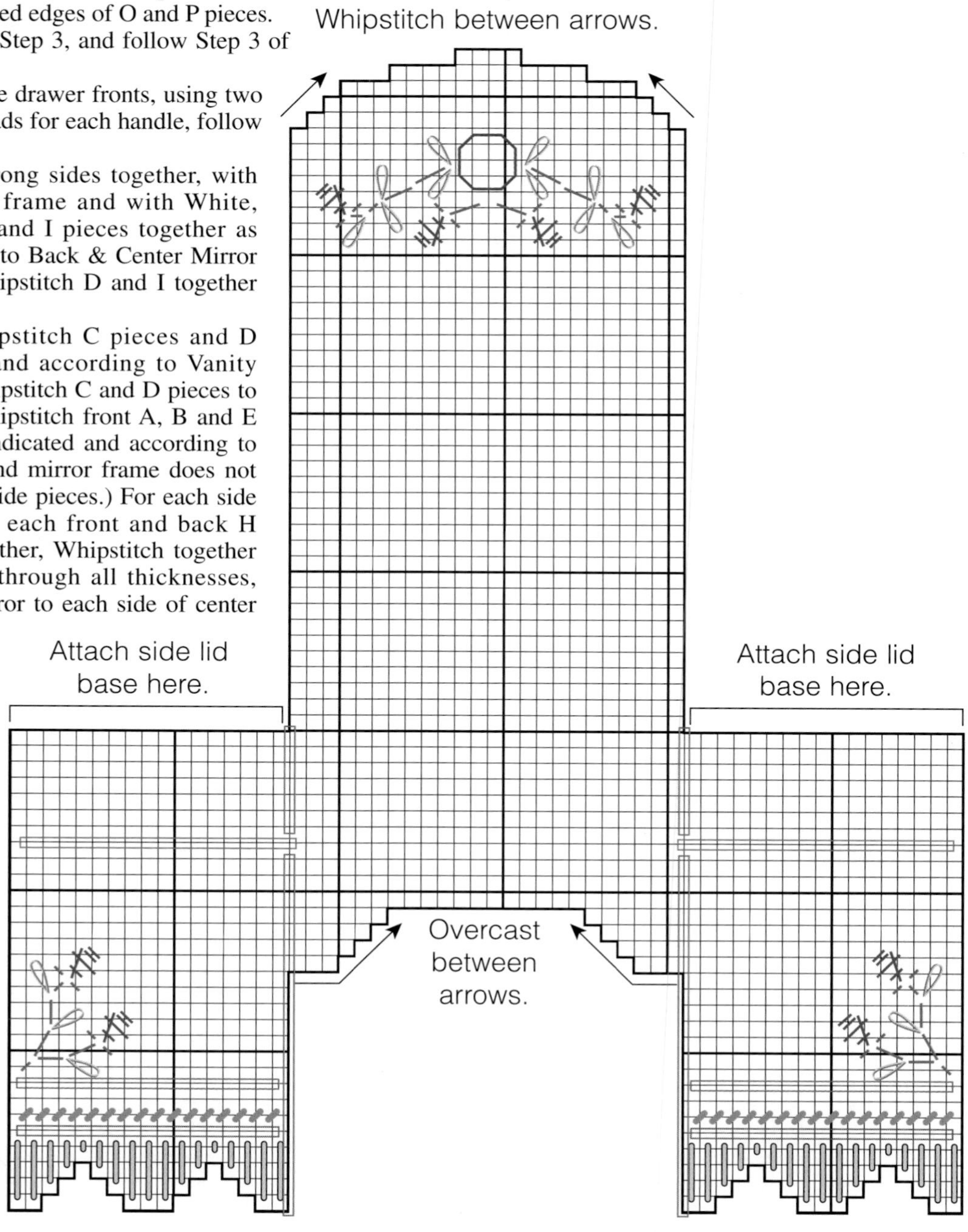

A – Front
(cut 1)
30 x 58 holes

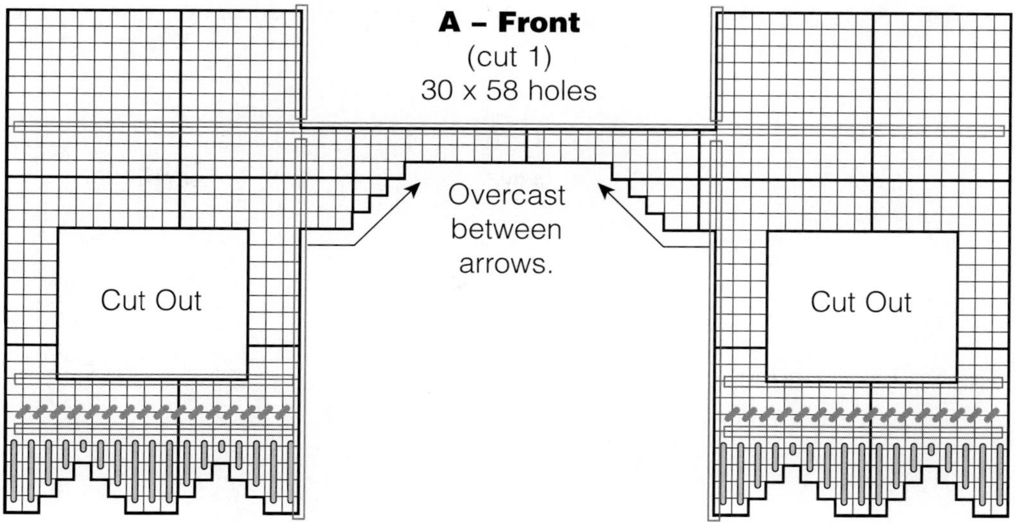

B – Outer Side
(cut 2) 17 x 30 holes

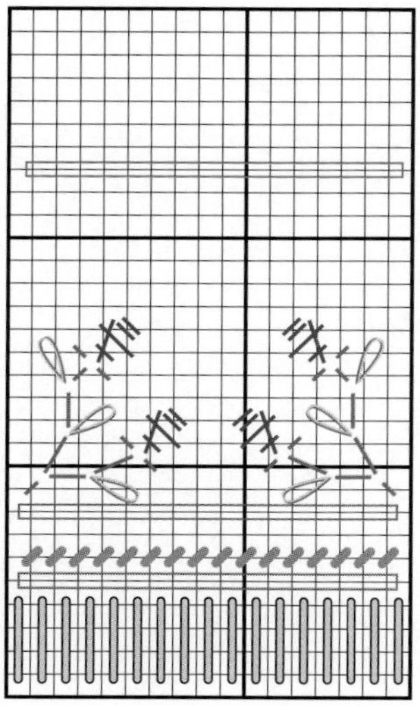

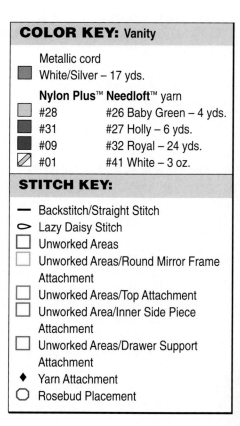

COLOR KEY: Vanity		
	Metallic cord	
■	White/Silver – 17 yds.	
	Nylon Plus™	**Needloft™** yarn
■	#28	#26 Baby Green – 4 yds.
■	#31	#27 Holly – 6 yds.
■	#09	#32 Royal – 24 yds.
▨	#01	#41 White – 3 oz.

STITCH KEY:

- — Backstitch/Straight Stitch
- ⬭ Lazy Daisy Stitch
- ☐ Unworked Areas
- ☐ Unworked Areas/Round Mirror Frame Attachment
- ☐ Unworked Areas/Top Attachment
- ☐ Unworked Area/Inner Side Piece Attachment
- ☐ Unworked Areas/Drawer Support Attachment
- ♦ Yarn Attachment
- ⬡ Rosebud Placement

D – Top (cut 1) 17 x 58 holes

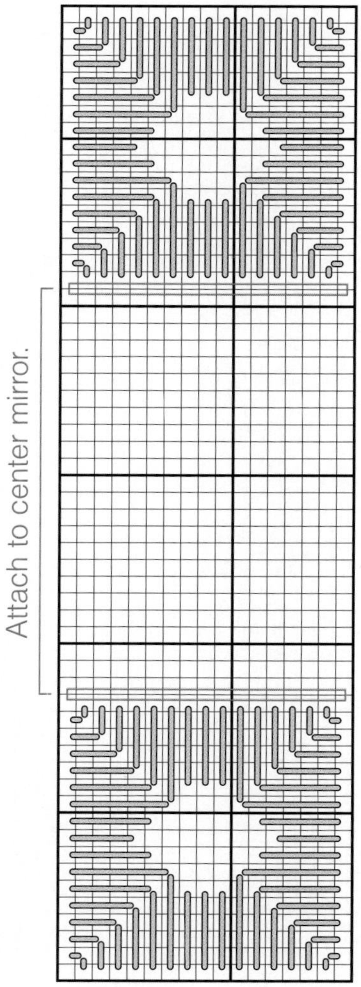

F – Side Lid Base
(cut 2) 18 x 19 holes

Do not Overcast;
attach to back.

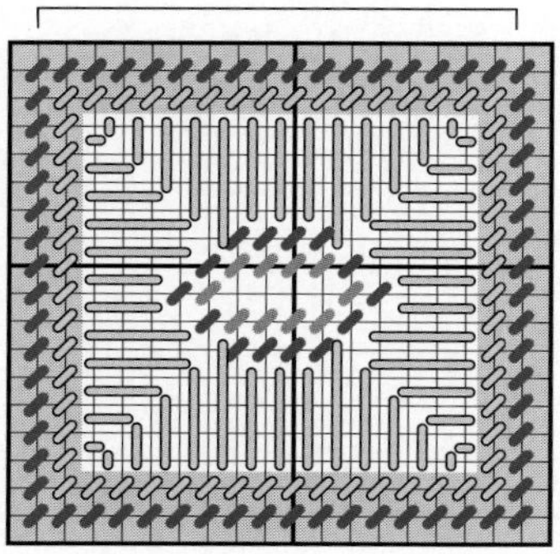

G – Round Mirror Frame
(cut 1) 19 x 22 holes

Do not Overcast; attach to center mirror.

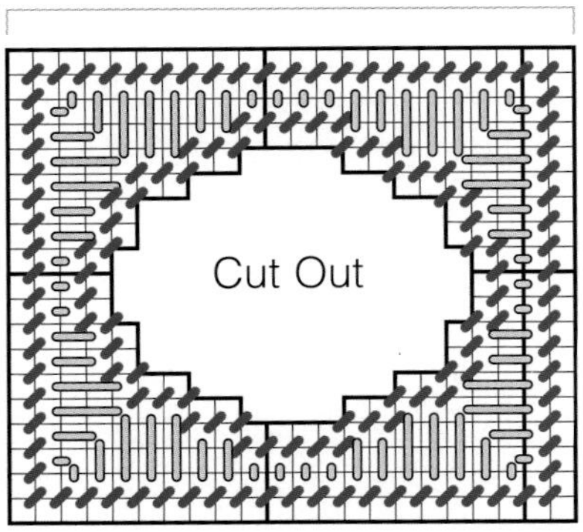

Back & Center Mirror Assembly Diagram

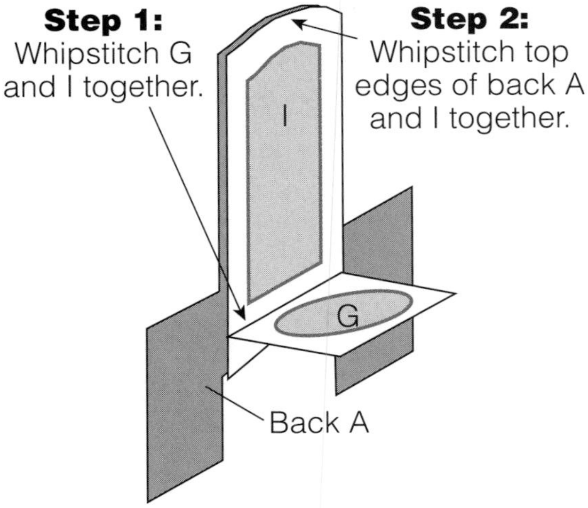

Large Drawer Assembly Diagram

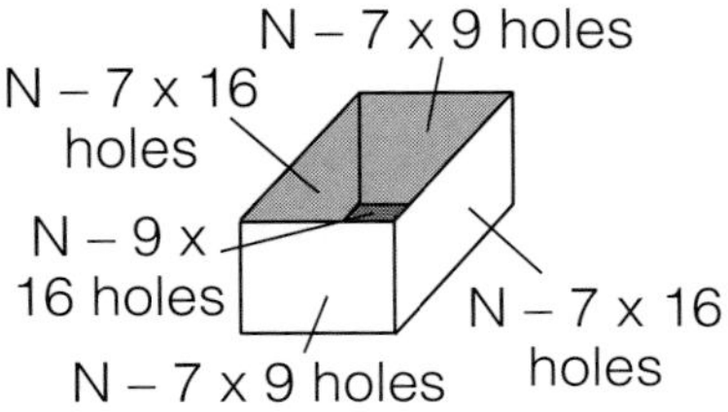

K – Outer Base Scallop Side
(cut 4) 4 x 21 holes

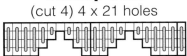

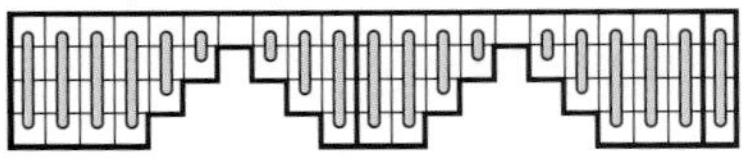

H – Side Mirror Back
(cut 2) 18 x 34 holes

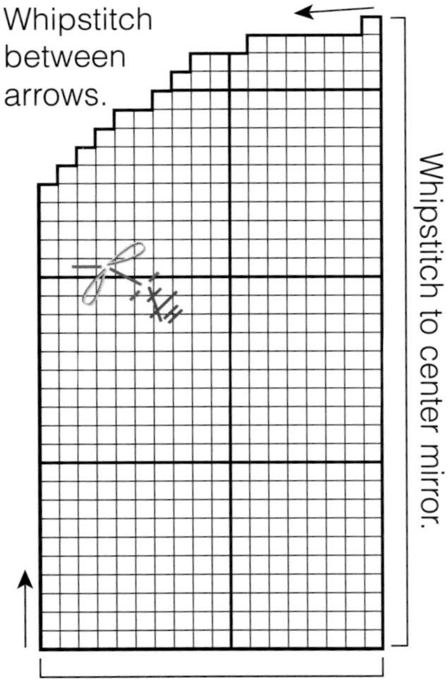

F – Side Lid Top
(cut 2) 14 x 15 holes

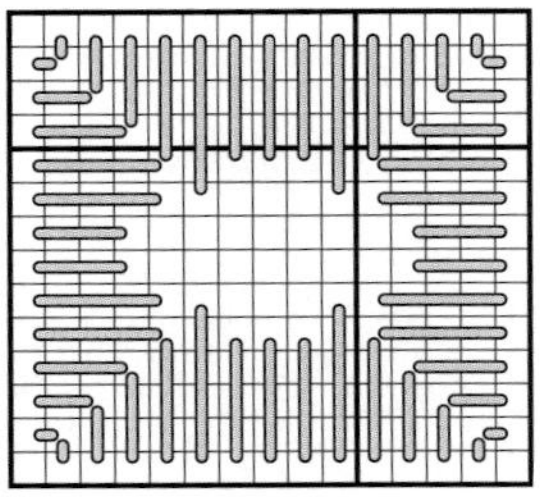

H – Side Mirror Front
(cut 2) 18 x 34 holes

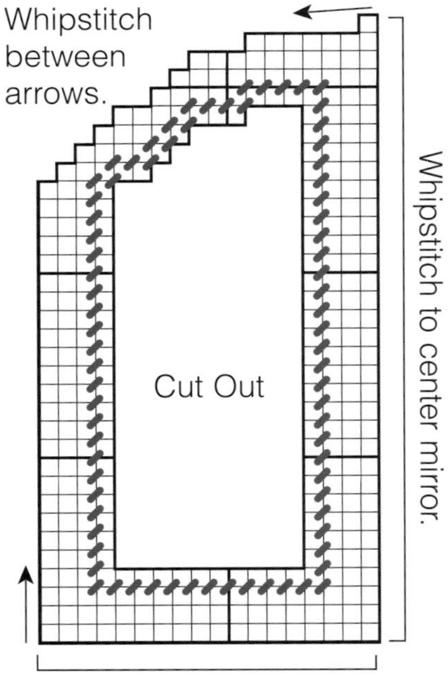

I – Center Mirror

(cut 1)
24 x 58 holes

Whipstitch between arrows.

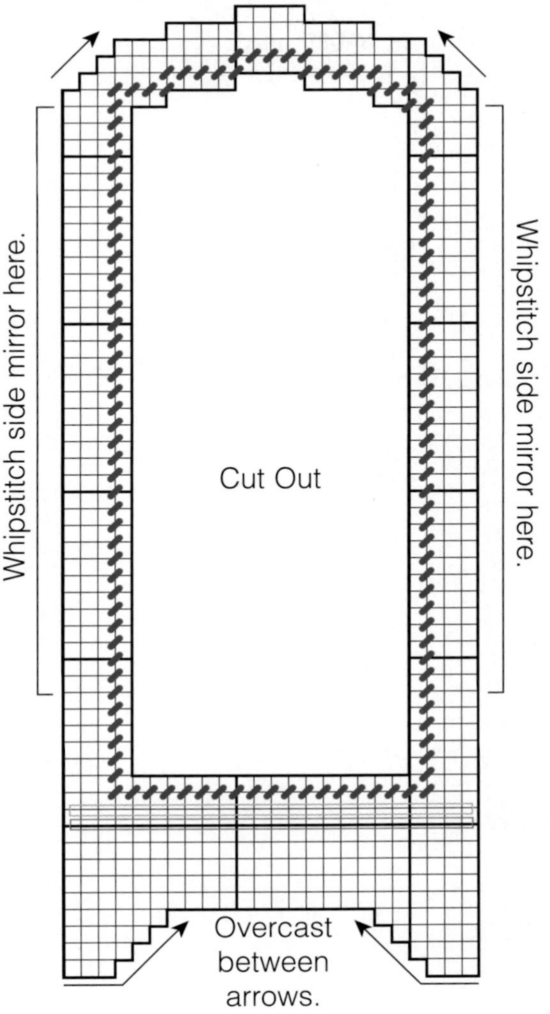

Vanity Assembly Diagram

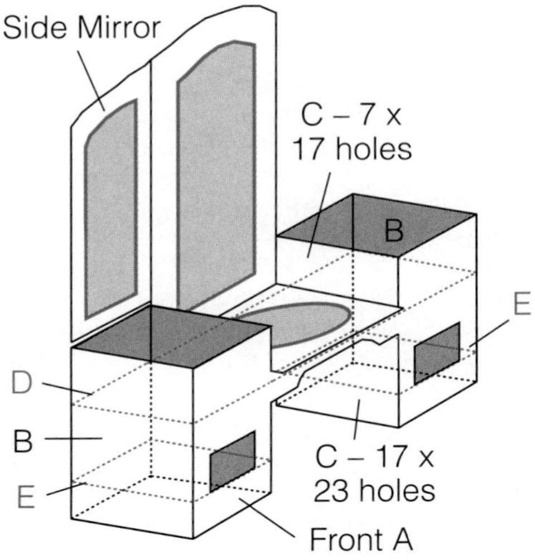

O – Small Handle Frame

(cut 2)
3 x 5 holes

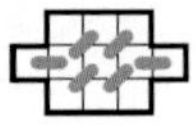

J – Inner Base Scallop Side

(cut 4) 5 x 19 holes

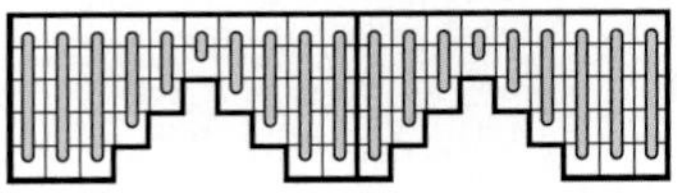

L – Small Drawer Facade

(cut 2) 7 x 13 holes

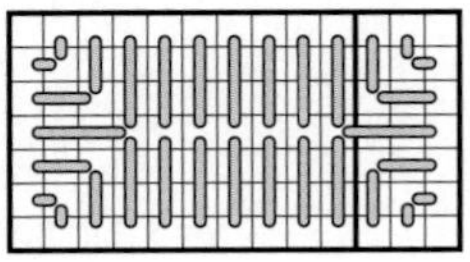

M – Large Drawer Front

(cut 2) 11 x 13 holes

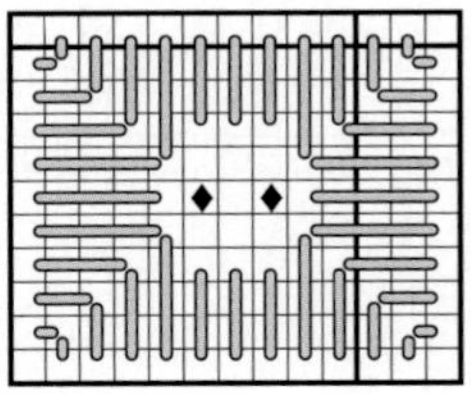

P – Large Handle Frame

(cut 4) 5 x 9 holes

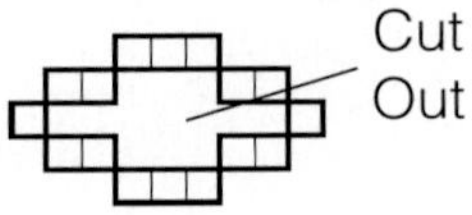

COLOR KEY: Vanity

Metallic cord
White/Silver – 17 yds.

Nylon Plus™	Needloft™ yarn
#28	#26 Baby Green – 4 yds.
#31	#27 Holly – 6 yds.
#09	#32 Royal – 24 yds.
#01	#41 White – 3 oz.

STITCH KEY:

- Backstitch/Straight Stitch
- Lazy Daisy Stitch
- Unworked Areas
- Unworked Areas/Round Mirror Frame Attachment
- Unworked Areas/Top Attachment
- Unworked Area/Inner Side Piece Attachment
- Unworked Areas/Drawer Support Attachment
- ♦ Yarn Attachment
- Rosebud Placement

VANITY STOOL

SIZE: 2¾" across x 3⅞" tall.

MATERIALS:

- ❑ ½ sheet of 7-count plastic canvas
- ❑ 7" white 1¼" pregathered lace
- ❑ Craft glue or glue gun
- ❑ Metallic cord; for amount see Color Key.
- ❑ Worsted-weight or plastic canvas yarn; for amounts see Color Key.

CUTTING INSTRUCTIONS:

A: For back, cut one according to graph.

B: For seat top and base, cut one each according to graphs.

C: For legs, cut eight according to graph.

D: For leg support pieces, cut two according to graph.

STITCHING INSTRUCTIONS:

1: Using colors indicated and Continental Stitch, work A (overlap five holes at ends as indicated on graph and work through both thicknesses to join) and one B piece for seat top according to graphs. Fill in uncoded areas (leave indicated area of A unworked), and work remaining B for base (leave indicated areas unworked) and C pieces using White and Continental Stitch.

2: See **NOTE** above Step 3, and follow Step 3 of Tissue Chest on page 32.

3: For each leg, holding two C pieces wrong sides together, with White, Whipstitch together as indicated. Whipstitch legs to seat base B as indicated. Holding D pieces together, Whipstitch together. With White for bottom of back and Royal for seat top, Overcast unfinished edges of A and seat top B.

4: With cord, Whipstitch seat base to unworked area of back as indicated (see Stool Assembly Diagram). With White, Overcast remaining unfinished edges of back. Glue ends of leg support to inner edges of legs according to diagram. Glue lace to seat base and back and seat top to base as shown.

B – Seat Top
(cut 1) 15 x 15 holes

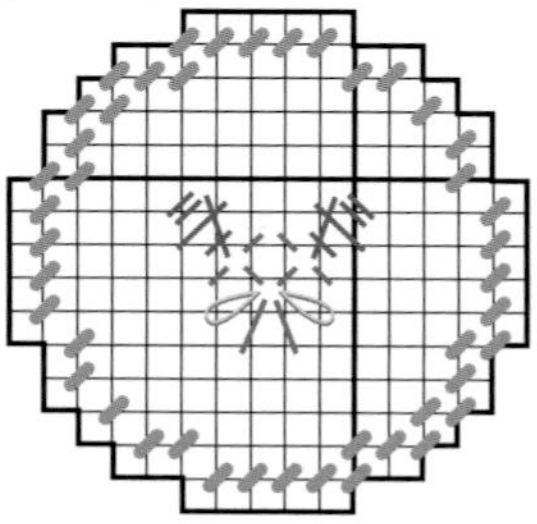

B – Seat Base
(cut 1) 17 x 17 holes

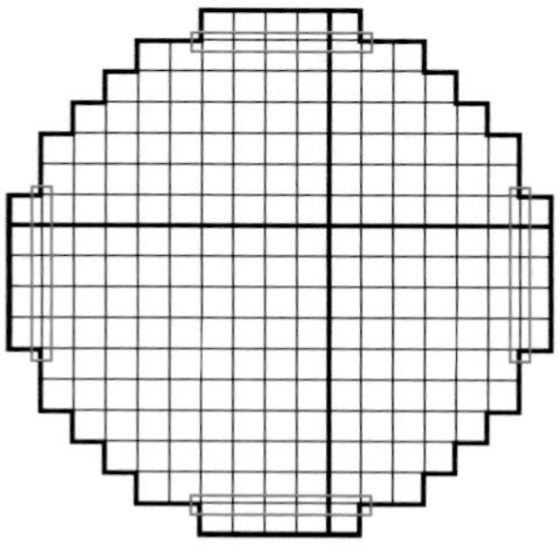

COLOR KEY: Vanity Stool

Metallic cord
- White/Silver – 7 yds.

Nylon Plus™	Needloft™ yarn
#28	#26 Baby Green – ½ yd.
#31	#27 Holly – 1 yd.
#09	#32 Royal – 6 yds.
#01	#41 White – 20 yds.

STITCH KEY:

- Backstitch/Straight Stitch
- Lazy Daisy Stitch
- Unworked Area/Seat Base Attachment
- Unworked Areas/Leg Attachments

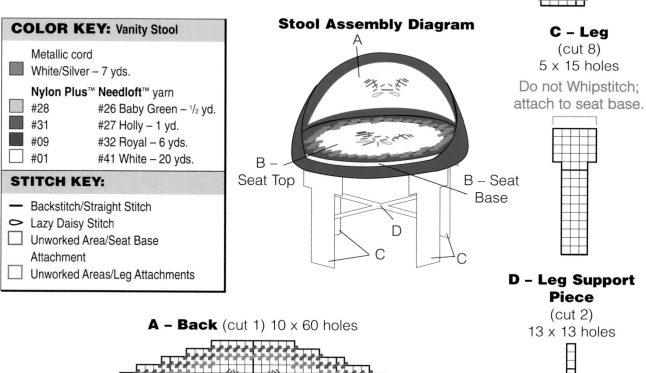

Stool Assembly Diagram

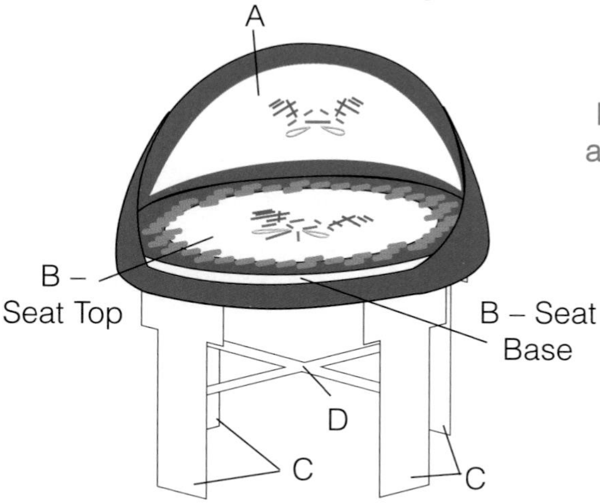

C – Leg
(cut 8)
5 x 15 holes

Do not Whipstitch; attach to seat base.

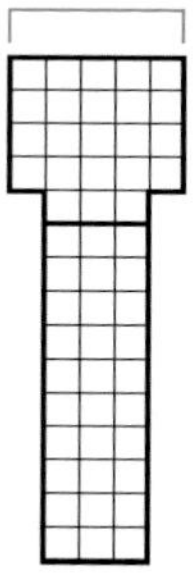

A – Back (cut 1) 10 x 60 holes

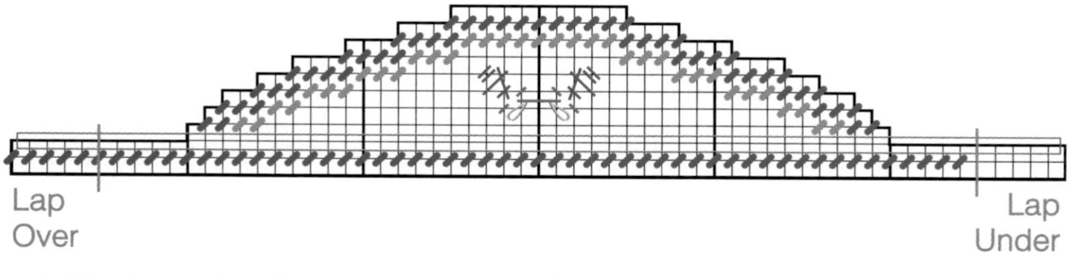

D – Leg Support Piece
(cut 2)
13 x 13 holes

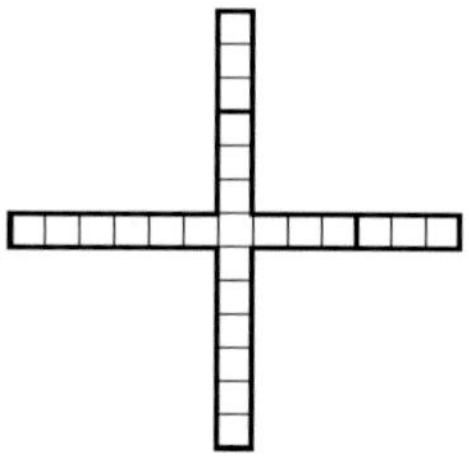

LAMP

SIZE: 3½" x 10½" tall.

MATERIALS:

- ❏ One sheet of 7-count plastic canvas
- ❏ 2" metal washer
- ❏ 8¼" wooden ⅛" dowel
- ❏ 3" string of 3-mm. silver beads
- ❏ ½ yd. blue ⅛" satin ribbon
- ❏ Metallic cord; for amount see Color Key.
- ❏ Worsted-weight or plastic canvas yarn; for amounts see Color Key.

CUTTING INSTRUCTIONS:

A: For shade pieces, cut six according to graph.

B: For pole pieces, cut three 2 x 55 holes (no graph).

C: For shade base top and bottom, cut two (one for top and one for bottom) according to graph.

D: For pole base top, cut one according to graph.

E: For pole base center, cut one according to graph.

F: For pole base bottom, cut two according to graph.

STITCHING INSTRUCTIONS:

1: Using colors and stitches indicated, work A pieces according to graph. Fill in uncoded areas and work one C for top, D, E and one F piece using White and Continental Stitch. Using metallic cord and Continental Stitch, work B and remaining C and F pieces. With matching colors for shade base top and bottom and with Royal for pole base top and center, Overcast unfinished edges of C, D and E pieces. Holding F pieces wrong sides together with washer between, with cord, Whipstitch together.

2: See **NOTE** above Step 3, and follow Step 3 of Tissue Chest on page 32.

3: With cord for top angled edges and with Royal, Whipstitch A pieces together as indicated, forming shade. With cord for top edges and with White, Overcast unfinished edges of shade.

4: Leaving about 4" of ribbon hanging, thread ribbon from front to back at one ◆ hole on one shade piece as indicated, then from back to front through neighboring ◆ hole on adjoining piece. Continue to thread ribbon through indicated holes around shade; tie in a bow as shown in photo and trim ends.

5: Holding B pieces wrong sides together with dowel between, with cord, Whipstitch together. Whipstitch one end of pole to center of bottom C and opposite end to center of D. Glue one end of bead string to bottom C next to pole. Glue C pieces wrong sides together. Center and glue E to silver side of pole base and D to center of E. Slip shade over shade base; glue to secure.

A – Shade Piece
(cut 6) 11 x 21 holes

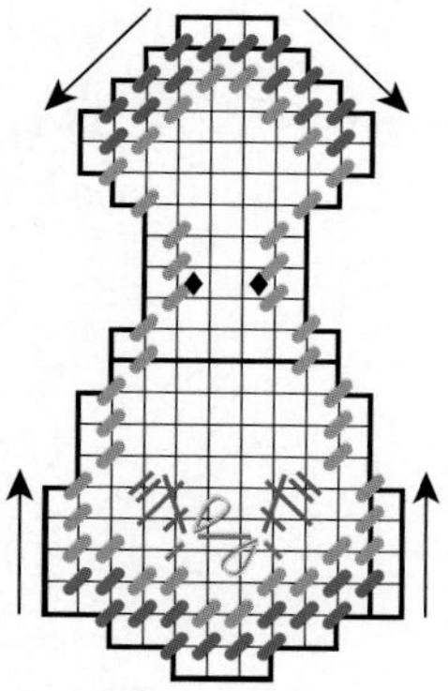

Whipstitch between arrows.

COLOR KEY: Lamp

Metallic cord
White/Silver – 24 yds.

Nylon Plus™	Needloft™ yarn
#28	#26 Baby Green – 1½ yds.
#31	#27 Holly – 2 yds.
#09	#32 Royal – 12 yds.
#01	#41 White – 17 yds.

STITCH KEY:

- — Backstitch/Straight Stitch
- ⬭ Lazy Daisy Stitch
- ◆ Ribbon Attachment

C – Shade Base Top & Bottom
(cut 1 each) 9 x 9 holes

D – Pole Base Top
(cut 1) 9 x 9 holes

E – Pole Base Center
(cut 1) 13 x 13 holes

F – Pole Base Bottom
(cut 2) 15 x 15 holes

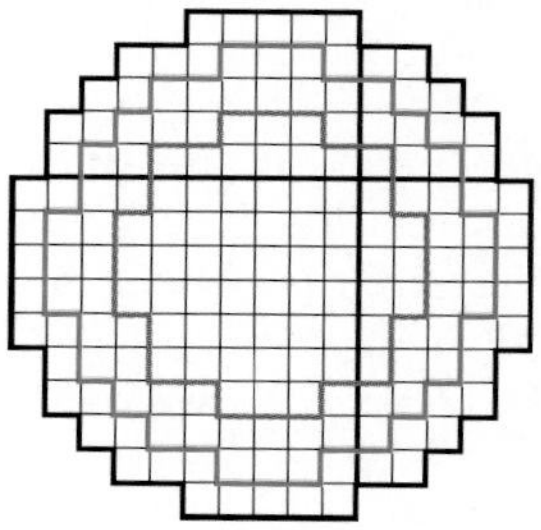

WARDROBE

SIZE: 3⅞" x 9" x 10¾" tall.

MATERIALS:

- ❏ Five sheets of 7-count plastic canvas
- ❏ Eight 5-mm. pearl beads
- ❏ 24 silver 4-mm. beads
- ❏ 2" drapery hook
- ❏ One white 9" x 12" felt square (optional)
- ❏ Two Velcro® closures
- ❏ Craft glue or glue gun
- ❏ Metallic cord; for amount see Color Key on page 49.
- ❏ Worsted-weight or plastic canvas yarn; for amounts see Color Key.
- ❏ Four Roses; see instructions on page 31.

CUTTING INSTRUCTIONS:

NOTE: Graphs and diagrams continued on pages 48-50.

A: For front and back, cut one each according to graphs.

B: For sides, cut two 18 x 59 holes.

C: For center divider, cut one 18 x 68 holes.

D: For supports, cut six 18 x 25 holes.

E: For doors, cut two 21 x 34 holes.

F: For top pieces, cut two 24 x 32 holes (no graph).

G: For top edging pieces, cut four according to graph and two 2 x 24 holes (no graph of 2 x 24-hole piece).

H: For inner base scallop and solid sides, cut two according to graph for scallop sides and two 5 x 19 holes for solid sides (no solid side graph).

I: For outer base scallop and solid sides, cut two according to graph for scallop sides and two 4 x 20 holes for solid sides (no solid side graph).

J: For stacking drawer fronts, cut three according to graph.

K: For stacking drawer inside pieces, cut six 8 x 16 holes, three 8 x 15 holes and three 15 x 16 holes (no graphs).

L: For large drawer fronts, cut two 13 x 21 holes.

M: For large drawer inside pieces, cut four 9 x 16 holes, four 9 x 17 holes and two 16 x 17 holes (no graphs).

N: For handle frames, cut two according to Nightstand F graph on page 38.

O: For motif frames, cut two according to Tissue Chest I graph on page 34.

P: For optional top support linings, using one D as a pattern, cut two from felt ⅛" smaller at all edges.

STITCHING INSTRUCTIONS:

1: Using colors and stitches indicated, work A-C, four D, E, scallop H, scallop I and L pieces according to graphs. Using Royal and Continental Stitch, work F pieces according to Top Stitch Pattern Guide, and work G pieces (work two angled pieces on opposite side of canvas). Fill in uncoded areas of A-C (leave indicated areas unworked), D, E, F and L pieces and work J, K and M pieces using White and Continental Stitch. Using White and Long Stitch over narrow width, work remaining H and I pieces.

2: With White, Overcast unfinished side and top edges of drawer cutouts and side edges of door cutouts on front A. With Royal for outer edges and metallic cord for inner edges of frames, Overcast unfinished edges of N and O pieces.

3: See **NOTE** above Step 3, and follow Step 3 of Tissue Chest on page 32.

4: For handles on large drawer fronts and doors (attach handle on one door on opposite side of motif), follow Step 4 of Tissue Chest.

5: With White, Whipstitch one long edge of each E (edge opposite handle) to front as indicated; Overcast unfinished edges of doors. Insert drapery hook from back to front through indicated hole on one D (see Drapery Hook Assembly Diagram). Whipstitch A, B, C and D (use unworked pieces for supports under drawers) according to Wardrobe Assembly Diagram; Overcast unfinished top edges of A and B pieces.

6: To attach edging to each top piece, with White, Whipstitch two angled and one straight G to one F according to Top Assembly Diagram; with Royal, Whipstitch ends of G pieces together. With cord, Overcast unfinished edges of edging. Holding top pieces wrong sides together and working through all thicknesses, with matching colors, Whipstitch unfinished edges of F pieces and top edge of C together according to diagram.

7: For base, using H and I pieces in place of F and G pieces, follow Step 8 of Tissue Chest.

8: For each stacking drawer, with White, Whipstitch J and K pieces together according to Stacking Drawer Assembly Diagram. For each large drawer, Whipstitch M pieces together as in Step 9 of Vanity on page 40. Center and glue one L to one long side of each assembly.

9: Glue Roses to front and doors as indicated, and handle and motif frames to drawer fronts and doors as shown in photo. Glue one closure to inside of each door behind handle and to corresponding area on front. If desired, glue one P to top of each support over doors.

Stacking Drawer Assembly Diagram

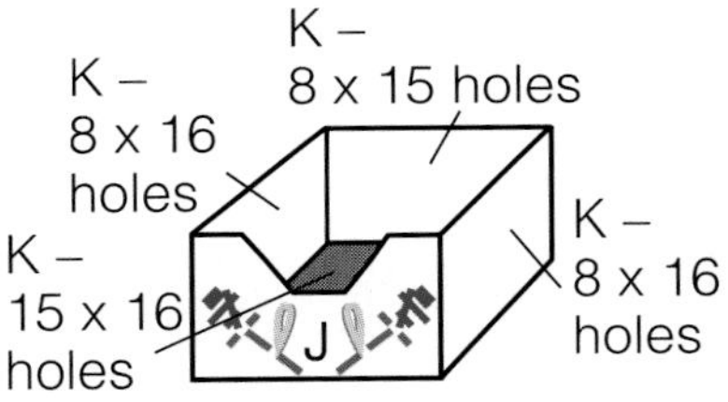

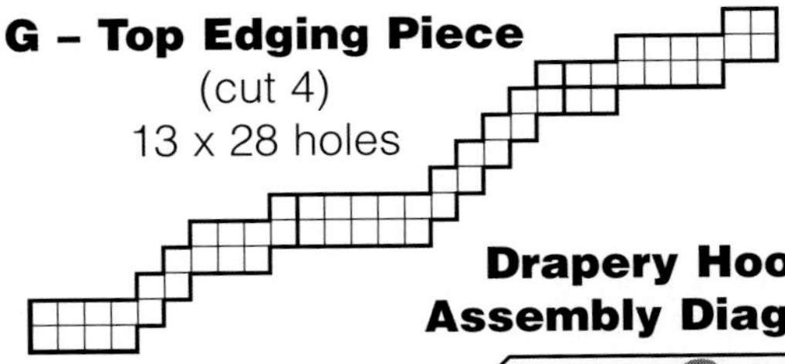

G – Top Edging Piece
(cut 4)
13 x 28 holes

Drapery Hook Assembly Diagram

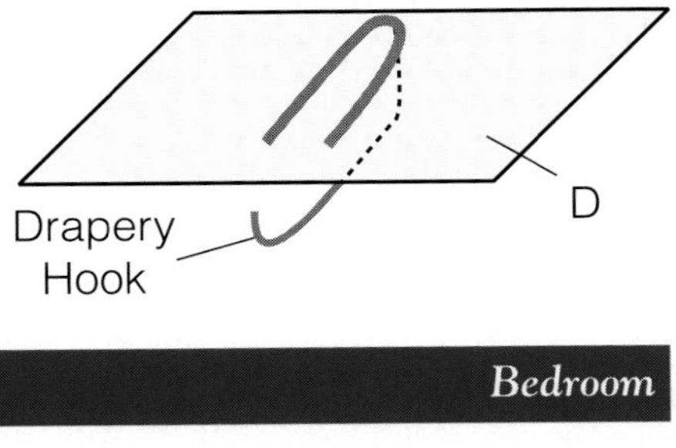

Hide tissues and treasures inside cleverly crafted fashion doll furnishings.

A – Front
(cut 1)
50 x 70 holes

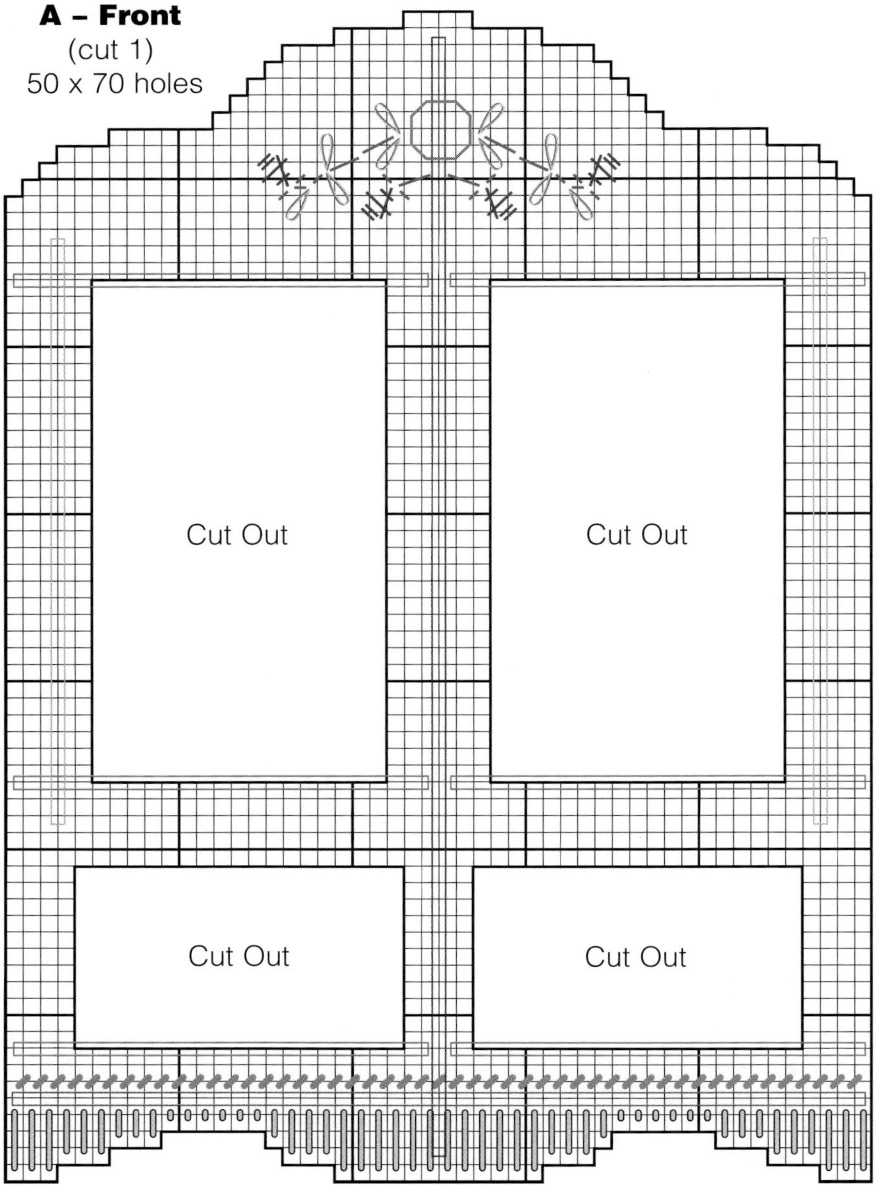

D – Inside Support
(cut 6) 18 x 25 holes

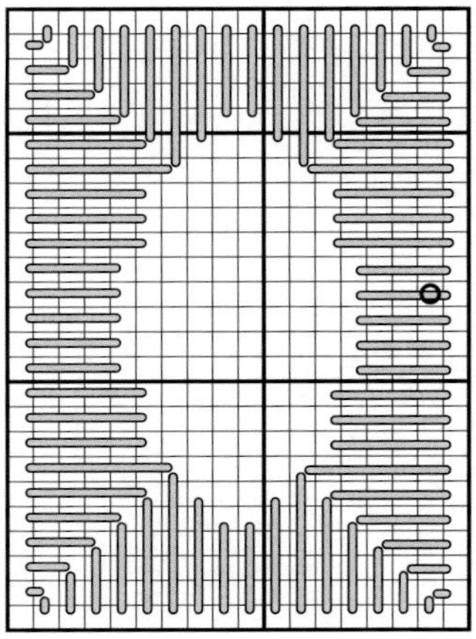

E – Door
(cut 2) 21 x 34 holes

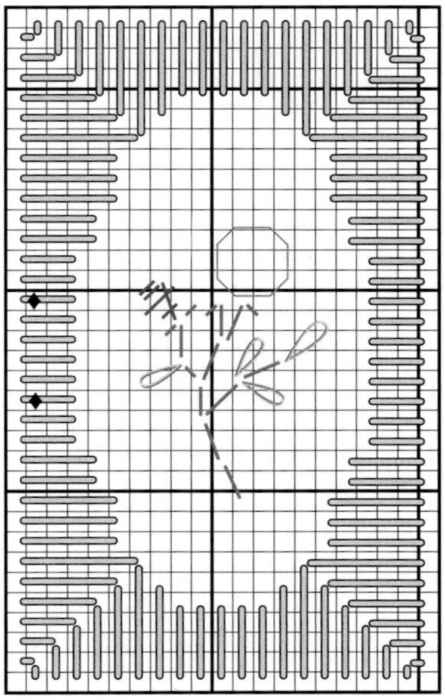

H – Inner Base Scallop Side (cut 2) 5 x 52 holes

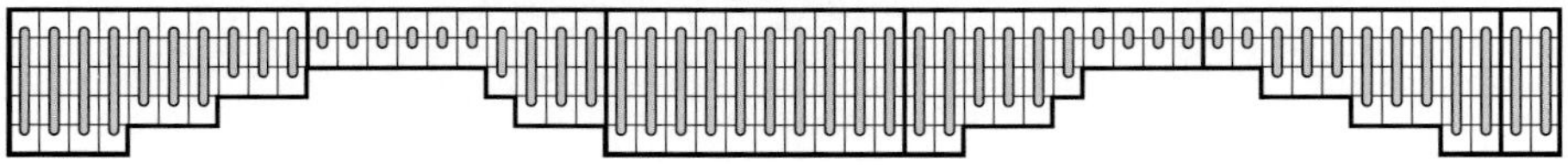

I – Outer Base Scallop Side (cut 2) 4 x 54 holes

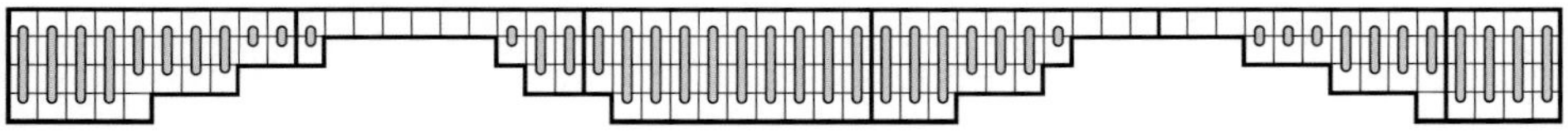

A – Back

(cut 1) 50 x 70 holes

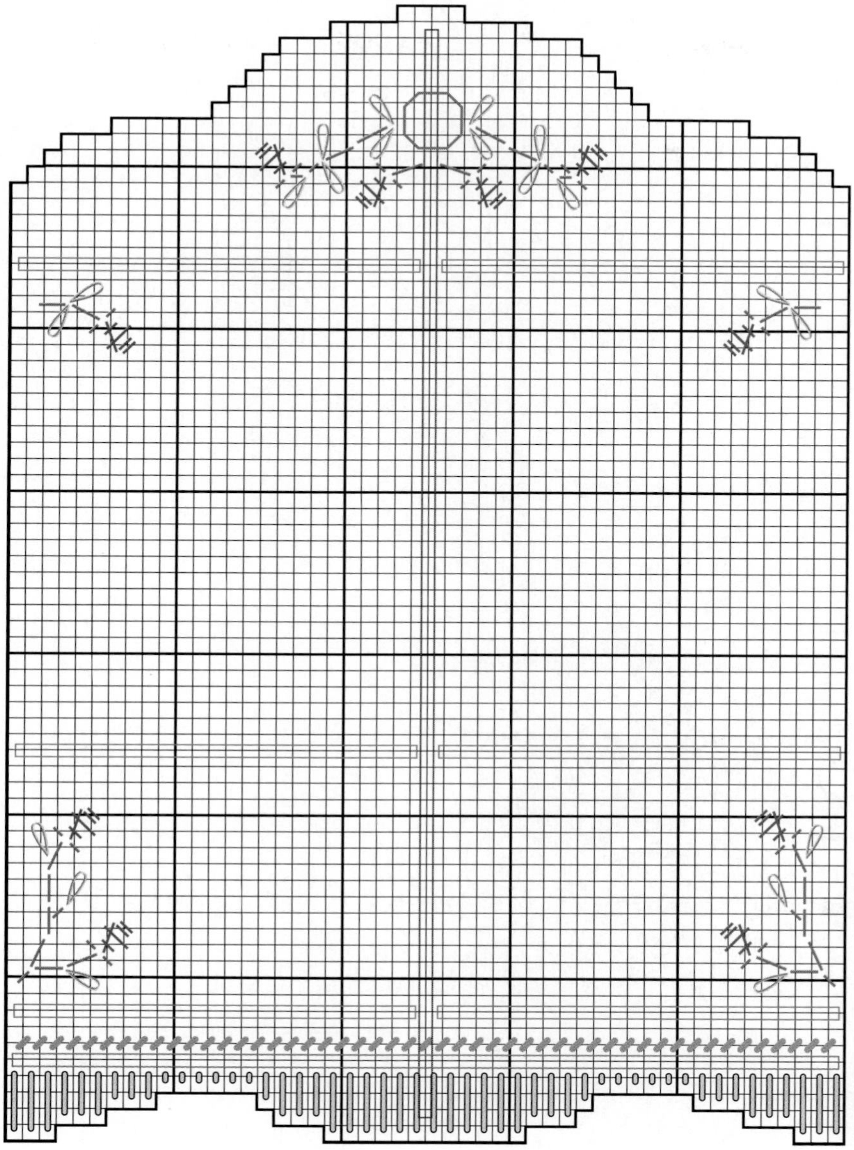

B – Side

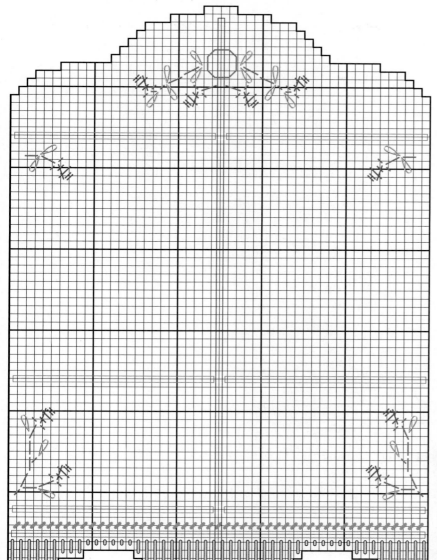

(cut 2)
18 x 59 holes

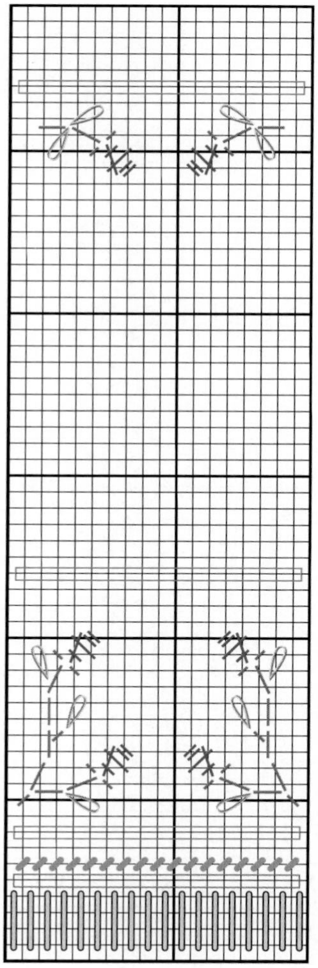

J – Stacking Drawer Front

(cut 3)
8 x 15 holes

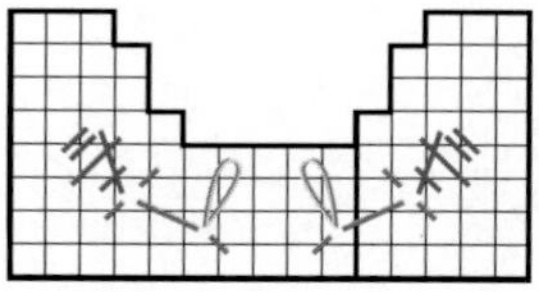

COLOR KEY: Wardrobe

Metallic cord
White/Silver – 20 yds.

Nylon Plus™	Needloft™ yarn
#28	#26 Baby Green – 8 yds.
#31	#27 Holly – 12 yds.
#09	#32 Royal – 30 yds.
#01	#41 White – 65 yds.

STITCH KEY:

- Backstitch/Straight Stitch
- Lazy Daisy Stitch
- Unworked Areas
- Unworked Areas/Door Attachment
- Unworked Areas/Center Divider Attachment
- Unworked Areas/Inside Support Attachments
- Drapery Hook Placement
- Yarn Attachment
- Rosebud Placement

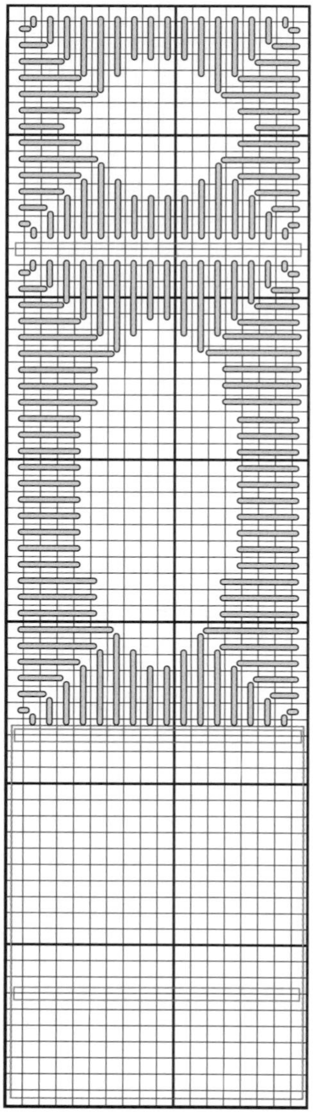

C – Center Divider
(cut 1)
18 x 68 holes

Wardrobe Assembly Diagram
(Attached doors not shown.)

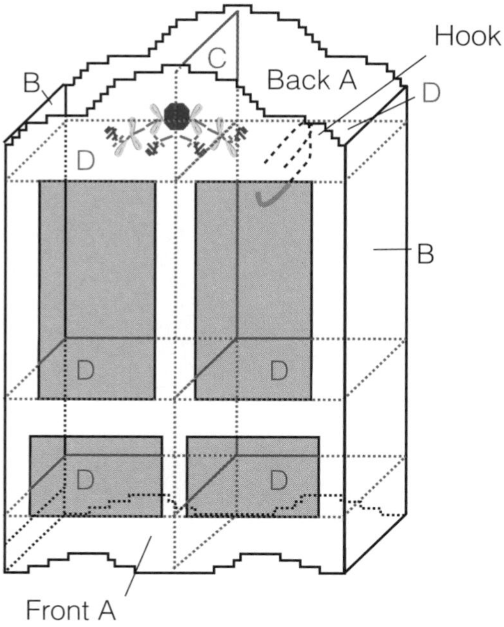

Top Assembly Diagram

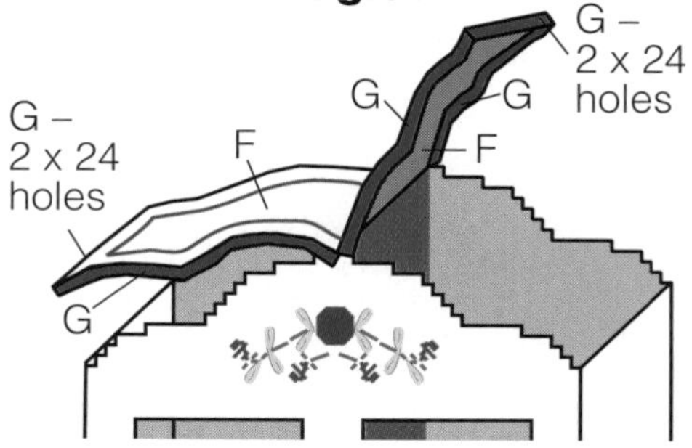

Top Stitch Pattern Guide

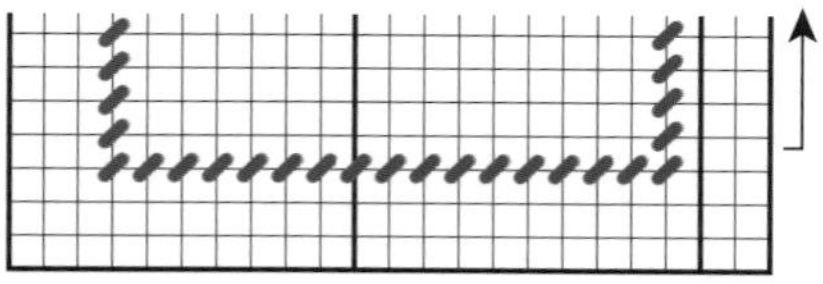

Continue Royal stitches to opposite edge.

L – Large Drawer Front
(cut 2)
13 x 21 holes

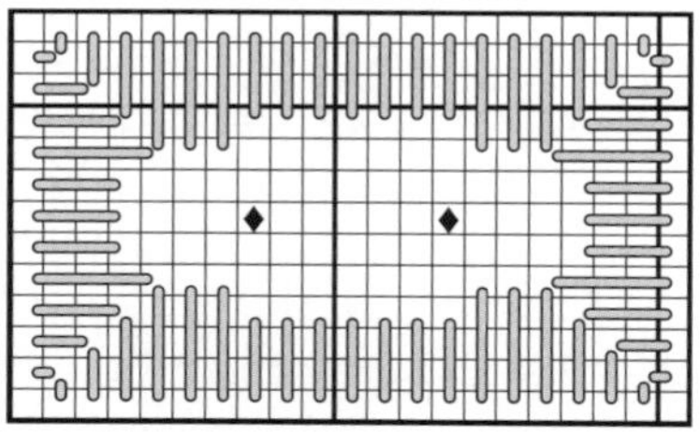

COLOR KEY: Wardrobe

Metallic cord
White/Silver – 20 yds.

Nylon Plus™	**Needloft™** yarn
#28	#26 Baby Green – 8 yds.
#31	#27 Holly – 12 yds.
#09	#32 Royal – 30 yds.
#01	#41 White – 65 yds.

STITCH KEY:

- Backstitch/Straight Stitch
- Lazy Daisy Stitch
- Unworked Areas
- Unworked Areas/Door Attachment
- Unworked Areas/Center Divider Attachment
- Unworked Areas/Inside Support Attachments
- Drapery Hook Placement
- Yarn Attachment
- Rosebud Placement

HOPE CHEST

SIZE: 3⅞" x 5¾" x 3⅛" tall.

MATERIALS:

- ❑ 1¼ sheets of 7-count plastic canvas
- ❑ Four 5-mm. pearl beads
- ❑ 12 silver 4-mm. beads
- ❑ Craft glue or glue gun
- ❑ Metallic cord; for amount see Color Key.
- ❑ Worsted-weight or plastic canvas yarn; for amounts see Color Key.
- ❑ One Rose; see instructions on page 31.

CUTTING INSTRUCTIONS:

A: For lid top and base, cut one 21 x 34 holes for top and one 25 x 38 holes for base.

B: For box scallop sides, cut two according to graph.

C: For box solid sides, cut two 18 x 21 holes.

D: For box bottom, cut one 21 x 34 holes.

E: For bottom support, cut one 6 x 21 holes (no graph).

F: For inner base scallop and solid sides, cut two according to graph for scallop sides and two 5 x 22 holes for solid sides (no solid side graph).

G: For outer base scallop and solid sides, cut two according to graph for scallop sides and two 4 x 23 holes for solid sides (no solid side graph).

H: For small motif frames, cut two according to Nightstand F graph on page 38.

I: For large motif frame, cut one according to Tissue Chest I graph on page 34.

STITCHING INSTRUCTIONS:

1: Using colors and stitches indicated, work A (work gray areas of base A on wrong side of canvas and leave indicated area unworked), B, C, D, scallop F and scallop G pieces according to graphs. Fill in uncoded areas of A-D (leave indicated areas unworked) pieces using White and Continental Stitch. Using White and Long Stitch over narrow width, work remaining F and G pieces.

2: With White for lid top A, metallic cord for outside edges of base A and inner edges of motif frames, and Royal for outer edges of motif frames, Overcast unfinished edges of A, H and I pieces.

3: See **NOTE** above Step 3, and follow Step 3 of Tissue Chest on page 32.

4: For each handle, follow Step 4 of Tissue Chest.

5: To attach lid base, follow Step 5 of Tissue Chest.

6: For box, alternating scallop and solid sides, with White, Whipstitch B and C pieces together. Whipstitch one long edge of unworked E to wrong side of D as indicated (see Tissue Chest Bottom & Support Assembly Diagram on page 32). Whipstitch bottom and bottom support to indicated areas on sides (see diagram); Overcast remaining unfinished top edges of box.

7: For base, follow Step 8 of Tissue Chest.

8: Holding wrong sides together, glue lid top to center of base (outer edge of base will have right side showing). Glue Rose to lid top as indicated and motif frames to front, back and lid top as shown in photo.

COLOR KEY: Hope Chest

Metallic cord		
White/Silver – 12 yds.		
Nylon Plus™	**Needloft™** yarn	
#28	#26 Baby Green – 4 yds.	
#31	#27 Holly – 8 yds.	
#09	#32 Royal – 16 yds.	
#01	#41 White – 40 yds.	

STITCH KEY:

- Backstitch/Straight Stitch
- Lazy Daisy Stitch
- Unworked Areas
- Unworked Area/Bottom Support Attachment
- Unworked Area/Bottom Attachment
- Unworked Area/Lid Attachment
- Yarn Attachment
- Rosebud Placement

A – Lid Base (cut 1) 25 x 38 holes

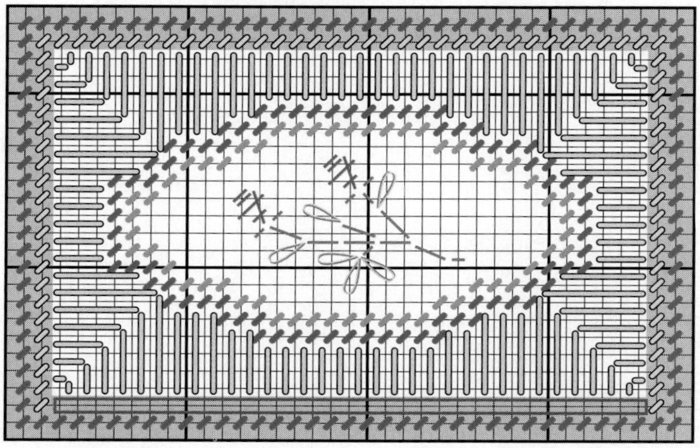

A – Lid Top (cut 1) 21 x 34 holes

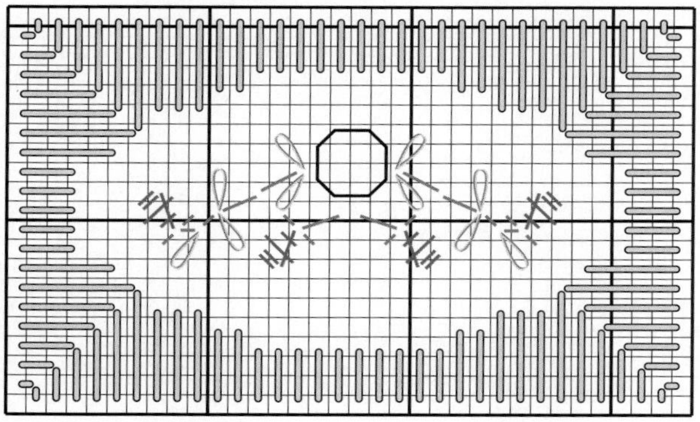

B – Box Scallop Side

(cut 2) 18 x 34 holes

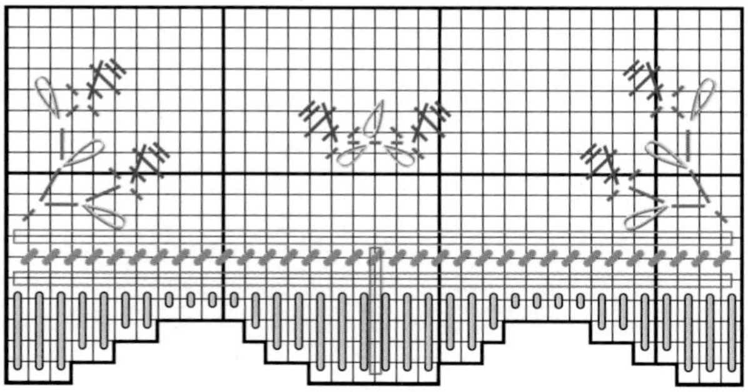

C – Box Solid Side

(cut 2)
18 x 21 holes

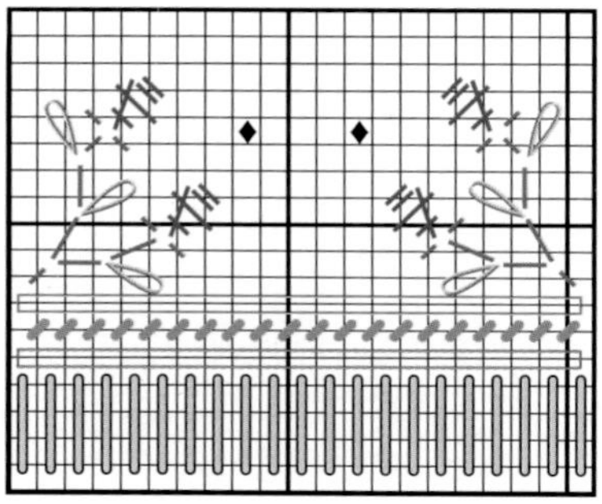

COLOR KEY: Hope Chest

Metallic cord
White/Silver – 12 yds.

Nylon Plus™ Needloft™ yarn

#28	#26 Baby Green – 4 yds.
#31	#27 Holly – 8 yds.
#09	#32 Royal – 16 yds.
#01	#41 White – 40 yds.

STITCH KEY:

- Backstitch/Straight Stitch
- Lazy Daisy Stitch
- Unworked Areas
- Unworked Area/Bottom Support Attachment
- Unworked Area/Bottom Attachment
- Unworked Area/Lid Attachment
- Yarn Attachment
- Rosebud Placement

D – Box Bottom

(cut 1) 21 x 34 holes

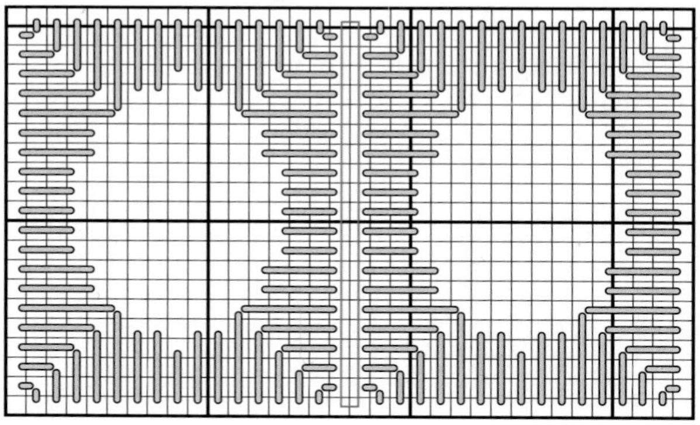

F – Box Inner Base Scallop Side

(cut 2) 5 x 36 holes

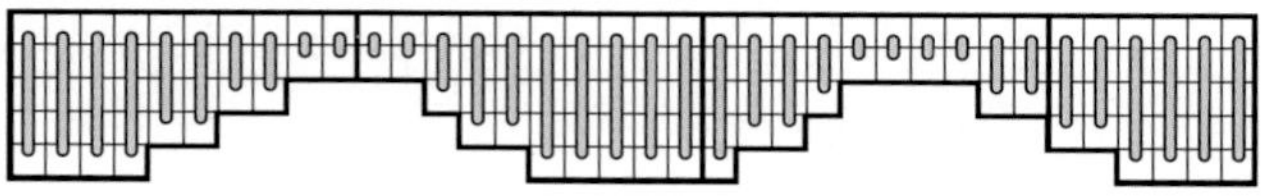

G – Box Outer Base Scallop Side

(cut 2) 4 x 38 holes

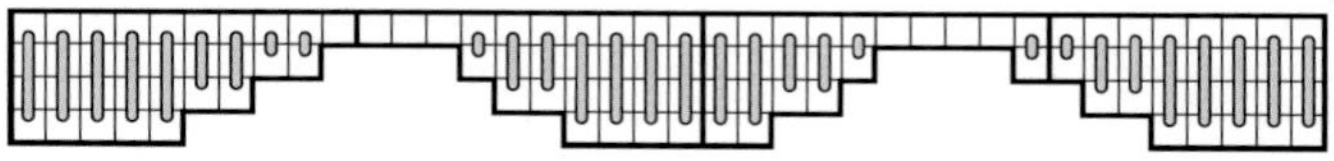

RUG

SIZE: 4¼" x 6".

MATERIALS:
- ❏ ½ sheet of 7-count plastic canvas
- ❏ Craft glue or glue gun
- ❏ Metallic cord; for amount see Color Key.
- ❏ Worsted-weight or plastic canvas yarn; for amounts see Color Key.
- ❏ One Rose; see instructions on page 31.

CUTTING INSTRUCTIONS:

A: For rug top and base, cut one each according to graph.

B: For motif frame, cut one according to Tissue Chest I graph on page 34.

STITCHING INSTRUCTIONS:

1: Holding A pieces together as indicated on graph and working through both thicknesses, using White and Continental Stitch, work A pieces. Using White and Modified Turkey Work (see Stitch Illustration), embroider A pieces as indicated on graph.

2: See **NOTE** above Step 3, and follow Step 3 of Tissue Chest on page 32.

3: With metallic cord for inner edges and Royal for outer edges of frame, Overcast B. Glue Rose as indicated and frame to rug top as shown in photo.

COLOR KEY: Rug		
	Metallic cord	
☐	White/Silver – 2 yds.	
	Nylon Plus™	**Needloft™** yarn
■	#28	#26 Baby Green – 1 yd.
■	#31	#27 Holly – 2 yds.
■	#09	#32 Royal – 3 yds.
☐	#01	#41 White – 20 yds.

STITCH KEY:
- Backstitch/Straight Stitch
- Lazy Daisy Stitch
- Modified Turkey Work
- Rosebud Placement

Modified Turkey Work Stitch Illustration

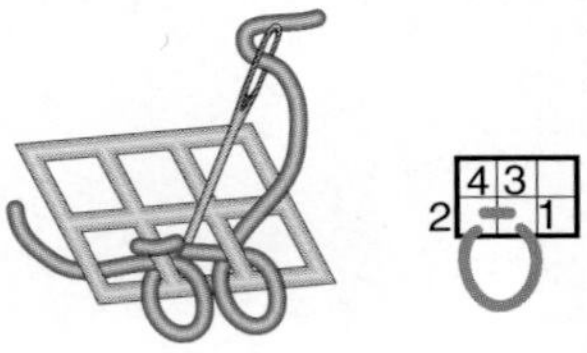

A – Rug Base
(cut 1) 19 x 32 holes
A – Rug Top
(cut 1) 15 x 28 holes

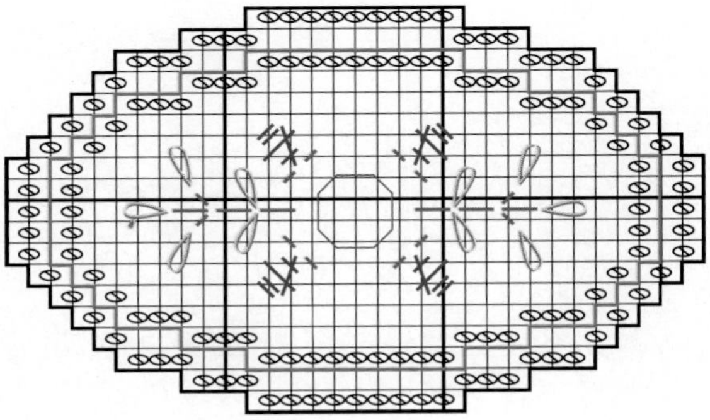

Clean up in style with state-of-the-art appliances, a wicker-look storage cabinet and a variety of housekeeping mops and tools.

BARBIE® doll and friends pictured with
permission of Mattel, Inc. ©1996 Mattel, Inc.

FASHION DOLL Laundry Room

Designed by
Diane T. Ray

MATERIALS FOR ENTIRE SET:

- ❑ 11¼ sheets of 7-count plastic canvas
- ❑ Two 12" x 18" or larger sheets of 7-count plastic canvas
- ❑ Two sheets of white 7-count plastic canvas
- ❑ Two each tan and white Velcro® closure strips
- ❑ 19 silver 5-mm. beads
- ❑ Six silver 4-mm. beads
- ❑ 16 black seed beads
- ❑ 1¼ yds. off-white 1" pregathered lace
- ❑ One 4", three 6" and five 6¼" lengths of clothes hanger or 16-gauge floral wire
- ❑ Pliers
- ❑ 6½" wooden ½" dowel
- ❑ ⅞" metal plumbing washer with ½" opening
- ❑ Rubber band
- ❑ Scraps of ⅜"-thick foam rubber
- ❑ Sewing needle and matching color thread
- ❑ Craft glue or glue gun
- ❑ Six-strand embroidery floss:
  - ❑ Black – 4 yds.
- ❑ Metallic cord:
  - ❑ White/Silver – 14 yds.
- ❑ Worsted-weight or plastic canvas yarn:

Nylon Plus™	Needloft™ yarn
❑ #02	#00 Black – 22 yds.
❑ #19	#02 Christmas Red – 1 yd.
❑ #44	#14 Cinnamon – 28½ yds.
❑ #47	#16 Sandstone – 6 oz.
❑ #30	#24 Mint – 11 yds.
❑ #01	#41 White – 8 oz.

For materials for individual items, see individual materials lists.

UTILITY CABINET

SIZE: 3½" x 7" x 10⅜" tall.

MATERIALS:

- ❑ Three sheets of 7-count plastic canvas
- ❑ Two sheets of 12" x 18" or larger 7-count plastic canvas
- ❑ ¾ yd. off-white 1" pregathered lace
- ❑ 10 silver 5-mm. beads
- ❑ Eight black seed beads
- ❑ Tan Velcro® closure strip
- ❑ Sewing needle and tan thread (optional)
- ❑ Craft glue or glue gun
- ❑ Six-strand embroidery floss; for amount see Color Key on page 56.
- ❑ Worsted-weight or plastic canvas yarn; for amounts see Color Key.

CUTTING INSTRUCTIONS:

NOTES: Graphs and diagrams on pages 56-58. Use large sheets for A pieces; see Cutting Guides below and on page 56. Use remainder of large sheets and standard-size sheets for remaining pieces.

A: For front and back, cut one each according to graphs.

B: For sides and center divider, cut three (two for sides and one for divider) according to graph.

C: For top and bottom, cut two (one for top and one for bottom) according to graph.

D: For shelf, cut one according to graph.

E: For doors, cut two according to graph.

F: For door motifs, cut two according to graph.

STITCHING INSTRUCTIONS:

1: Using colors and stitches indicated, work front A and F pieces according to graphs. Fill in uncoded areas of F pieces using White and Continental Stitch. With Sandstone, Overcast unfinished edges of F pieces and unfinished cutout edges on front A.

NOTE: Separate Mint into 1-ply or worsted-weight into 2-ply and floss into 3-ply strands.

2: Using 1-ply Mint, Backstitch and Straight Stitch, embroider plants as indicated on F graph. Using three strands floss, Backstitch and Straight Stitch and attaching one seed bead at each indicated hole as you work, embroider hanger and bracket hook on each F (reverse direction of hook on second piece) as indicated.

3: Using Sandstone and Wicker Stitch (see Stitch Illustrations on page 58), work one B for right side, top C, D and E pieces according to graphs. Overcast unfinished edges of D and one E piece as indicated;

Utility Cabinet Cutting Guide #1
(80 x 120 holes)

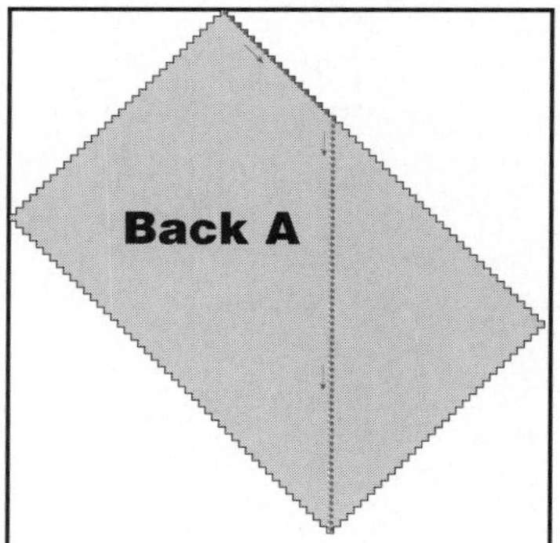

Red dotted line illustrates method of determining vertical hole count for pieces cut on the diagonal.

Utility Cabinet Cutting Guide #2
(80 x 120 holes)

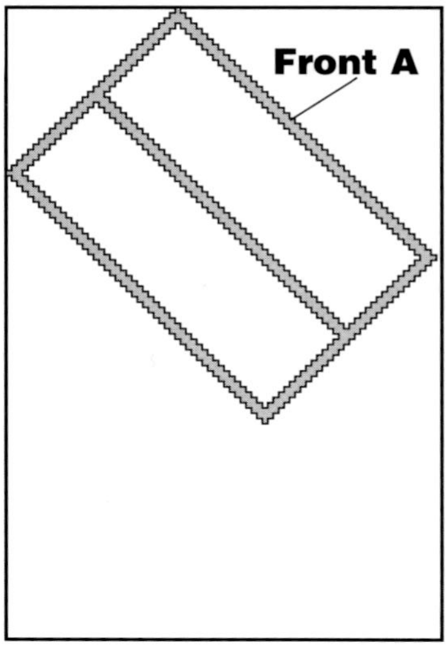

leaving opposite long edge unfinished, Overcast remaining E as indicated.

4: Whipstitch D and one unworked B for center divider together as indicated and according to Cabinet Assembly Diagram. Using Wicker Stitch, work center divider on side opposite shelf according to graph.

5: Whipstitching pieces together and then working pieces as established in Step 3, assemble pieces as indicated in the following order (see diagram): shelf and center divider to unworked back A; shelf to remaining unworked B for left side; center divider and unworked bottom C. Whipstitch left side, bottom and back together. Whipstitch assembly, top C and right B together.

6: Whipstitch unfinished edge of each door to right side of front A as indicated. For each door handle (attach second handle on opposite side of piece), thread needle from back to front at one ✚ hole as indicated on E

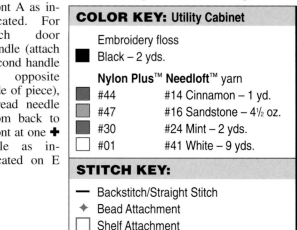

COLOR KEY: Utility Cabinet

Embroidery floss

■	Black – 2 yds.	

Nylon Plus™ Needloft™ yarn

■	#44	#14 Cinnamon – 1 yd.
■	#47	#16 Sandstone – 4½ oz.
■	#30	#24 Mint – 2 yds.
□	#01	#41 White – 9 yds.

STITCH KEY:

- — Backstitch/Straight Stitch
- ✦ Bead Attachment
- □ Shelf Attachment
- □ Center Divider Attachment
- □ Door Attachment
- ✚ Handle Attachment
- □ Motif Placement
- □ Closure Placement

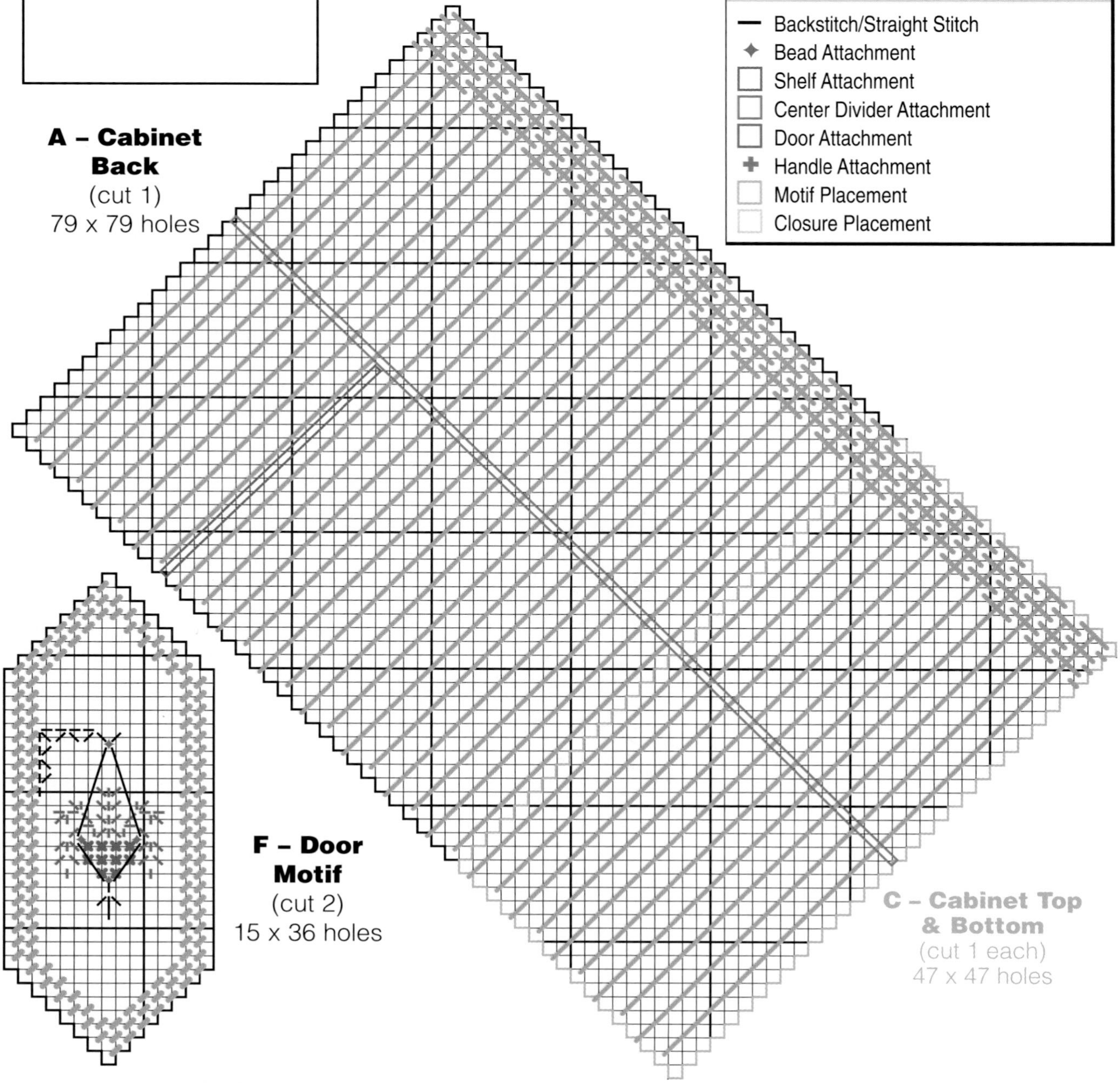

A – Cabinet Back
(cut 1)
79 x 79 holes

C – Cabinet Top & Bottom
(cut 1 each)
47 x 47 holes

F – Door Motif
(cut 2)
15 x 36 holes

graph; thread five silver beads onto yarn. Thread needle from front to back through remaining ✚ hole; pull ends firmly to align beads, and knot ends together on wrong side.

NOTES: Cut closure into two 3/8" x 1" pieces; cut each sticky side into two 3/8" x 1/2" pieces. Cut lace into two 13½" lengths.

7: Glue or sew fuzzy sides of closure pieces to top and bottom on right side of front as indicated; glue or sew one sticky side at top and bottom corners of each door. Glue one length of lace to back of each motif as shown in photo and one motif to front of each door as indicated.

B – Cabinet Side & Center Divider
(cut 3) 63 x 63 holes

D – Shelf
(cut 1) 31 x 31 holes

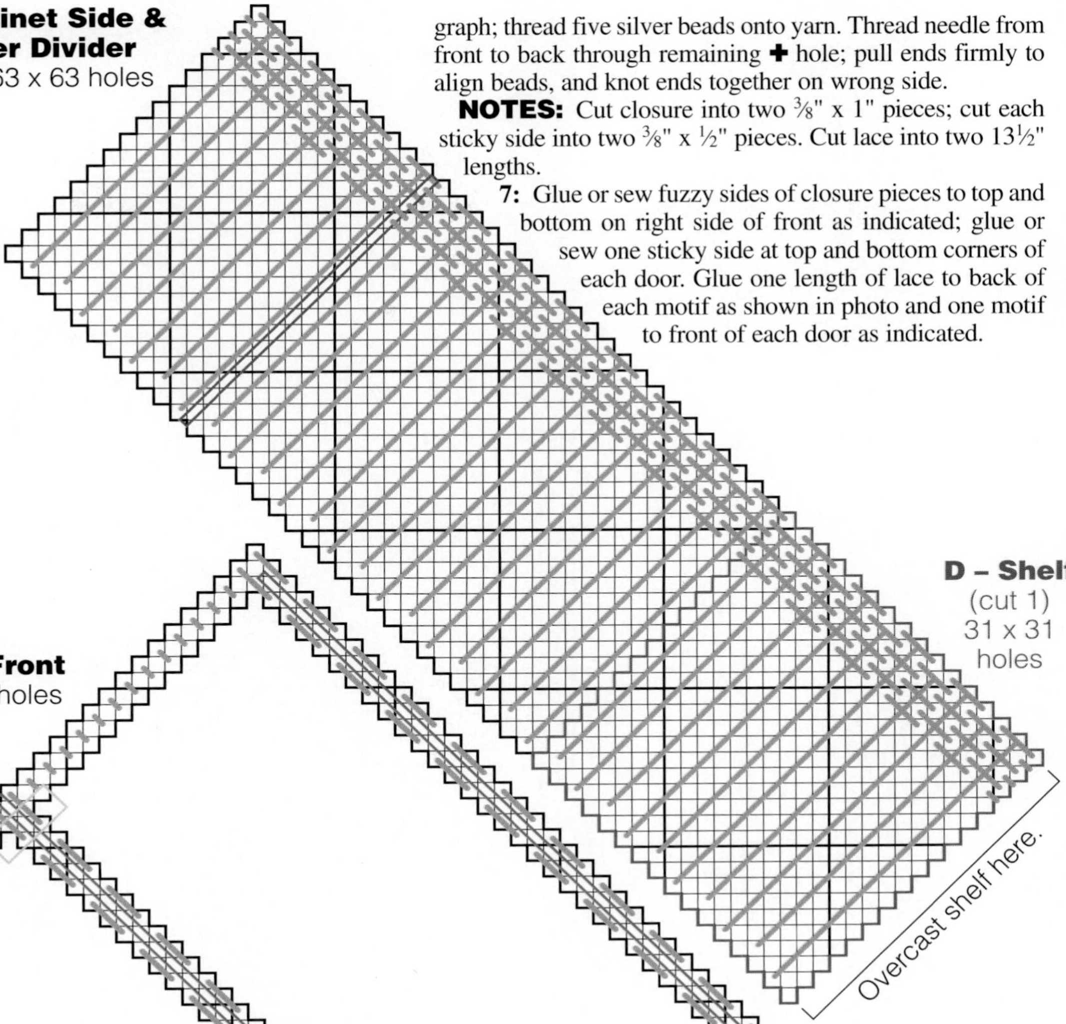

A – Cabinet Front
(cut 1) 79 x 79 holes

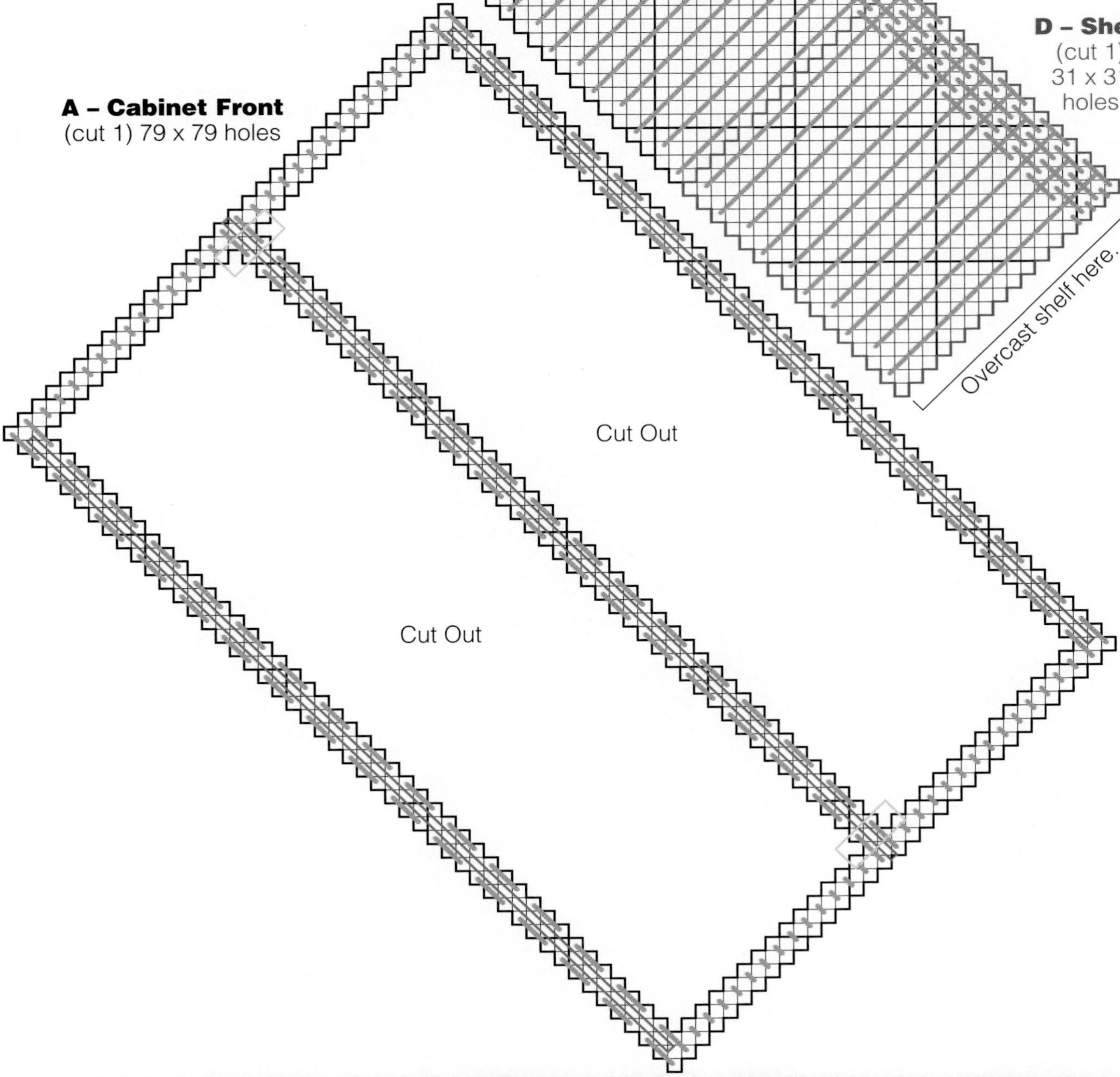

E – Cabinet Door

(cut 2)
60 x 60 holes

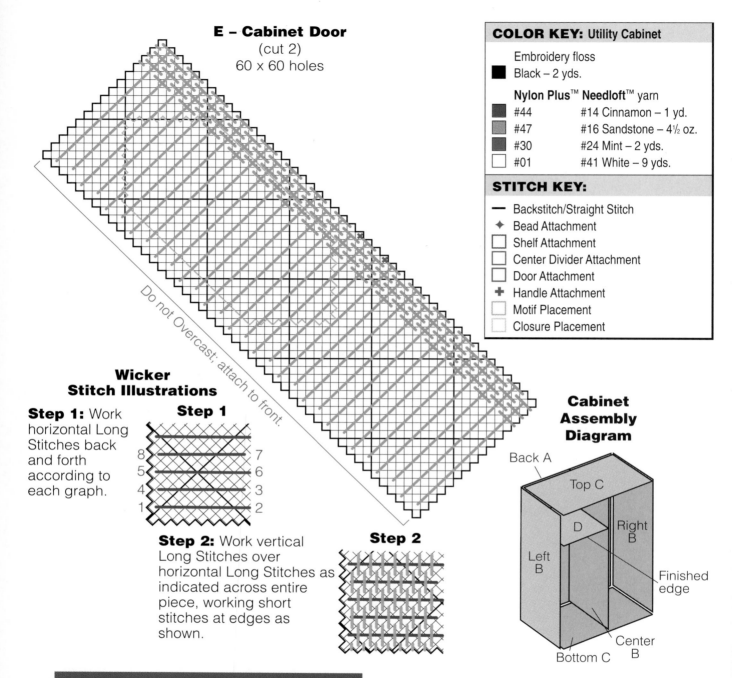

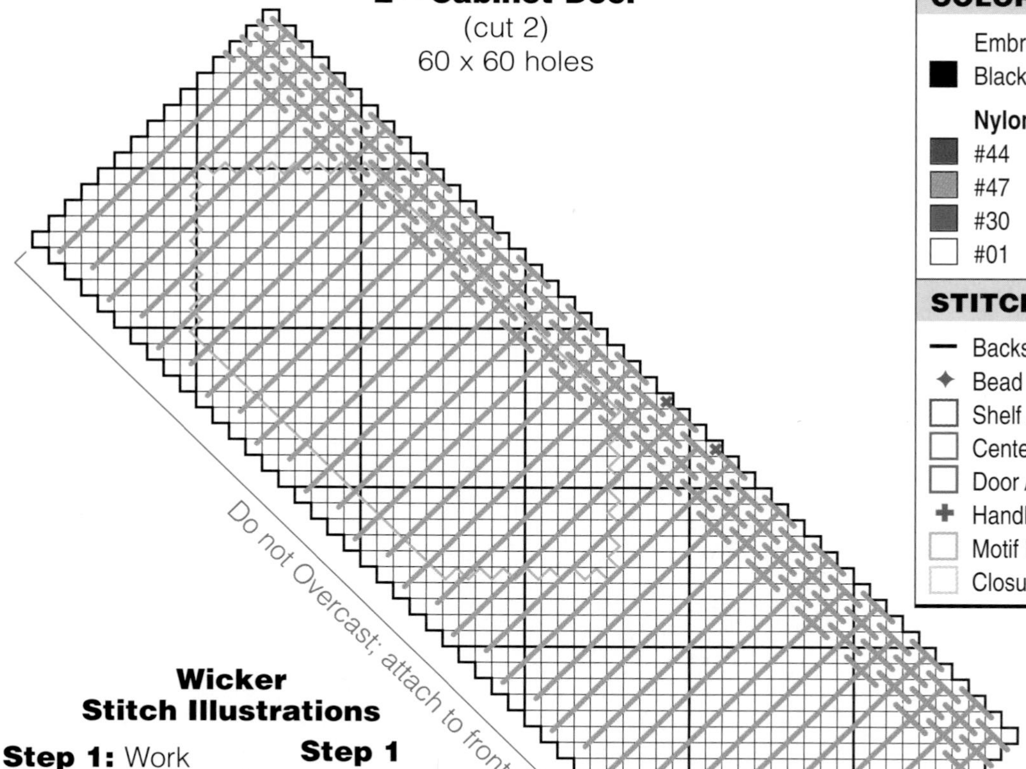

COLOR KEY: Utility Cabinet		
	Embroidery floss	
■	Black – 2 yds.	
	Nylon Plus™ Needloft™ yarn	
■	#44	#14 Cinnamon – 1 yd.
■	#47	#16 Sandstone – 4½ oz.
■	#30	#24 Mint – 2 yds.
□	#01	#41 White – 9 yds.

STITCH KEY:

- Backstitch/Straight Stitch
- Bead Attachment
- Shelf Attachment
- Center Divider Attachment
- Door Attachment
- Handle Attachment
- Motif Placement
- Closure Placement

Wicker Stitch Illustrations

Step 1: Work horizontal Long Stitches back and forth according to each graph.

Step 1

Step 2: Work vertical Long Stitches over horizontal Long Stitches as indicated across entire piece, working short stitches at edges as shown.

Step 2

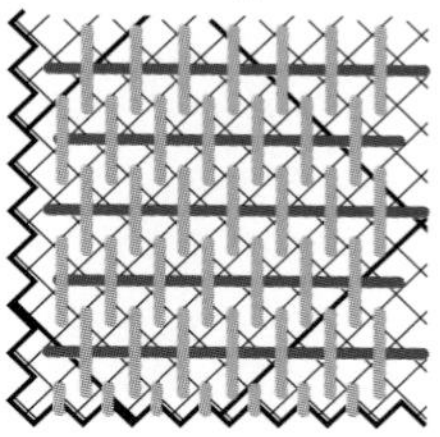

Cabinet Assembly Diagram

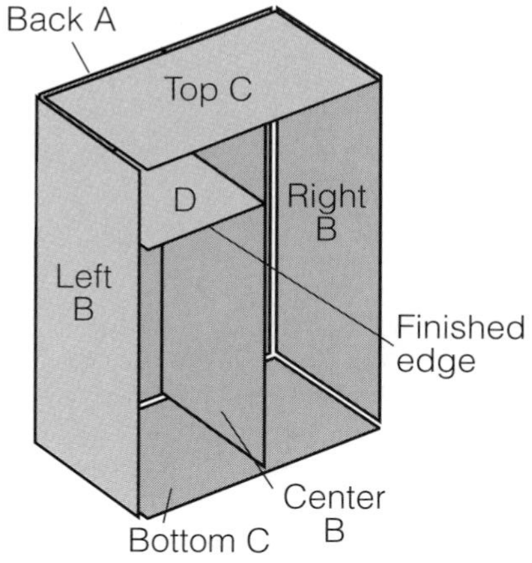

VACUUM CLEANER

SIZE: 1½" x 2½" x about 7" tall.

MATERIALS:

- ❑ ½ sheet of 7-count plastic canvas
- ❑ Tan Velcro® closure strip
- ❑ 6¼" length of clothes hanger or 16-gauge floral wire
- ❑ Craft glue or glue gun
- ❑ Worsted-weight or plastic canvas yarn; for amounts see Color Key.

CUTTING INSTRUCTIONS:

A: For top and bottom, cut one 10 x 25 holes for top and one 10 x 15 holes for bottom.

B: For sides, cut two according to graph.

C: For bag front and back, cut one each according to graphs.

D: For bag sides, cut two according to graph.

E: For bag brace, cut one 2 x 15 holes.

STITCHING INSTRUCTIONS:

1: Using colors and stitches indicated, work A, C, D (one on opposite side of canvas) and E pieces according to graphs. Fill in uncoded areas (leave indicated area of top A unworked) and work B pieces (one on opposite side of canvas) using Camel and Continental Stitch. With Cinnamon, Overcast E as indicated on graph.

NOTE: Separate 2 yds. of Black and 1 yd. of Cinnamon into 1-ply or worsted-weight into 2-ply.

2: Using 1-ply colors indicated, Backstitch and Running Stitch, embroider detail on A-D pieces as indicated.

3: With Sandstone, easing top to fit, Whipstitch top A and B pieces together as indicated and according to Vacuum Cleaner Assembly Diagram. With 1-ply Black, work one stitch over each corner seam to match stitching on sides and top.

4: With Cinnamon, Whipstitch front C and D pieces together and E and back C together as indicated.

NOTE: Bend wire slightly 1" from one end.

5: Easing back to fit, with Cinnamon for bag and with matching colors, Whipstitch bag front, back and sides together, inserting wire between pieces as indicated before closing handle.

6: With Sandstone, Whipstitch bottom edge of bag and top A together as indicated; with Cinnamon, Whipstitch assembly and bottom together. Trim closure to fit, and glue to wrong side of brace and to back of bag as indicated.

A – Vacuum Cleaner Bottom
(cut 1) 10 x 15 holes

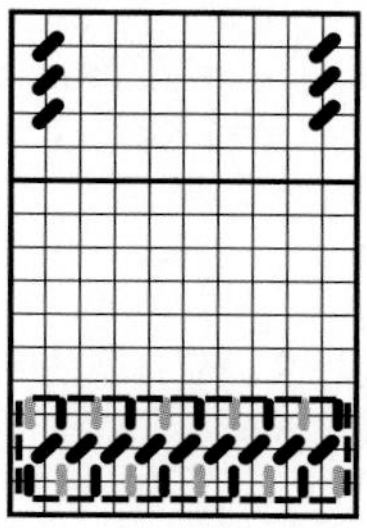

Front

COLOR KEY: Vacuum Cleaner		
	Nylon Plus™	**Needloft™** yarn
■	#02	#00 Black – 7 yds.
■	#44	#14 Cinnamon –10 yds.
■	#47	#16 Sandstone – 12 yds.
▨	#01	#41 White – 1/2 yd.

STITCH KEY:

- Backstitch/Straight Stitch
- Wire Placement
- Brace Attachment
- Unworked Area/Bag Attachment
- Closure Placement

A – Vacuum Cleaner Top
(cut 1) 10 x 25 holes

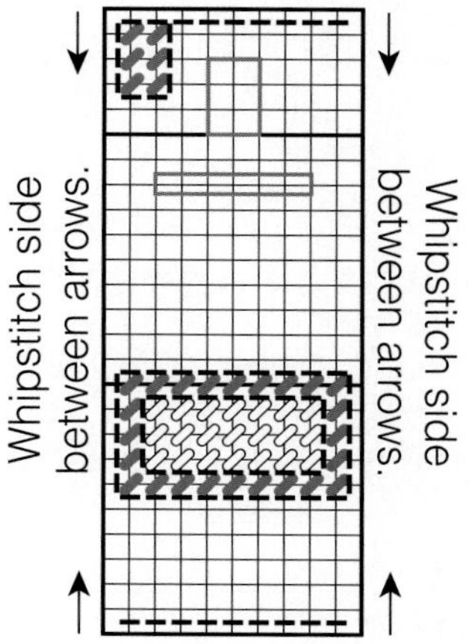

Front

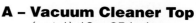

B – Vacuum Cleaner Side
(cut 2) 6 x 15 holes

Whipstitch top between arrows.

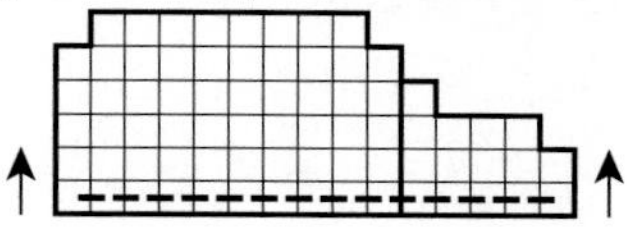

C – Vacuum Bag Front
(cut 1)
10 x 42 holes

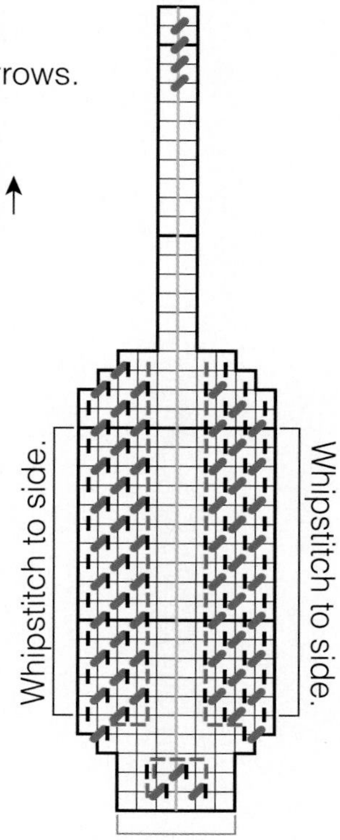

Whipstitch to top.

C – Vacuum Bag Back
(cut 1)
10 x 42 holes

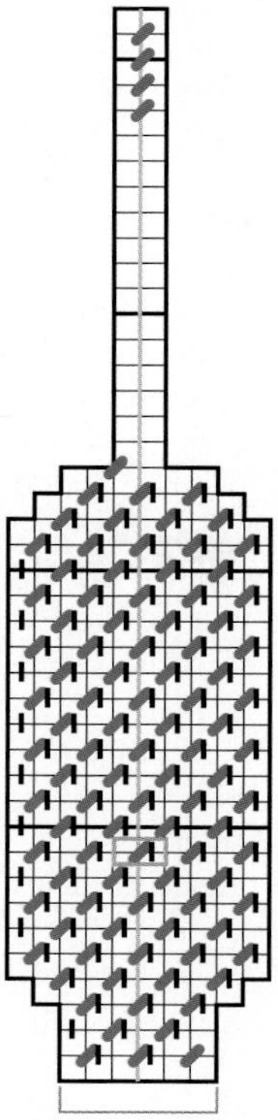

Whipstitch to top.

D – Vacuum Bag Side
(cut 2)
3 x 15 holes

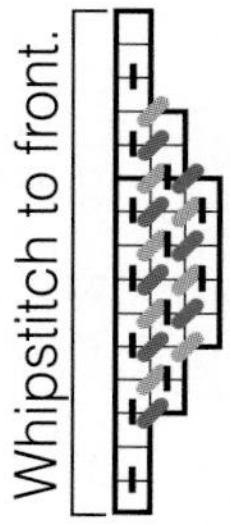

E – Vacuum Bag Brace
(cut 1)
2 x 15 holes

Do not Overcast; attach to bag back.

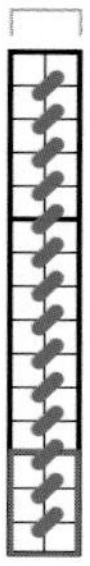

Vacuum Cleaner Assembly Diagram

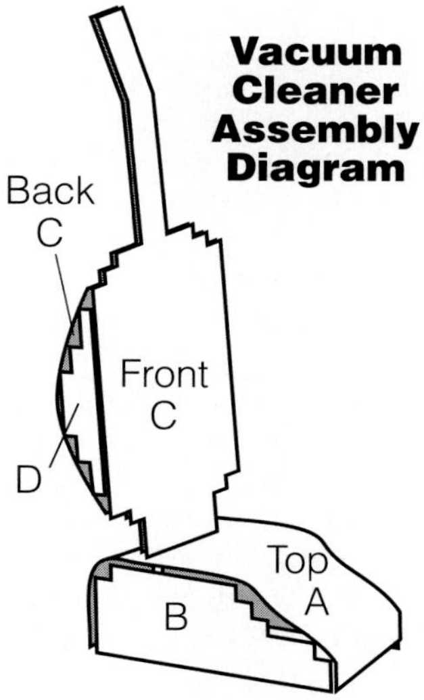

WASHER

SIZE: $3\frac{7}{8}$" x $4\frac{1}{2}$" x $6\frac{3}{4}$" tall.

MATERIALS:

- ❑ $1\frac{1}{2}$ sheets of 7-count plastic canvas
- ❑ One sheet of white 7-count plastic canvas
- ❑ One silver 5-mm. bead
- ❑ Two silver 4-mm. beads
- ❑ $\frac{7}{8}$" metal plumbing washer with $\frac{1}{2}$" opening
- ❑ 5" wooden $\frac{1}{2}$" dowel
- ❑ Rubber band
- ❑ Sewing needle and black thread
- ❑ Metallic cord; for amount see Color Key.
- ❑ Worsted-weight or plastic canvas yarn; for amounts see Color Key.

CUTTING INSTRUCTIONS:

NOTES: Graphs and diagrams continued on page 62. Use white canvas for H-J pieces.

A: For front and back, cut one 29 x 36 holes for front and one according to graph for back.

B: For sides, cut two 25 x 36 holes.

C: For top, cut one according to graph.

D: For lid and hinge, cut one according to graph for lid and one 1 x 13 holes for hinge.

E: For control panel front and top, cut one 8 x 26 holes for front and one 4 x 27 holes for top.

F: For control panel ends, cut two according to graph.

G: For bottom support, cut one according to graph.

H: For tub side, cut one from white 26 x 83 holes (no graph).

I: For tub bottom, cut one from white according to graph.

J: For agitator sides and top, cut four according to graph for sides and one 3 x 3 holes for top (no top graph).

STITCHING INSTRUCTIONS:

NOTE: G-J pieces are unworked.

1: Using colors and stitches indicated, work A, B, C and E (leave indicated area of top unworked) pieces according to graphs. Fill in uncoded areas (leave indicated areas unworked) of A, B and C pieces and work lid D using White and Continental Stitch. Fill in uncoded areas of front E and work F (one on opposite side of canvas) pieces using Black and Continental Stitch. With Black for front E and with matching colors, Overcast unfinished cutout edges of C and unfinished edges of lid D, E, and F pieces as indicated on graphs.

NOTE: Separate Christmas Red into 1-ply or worsted-weight into 2-ply.

2: Using metallic cord, 1-ply Christmas Red, Backstitch and Straight Stitch, embroider detail on front E as indicated. With thread, sew beads to front E as indicated.

3: With White, Whipstitch side J pieces together as indicated, forming agitator. Whipstitch sides and top J together.

4: Overlapping six holes, Whipstitch short ends of H together, forming tub. Easing to fit, Whipstitch tub and I together.

5: Holding tub bottom and G together at matching cutouts, Whipstitch cutout edges together. Whipstitch G to wrong side of A and B pieces as indicated and according to Washer Assembly Diagram; Whipstitch sides and front together.

6: Insert dowel into agitator; place agitator inside tub with dowel extending through bottom opening. Slide washer onto dowel to bottom support; secure by wrapping rubber band around dowel next to washer.

7: With Cinnamon, Whipstitch front E to wrong side of top E as indicated and according to Control Panel Assembly Diagram. With Black, Whipstitch front E and C together as indicated; Whipstitch one F to each end of top E and to C as indicated.

8: Whipstitch hinge D and lid together as indicated; with right sides up, Whipstitch hinge to washer top as indicated. Whipstitch washer top, front and sides together.

9: With Cinnamon for control panel top and with matching colors, Whipstitch assembly and back A together as indicated. With White, Overcast unfinished bottom edges.

E – Washer Control Panel Front
(cut 1)
8 x 26 holes

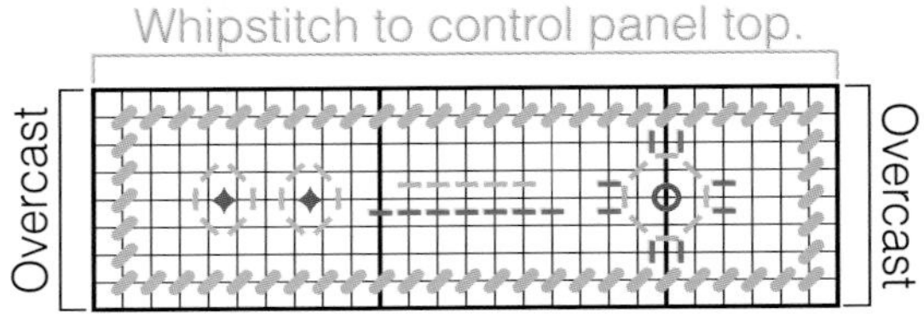

A – Washer Front
(cut 1)
29 x 36 holes
B – Washer Side
(cut 2)
25 x 36 holes

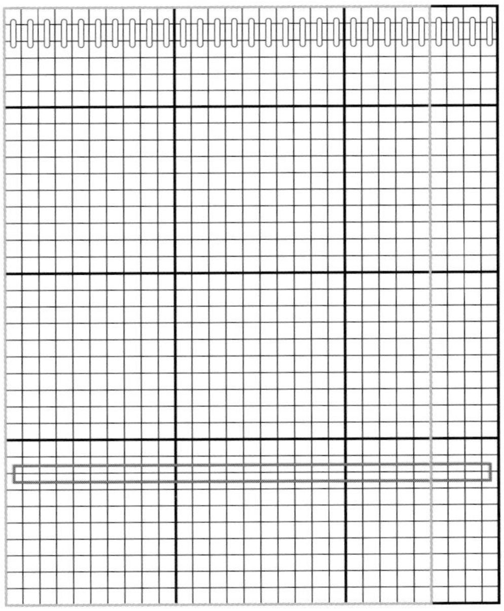

COLOR KEY: Washer		
	Metallic cord	
▨	White/Silver – 2½ yds.	
	Nylon Plus™ Needloft™ yarn	
■	#02	#00 Black – 7 yds.
■	#19	#02 Christmas Red – ½ yd.
▨	#44	#14 Cinnamon – 3 yds.
▨	#01	#41 White – 2½ oz.

STITCH KEY:

- — Backstitch/Straight Stitch
- ✦ 4-mm. Bead Attachment
- ○ 5-mm. Bead Attachment
- ☐ Unworked Area/Bottom Support Attachment
- ☐ Unworked Area/Panel Front To Panel Top Attachment
- ☐ Unworked Area/Panel Front To Washer Top Attachment
- ☐ Unworked Area/Panel End Attachment
- ☐ Unworked Area/Hinge Attachment
- ☐ Unworked Area/Washer Top Attachment

C – Washer Top
(cut 1)
25 x 29 holes

Whipstitch to back.

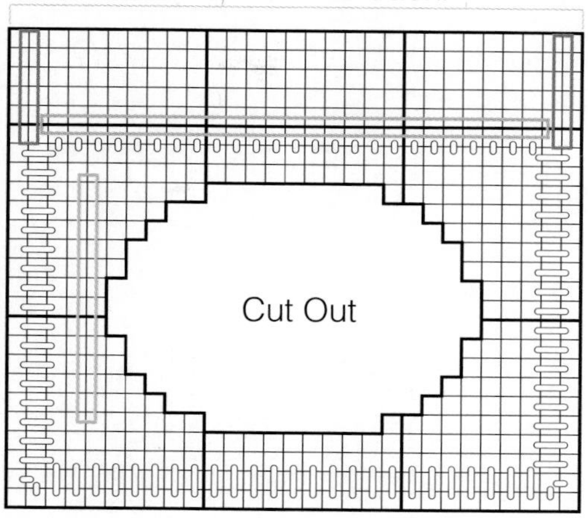

F – Washer Control Panel End
(cut 2)
6 x 8 holes

Whipstitch to top E.

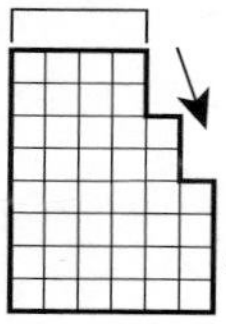

Overcast between arrows.

E – Washer Control Panel Top
(cut 1) 4 x 27 holes

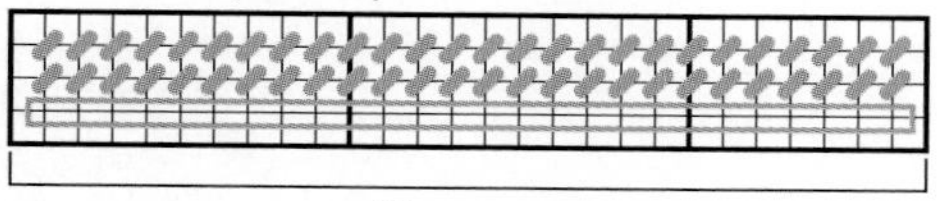

Overcast

J – Agitator Side
(cut 4 from white)
17 x 26 holes

Whipstitch between arrows.

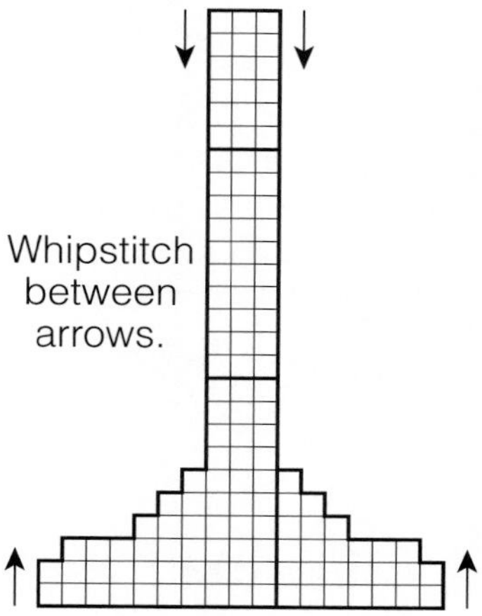

D – Washer Lid
(cut 1)
13 x 19 holes

Do not Overcast; Whipstitch to hinge.

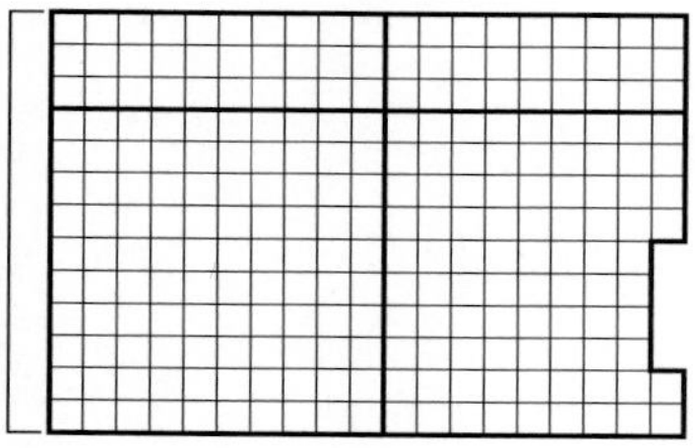

A – Washer Back
(cut 1)
29 x 44 holes

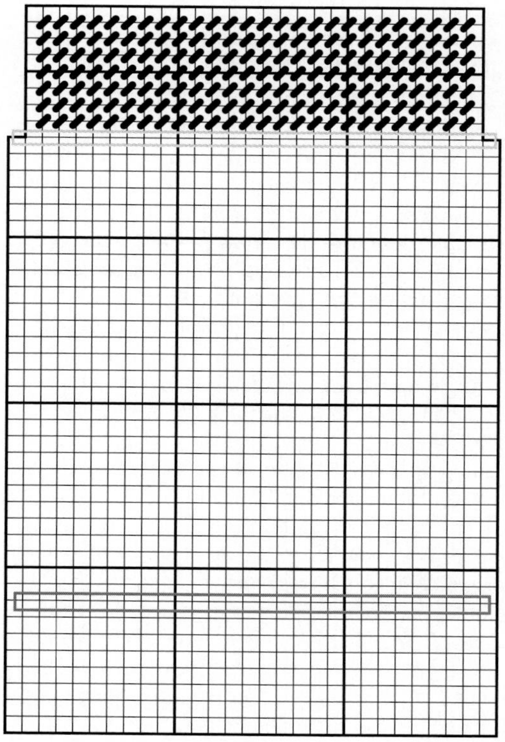

G – Washer Bottom Support
(cut 1) 25 x 29 holes

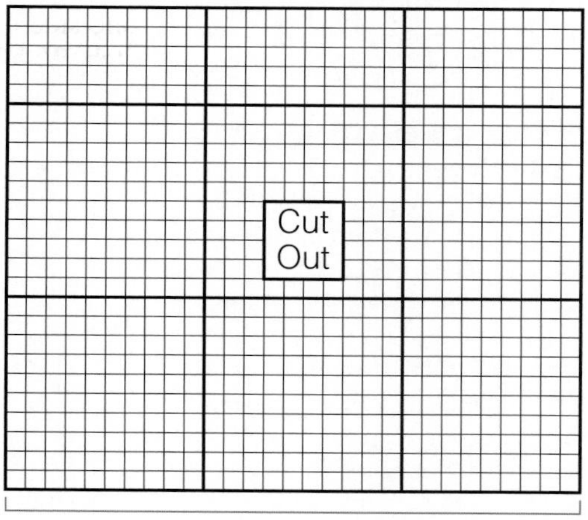

Whipstitch to front.

COLOR KEY: Washer

	Metallic cord	
	White/Silver – 2½ yds.	
	Nylon Plus™	**Needloft™** yarn
	#02	#00 Black – 7 yds.
	#19	#02 Christmas Red – ½ yd.
	#44	#14 Cinnamon – 3 yds.
	#01	#41 White – 2½ oz.

STITCH KEY:

- Backstitch/Straight Stitch
- 4-mm. Bead Attachment
- 5-mm. Bead Attachment
- Unworked Area/Bottom Support Attachment
- Unworked Area/Panel Front To Panel Top Attachment
- Unworked Area/Panel Front To Washer Top Attachment
- Unworked Area/Panel End Attachment
- Unworked Area/Hinge Attachment
- Unworked Area/Washer Top Attachment

I – Washer Tub Bottom
(cut 1 from white)
24 x 24 holes

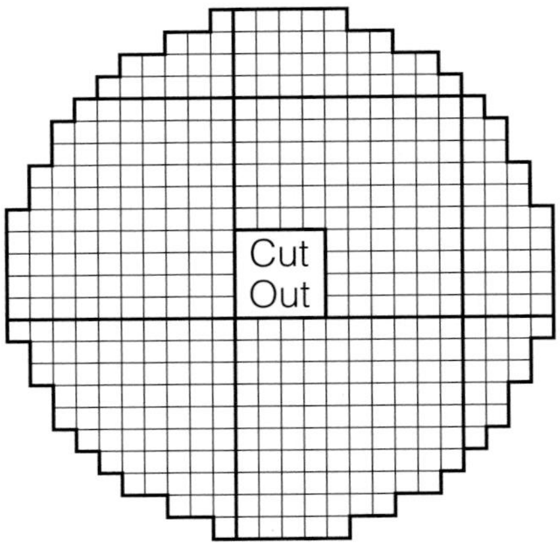

Washer Assembly Diagram

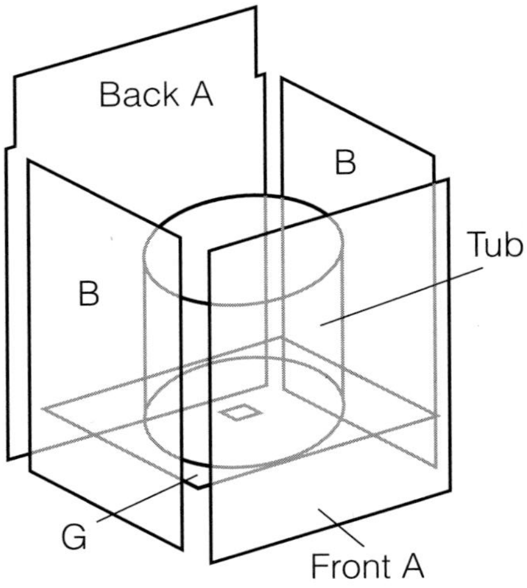

Control Panel Assembly Diagram

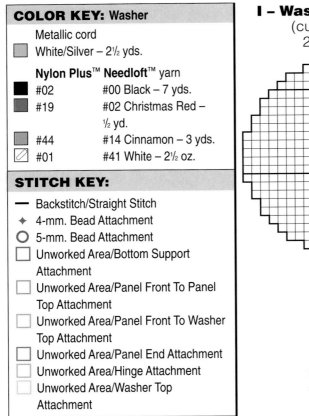

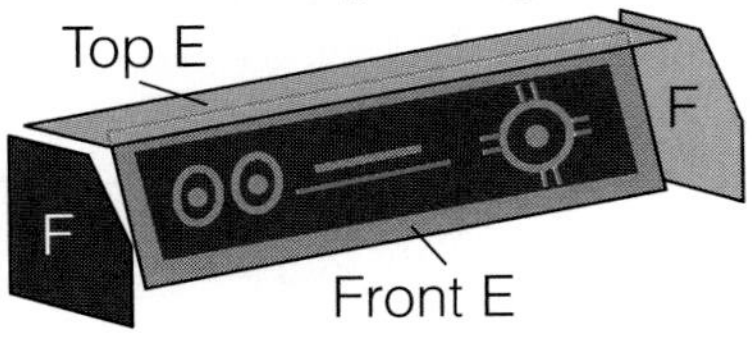

DRYER

SIZE: 3⅞" x 4½" x 6¾" tall.

MATERIALS:

- ❑ 1½ sheets of 7-count plastic canvas
- ❑ One sheet of white 7-count plastic canvas
- ❑ One silver 5-mm. bead
- ❑ Two silver 4-mm. beads
- ❑ 1½" wooden ½" dowel
- ❑ White Velcro® closure strip
- ❑ Sewing needle and black and white thread (white thread optional)
- ❑ Metallic cord; for amount see Color Key.
- ❑ Worsted-weight or plastic canvas yarn; for amounts see Color Key.

CUTTING INSTRUCTIONS:

NOTES: Graphs and diagrams continued on pages 64 & 65. Use white canvas for J-N pieces.

A: For front and back, cut one each according to graphs.

B: For sides, cut two 25 x 36 holes.

C: For top, cut one according to graph.

D: For door, hinge and handle, cut one 15 x 23 holes for door, one 1 x 23 holes for hinge and one 1 x 9 holes for handle (no hinge and handle graphs).

E-F: Follow Steps E-F of Washer on page 60.

G: For bottom support, cut one 25 x 29 holes (no graph).

H: For tub support, cut one 23 x 65 holes (no graph).

I: For heating element, cut one 3 x 6 holes.

J: For lint filter screen and top, cut one 4 x 6 holes for screen and one 2 x 6 holes for top (no screen graph).

K: For tub side, cut one 22 x 83 holes.

L: For tub paddle pieces, cut six 4 x 20 holes (no graph).

M: For tub back, cut one according to graph.

N: For tub spindle rod side and end, cut one 12 x 14 holes for side and one according to graph for end (no side graph).

STITCHING INSTRUCTIONS:

NOTE: G, H and J-N pieces are unworked.

1: Using colors and stitches indicated, work A, B, C, E (work according to Washer E graphs) and I pieces according to graphs. Fill in uncoded areas (leave indicated areas unworked) of A, B and C, and work door D using White and Continental Stitch. Fill in uncoded areas of front E and work F (one on opposite side of canvas) pieces using Black and Continental Stitch. With black for front E and with matching colors, Overcast unfinished cutout edges of A and C pieces and unfinished edges of D, E and F pieces as indicated on graphs. With White for handle and metallic cord for element, Overcast unfinished edges of handle D and I pieces.

2: Follow **NOTE** above Step 2 and Step 2 of Washer on page 60, reversing position of embroidery as shown in photo.

3: With White, Whipstitch one long edge of each L piece to K as indicated. For each paddle, Whipstitch two adjacent L pieces together. Overlapping six holes as indicated with paddles on inside, Whipstitch ends of K together.

4: For spindle rod, overlapping two holes, Whipstitch short ends of side N together; Whipstitch one end of spindle and end N together. Insert dowel into spindle; Whipstitch unfinished end to M as indicated. Glue heating element to opposite side of M over spindle attachment.

5: Tack ends of handle to door as indicated. Whipstitch hinge and door together as indicated; Whipstitch hinge and front A together as indicated.

NOTE: Cut one 12" length of metallic cord.

6: For door support, thread 12" strand of cord from back to front on front A at one ✦ hole; knot end. Run cord through back of stitches on door, then thread needle from front to back through remaining ✦ hole on front. Pull cord, leaving about ¾" between door and front on each side. Knot end; trim excess.

7: Follow Step 7 of Washer on page 60.

8: With White, Whipstitch G to wrong side of A and B pieces as indicated and according to Dryer Assembly Diagram. Whipstitch ends of H to wrong side of B pieces as indicated (see diagram). Place tub inside dryer with spindle extending through back opening; Whipstitch front and sides together.

9: Whipstitch dryer top, front and sides together. With Cinnamon for control panel top and with matching colors, Whipstitch assembly and back together; with White, Overcast unfinished bottom edges.

NOTE: Cut closure strip into two ½" x ¾" pieces.

10: With White, Whipstitch J pieces together as indicated on top J graph; Overcast unfinished edges of top. Insert lint filter into cutout on dryer top. Glue or sew closure pieces to inside top corners of door and corresponding areas on front.

A – Dryer Back (cut 1) 29 x 44 holes

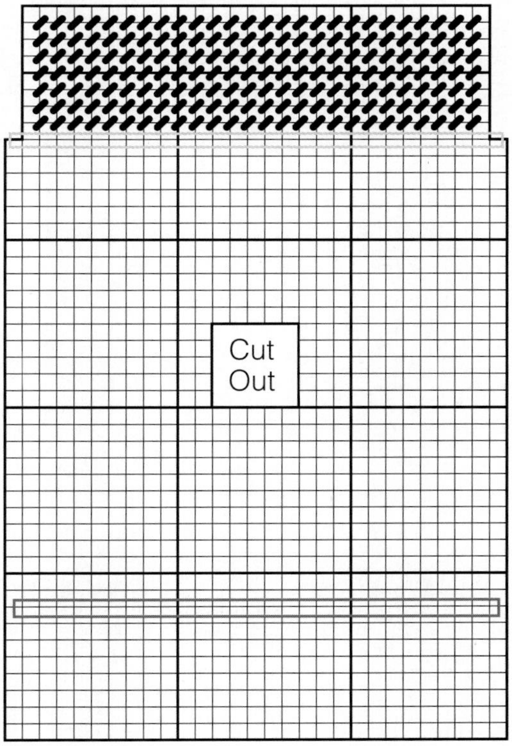

I – Dryer Heating Element
(cut 1) 3 x 6 holes

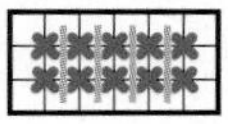

COLOR KEY: Dryer

Metallic cord
White/Silver – 2½ yds.

Nylon Plus™	Needloft™ yarn
#02	#00 Black – 7 yds.
#19	#02 Christmas Red – ½ yd.
#44	#14 Cinnamon – 3 yds.
#01	#41 White – 2½ oz.

STITCH KEY:

- Backstitch/Straight Stitch
- 4-mm. Bead Attachment
- 5-mm. Bead Attachment
- Paddle Attachment
- Spindle Rod Attachment
- Handle Attachment
- Unworked Area/Hinge Attachment
- Door Support Attachment
- Unworked Area/Panel Front To Panel Top Attachment
- Unworked Area/Panel Front To Dryer Top Attachment
- Unworked Area/Panel End Attachment
- Unworked Area/Bottom Support Attachment
- Unworked Area/Tub Support Attachment
- Unworked Area/Dryer Top Attachment
- Lint Filter Screen Attachment

J – Dryer Lint Filter Top
(cut 1 from white)
2 x 6 holes

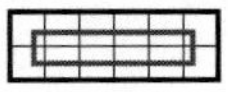

A – Dryer Front (cut 1) 29 x 36 holes

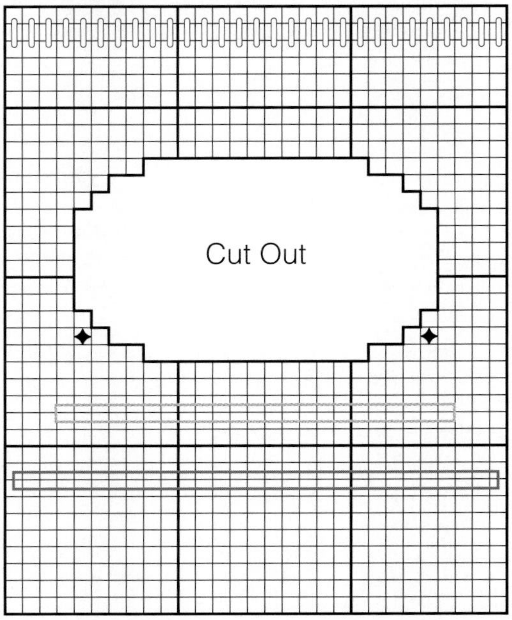

N – Dryer Tub Spindle Rod End
(cut 1 from whtie)
4 x 4 holes

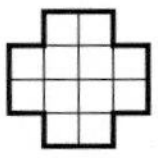

B – Dryer Side
(cut 2)
25 x 36 holes

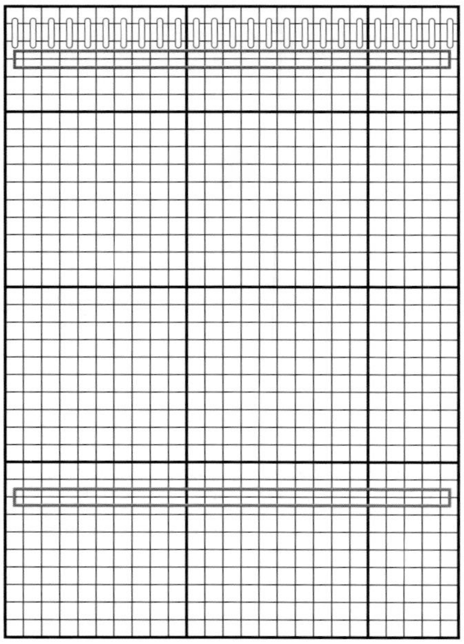

D – Dryer Door
(cut 1)
15 x 23 holes
Overcast between arrows.

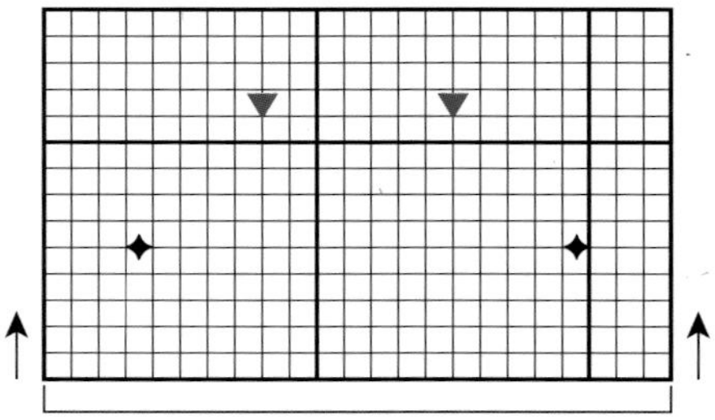

Whipstitch to hinge.

COLOR KEY: Dryer		
	Metallic cord	
	White/Silver – 2½ yds.	
	Nylon Plus™ Needloft™ yarn	
	#02	#00 Black – 7 yds.
	#19	#02 Christmas Red – ½ yd.
	#44	#14 Cinnamon – 3 yds.
	#01	#41 White – 2½ oz.

STITCH KEY:
Backstitch/Straight Stitch
4-mm. Bead Attachment
5-mm. Bead Attachment
Paddle Attachment
Spindle Rod Attachment
Handle Attachment
Unworked Area/Hinge Attachment
Door Support Attachment
Unworked Area/Panel Front To Panel Top Attachment
Unworked Area/Panel Front To Dryer Top Attachment
Unworked Area/Panel End Attachment
Unworked Area/Bottom Support Attachment
Unworked Area/Tub Support Attachment
Unworked Area/Dryer Top Attachment
Lint Filter Screen Attachment

C – Dryer Top (cut 1) 25 x 29 holes
Whipstitch to back.

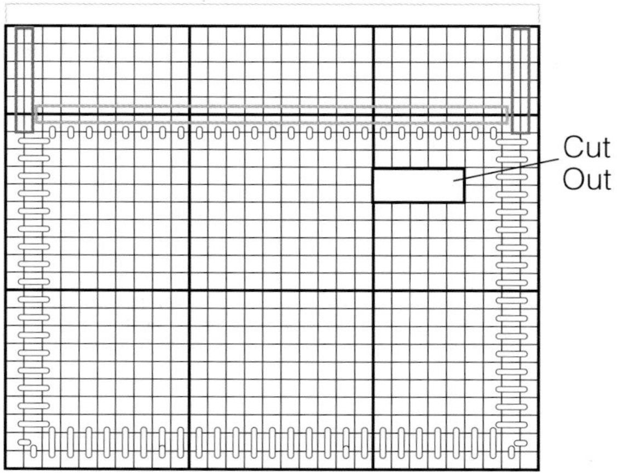

Lap Under

K – Dryer Tub Side (cut 1 from white) 22 x 83 holes

Lap Over

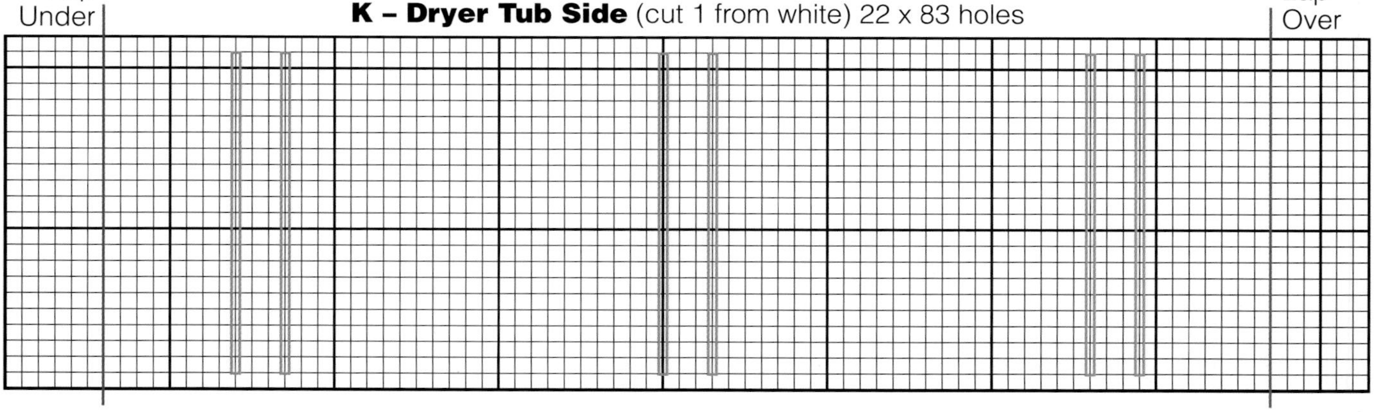

M – Dryer Tub Back
(cut 1 from white)
24 x 24 holes

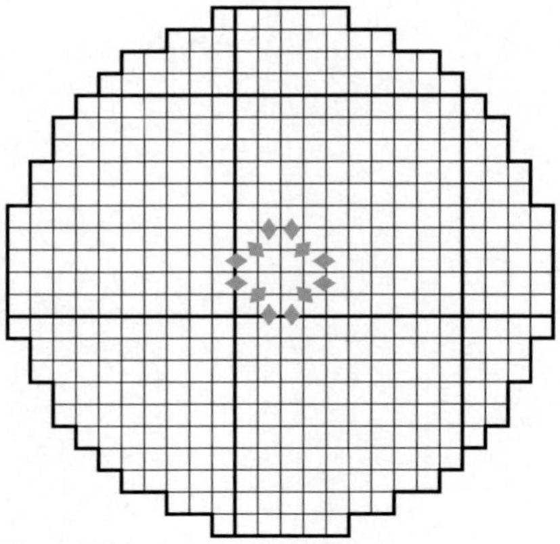

Dryer Assembly Diagram

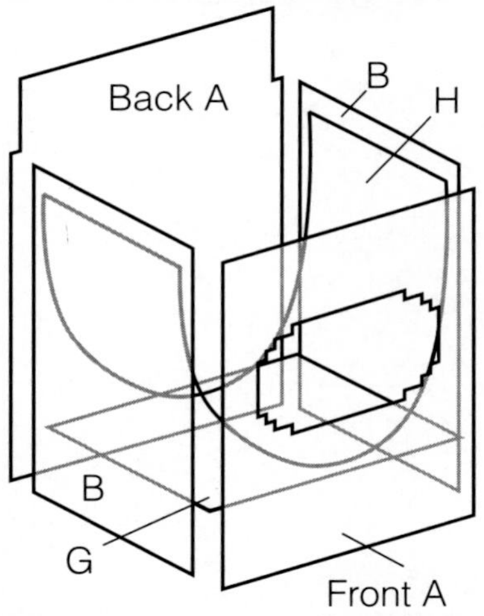

MOP & BUCKET

SIZE: Dust Mop is about 7¼" long; Sponge Mop is about 7¼" long; Wet Mop is about 8" long; Bucket is 1⅜" across x 1⅜" tall, not including handle.

MATERIALS:

- ❑ ½ sheet of 7-count plastic canvas
- ❑ Scraps of ⅜"-thick foam rubber
- ❑ One 4" and three 6¼" lengths of clothes hanger or 16-gauge floral wire
- ❑ Pliers
- ❑ Craft glue or glue gun
- ❑ Metallic cord; for amount see Color Key on page 66.
- ❑ Worsted-weight or plastic canvas yarn; for amounts see Color Key.

CUTTING INSTRUCTIONS:

NOTE: Graphs on pages 66.

A: For Dust Mop top and bottom, cut one each according to graphs.

B: For Sponge Mop sponge press and top, cut two according to graph for press and one 2 x 7 holes for top.

C: For Dust Mop and Sponge Mop handle pieces, cut four (two for dust mop and two for sponge mop) 1 x 45 holes (no graphs).

D: For Wet Mop, cut two according to graph.

E: For Bucket bottom and side, cut one according to graph for bottom and one 8 x 30 holes for side (no side graph).

STITCHING INSTRUCTIONS:

1: Using Mint for Dust Mop, White for Wet Mop and Modified Turkey Work (see Stitch Illustration), work bottom A with ½" loops and D pieces with 2" loops according to graphs. Cut through loops on D pieces. Using colors and stitches indicated, work top A, B and bottom E pieces according to graphs.

2: For Dust Mop, holding two C pieces together with one 6¼" wire between, with Cinnamon, loosely Whipstitch together along one side; make a ½" loop at end for hanger, then Whipstitch down other side. Tack end of handle to center of top A as indicated on graph. Holding A pieces wrong sides together, with White, Whipstitch together.

NOTE: Cut foam rubber into one ½" x 1¼" and two ⅝" x 1" pieces.

3: For Sponge Mop, holding sponge press B pieces wrong sides together, with cord, Whipstitch together as indicated. Working through all thicknesses, Whipstitch sponge press and top B together; Overcast unfinished edges of top. Holding one 6¼" wire between remaining two C pieces, Whipstitch together as for Dust Mop in Step 2; tack to right side center of top. Glue ½" x 1¼" piece of foam to wrong side of top.

4: For Wet Mop, holding D pieces wrong sides together, with White, Whipstitch bottom edges together as indicated. Using metallic cord and Straight Stitch and working through both thicknesses, embroider detail as indicated. Holding remaining 6¼" wire between handle edges, with Mint, Whipstitch together as for Dust Mop in Step 2.

5: For Bucket, overlapping two holes at short ends and working through both thicknesses to join, using Sandstone and Continental Stitch, work side E. Whipstitch side and bottom E together; Overcast unfinished edge. With pliers, bend 4" wire as shown in Bucket Handle Diagram. Insert ends of handle through top hole on opposite sides of bucket as shown in photo. Place remaining scraps of foam rubber in Bucket for sponges.

Bucket Handle Diagram

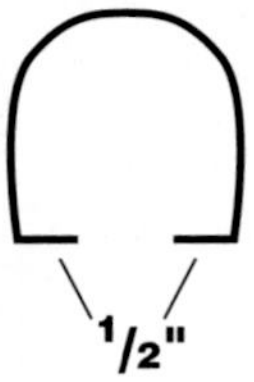

Modified Turkey Work Stitch Illustration

A – Dust Mop Bottom
(cut 1) 7 x 7 holes

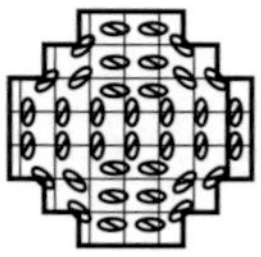

A – Dust Mop Top
(cut 1) 7 x 7 holes

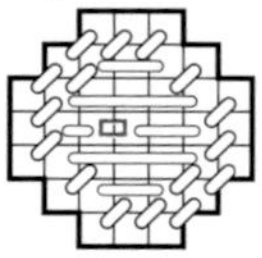

B – Sponge Mop Sponge Press
(cut 2)
7 x 7 holes

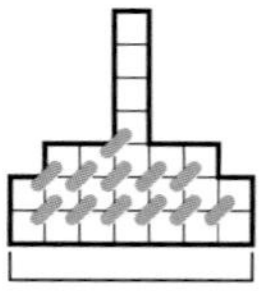

Do not Whipstitch; attach to top.

B – Sponge Mop Top
(cut 1) 2 x 7 holes

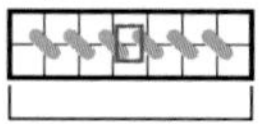

Whipstitch to sponge press.

COLOR KEY: Mops & Bucket		
	Metallic cord	
■	White/Silver – 2½ yds.	
	Nylon Plus™ Needloft™ yarn	
□	#44	#14 Cinnamon – 5½ yds.
■	#47	#16 Sandstone – 8 yds.
□	#30	#21 Mint – 4½ yds.
▨	#01	#41 White – 3 yds.

STITCH KEY:	
—	Backstitch/Straight Stitch
⊘	Modified Turkey Work
□	Handle Attachment

D – Wet Mop
(cut 2)
3 x 49 holes

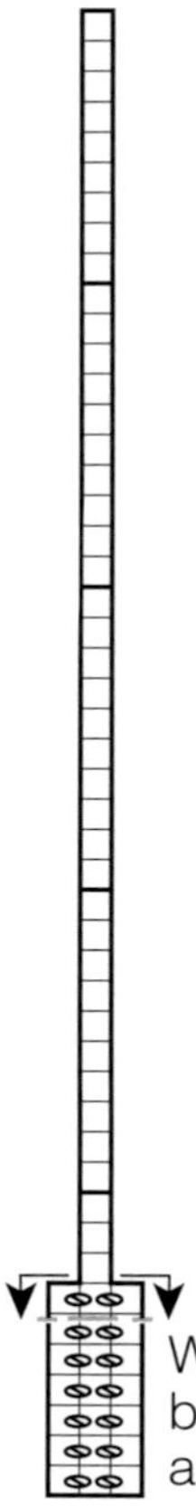

Whipstitch between arrows.

E – Bucket Bottom
(cut 1) 8 x 8 holes

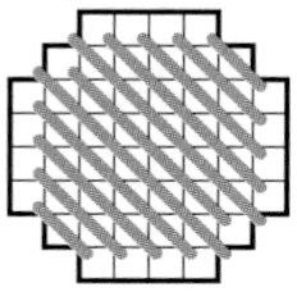

BROOM & DUST PAN

SIZE: Broom is 1⅛" x 7⅜", not including loop hanger; Dustpan is 1½" x 1⅝".

MATERIALS:
- ❑ ¼ sheet of 7-count plastic canvas
- ❑ 6¼" length of clothes hanger or 16-gauge floral wire
- ❑ Worsted-weight or plastic canvas yarn; for amounts see Color Key.

CUTTING INSTRUCTIONS:

A: For Broom, cut two according to graph.

B: For Dustpan top and bottom, cut one each according to graphs.

C: For Dustpan side, cut one 1 x 14 holes (no graph).

STITCHING INSTRUCTIONS:

1: Using colors and stitches indicated, work A and B pieces according to graphs. With Cinnamon, Overcast top B as indicated on graph.

NOTE: Separate 1 yd. of Cinnamon into 1-ply or worsted-weight into 2-ply.

2: Using 1-ply Cinnamon and Backstitch, embroider detail on A pieces as indicated.

3: For Broom, holding A pieces wrong sides together with wire between at handle end, with Mint for handle and with matching colors, Whipstitch together, making a ½" loop at top of handle for hanger as you work.

4: For Dustpan, with right sides of B pieces facing up and C between as indicated, with Cinnamon, Whipstitch B and C pieces together, Overcasting unfinished edges of bottom as you work.

A – Broom
(cut 2)
7 x 48 holes

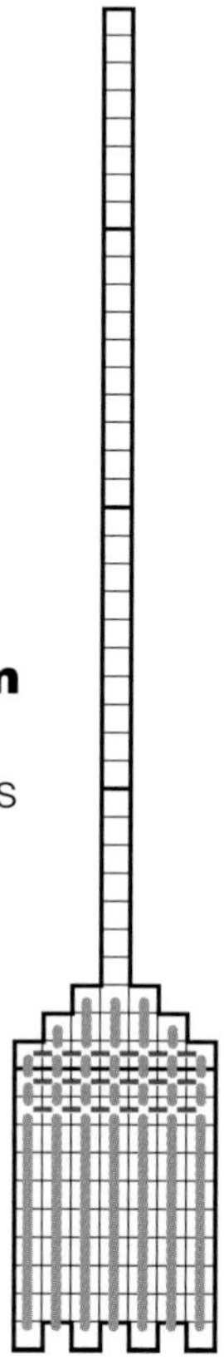

COLOR KEY: Broom & Dustpan		
	Nylon Plus™ Needloft™ yarn	
■	#44	#14 Cinnamon – 5 yds.
■	#47	#16 Sandstone – 4 yds.
□	#30	#24 Mint – 2½ yds.

STITCH KEY:

— Backstitch/Straight Stitch

— Dustpan Side Attachment

B – Dustpan Top
(cut 1)
4 x 9 holes

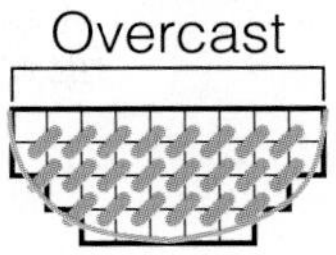

B – Dustpan Bottom
(cut 1)
9 x 9 holes

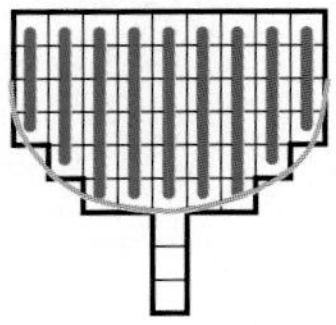

SINK

SIZE: 3⅜" x 3⅞" x 6⅞" tall.

MATERIALS:

- ❏ 1½ sheets of 7-count plastic canvas
- ❏ Two silver 4-mm. beads
- ❏ Seven silver 5-mm. beads
- ❏ White Velcro® closure strip
- ❏ Sewing needle and white thread
- ❏ Metallic cord; for amount see Color Key on page 68.
- ❏ Worsted-weight or plastic canvas yarn; for amount see Color Key.

CUTTING INSTRUCTIONS:

NOTE: Graphs on page 68.

A: For cabinet front and back, cut one according to graph for front and one 22 x 36 holes for back (no back graph).

B: For cabinet sides, cut two 25 x 36 holes.

C: For cabinet top and bottom, cut one according to graph for top and one 22 x 25 holes for bottom (no bottom graph).

D: For basin bottom and bottom support, cut one 18 x 18 holes for basin bottom and one 22 x 25 holes for bottom support (no support graph).

E: For basin walls, cut four 17 x 18 holes (no graph).

F: For cabinet door, cut one 15 x 18 holes.

G: For cabinet door hinge and handle, cut one 1 x 18 holes for hinge and one 1 x 9 holes for handle (no graphs).

H: For basin cover, cut one 17 x 18 holes.

I: For basin cover lip pieces, cut four 2 x 15 holes (no graph).

J: For faucet pieces, cut two according to graph.

K: For faucet base, cut one 3 x 14 holes.

L: For faucet base sides, cut two 1 x 3 holes and two 1 x 14 holes (no graphs).

STITCHING INSTRUCTIONS:

NOTE: D pieces are unworked.

1: Using colors and stitches indicated, work front A, B, top C, basin D and H pieces according to graphs. Fill in uncoded areas (leave indicated areas unworked) on front A, B, basin D and H pieces and work back A, bottom C, E, F and I pieces using White and Continental Stitch. With White, Overcast unfinished edges of F as indicated on graph, handle G and H pieces, and unfinished cutout edges of front A. With metallic cord, work K and J (one on opposite side of canvas) pieces.

2: With White, tack ends of handle G to right side of F as indicated. Whipstitch hinge G and F together as indicated; Whipstitch hinge to front A as indicated and according to Sink Assembly Diagram.

3: Whipstitch support D to wrong side of A and B pieces as indicated and according to diagram. Whipstitch A, B and bottom C pieces together. With right sides facing in, Whipstitch basin bottom D and E pieces together, forming basin. Whipstitch basin to wrong side of top C at cutout.

4: With metallic cord, holding J pieces wrong sides together, Whipstitch together as indicated; Whipstitch faucet and K together as indicated and according to Faucet Assembly Diagram. For each faucet handle, sew three 5-mm. beads and one 4-mm. bead to each side of base as indicated and according to diagram.

5: With cord, Whipstitch L and K pieces together according to diagram; Whipstitch to top C as indicated. With White, Whipstitch top and cabinet together.

6: For cover, Whipstitch I pieces to wrong side of H as indicated; tack ends of I pieces together, and Overcast unfinished edges. Sew remaining 5-mm. bead to top of cover as indicated.

NOTE: Cut closure strip into one ⅜" x ¾" piece.

7: Glue or sew closure to inside top of door and corresponding area on front.

Sink Assembly Diagram

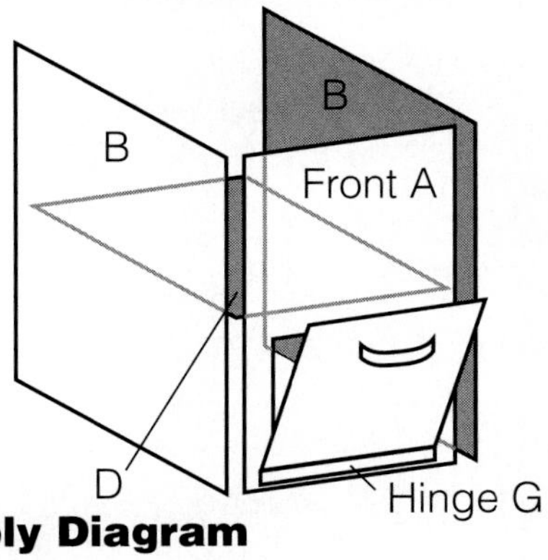

Faucet Assembly Diagram

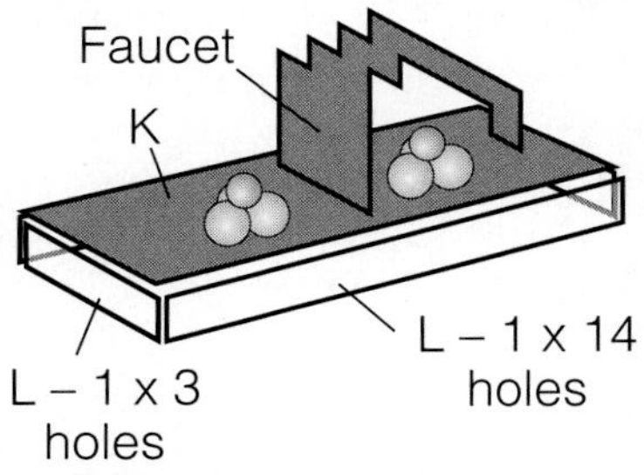

COLOR KEY: Sink

Metallic cord
White/Silver – 5 yds.

Nylon Plus™ Needloft™ yarn
#01 #41 White – 90 yds.

STITCH KEY:

- Backstitch/Straight Stitch
- Handle Attachment
- Unworked Area/Hinge Attachment
- Unworked Area/Bottom Support Attachment
- Unworked Area/Faucet Attachment
- 5-mm. Bead Attachment
- 4-mm. Bead Attachment
- Unworked Area/Faucet Base Attachment
- Unworked Area/Cover Lip Attachment

C – Cabinet Top
(cut 1) 22 x 25 holes

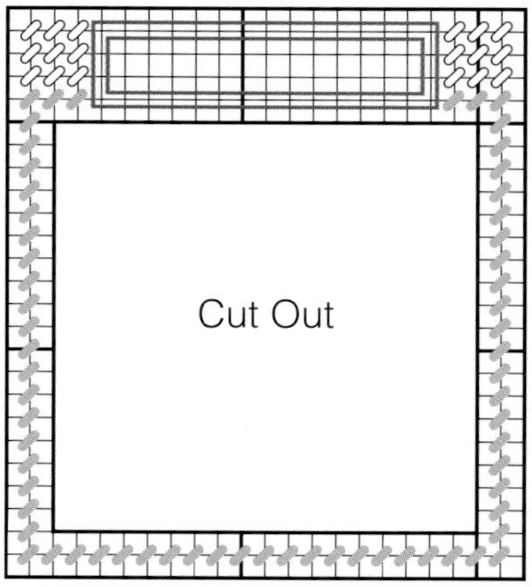

A – Cabinet Front
(cut 1)
22 x 36 holes

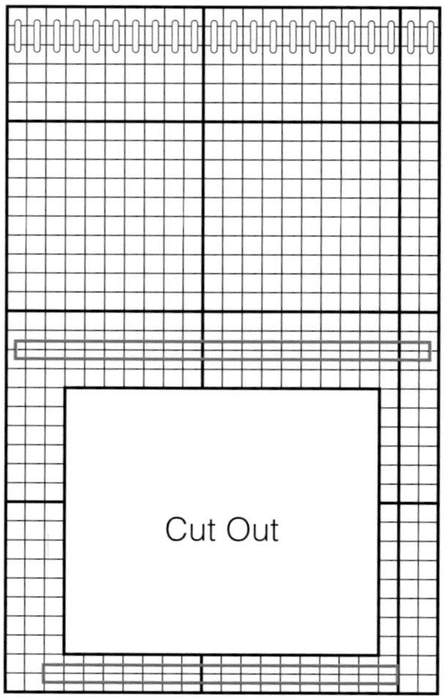

D – Basin Bottom
(cut 1) 18 x 18 holes

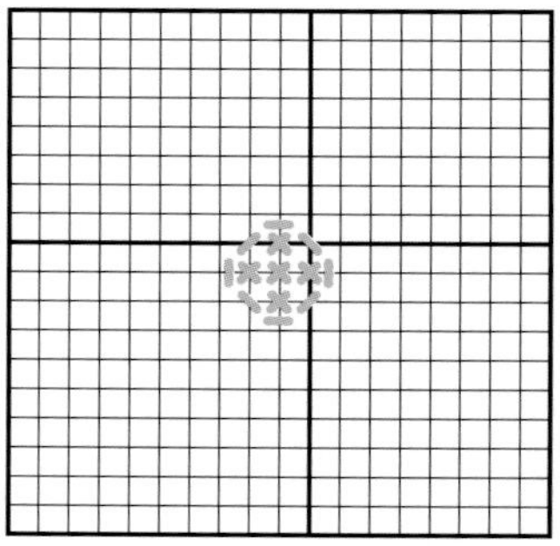

F – Cabinet Door
(cut 1) 15 x 18 holes
Overcast between arrows.

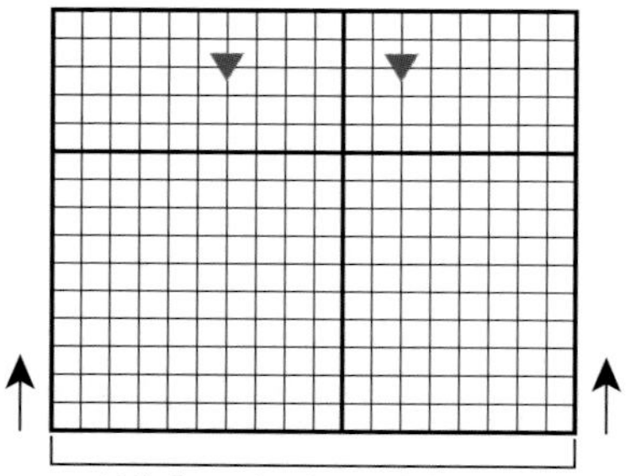

Whipstitch to hinge.

B – Cabinet Side
(cut 2) 25 x 36 holes

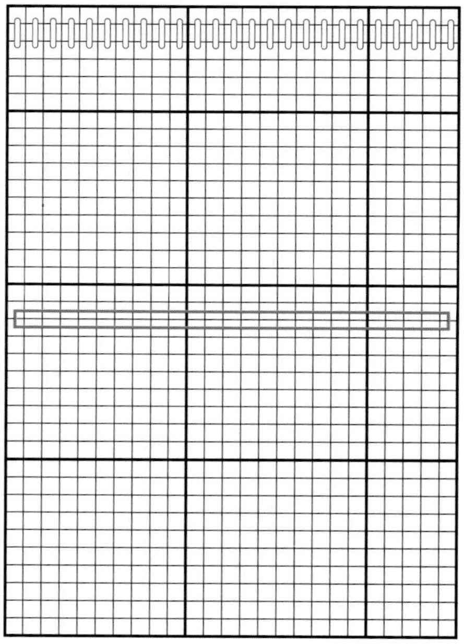

K – Faucet Base
(cut 1) 3 x 14 holes

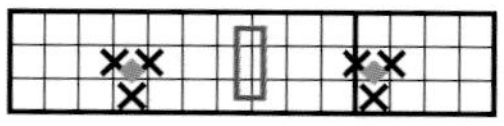

H – Basin Cover
(cut 1) 17 x 18 holes

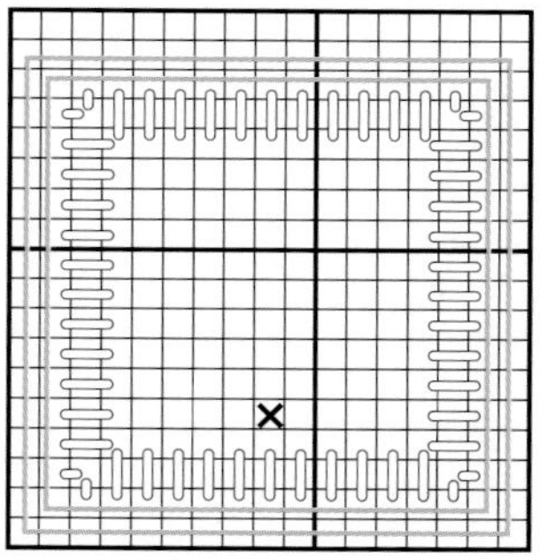

J – Faucet Piece
(cut 2) 6 x 8 holes

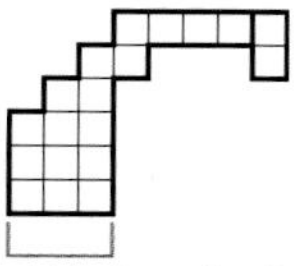

Do not Whipstitch;
attach to base.

IRONING BOARD & IRON

SIZE: Board is 2⅜" x 7¼" x about 5¾" tall when standing; Iron is ⅜" x 1⅛" x ¾" tall.

MATERIALS:

- ❏ One sheet of 7-count plastic canvas
- ❏ Four black seed beads
- ❏ Three 6" lengths of clothes hanger or 16-gauge floral wire
- ❏ Six-strand embroidery floss; for amount see Color Key.
- ❏ Metallic cord; for amount see Color Key.
- ❏ Worsted-weight or plastic canvas yarn; for amounts see Color Key.

CUTTING INSTRUCTIONS:

A: For Board top and bottom, cut two (one for top and one for bottom) according to graph.

B: For Board large and small legs, cut two each according to graphs.

C: For Iron top and bottom, cut two (one for top and one for bottom) according to graph.

D: For Iron sides and back, cut two 1 x 7 holes for sides and one 1 x 3 holes for back (no graphs).

E: For Iron handle, cut two according to graph.

STITCHING INSTRUCTIONS:

1: For Board, using colors and stitches indicated, work one A for top and B pieces according to graphs. Fill in uncoded areas of top A and B pieces using White and Continental Stitch. Using Sandstone and Continental Stitch, work remaining A for bottom.

NOTE: Separate Mint into 1-ply or worsted-weight into 2-ply and floss into 3-ply strands.

2: Using 1-ply Mint, Backstitch and Straight Stitch, embroider plant as indicated on graph. Using three strands floss, Backstitch and Straight Stitch and attaching one bead at each indicated hole as you work, embroider hanger and bracket hook as indicated.

3: Holding small B pieces wrong sides together with one 6" length of wire between as indicated, with matching colors, Whipstitch together as indicated; repeat with large B pieces and remaining lengths of wire.

4: Insert small leg through cutout on large leg, forming an X. With Sandstone, Whipstitch top of each leg to right side of bottom A as indicated. Holding Board top and bottom wrong sides together, with Sandstone, Whipstitch together.

5: For Iron, using Black for top, metallic cord for bottom and Continental Stitch, work one C in each color. Holding E pieces together, with Black, Whipstitch together, and tack to top C as indicated and according to Iron Assembly Diagram. Bending side D pieces to fit, with cord, Whipstitch C and D pieces together according to diagram.

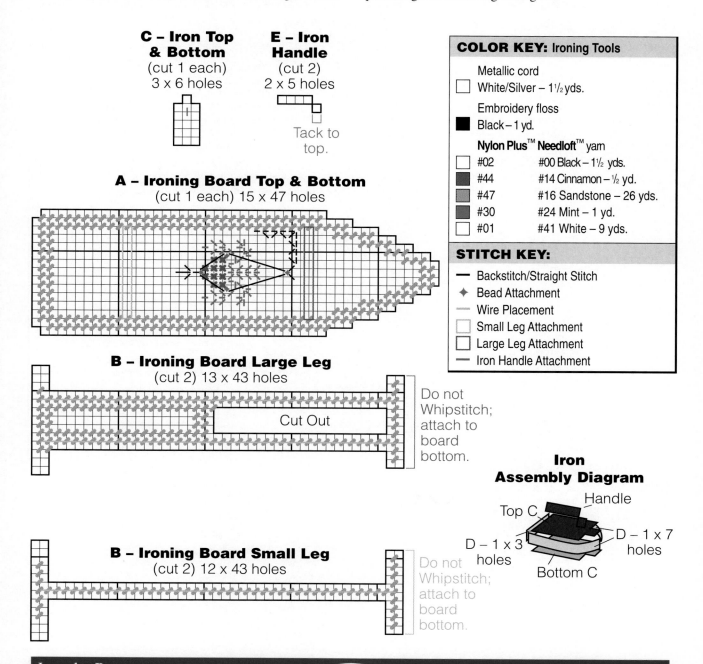

C – Iron Top & Bottom
(cut 1 each)
3 x 6 holes

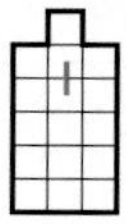

E – Iron Handle
(cut 2)
2 x 5 holes

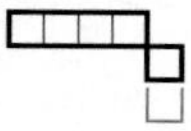

COLOR KEY: Ironing Tools

Metallic cord
☐ White/Silver – 1½ yds.

Embroidery floss
■ Black – 1 yd.

Nylon Plus™	Needloft™ yarn
#02	#00 Black – 1½ yds.
#44	#14 Cinnamon – ½ yd.
#47	#16 Sandstone – 26 yds.
#30	#24 Mint – 1 yd.
#01	#41 White – 9 yds.

STITCH KEY:
- Backstitch/Straight Stitch
- Bead Attachment
- Wire Placement
- Small Leg Attachment
- Large Leg Attachment
- Iron Handle Attachment

A – Ironing Board Top & Bottom
(cut 1 each) 15 x 47 holes

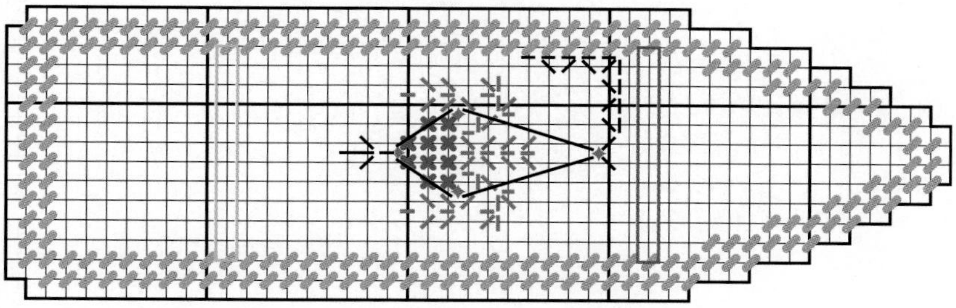

B – Ironing Board Large Leg
(cut 2) 13 x 43 holes

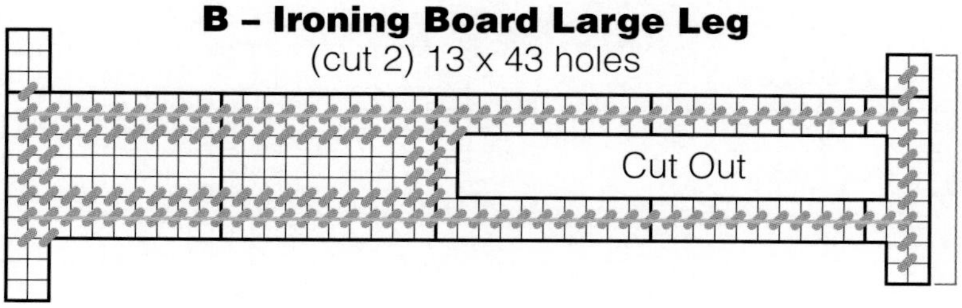

Iron Assembly Diagram

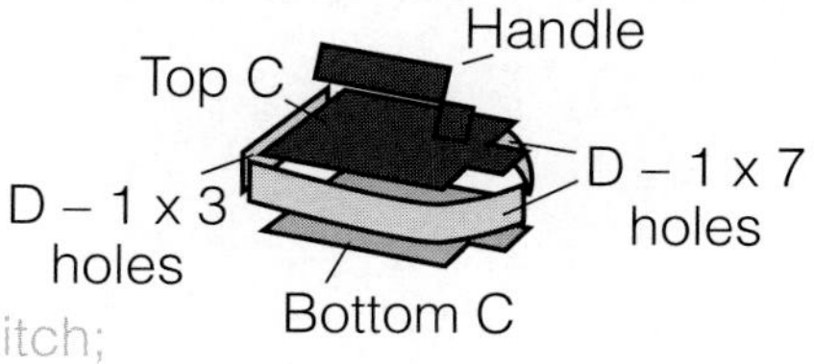

B – Ironing Board Small Leg
(cut 2) 12 x 43 holes

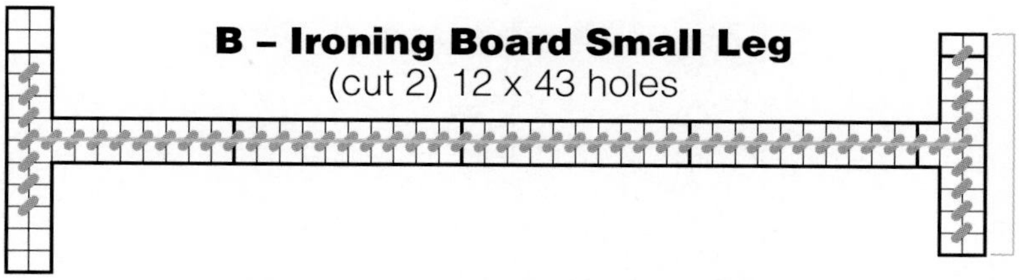

HAMPER & BASKET

SIZE: Hamper is 2⅜" x 3¼" x 5⅛" tall; Basket is 2⅝" x 3⅞" x 2" tall, not including handles.

MATERIALS:

- ❑ 1½ sheets of 7-count plastic canvas
- ❑ ½ yd. off-white 1" pregathered lace
- ❑ Four black seed beads
- ❑ Craft glue or glue gun
- ❑ Six-strand embroidery floss; for amount see Color Key.
- ❑ Worsted-weight or plastic canvas yarn; for amounts see Color Key.

CUTTING INSTRUCTIONS:

A: For Hamper front and back, cut one each according to graph.

B: For Hamper lid and bottom, cut one each according to graphs.

C: For Hamper lid hinge, cut one 2 x 19 holes (no graph).

D: For Basket side, cut one according to graph.

E: For Basket bottom, cut one according to graph.

F: For Basket handles, cut two according to graph.

STITCHING INSTRUCTIONS:

1: Using Sandstone and Wicker Stitch (see Stitch Illustrations on page 58), work A pieces according to graph. Using colors and stitches indicated, work lid B according to graph. Fill in uncoded areas of lid B using White, and work bottom B, C and E pieces using Sandstone and Continental Stitch; Overcast unfinished edges of lid B as indicated.

NOTE: Separate Mint into 1-ply or worsted-weight into 2-ply and floss into 3-ply strands.

2: Using 1-ply Mint, Backstitch and Straight Stitch, embroider plant as indicated on lid B graph. Using three strands floss and Straight Stitch and attaching one bead at each indicated hole as you work, embroider hanger as indicated.

3: Bending front according to Hamper Assembly Diagram, with Sandstone, Whipstitch A pieces together. Whipstitch assembly and bottom B together; Overcast unfinished top edges of Hamper. Holding right side of C to wrong side of lid, Whipstitch together (see diagram).

NOTE: Cut lace into one 5½" and one 10" length.

4: Glue wrong side of hinge to inside back of Hamper according to diagram, and 5½" length of lace to inside as shown in photo.

5: For Basket, overlapping ends of D as indicated and working through both thicknesses at overlap area to join, work vertical Long Stitches according to Step 2 of Wicker Stitch Illustrations; working under vertical stitches, work horizontal Long Stitches according to D graph and Step 1 of Wicker Stitch Illustrations, pulling yarn snug against canvas.

6: Easing to fit, Whipstitch D and E pieces together. Using Herringbone Overcast (see Stitch Illustration), Overcast unfinished top edges. For each handle, Overcast unfinished edges of one F, and tack to basket side as indicated.

B – Hamper Lid
(cut 1) 14 x 21 holes
Do not Overcast; Whipstitch to hinge.

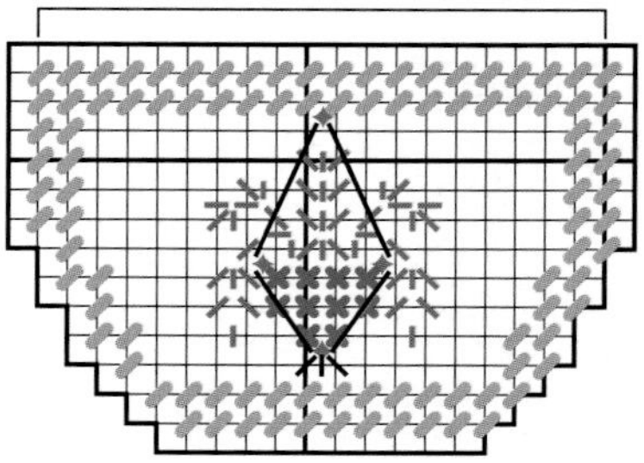

B – Hamper Bottom
(cut 1) 12 x 20 holes

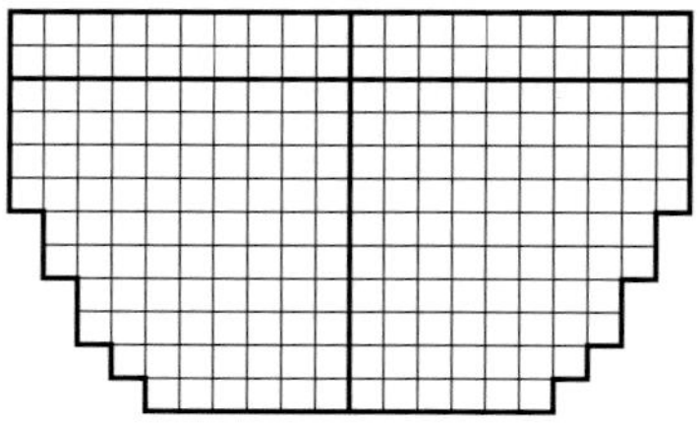

Hamper Assembly Diagram

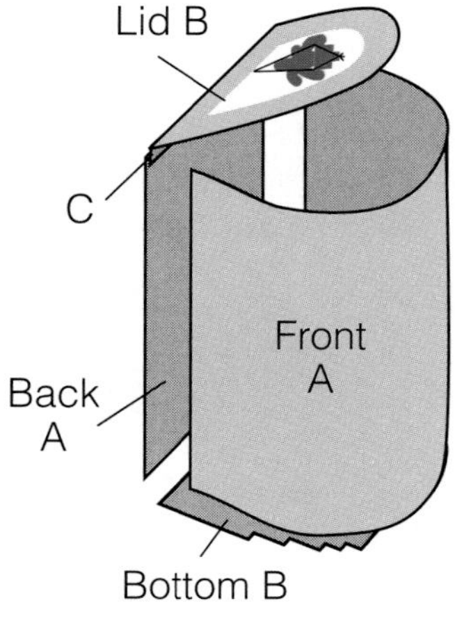

Herringbone Overcast Stitch Illustration

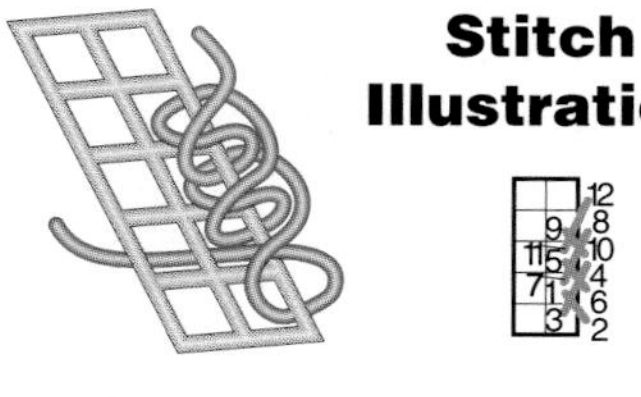

COLOR KEY: Hamper & Basket

Embroidery floss

- Black – 1 yd.

Nylon Plus™ Needloft™ yarn

#44	#14 Cinnamon – ½ yd.
#47	#16 Sandstone – 55 yds.
#30	#24 Mint – 1 yd.
#01	#41 White – 2½ yds.

STITCH KEY:

- Backstitch/Straight Stitch
- Bead Attachment
- Handle Attachment

D – Basket Side (cut 1)
58 x 58 holes

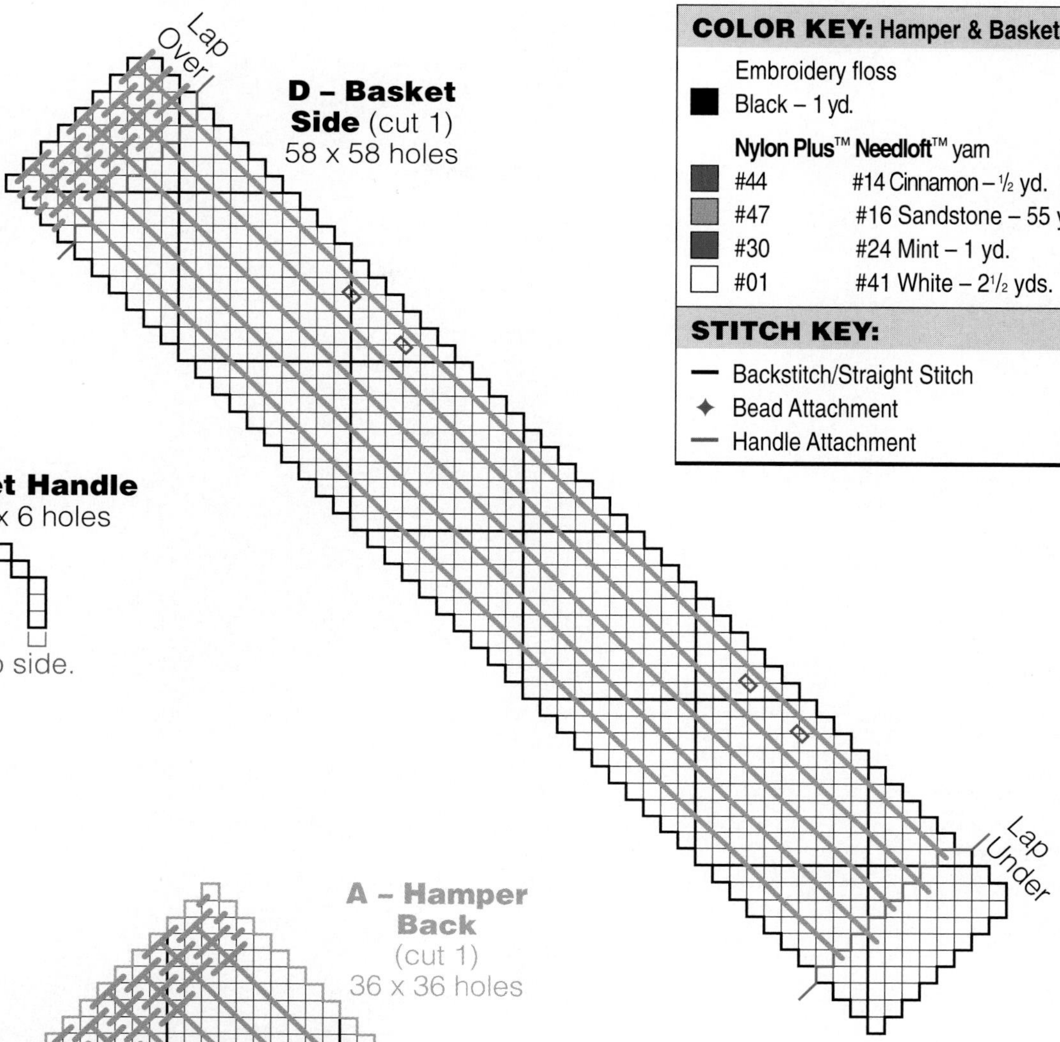

F – Basket Handle
(cut 2) 5 x 6 holes

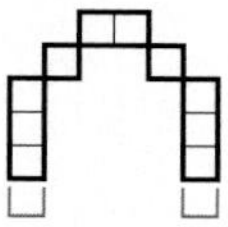

Tack to side.

A – Hamper Back
(cut 1)
36 x 36 holes

A – Hamper Front
(cut 1)
50 x 50 holes

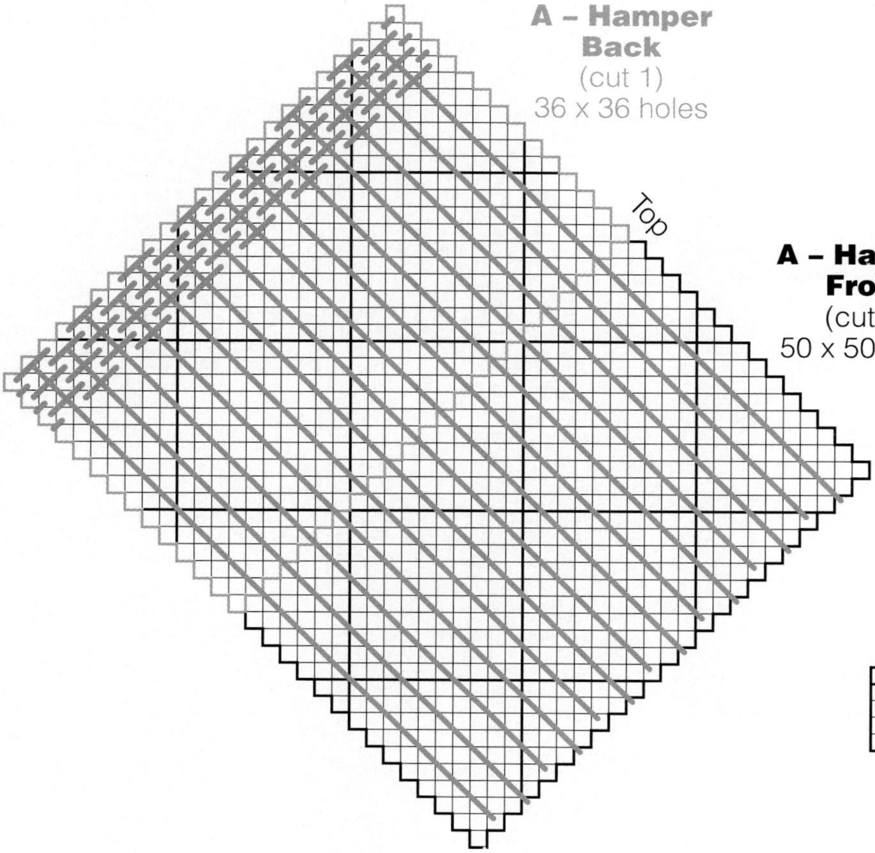

E – Basket Bottom
(cut 1) 17 x 25 holes

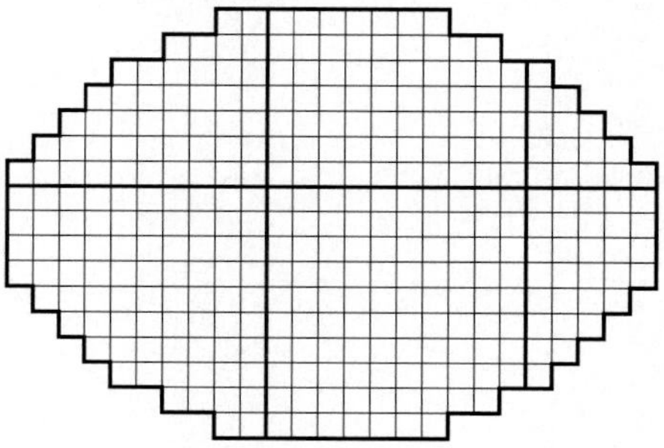

BARBIE® doll and friends
pictured with permission of
Mattel, Inc. ©1996 Mattel, Inc.
All rights reserved.

FASHION DOLL Bathroom

Designed by
Diane T. Ray

MATERIALS FOR ENTIRE SET:
- ❑ Six sheets of 7-count plastic canvas
- ❑ Five 12" x 18" or larger sheets of 7-count plastic canvas
- ❑ Scraps of white 7-count plastic canvas
- ❑ One sheet of 10-count plastic canvas
- ❑ Five white 15-mm. aurora-borealis berry beads
- ❑ 20 silver 5-mm. beads
- ❑ 14 silver 4-mm. beads
- ❑ 44 black seed beads
- ❑ $3\frac{3}{4}$ yds. off-white 1" pregathered lace
- ❑ 2 yds. off-white $\frac{1}{2}$" pregathered lace
- ❑ 8" x 9" piece of white 14-count Aida cloth
- ❑ 15" square piece of off-white lace fabric
- ❑ $2\frac{1}{2}$ white 9" x 12" sheets of felt
- ❑ 1" tan $\frac{3}{4}$" Velcro® closure strip
- ❑ $\frac{1}{2}$" pink pom-pom
- ❑ Polyester fiberfill
- ❑ Facial tissues
- ❑ 3" x 7" foil loaf pan (optional)
- ❑ $11\frac{1}{2}$" wooden $\frac{3}{16}$" dowel
- ❑ Round wooden toothpick
- ❑ $\frac{5}{16}$" x 2" hex-head cap screw or bolt
- ❑ $5\frac{1}{2}$" x 8" aluminum or craft foil
- ❑ $5\frac{1}{2}$" x 8" poster board
- ❑ Sewing needle or machine and white, brown and off-white thread
- ❑ Fabric glue or iron-on hem tape (optional)
- ❑ Craft glue or glue gun
- ❑ Six-strand embroidery floss:
  - ❑ Black – $11\frac{1}{2}$ yds.
  - ❑ Avocado – $6\frac{1}{2}$ yds.
  - ❑ Brown – 3 yds.
- ❑ Metallic cord:
  - ❑ Silver – $10\frac{1}{2}$ yds.
- ❑ Worsted-weight or plastic canvas yarn:

Nylon Plus™	Needloft™ yarn
❑ #02	#00 Black – $2\frac{1}{2}$ yds.
❑ #19	#02 Christmas Red – small amount
❑ #44	#14 Cinnamon – $14\frac{1}{2}$ yds.
❑ #47	#16 Sandstone – $8\frac{1}{4}$ oz.
❑ #30	#24 Mint – 11 yds.
❑ #43	#40 Beige – 4 yds.
❑ #01	#41 White – $8\frac{1}{2}$ oz.

For materials for individual items, see individual materials lists.

SINK CABINET

SIZE: $4\frac{1}{4}$" x $5\frac{5}{8}$" x 14" tall.

MATERIALS:
- ❑ $1\frac{1}{2}$ sheets of 7-count plastic canvas
- ❑ One sheet of 12" x 18" or larger 7-count plastic canvas
- ❑ $\frac{1}{4}$ sheet of 10-count plastic canvas
- ❑ Two white 15-mm. aurora-borealis berry beads
- ❑ 10 silver 5-mm. beads
- ❑ Four silver 4-mm beads
- ❑ Eight black seed beads
- ❑ 1 yd. off-white $\frac{1}{2}$" pregathered lace
- ❑ $5\frac{1}{2}$" x 8" aluminum or craft foil
- ❑ $5\frac{1}{2}$" x 8" poster board
- ❑ $\frac{1}{2}$" tan $\frac{3}{4}$" Velcro® closure strip
- ❑ Sewing needle and white thread
- ❑ Craft glue or glue gun
- ❑ Six-strand embroidery floss; for amounts see Color Key on page 75.
- ❑ Metallic cord; for amount see Color Key.
- ❑ Worsted-weight or plastic canvas yarn; for amounts see Color Key.

CUTTING INSTRUCTIONS:

NOTES: Graphs and diagrams on pages 75-77.

Use 10-count canvas for G pieces. Though graphs are positioned vertically and horizontally, pieces (except G and spout N) are cut on the diagonal; see Cutting Guides on page 75. Cut K from remaining half sheet.

A: For cabinet front, cut one according to graph.

B: For cabinet sides, cut two according to graph.

C: For cabinet bottom panel, cut one according to graph.

D: For cabinet bottom shelf, cut one according to graph.

E: For cabinet bottom, cut one according to graph.

F: For cabinet doors, cut two according to graph.

G: For door motifs, cut two according to graph.

H: For drawer facades, cut two according to graph.

I: For cabinet back/mirror front, cut one according to graph.

J: For mirror back, cut one according to graph.

K: For cabinet top, cut one according to graph.

L: For basin long and short sides, cut two each according to graphs.

M: For basin bottom, cut one according to graph.

N: For faucet base and faucet spout, cut two each

according to graphs.

O: For towel bar, cut one according to graph.

P: For mirror and backing, using J as a pattern, cut foil and poster board each ¼" smaller at all edges.

STITCHING INSTRUCTIONS:

NOTES: One base N piece is unworked.

Separate Cinnamon and 3 yds. each of Sandstone and White into 1-ply or worsted-weight into 2-ply strands.

1: Using 1-ply colors and stitches indicated, work G pieces according to graph; fill in uncoded areas using 1-ply White and Continental Stitch. With 1-ply Sandstone, Overcast unfinished edges.

NOTE: Separate floss into 2-ply strands.

2: Using two strands avocado floss, Backstitch and Straight Stitch, embroider plants as indicated on G graph. Using two strands black, Backstitch and Straight Stitch and attaching one seed bead at each indicated hole as you work, embroider hanger and bracket hook (reverse direction of hook on second piece) as indicated.

3: Using Sandstone and Wicker Stitch, work A, C, E, F, H and J pieces according to graphs. Using colors and stitches indicated, work upper section only of I as indicated, L, M, one base N and spout N (one on opposite side of canvas) pieces according to graphs. Using White and Continental Stitch, work K. (**NOTE:** Remaining cabinet pieces will be Whipstitched together before being worked.)

4: With matching colors, Overcast unfinished cutout edges of A, cutout and outer top edges of I as indicated, unfinished edges of H and J pieces, and one F and O as indicated; leaving opposite long edge unworked, Overcast remaining F as indicated.

5: With Sandstone, Whipstitch C and D pieces together as indicated and according to Sink Cabinet Assembly Diagram; using Wicker Stitch, work D on side opposite panel according to graph.

6: Whipstitching pieces together and then stitching unworked pieces as established in Step 5, Whipstitch B and I pieces to D as indicated and according to diagram; Whipstitch sides to bottom panel and back. Whipstitch assembly and E together.

7: With metallic cord, tack O to one cabinet side as indicated. With Sandstone, Whipstitch unfinished edge of each F to A as indicated; Whipstitch assembly and A together.

8: Holding right sides together, with White, Whipstitch L and M pieces together as indicated and according to Basin Assembly Diagram; Whipstitch basin to wrong side of K at cutout. Whipstitch K and I together as indicated; Whipstitch top, front and sides together.

9: Holding spout N pieces wrong sides together, with cord, Whipstitch together and tack to worked base N as indicated; holding unworked base N to wrong side of worked piece, Whipstitch together.

NOTE: Gently pry each berry bead apart and discard center sections of each (see Step 1 of Berry Bead Diagram).

10: For each faucet handle, with sewing thread, insert needle from back to front through faucet base at one indicated hole, through shank of one berry bead end (see Step 2 of diagram), through one silver 4-mm. bead, back through berry bead and same hole on base; knot ends of thread together on wrong side.

11: For handle on each drawer facade, follow Step 10.

12: For each door handle (position handle on edge opposite door attachment), with sewing thread, insert needle from back to front through one ✚ hole as indicated on F graph; thread five 5-mm. beads on thread. Insert needle from front to back through remaining ✚ hole; pull thread to align beads, and knot ends together on wrong side.

NOTES: Cut one 18" and two 8" lengths of lace. Cut closure strip into two ¼" x ¾" pieces.

13: Glue 8" lace to wrong side of each door motif as shown in photo. Glue drawer facades to front and faucet base to top as indicated and one motif to each door as shown. Glue or sew one closure piece to inside of each door behind handle and remaining two pieces to corresponding areas on front.

14: Glue 18" lace to wrong side of mirror front as shown. Matching top edges and leaving bottom edge of back unattached, glue edges of mirror front and back wrong sides together. For mirror, glue P pieces together; insert between mirror front and back.

A – Cabinet Front
(cut 1)
48 x 48 holes

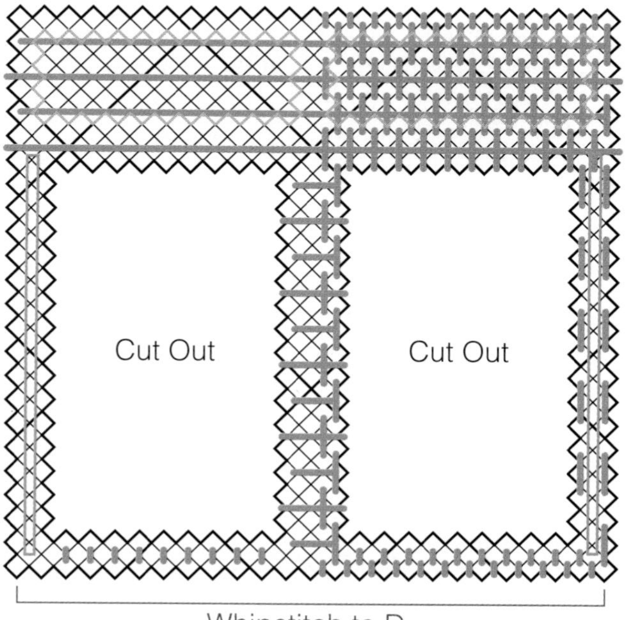

B – Cabinet Side
(cut 2) 41 x 44 holes

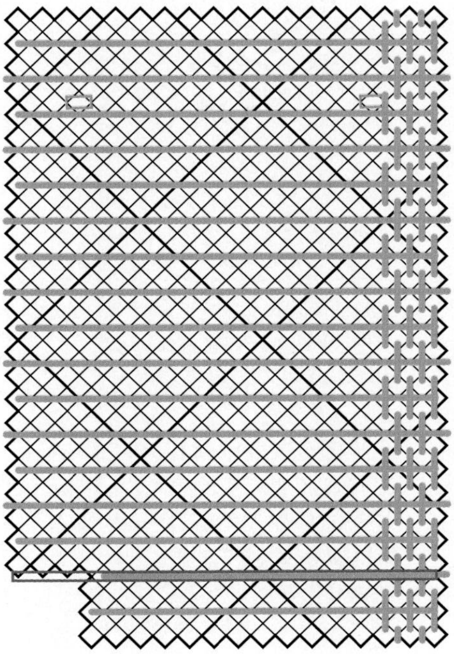

COLOR KEY: Sink Cabinet

Embroidery floss
- Avocado – 1 yd.
- Black – 1/2 yd.

Metallic cord
- Silver – 5 yds.

Nylon Plus™ Needloft™ yarn

#44	#14 Cinnamon – 1/2 yd.
#47	#16 Sandstone – 2 oz.
#01	#41 White – 20 yds.

STITCH KEY:
- Backstitch/Straight Stitch
- Seed Bead Attachment
- Bottom Panel Attachment
- Bottom Shelf Attachment
- Towel Bar Attachment
- Door Attachment
- Top Attachment
- Spout Attachment
- Berry Bead Attachment
- Door Handle Attachment
- Drawer Facade Placement
- Faucet Base Placement

Sink Cabinet Cutting Guide #2
(70 x 90 holes)

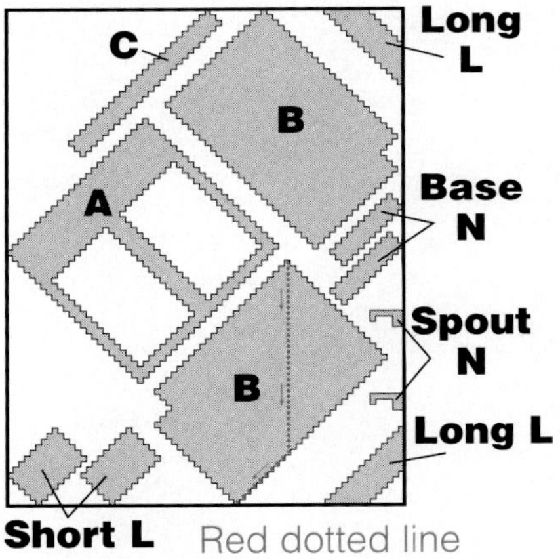

Red dotted line illustrates method of determining vertical hole count for pieces cut on the diagonal.

Sink Cabinet Cutting Guide #1
(80 x 120 holes)

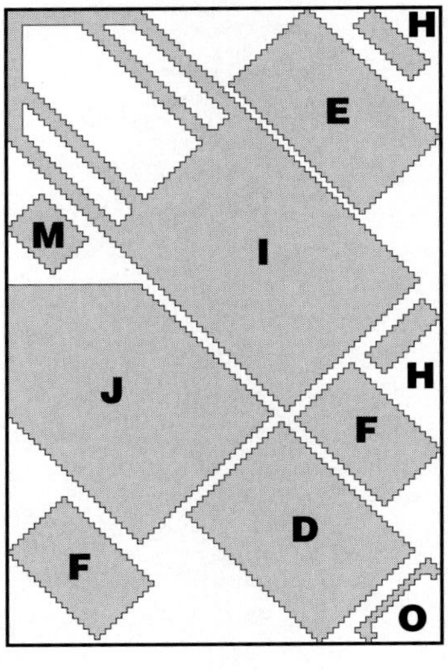

Wicker Stitch Illustrations

Step 1

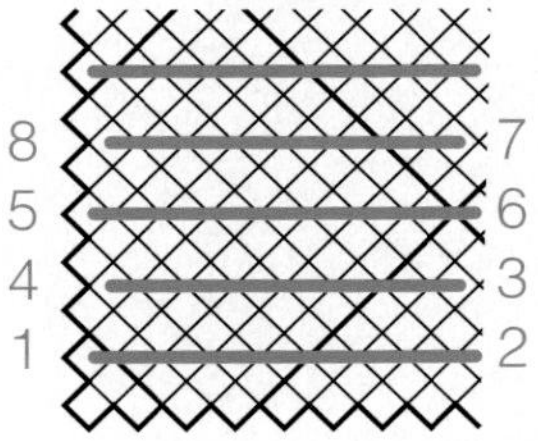

Step 1: Work horizontal Long Stitches back and forth according to each graph.

Step 2

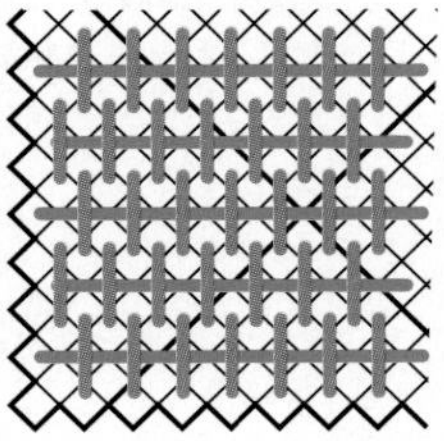

Step 2: Work vertical Long Stitches over horizontal Long Stitches as indicated across entire piece, working short stitches at edges when indicated.

I – Cabinet Back/ Mirror Front
(cut 1)
76 x 76 holes

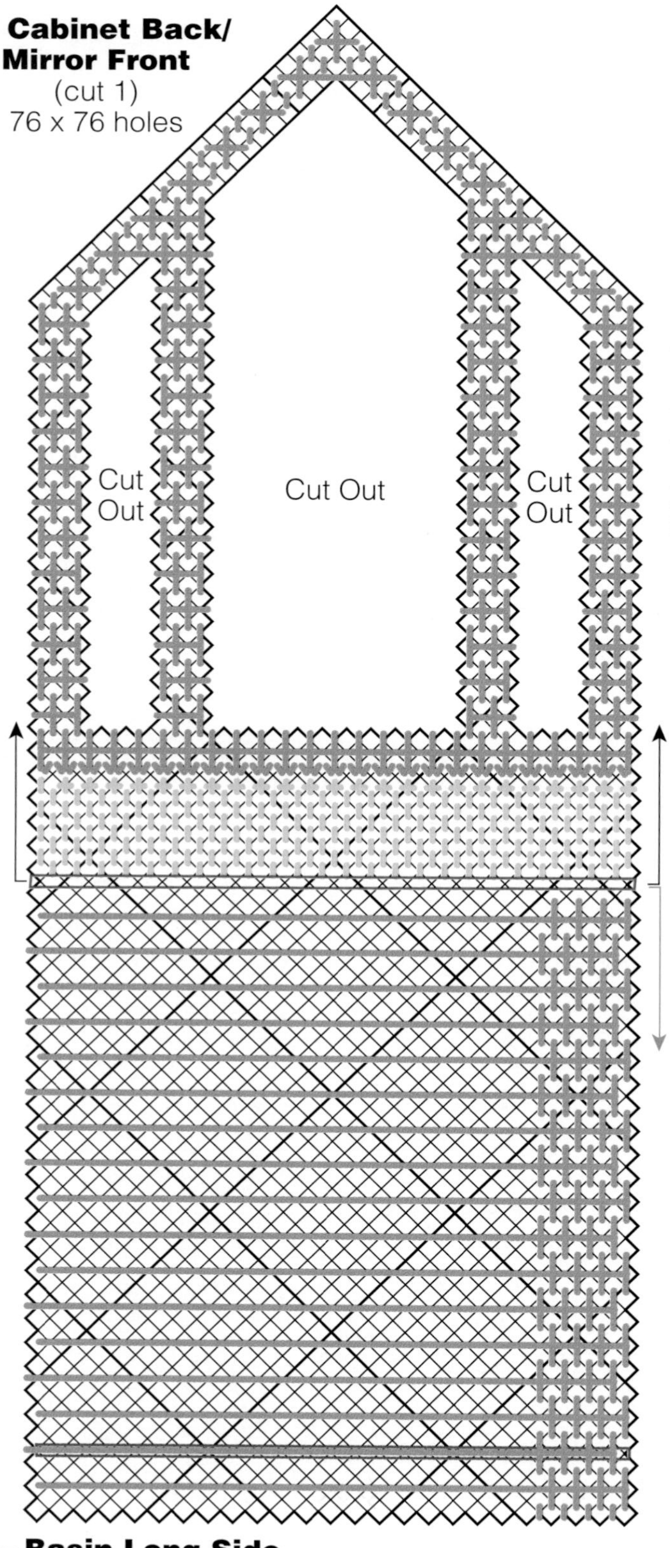

D – Cabinet Bottom Shelf
(cut 1)
42 x 42 holes

C – Cabinet Bottom Panel
(cut 1)
27 x 27 holes

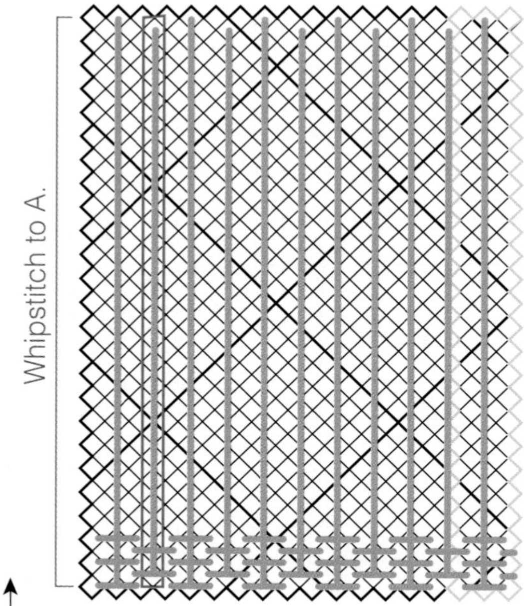

Berry Bead Diagram

Step 1:
Discard center sections.

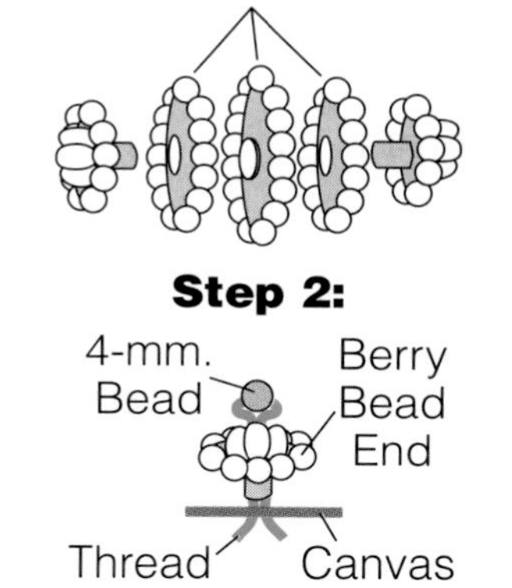

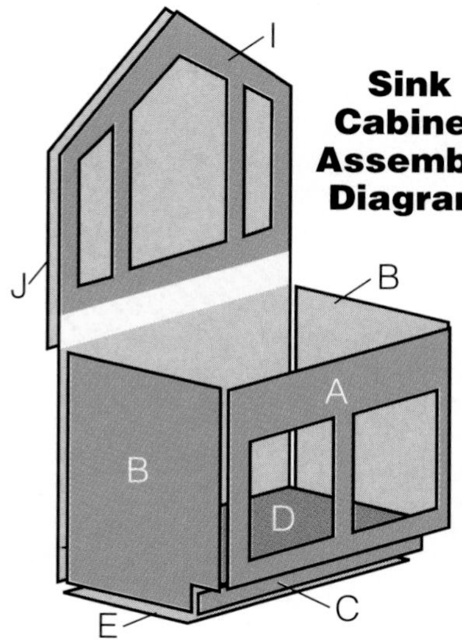

Sink Cabinet Assembly Diagram

L – Basin Long Side
(cut 2) 14 x 14 holes

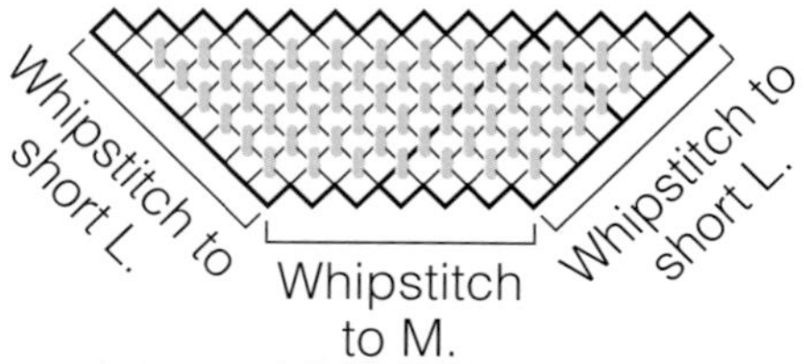

O – Towel Bar
(cut 1) 16 x 16 holes

Do not Overcast; tack to cabinet side.

Basin Assembly Diagram

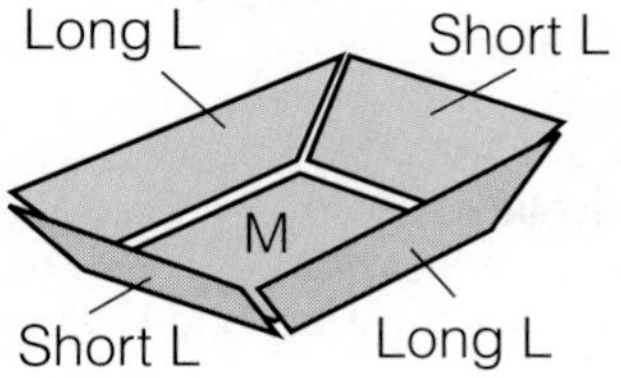

N – Faucet Spout
(cut 2) 3 x 6 holes

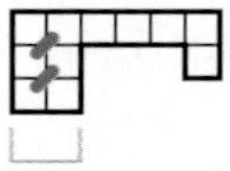

Do not Overcast; tack to base.

G – Door Motif
(cut 2 from 10-count)
15 x 30 holes

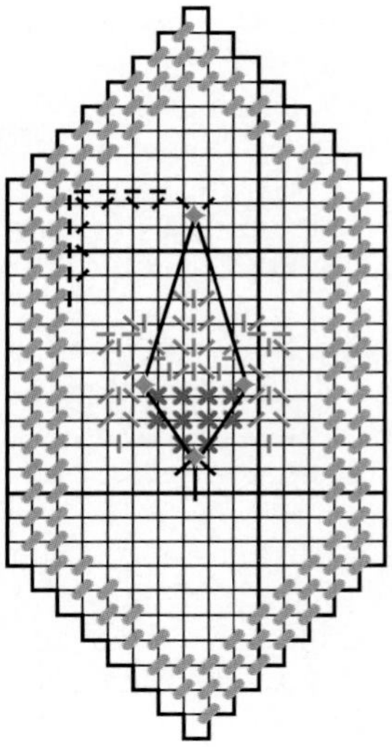

H – Drawer Facade
(cut 2)
14 x 14 holes

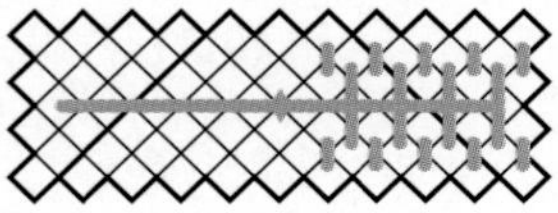

J – Mirror Back
(cut 1)
49 x 49 holes

E – Cabinet Bottom
(cut 1)
39 x 39 holes

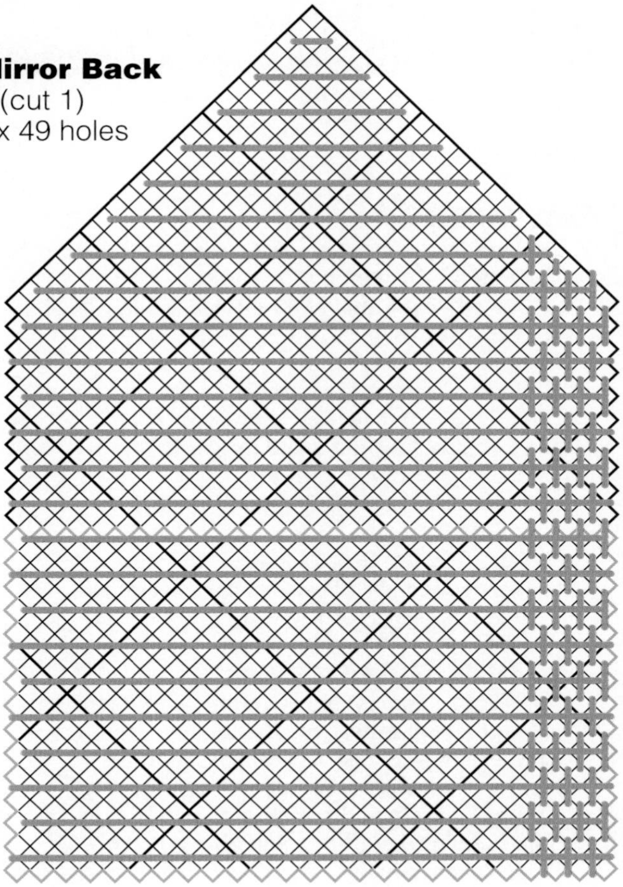

M – Basin Bottom
(cut 1) 15 x 15 holes

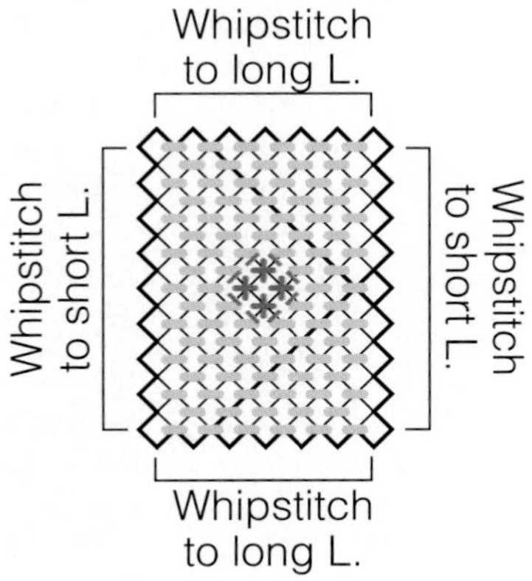

N – Faucet Base
(cut 2) 13 x 13 holes

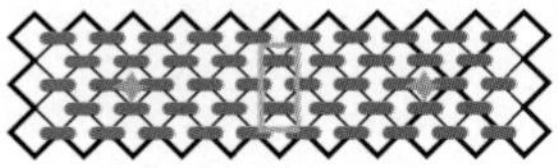

K – Cabinet Top
(cut 1) 42 x 42 holes

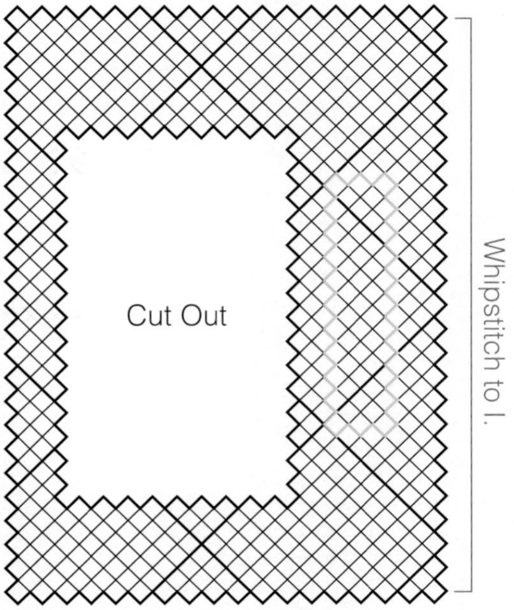

F – Cabinet Door
(cut 2)
27 x 27 holes

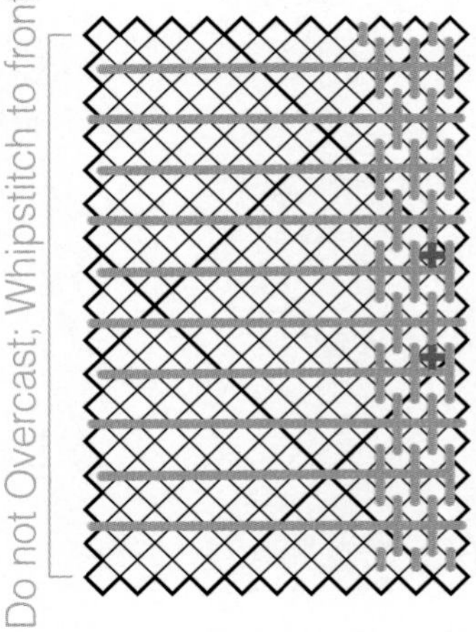

L – Basin Short Side
(cut 2) 14 x 14 holes

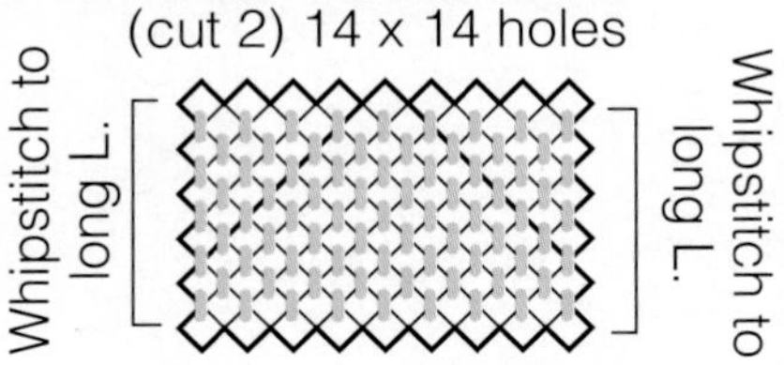

COMMODE

Photo on page 93.

SIZE: 3¾" x 5¼" x 5⅞" tall.

MATERIALS:

- ❑ One sheet of 7-count plastic canvas
- ❑ Scrap of 10-count plastic canvas
- ❑ One white 15-mm. aurora-borealis berry bead
- ❑ One silver 4-mm. bead
- ❑ Four black seed beads
- ❑ ¼ yd. off-white ½" pregathered lace
- ❑ 5/16" x 2" hex-head cap screw or bolt
- ❑ Sewing needle and white thread
- ❑ Craft glue or glue gun
- ❑ Six-strand embroidery floss; for amounts see Color Key.
- ❑ Metallic cord; for amount see Color Key.
- ❑ Worsted-weight or plastic canvas yarn; for amounts see Color Key.

CUTTING INSTRUCTIONS:

NOTES: Graphs and diagrams continued on page 80. Use 10-count canvas for J piece.

A: For bowl, cut one according to graph.

B: For bowl rim, cut one according to graph.

C: For base top and bottom, cut two (one for top and one for bottom) according to graph.

D: For tank support bottom and sides, cut one 7 x 14 holes for bottom (no graph) and two for sides according to graph.

E: For tank front and back, cut two (one for front and one for back) according to graph.

F: For tank side, cut one 7 x 52 holes (no graph).

G: For tank lid top, cut one 9 x 24 holes.

H: For tank lid lip pieces, cut two 2 x 9 holes and two 2 x 24 holes (no graphs).

I: For seat lid and seat, cut two (one for lid and one for seat) according to graph.

J: For lid motif, cut one according to graph.

STITCHING INSTRUCTIONS:

NOTE: Separate 2½ yds. of White, 2 yds. of Sandstone and Cinnamon into 1-ply or worsted-weight into 2-ply strands.

1: Using 1-ply colors and stitches indicated, work J according to graph; fill in uncoded areas using 1-ply White and Continental Stitch. With 1-ply Sandstone, Overcast unfinished edges.

NOTE: Separate floss into 2-ply strands.

2: Using two strands avocado floss, Backstitch and Straight Stitch, embroider plant as indicated on J graph. Using two strands black and Straight Stitch and attaching one seed bead at each indicated hole as you work, embroider hanger as indicated.

3: Overlapping one hole at ends as indicated and working through both thicknesses at overlap area to join, using White and Continental Stitch, work A; Whipstitch X edges together as indicated.

4: Using Sandstone, White and stitches indicated (do not work metallic cord), work B (leave indicated areas unworked), one C for top (leave indicated area unworked), E, G and seat I piece according to graphs. Fill in uncoded areas of E and G and work bottom C, D (one side D on opposite side of canvas), F and H pieces using White and Continental Stitch; Overcast unfinished edges of side D pieces, long edges of bottom D, each side edge of B as indicated and cutout edges of B. Omitting metallic cord stitches, using Sandstone and Continental Stitch, work lid I.

5: Using metallic cord and Long Stitch, work I pieces (work on opposite side of canvas for seat lid) according to graph, Overcasting edges as indicated as you work. With Sandstone, Overcast remaining unfinished edges of seat and seat lid as indicated.

6: With White, Whipstitch one unfinished short edge of bottom D to bowl over seam as indicated and according to Commode Assembly Diagram. Placing seam at back, Whipstitch bottom edge of bowl and top C together as indicated and according to diagram; holding base top and bottom wrong sides together, Whipstitch C pieces together.

7: With White, Whipstitch bowl and rim together as indicated and according to diagram. Holding seat and seat lid right sides together and working through all thicknesses, with cord, Whipstitch unfinished edges of I pieces together and to bowl rim as indicated on B graph. With White, Whipstitch unattached end of bottom D and B together as indicated.

8: For flush handle, attaching one section of berry bead to front E as indicated, follow **NOTE** and Step 10 of Sink Cabinet on page 74.

9: For tank, easing side to fit, with White, Whipstitch E and F pieces together as indicated and according to Tank Assembly Diagram; Overcast unfinished edges. For lid, Whipstitch G and H pieces together; Overcast unfinished edges.

10: For counterweight, glue bolt head down to inside front of bowl and base. Glue tank support side pieces to assembly according to Support Side Placement Diagram, and center bottom of tank to back of bowl rim as indicated on B graph. Glue lace to wrong side of lid motif as shown and motif to center top of seat lid. Place tank lid on tank.

Commode Assembly Diagram

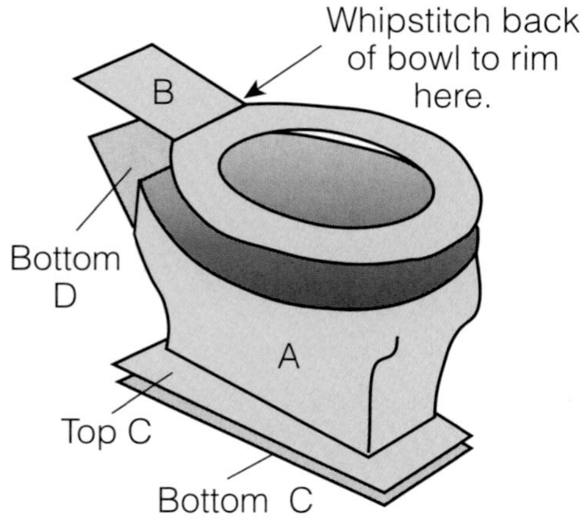

B – Bowl Rim
(cut 1) 19 x 33 holes

Whipstitch to bottom D.

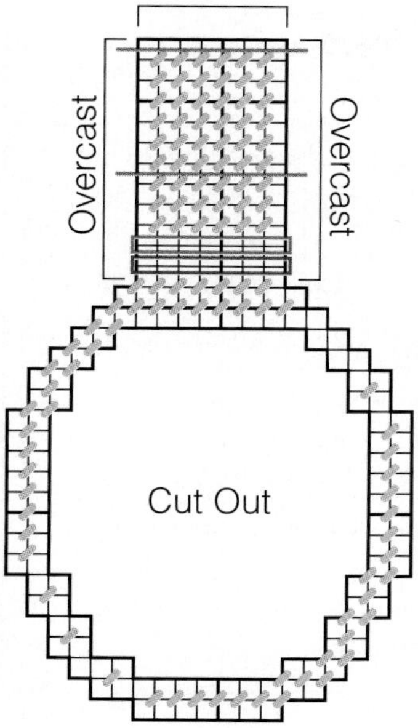

C – Base Top & Bottom
(cut 1 each)
13 x 21 holes

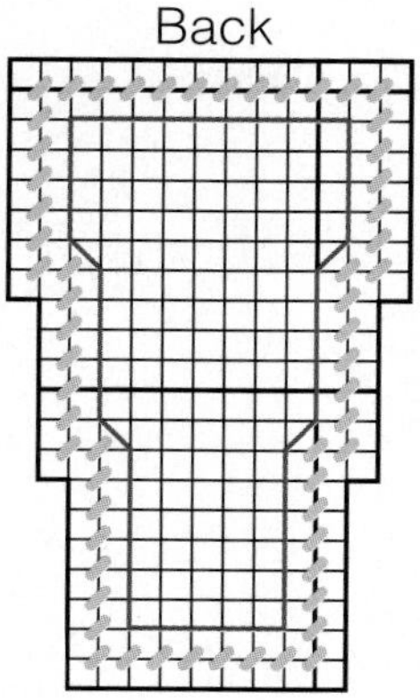

E – Tank Front & Back
(cut 1 each) 16 x 22 holes

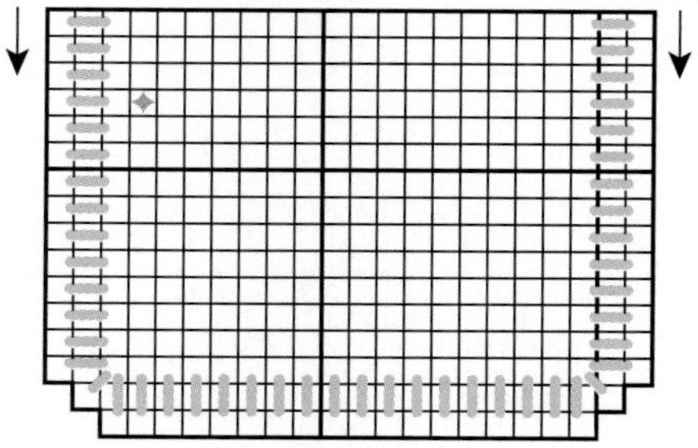

Whipstitch to F between arrows.

Tank Assembly Diagram

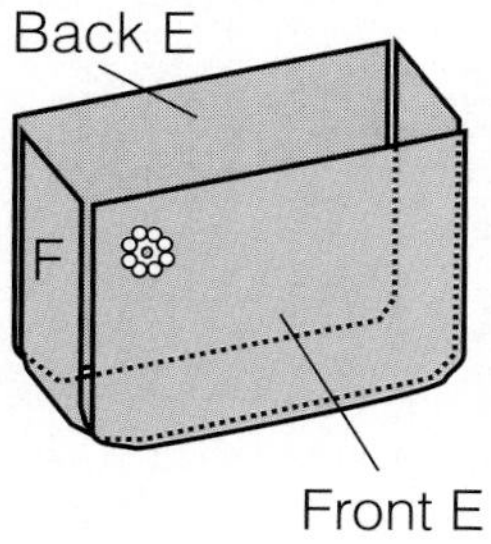

D – Tank Support Side
(cut 2) 7 x 10 holes

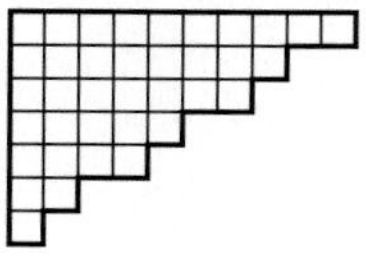

COLOR KEY: Commode

Embroidery floss
- Avocado – 1/2 yd.
- Black – 1/4 yd.

Metallic cord
- Silver – 1 1/2 yds.

Nylon Plus™ Needloft™ yarn

#44	#14 Cinnamon – 1/2 yd.
#47	#16 Sandstone – 12 yds.
#01	#41 White – 40 yds.

STITCH KEY:
- Backstitch/Straight Stitch
- Seed Bead Attachment
- Tank Support Bottom Attachment
- Unworked Area/Bowl Attachment
- Unworked Area/Seat & Lid Attachment
- Berry Bead Attachment
- Tank Placement

G – Tank Lid Top
(cut 1) 9 x 24 holes

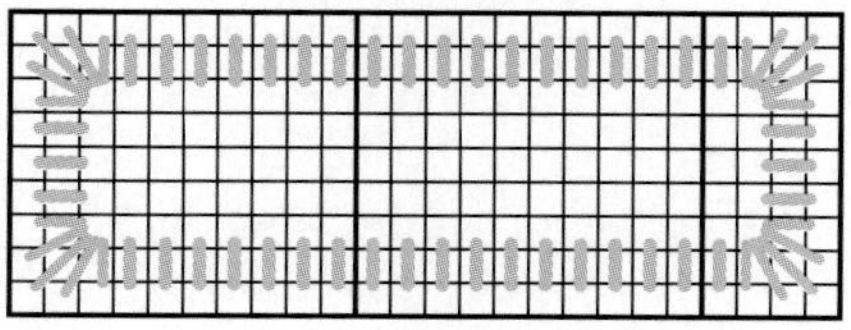

A – Bowl (cut 1) 18 x 69 holes

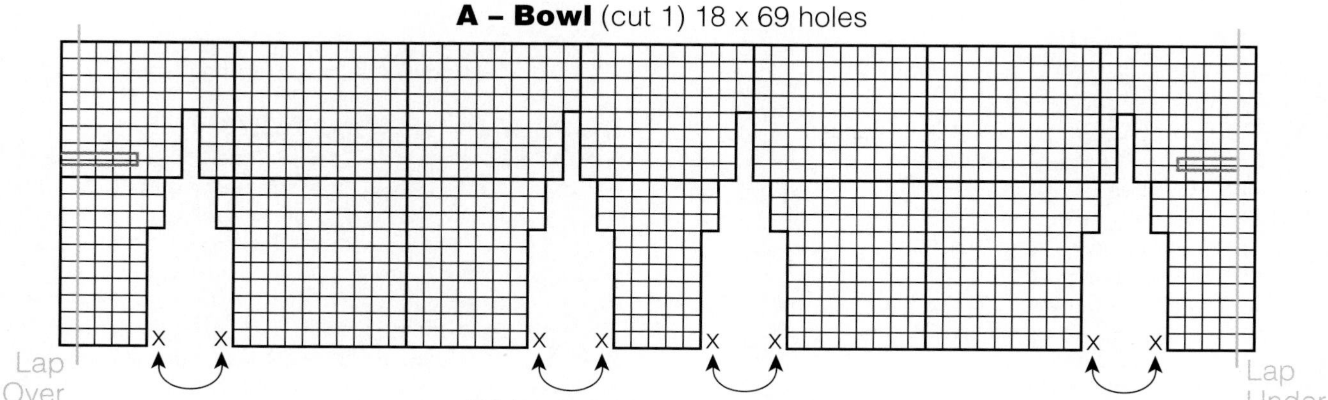

Whipstitch X edges together.

I – Seat Lid & Seat
(cut 1 each)
19 x 23 holes

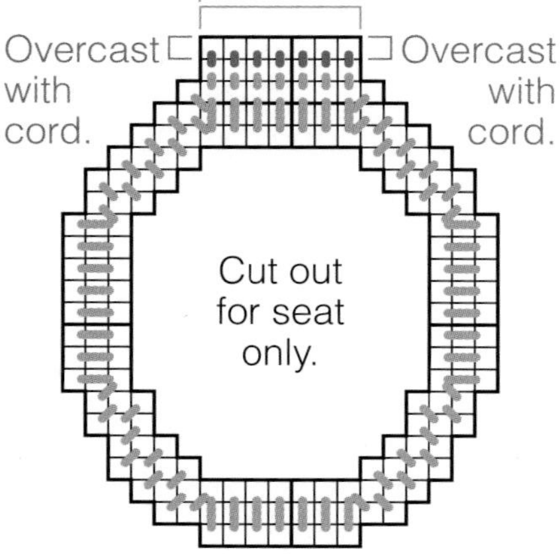

Support Side Placement Diagram

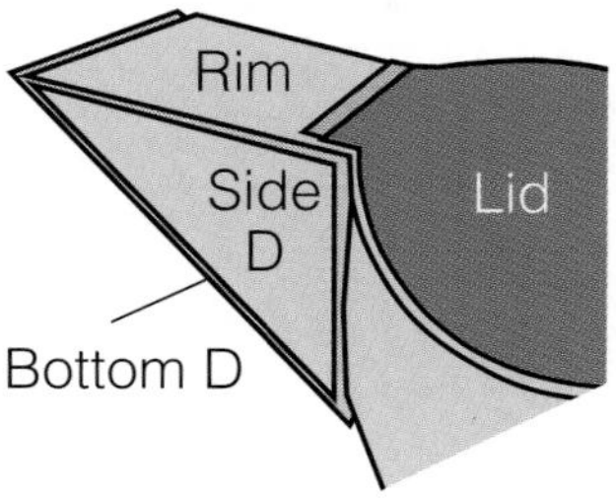

COLOR KEY: Commode		
	Embroidery floss	
■	Avocado – 1/2 yd.	
■	Black – 1/4 yd.	
	Metallic cord	
■	Silver – 1 1/2 yds.	
	Nylon Plus™ Needloft™ yarn	
■	#44	#14 Cinnamon – 1/2 yd.
■	#47	#16 Sandstone – 12 yds.
■	#01	#41 White – 40 yds.

STITCH KEY:	
—	Backstitch/Straight Stitch
✦	Seed Bead Attachment
□	Tank Support Bottom Attachment
□	Unworked Area/Bowl Attachment
□	Unworked Area/Seat & Lid Attachment
✦	Berry Bead Attachment
—	Tank Placement

J – Lid Motif
(cut 1 from 10-count)
23 x 26 holes

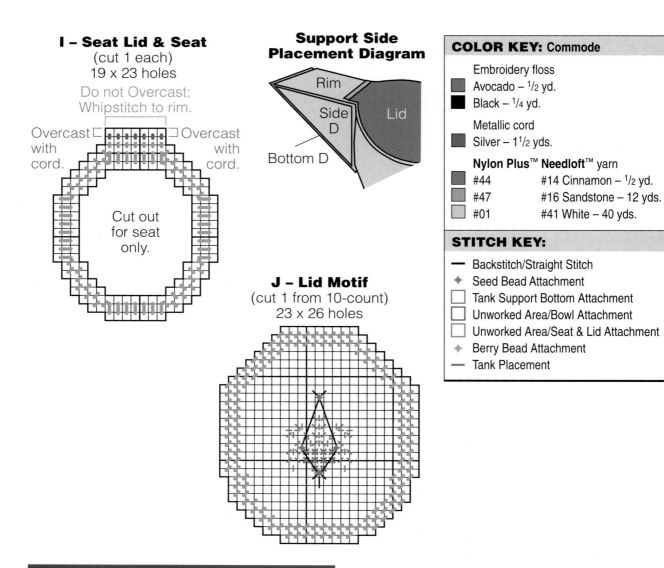

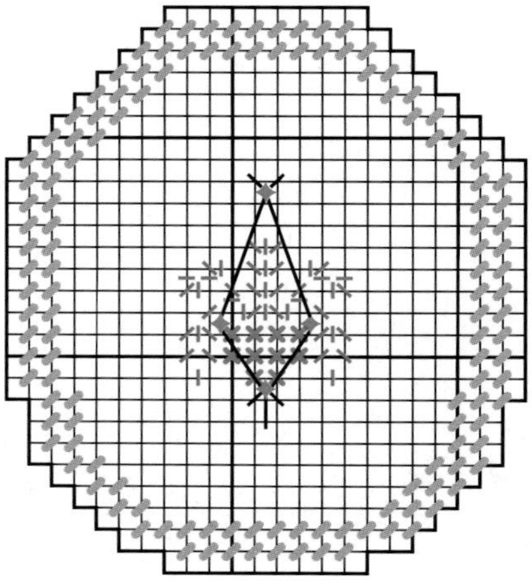

SPACE SAVER UNIT

Photo on page 93.

SIZE: 1¾" x 4½" x 12¼" tall.

MATERIALS:

- ❏ One sheet of 12" x 18" or larger 7-count plastic canvas
- ❏ Scraps of 10-count plastic canvas
- ❏ 10 silver 5-mm. beads
- ❏ Eight black seed beads
- ❏ ⅓ yd. off-white ½" pregathered lace
- ❏ ½" tan ¾" Velcro® closure strip
- ❏ Sewing needle and thread
- ❏ Craft glue or glue gun
- ❏ Six-strand embroidery floss; for amounts see Color Key on page 81.
- ❏ Worsted-weight or plastic canvas yarn; for amounts see Color Key.

CUTTING INSTRUCTIONS:

NOTES: Graphs on pages 81 & 82.

Use 10-count canvas for F pieces. Though graphs are positioned vertically and horizontally, A-E pieces are cut on the diagonal; see Cutting Guide on page 81.

A: For front and back, cut one each according to graphs.

B: For sides, cut two according to graph.

C: For cabinet top and bottom, cut two (one for top and one for bottom) according to graph.

D: For unit top and bottom, cut one each according to graphs.

E: For doors, cut two according to graph.

F: For door motifs, cut two according to graph.

STITCHING INSTRUCTIONS:

NOTES: Separate White, Cinnamon and ½ yd. of Sandstone into 1-ply or worsted-weight into 2-ply strands. Separate floss into 2-ply strands.

1: Using 1-ply Cinnamon and Cross Stitch, work F pieces according to graph; fill in uncoded areas using 1-ply White and Continental Stitch. With 1-ply Sandstone, Overcast unfinished edges. Using two strands avocado floss, Backstitch and Straight Stitch, embroider plants as indicated on graph. Using two strands black and Straight Stitch and attaching one seed bead at each indicated hole as you work, embroider hangers as indicated.

2: Using Sandstone, Continental Stitch and Wicker Stitch, work front A and C-E pieces according to graphs. Overcast cutout edges of A and bottom D pieces and unfinished edges of E pieces as indicated. (**NOTE:** Remaining pieces will be Whipstitched together before being worked.)

3: Holding wrong sides of cabinet top and bottom facing in, with Sandstone, Whipstitch C pieces to back A as indicated; using Wicker Stitch (see Illustrations on page 75), work back A on side opposite C pieces according to graph.

4: Whipstitching pieces together and then stitching unworked pieces as established in Step 3, Whipstitch B and C pieces together. Whipstitch sides and back together; Whipstitch assembly and D pieces together.

5: Whipstitch unfinished edge of each E to front A as indicated; Whipstitch assembly and front A together; Overcast unfinished edges.

6: For door handles, follow Step 12 of Sink Cabinet on page 74.

NOTES: Cut lace into two 6" lengths. Cut closure strip into two 1/4" x 3/4" pieces.

7: Glue 6" lace to each motif and one motif to each door as shown in photo. Glue one closure piece to inside of each door behind handle and remaining pieces to corresponding areas on front.

Space Saver Unit Cutting Guide

(80 x 120 holes)

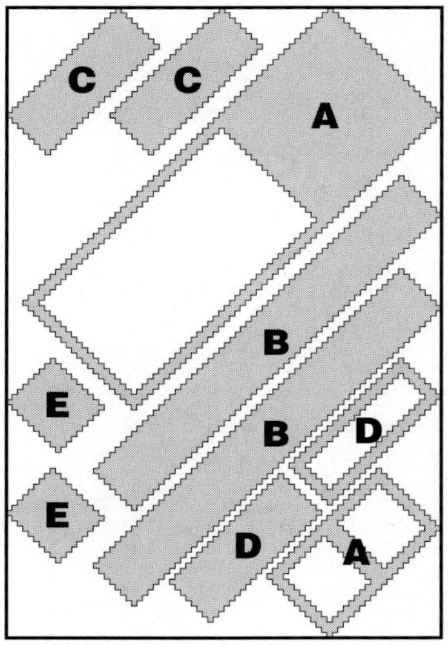

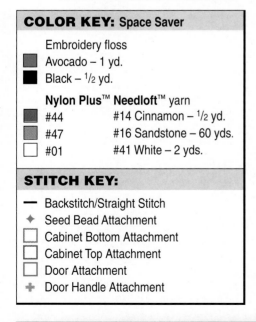

COLOR KEY: Space Saver

Embroidery floss
- Avocado – 1 yd.
- Black – 1/2 yd.

Nylon Plus™ Needloft™ yarn

#44	#14 Cinnamon – 1/2 yd.
#47	#16 Sandstone – 60 yds.
#01	#41 White – 2 yds.

STITCH KEY:

- Backstitch/Straight Stitch
- Seed Bead Attachment
- Cabinet Bottom Attachment
- Cabinet Top Attachment
- Door Attachment
- Door Handle Attachment

B – Side

(cut 2)
64 x 64 holes

A – Back

(cut 1)
77 x 77 holes

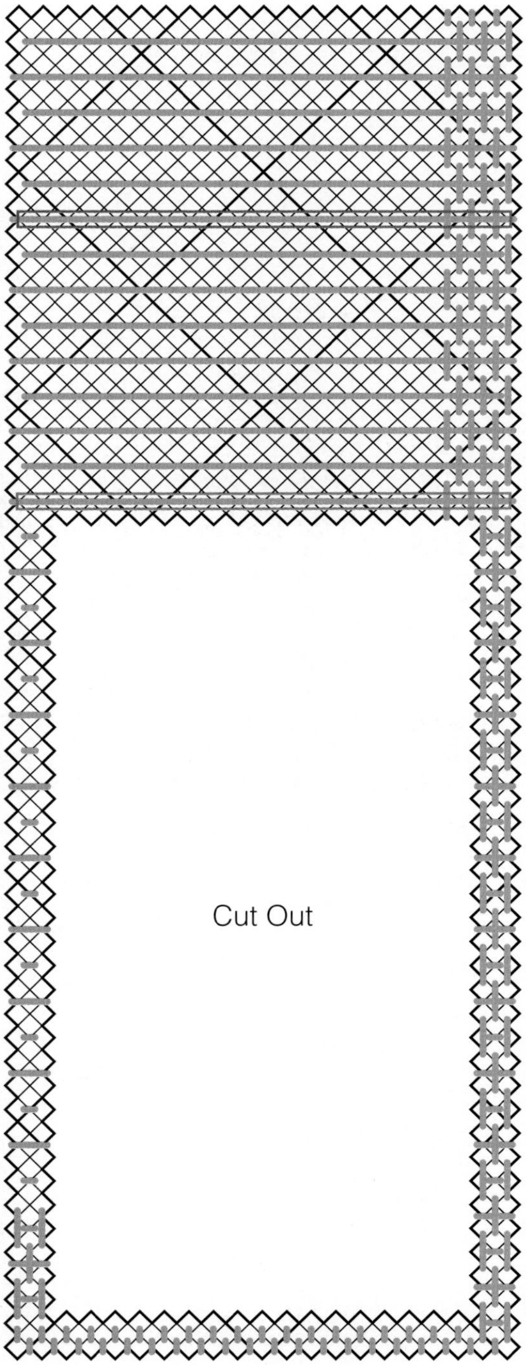

COLOR KEY: Space Saver

Embroidery floss
- Avocado – 1 yd.
- Black – 1/2 yd.

Nylon Plus™ Needloft™ yarn

#44	#14 Cinnamon – 1/2 yd.	
#47	#16 Sandstone – 60 yds.	
#01	#41 White – 2 yds.	

STITCH KEY:
- Backstitch/Straight Stitch
- Seed Bead Attachment
- Cabinet Bottom Attachment
- Cabinet Top Attachment
- Door Attachment
- Door Handle Attachment

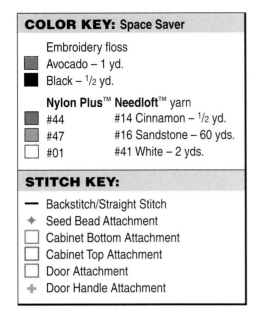

A – Front
(cut 1) 32 x 32 holes

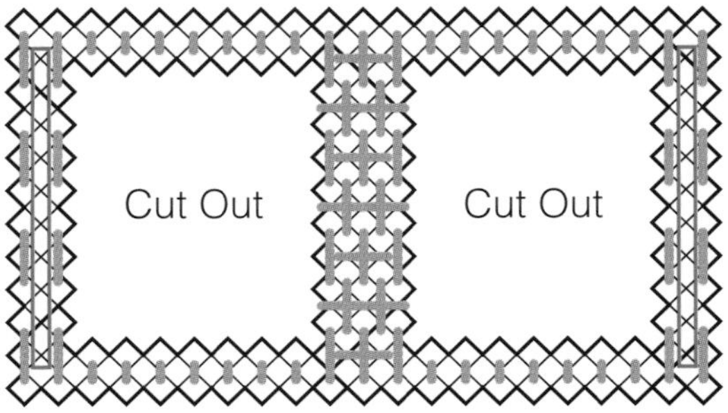

C – Cabinet Top & Bottom
(cut 1 each) 28 x 28 holes

D – Unit Top
(cut 1) 28 x 28 holes

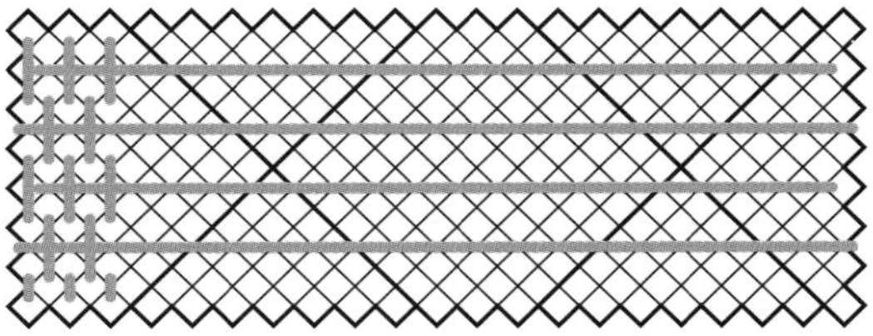

F – Door Motif
(cut 2 from 10-count)
9 x 16 holes

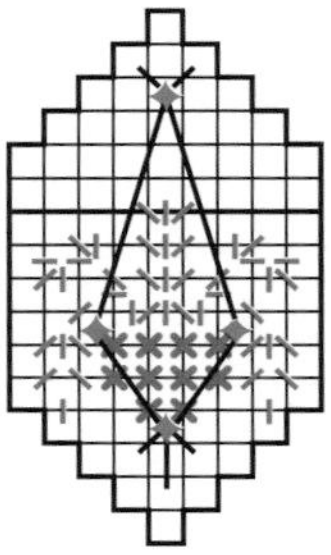

E – Door
(cut 2)
18 x 18 holes

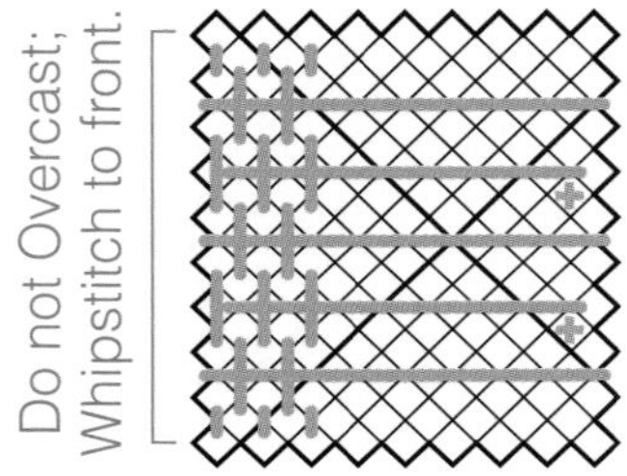

D – Unit Bottom
(cut 1) 28 x 28 holes

SHOWER CURTAINS

NOTE: If Shower Curtains are desired, they must be made before Bathtub & Enclosure.

MATERIALS:
- ❑ Scraps of white 7-count plastic canvas
- ❑ 15" square piece of off-white lace fabric
- ❑ 11½" wooden 3/16" dowel
- ❑ Two silver 4-mm. beads
- ❑ 2 yds. off-white 1" pregathered lace
- ❑ Craft or fabric glue or iron-on hem tape (optional)
- ❑ Sewing needle or machine and off-white thread

CUTTING INSTRUCTIONS:

A: For curtains, cut two 7½" x 13" pieces from fabric (see Fabric Cutting Guide).

B: For center swag, cut one 2" x 7½" piece from fabric (see Fabric Cutting Guide).

C: For curtain trim, cut two 18" lengths of lace.

D: For center swag trim, cut one 7½" length of lace.

E: For for curtain tiebacks, cut two 5" lengths of lace.

F: For curtain tieback rings, cut two from plastic canvas according to graph.

G: For valance, cut one 12" length of lace.

STITCHING INSTRUCTIONS:

1: Placing A pieces wrong sides together, cut through both thicknesses to round one bottom corner of each piece (see guide). Finish side and bottom edges by pressing under ¼" twice; secure using glue or iron-on hem tape, or press and then sew.

2: With ends of lace folded under ½" to wrong side, sew or glue one C to each A as shown. For rod pockets, fold top edge of each A under ½" twice; sew or glue through all thicknesses at first fold. Run dowel through rod pockets.

3: For each tieback, with ends of lace folded under ¼" to wrong side, fold one E wrong sides together. With one corner of one F between, glue ends of lace together. Sew one bead over each ring (sew second piece on opposite side).

4: For center swag, finish one long edge of B as in Step 1; sew or glue D to finished edge. Run a line of gathering stitches along unfinished long edge of swag;

pull thread tightly to gather, and knot ends of thread together. (**NOTE:** Pieces are assembled with Bathtub & Enclosure.)

F – Curtain Tieback Ring
(cut 2)
3 x 3 holes
Cut around black bars.

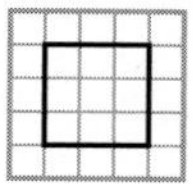

Fabric Cutting Guide

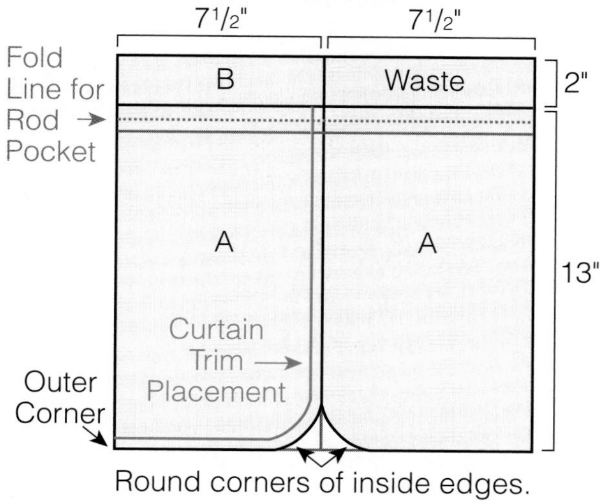

BATHTUB & ENCLOSURE

SIZE: 5½" x 12¼" x 12¼" tall.

MATERIALS:

- ❑ One sheet of 7-count plastic canvas
- ❑ Three sheets of 12" x 18" or larger 7-count plastic canvas
- ❑ Two white 15-mm. aurora-borealis berry beads
- ❑ Four silver 4-mm. beads
- ❑ Two white 9" x 12" sheets of felt
- ❑ Polyester fiberfill
- ❑ 3" x 7" foil loaf pan (optional)
- ❑ Sewing needle and white thread
- ❑ Craft glue or glue gun
- ❑ Six-strand embroidery floss; for amount see Color Key on page 84.
- ❑ Metallic cord; for amount see Color Key.
- ❑ Worsted-weight or plastic canvas yarn; for amounts see Color Key.

CUTTING INSTRUCTIONS:

NOTES: Graphs and diagrams on pages 84-88.

Cut A from standard-size sheet; from large sheets, cut F pieces first.

A: For bathtub bottom, cut one 35 x 80 holes.

B: For bathtub end and side walls, cut two 14 x 31 holes for end walls and two 14 x 50 holes for side walls (no graphs).

C: For bathtub top, cut one according to graph.

D: For enclosure right and left inner end walls, cut one each according to graphs.

E: For enclosure outer end walls, cut two 35 x 80 holes.

F: For enclosure front and back, cut one according to graph for front and one 80 x 80 holes for back.

G: For top center support and top ends, cut one 5 x 70 holes for center and two 5 x 35 holes for ends (no graphs).

H: For shower pipe and pipe base, cut one according to graph for pipe and one 2 x 2 holes for base (no graph).

I: For shower head outer sides and inner support, cut two according to graph for outer sides and one 3 x 3 holes for inner support (no graph).

J: For faucet, cut two according to graph.

K: For drain control base and drain control handle, cut one according to graph for base and one 1 x 2 holes for handle.

L: For soap dish back and bottom, cut one each according to graphs.

M: For soap dish sides, cut two according to graph.

STITCHING INSTRUCTIONS:

NOTE: Inner support I piece is unworked.

1: Using colors and stitches indicated, work A, D (leave indicated areas unworked), E (move pot 2 holes right on second piece), F, (leave indicated areas unworked) outer I, J (one on opposite side of canvas), base K and L pieces according to graphs. Fill in uncoded areas of E and F (center only on back) pieces and work B and C pieces using White and Continental Stitch. Using White and Long Stitch over narrow width, work G pieces; Overcast top cutout edge of front F as indicated on graph and one long edge of 5 x 70-hole center G.

2: Using White and Backstitch, embroider tile outlines on D and back F pieces as indicated. Using Mint, Backstitch and Straight Stitch, embroider plants on outer E and F pieces as indicated. Using six strands floss, Backstitch, Straight Stitch and French Knot, embroider hangers and bracket hooks as indicated, reversing direction of hanger hook on second E piece.

3: Holding right sides of inner tub pieces facing in, with White, Whipstitch A-C pieces together as indicated and according to Bathtub Assembly Diagrams #1 and #2.

4: For each faucet handle and tieback anchor, attaching berry bead sections to left D and front F as indicated, follow **NOTE** and Step 10 of Sink Cabinet on page 74.

5: Holding right sides facing in, with White, Whipstitch D pieces to tub assembly as indicated and according to Diagram #2.

6: Glue 12" lace (G piece in Shower Curtain Instructions) for valance and swag to wrong side of finished edge on center G according to Bathtub Assembly Diagram #3. Holding wrong sides together, Whipstitch center G and front F together at top as indicated and according to Bathtub Assembly Diagram #4. Working through all thicknesses at support ends, Whipstitch enclosure front and back, remaining G pieces and tub assembly together as indicated (see Diagram #5), stuffing fiberfill around tub before closing.

7: With right sides of curtain facing front, insert one end of dowel through cutouts on each inner end wall. Whipstitch outer end walls and assembly together; Overcast unfinished edge of enclosure back.

8: For faucet, holding J pieces wrong sides together, with cord, Whipstitch together.

9: For shower head, holding outer I pieces wrong sides together with inner I between (see Step 1 of Shower Plumbing Assembly Diagram) and working through all thicknesses, with Black, Whipstitch bottom edges together as indicated.

10: Holding pipe H between I pieces as indicated (see Step 2 of diagram) and working through all thicknesses, with cord, assemble shower plumbing pieces in the following order (see diagram): Whipstitch shower head pieces together, catching end of pipe H to join; Overcast top edge of pipe; tack H pieces together as indicated and according to diagram; Overcast unfinished edges of base H and continue Overcasting bottom of pipe; Whipstitch remaining unfinished edges of shower head together.

11: Overcasting unfinished edges as you assemble pieces, with cord, tack K pieces together as indicated for drain control; Whipstitch L and M pieces together as indicated and according to Soap Dish Assembly Diagram.

NOTE: For backing, sew felt sheets together, and trim one end according to Felt Backing Diagram.

12: Glue shower plumbing, faucet and soap dish to enclosure as indicated, drain control base to bathtub end wall below faucet and backing to back and bottom of enclosure. Place one tieback over each curtain; hook rings over tieback anchors.

Bathtub Assembly Diagram #4

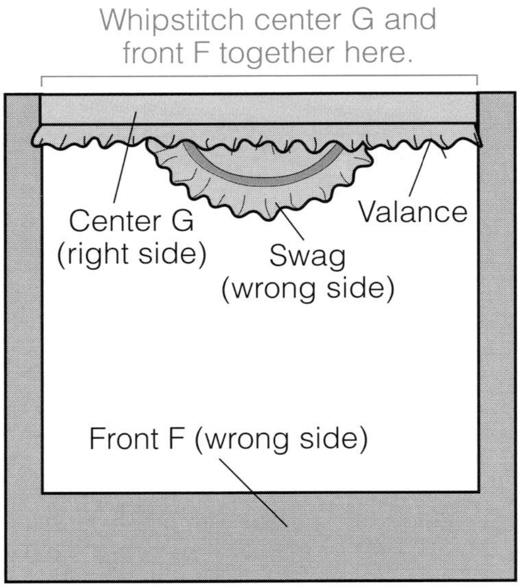

Bathtub Assembly Diagram #2

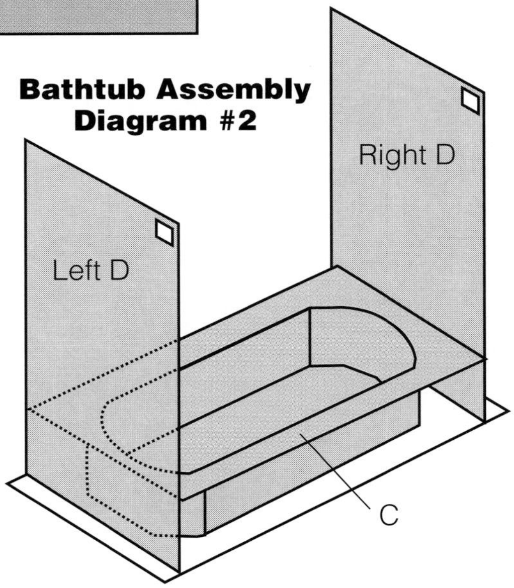

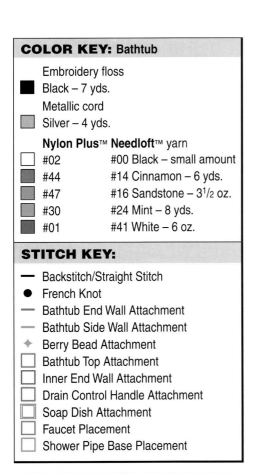

COLOR KEY: Bathtub

Embroidery floss
- Black – 7 yds.

Metallic cord
- Silver – 4 yds.

Nylon Plus™	Needloft™ yarn
#02	#00 Black – small amount
#44	#14 Cinnamon – 6 yds.
#47	#16 Sandstone – 3½ oz.
#30	#24 Mint – 8 yds.
#01	#41 White – 6 oz.

STITCH KEY:

- Backstitch/Straight Stitch
- French Knot
- Bathtub End Wall Attachment
- Bathtub Side Wall Attachment
- Berry Bead Attachment
- Bathtub Top Attachment
- Inner End Wall Attachment
- Drain Control Handle Attachment
- Soap Dish Attachment
- Faucet Placement
- Shower Pipe Base Placement

D – Enclosure Right Inner End Wall

(cut 1) 35 x 80 holes

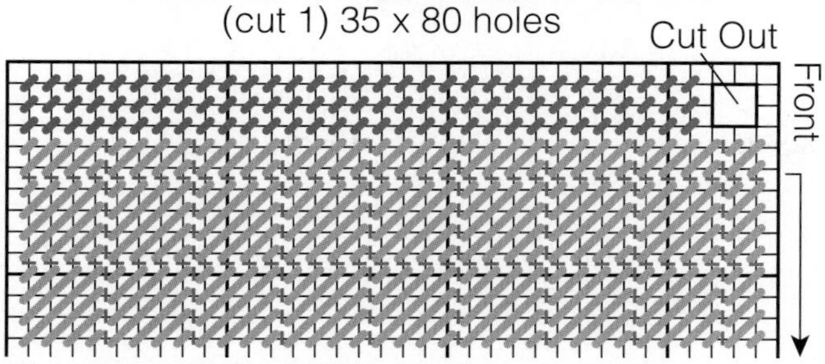

Cut opposite end 80 holes from top edge.

Continue established pattern, leaving unworked area at bottom to match left end.

Bathtub Assembly Diagram #5

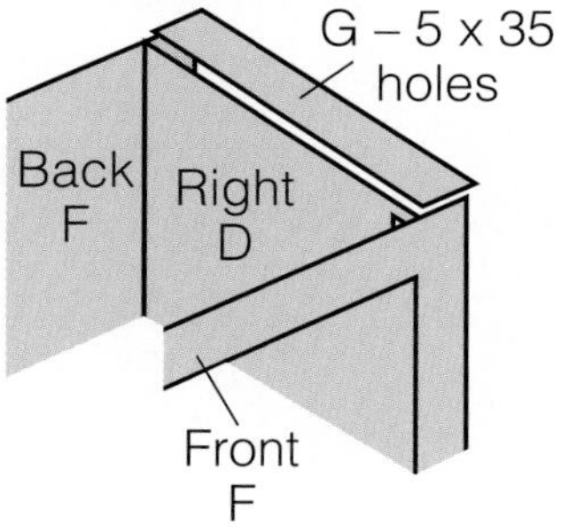

A – Bathtub Bottom (cut 1) 35 x 80 holes

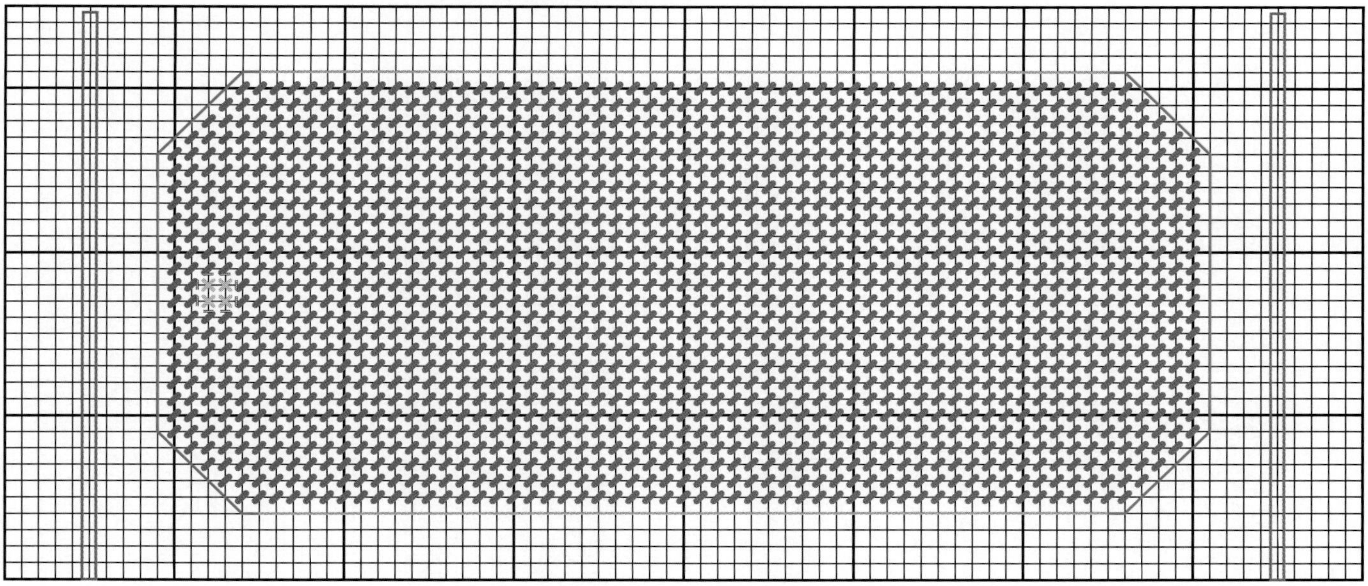

C – Bathtub Top (cut 1) 35 x 70 holes

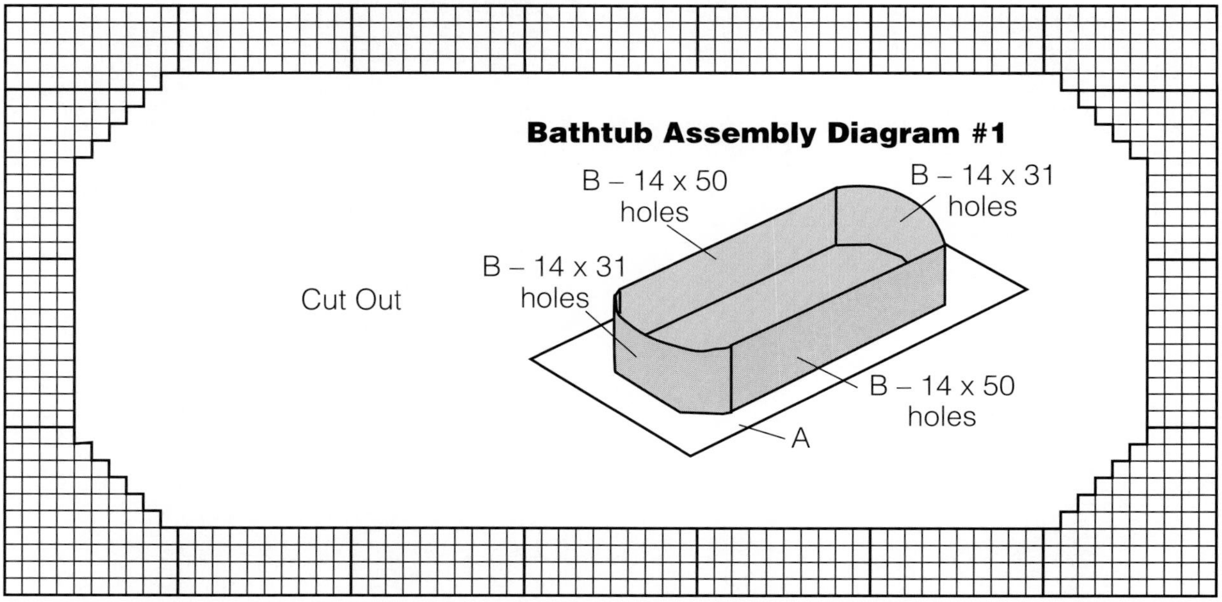

D – Enclosure Left Inner End Wall
(cut 1) 35 x 80 holes

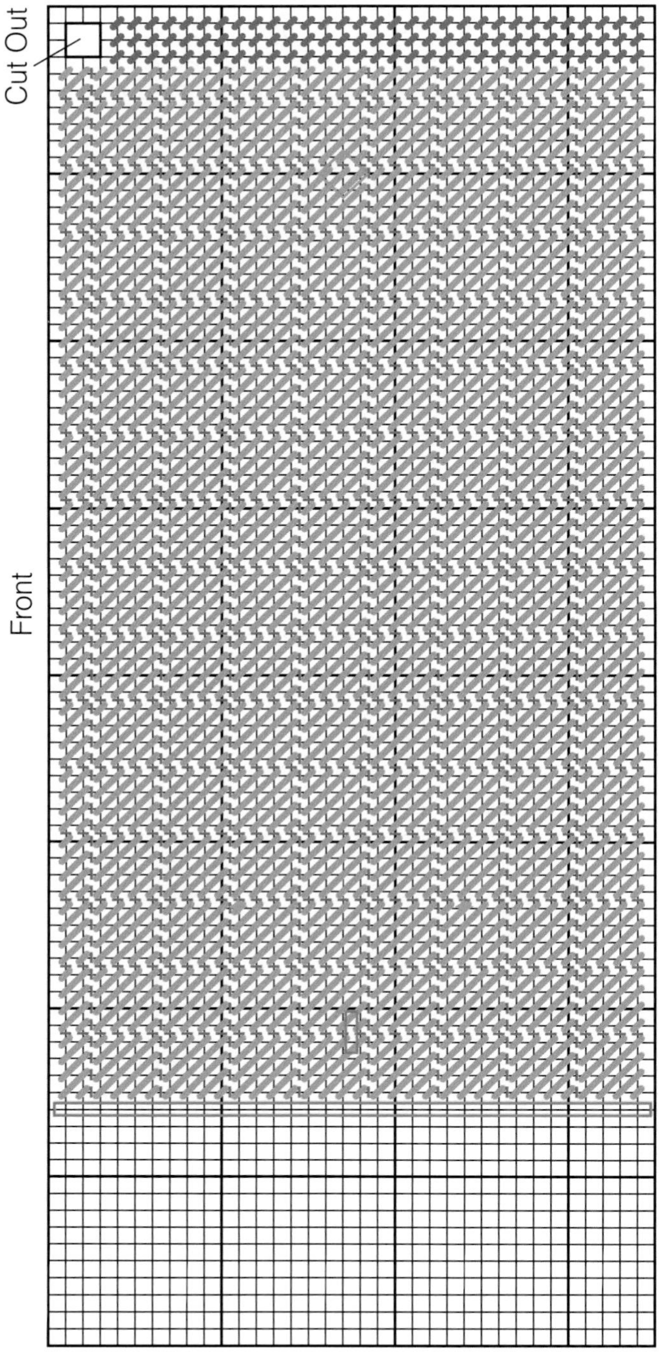

E – Enclosure Outer End Wall
(cut 2) 35 x 80 holes

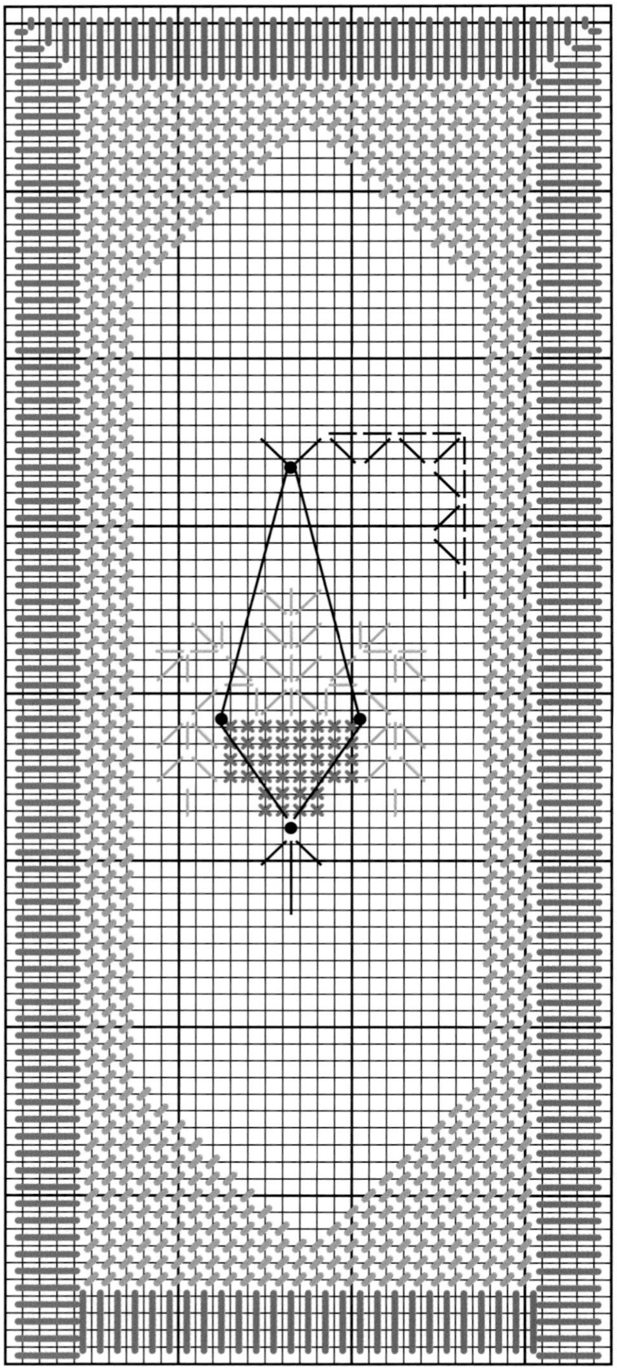

H – Shower Pipe
(cut 1) 3 x 5 holes

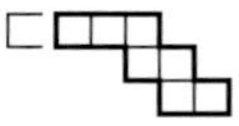

I – Shower Head Outer Side
(cut 2)
3 x 4 holes

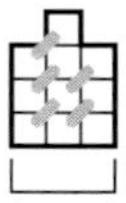

J – Faucet
(cut 2)
3 x 7 holes

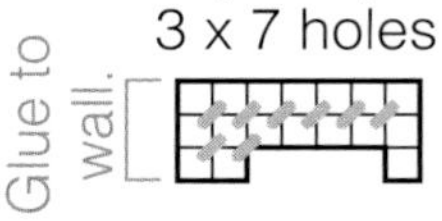

Bathtub Assembly Diagram #3

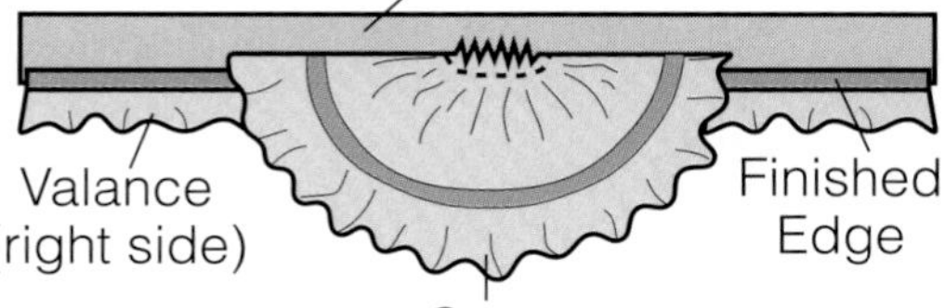

F – Enclosure Front (cut 1) 80 x 80 holes

Whipstitch to top center support G.

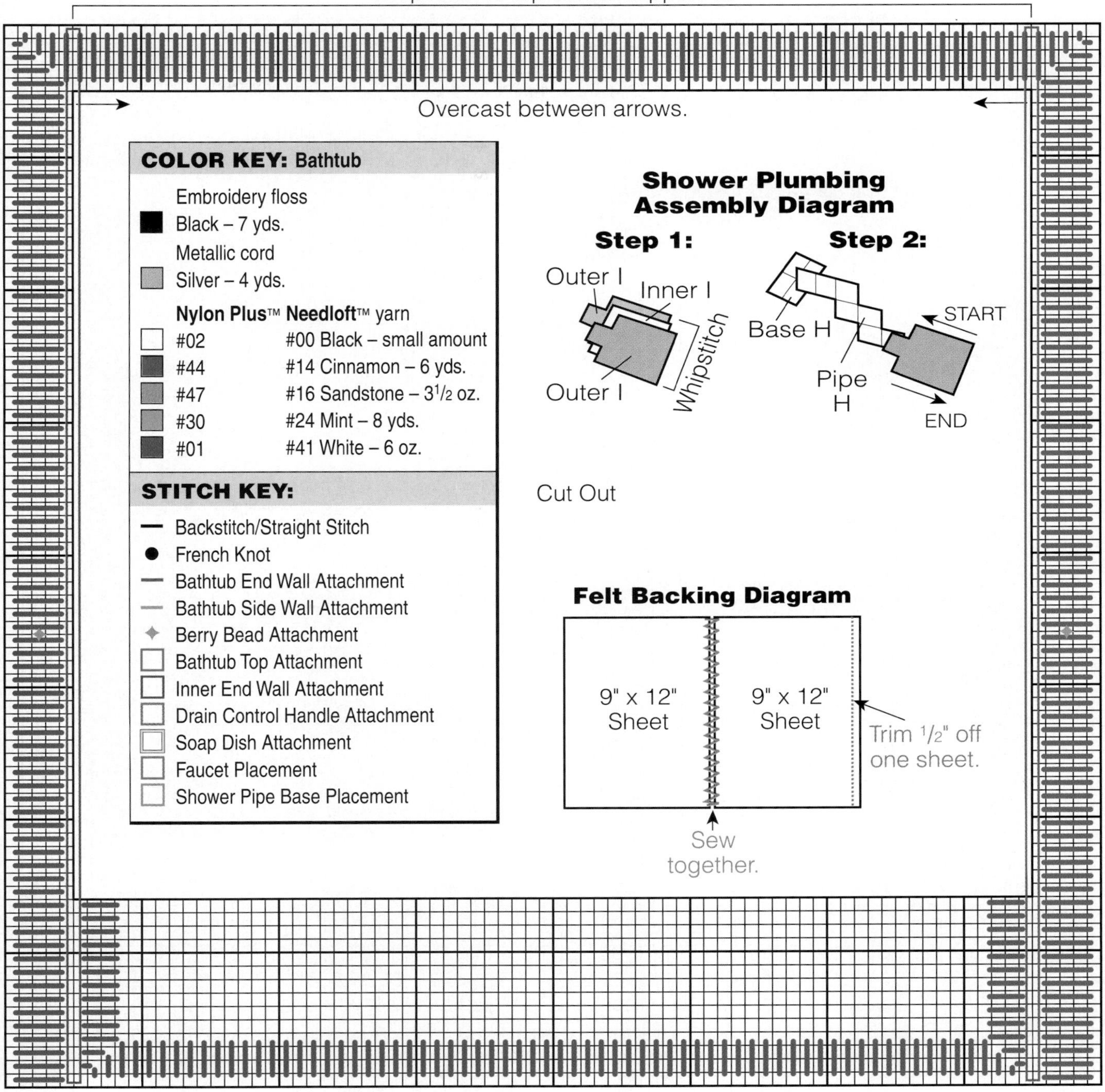

COLOR KEY: Bathtub

	Embroidery floss	
■	Black – 7 yds.	
	Metallic cord	
■	Silver – 4 yds.	
	Nylon Plus™	**Needloft™** yarn
□	#02	#00 Black – small amount
■	#44	#14 Cinnamon – 6 yds.
■	#47	#16 Sandstone – 3 1/2 oz.
■	#30	#24 Mint – 8 yds.
■	#01	#41 White – 6 oz.

STITCH KEY:

- Backstitch/Straight Stitch
- French Knot
- Bathtub End Wall Attachment
- Bathtub Side Wall Attachment
- Berry Bead Attachment
- Bathtub Top Attachment
- Inner End Wall Attachment
- Drain Control Handle Attachment
- Soap Dish Attachment
- Faucet Placement
- Shower Pipe Base Placement

Shower Plumbing Assembly Diagram

Felt Backing Diagram

K – Drain Control Handle
(cut 1) 1 x 2 holes
Do not Overcast; tack to base.

K – Drain Control Base
(cut 1) 4 x 4 holes

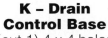

Soap Dish Assembly Diagram

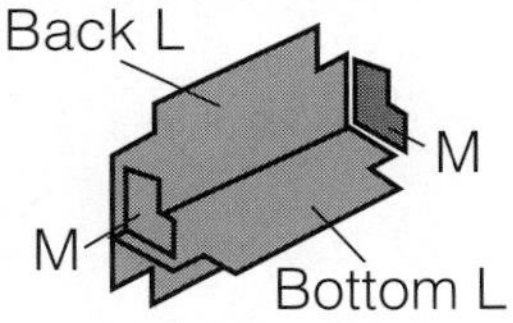

L – Soap Dish Back
(cut 1) 5 x 6 holes

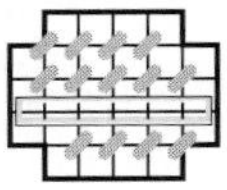

M – Soap Dish Side
(cut 2)
2 x 2 holes

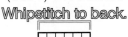

L – Soap Dish Bottom
(cut 1) 3 x 6 holes
Whipstitch to back.

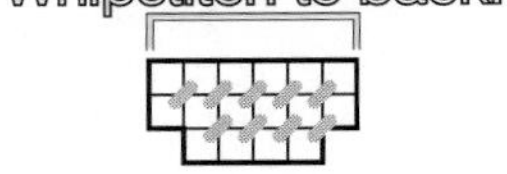

F – Enclosure Back (cut 1) 80 x 80 holes

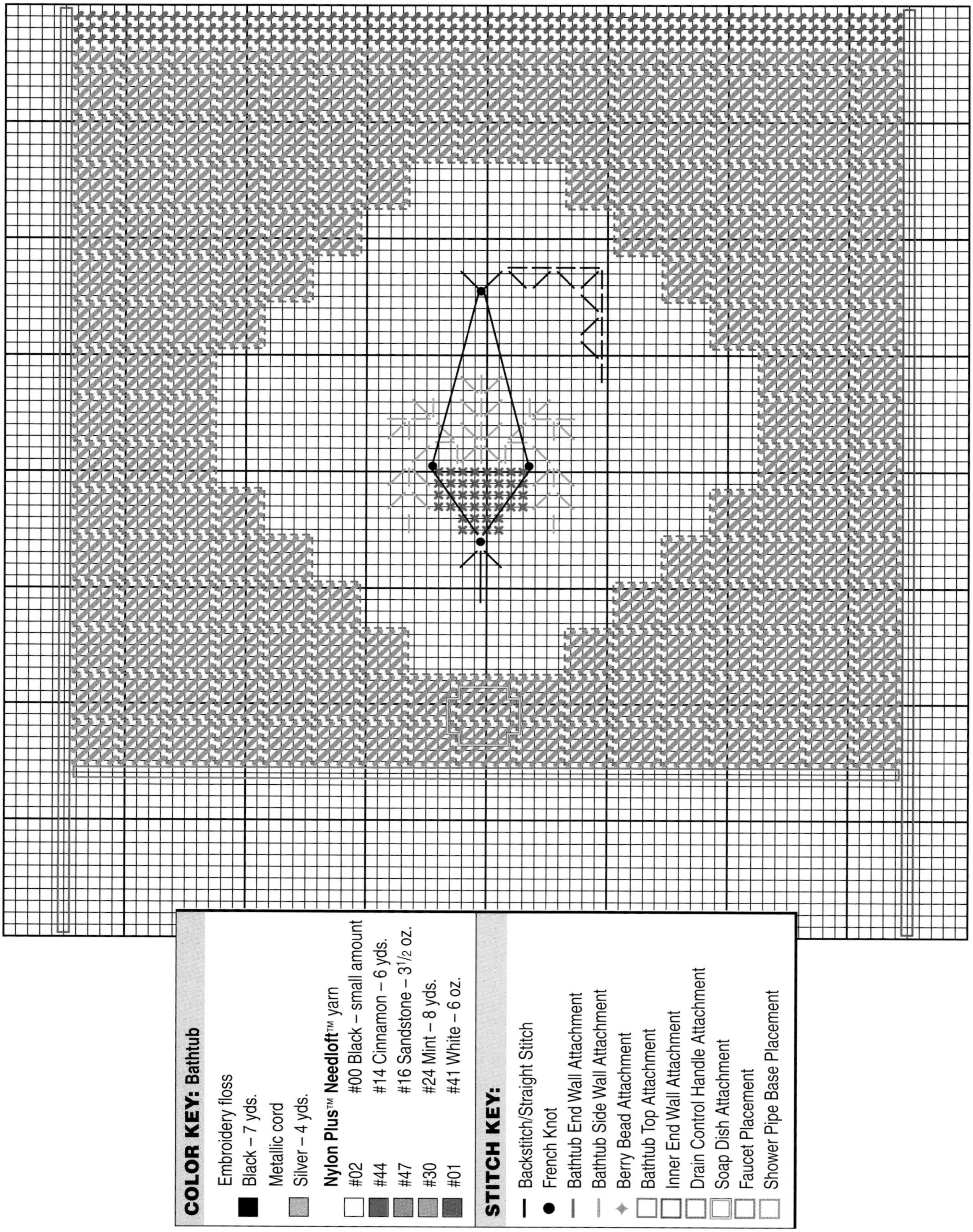

COLOR KEY: Bathtub

Embroidery floss
- Black – 7 yds.

Metallic cord
- Silver – 4 yds.

Nylon Plus™ Needloft™ yarn

#02	#00 Black – small amount	
#44	#14 Cinnamon – 6 yds.	
#47	#16 Sandstone – $3^1/_2$ oz.	
#30	#24 Mint – 8 yds.	
#01	#41 White – 6 oz.	

STITCH KEY:
- Backstitch/Straight Stitch
- French Knot
- Bathtub End Wall Attachment
- Bathtub Side Wall Attachment
- Berry Bead Attachment
- Bathtub Top Attachment
- Inner End Wall Attachment
- Drain Control Handle Attachment
- Soap Dish Attachment
- Faucet Placement
- Shower Pipe Base Placement

ACCESSORIES

SIZE: Scale is 1⅝" x 2¼"; Soap Dish is ⅝" x ⅞" x ¼" tall; Soap is ⅜" x ½"; Small Toiletry Canister is ⅝" across x 1" tall; Large Toiletry Canister is ¾" across x ¾" tall; Bathroom Tissue Cover is ⅝" across x ⅞" tall; Facial Tissue Cover is ¾" x 1½" x ½" tall; Cup is ⅜" across x ¾" tall.

MATERIALS:
- ❑ ¼ sheet of 7-count plastic canvas
- ❑ ¼ sheet of 10-count plastic canvas
- ❑ Three silver 4-mm. beads
- ❑ Pink ½" pom-pom
- ❑ Polyester fiberfill
- ❑ Facial tissues
- ❑ Round wooden toothpick
- ❑ Sewing needle and brown thread
- ❑ Craft glue or glue gun
- ❑ Worsted-weight or plastic canvas yarn; for amounts see Color Key on page 90.

SCALE & SOAP DISH

CUTTING INSTRUCTIONS:

NOTES: Graphs on page 90.

Use 7-count canvas for all pieces.

A: For Scale pieces, cut three 10 x 14 holes.

B: For Scale face, cut one according to graph.

C: For Soap Dish bottom, cut one 3 x 5 holes (no graph).

D: For Soap Dish sides, cut two 1 x 3 holes and two 1 x 5 holes (no graphs).

E: For Soap, cut two 2 x 3 holes (no graph).

STITCHING INSTRUCTIONS:

NOTE: One A piece is unworked.

1: Using Black and Continental Stitch, work one A for top according to graph; fill in uncoded areas and work one A for bottom and B piece using White and Continental Stitch. Overcast unfinished edges of B.

NOTE: Separate Christmas Red and ½ yd. of Black into 1-ply or worsted-weight into 2-ply strands.

2: Using 1-ply colors indicated and Straight Stitch, embroider detail on B as indicated on graph. Holding top and bottom A wrong sides together with unworked A between, with White, Whipstitch together, forming Scale. Glue face to top as indicated.

3: Using Beige for Soap Dish bottom, White for Soap and Long Stitch over narrow width, work C and E pieces.

4: For Soap Dish, with Beige, Whipstitch C and D pieces together; Overcast unfinished edges.

5: For Soap, holding E pieces wrong sides together, with White, Whipstitch together.

CANISTERS & BATHROOM TISSUE COVER

CUTTING INSTRUCTIONS:

NOTES: Graphs on page 90.

Use 10-count canvas for all pieces.

A: For Small Canister lid and bottom, cut two (one for lid and one for bottom) according to graph.

B: For Small Canister side, cut one 6 x 21 holes.

C: For Large Canister lid and bottom, cut two (one for lid and one for bottom) according to graph.

D: For Large Canister side, cut one 4 x 25 holes.

E: For Bathroom Tissue Cover top and side, cut one according to graph for top and one 6 x 21 holes for side.

STITCHING INSTRUCTIONS:

NOTE: Separate Cinnamon and 1 yd. of White into 1-ply or worsted-weight into 2-ply strands.

1: Using 1-ply Cinnamon and stitches indicated, work A, C and top E pieces according to graphs; Overcast unfinished edges of lid A and lid C.

2: Overlapping three holes at short ends of each piece as indicated on graphs and working through both thicknesses at overlap area to join, using 1-ply colors and stitches indicated, work B, D and side E according to graphs.

3: For each Canister, with 1-ply Cinnamon, Whipstitch corresponding side and bottom pieces together; Overcast unfinished edges. With thread, sew one bead to each lid as indicated. Stuff a small amount of fiberfill inside Small Canister, and place pom-pom inside Large Canister.

4: For Bathroom Tissue Cover, sew remaining bead to top E as indicated; Whipstitch E pieces together; Overcast unfinished edge. For tissue roll, from facial tissue, cut ½"-wide strips. Wrap strips tightly around toothpick until roll is about ½" across; glue end of strip to secure. Trim ends off toothpick. Place roll inside Cover.

FACIAL TISSUE COVER & CUP

CUTTING INSTRUCTIONS:

NOTES: Graphs on page 90.

Use 10-count canvas for all pieces.

A: For Facial Tissue Cover top and bottom, cut one according to graph for top and one 6 x 13 holes for bottom (no graph).

B: For Facial Tissue Cover sides and ends, cut two 4 x 13 holes for sides and two 4 x 6 holes for ends (no graphs).

C: For Cup bottom and side, cut one according to graph for bottom and one 6 x 13 holes for side (no graph).

STITCHING INSTRUCTIONS:

NOTE: Separate Beige into 1-ply or worsted-weight into 2-ply strands.

1: Using 1-ply Beige and stitches indicated, work top A and bottom C pieces according to graphs; Overcast cutout edges of top A. Using Long Stitch over narrow width, work bottom A, B and side C pieces.

2: For Tissue Cover, Whipstitch top A and B pieces together. Whipstitch bottom A to one side; Overcast unfinished edges.

3: For tissues, from facial tissue, cut 1¼" strips. Fold each strip across width every ½", forming a ¼" stack. Insert stack inside Cover, pulling one end through top cutout.

4: For Cup, Whipstitch short ends of side C together. Whipstitch C pieces together; Overcast top edge.

COLOR KEY: Accessories		
	Nylon Plus™	Needloft™ yarn
■	#02	#00 Black – 2 yds.
■	#19	#02 Christmas Red – small amount
■	#44	#14 Cinnamon – 5 yds.
■	#43	#40 Beige – 4 yds.
□	#01	#41 White – 3 yds.

STITCH KEY:	
—	Backstitch/Straight Stitch
□	Scale Face Placement
○	Bead Placement

A – Facial Tissue Cover Top
(cut 1) 6 x 13 holes

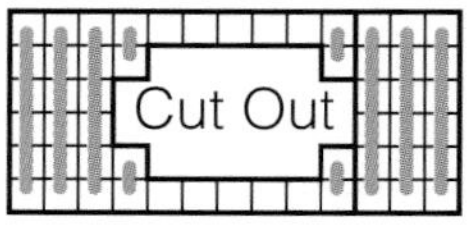

A – Scale Top Piece
(cut 3)
10 x 14 holes

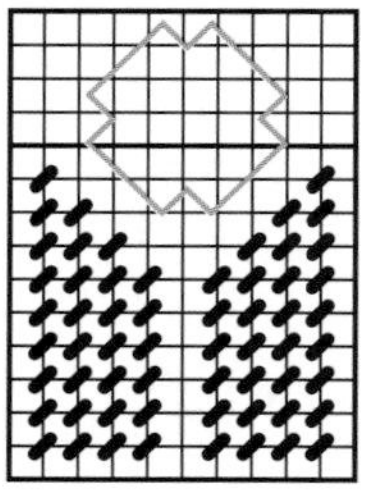

B – Scale Face
(cut 1)
5 x 5 holes

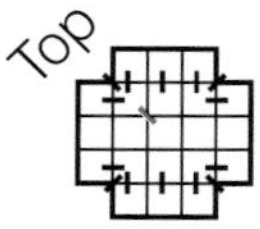

C – Cup Bottom
(cut 1)
4 x 4 holes

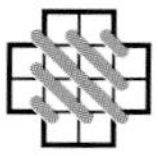

A – Small Canister Lid & Bottom
(cut 1 each) 5 x 5 holes

E – Bathroom Tissue Cover Top
(cut 1) 5 x 5 holes

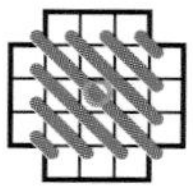

C – Large Canister Lid & Bottom
(cut 1 each)
7 x 7 holes

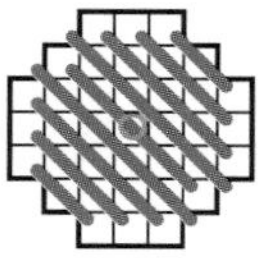

B – Small Canister Side
(cut 1) 6 x 21 holes

E – Bathroom Tissue Cover Side
(cut 1) 6 x 21 holes

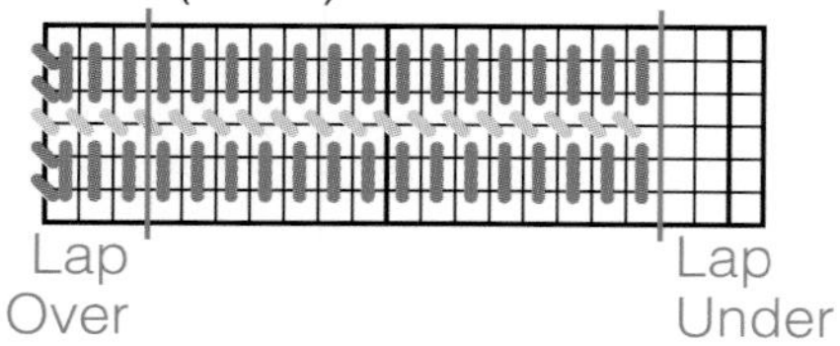

D – Large Canister Side
(cut 1) 4 x 25 holes

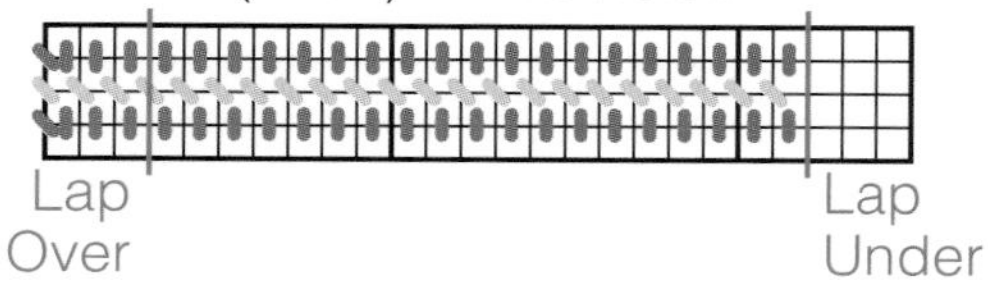

RUGS

SIZE: Contour Rug is 3⅞" x 4⅝"; Half Rug is 4" x 4½"; Full Rug is 3½" x 6⅞", not including lace.

MATERIALS:
- ❑ One sheet of 7-count plastic canvas
- ❑ 12 black seed beads
- ❑ 1¼ yds. off-white 1" pregathered lace
- ❑ Craft glue or glue gun
- ❑ Six-strand embroidery floss; for amount see Color Key.
- ❑ Worsted-weight or plastic canvas yarn; for amounts see Color Key.

CUTTING INSTRUCTIONS:
A: For Contour Rug, cut one according to graph.
B: For Half Rug, cut one according to graph.
C: For Full Rug, cut one according to graph.

STITCHING INSTRUCTIONS:
1: Using colors indicated, Continental Stitch and Cross Stitch, work A-C pieces according to graphs; fill in uncoded areas using White and Continental Stitch. With Sandstone, Overcast unfinished edges.

NOTES: Separate Mint into 1-ply or worsted-weight into 2-ply strands. Separate floss into 3-ply strands.

2: Using 1-ply Mint, Backstitch and Straight Stitch, embroider plants as indicated on graphs. Using three strands floss, Backstitch and Straight Stitch and attaching one seed bead at each indicated hole as you work, embroider plant hangers as indicated.

NOTE: Cut one 18" and two 12" lengths of lace.

3: Glue 18" lace around Full Rug and 12" lace around each remaining Rug as shown in photo.

B – Half Rug
(cut 1)
26 x 29 holes

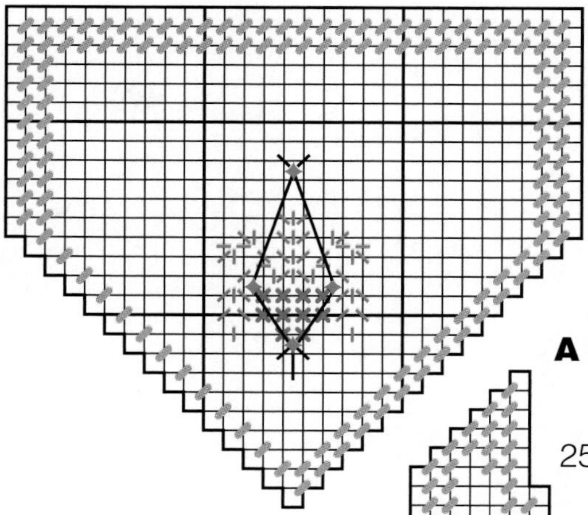

COLOR KEY: Rugs

Embroidery floss
Black – 1½ yds.

Nylon Plus™ Needloft™ yarn

#44	#14 Cinnamon – 1½ yds.	
#47	#16 Sandstone – 18 yds.	
#30	#24 Mint – 3 yds.	
#01	#41 White – 28 yds.	

STITCH KEY:

— Backstitch/Straight Stitch
✦ Bead Attachment

A – Contour Rug
(cut 1)
25 x 30 holes

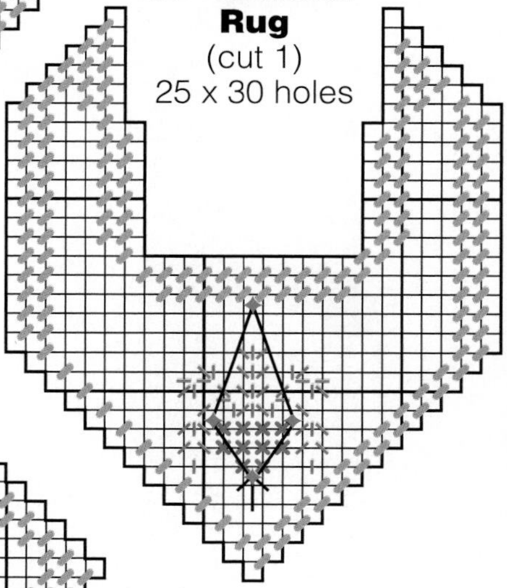

C – Full Rug
(cut 1) 23 x 45 holes

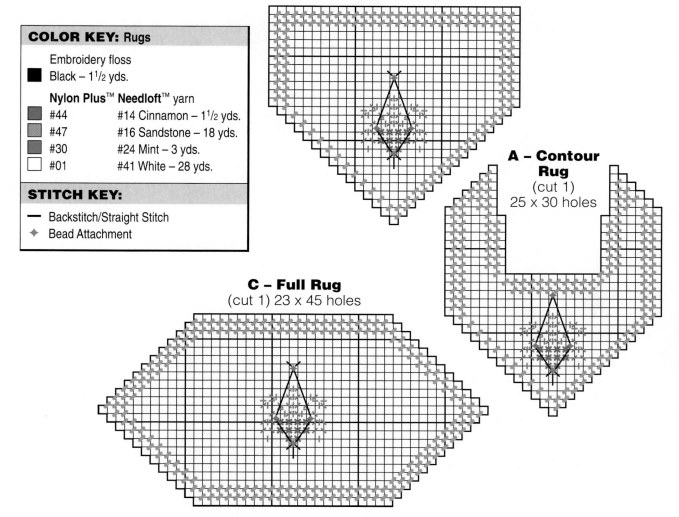

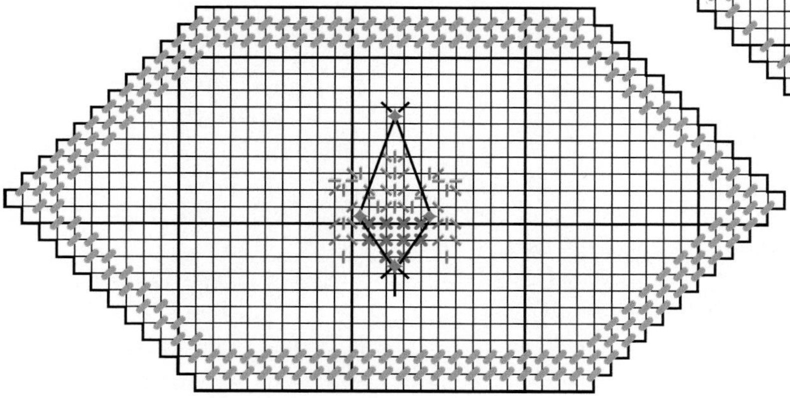

BENCH & BASKET

NOTE: Wastebasket is not shown.

SIZE: Bench is 2⅞" x 3⅜" x 2⅝" tall; Wastebasket is 1⅛" x 2" x 2⅜" tall.

MATERIALS:
- ❑ One sheet of 7-count plastic canvas
- ❑ Scraps of 10-count plastic canvas
- ❑ Eight black seed beads
- ❑ ⅓ yd. off-white ½" pregathered lace
- ❑ Craft glue or glue gun
- ❑ Six-strand embroidery floss; for amount see Color Key on page 92.
- ❑ Worsted-weight or plastic canvas yarn; for amounts see Color Key.

CUTTING INSTRUCTIONS:
NOTE: Graphs on page 92.

A: For Bench top, cut one according to graph.
B: For Bench sides and ends, cut two each according to graphs.
C: For Wastebasket sides, cut two according to graph.
D: For Wastebasket ends, cut two according to graph.
E: For Wastebasket bottom, cut one according to graph.
F: For motifs, cut two according to Space Saver Unit F graph on page 82.

STITCHING INSTRUCTIONS:
1: For motifs, follow **NOTES** and Step 1 of Space Saver Unit on page 80.
2: Using Sandstone and stitches indicated, work A-E pieces according to graphs.
3: Whipstitch A and B pieces together, forming Bench, and Whipstitch C-E pieces together, forming Wastebasket; Overcast unfinished edges.
NOTE: Cut lace into two 6" lengths.
4: Glue one length of lace to each motif, and motifs to Bench as shown in photo and to one side of Wastebasket.

A – Bench Top
(cut 1) 27 x 27 holes

B – Bench Side
(cut 2) 26 x 26 holes

COLOR KEY: Bench & Basket		
	Embroidery floss	
■	Avocado – 1 yd.	
■	Black – 1/2 yd.	
	Nylon Plus™	**Needloft™** yarn
■	#44	#14 Cinnamon – 1/2 yd.
■	#47	#16 Sandstone – 10 yds.
□	#01	#41 White – 2 yds.

B – Bench End
(cut 2) 24 x 24 holes

C – Wastebasket Side
(cut 2) 19 x 19 holes

D – Wastebasket End
(cut 2) 15 x 15 holes

E – Wastebasket Bottom
(cut 1) 13 x 13 holes

TOWELS

SIZE: Large Towel is 3⅜" x 7½"; Small Towel is 1¾" x 3¾", not including lace; Guest Towel is 1½" x 2⅜".

MATERIALS FOR ONE OF EACH:

- ❑ 8" x 9" piece of white 14-count Aida cloth
- ❑ ½ yd. off-white 1" pregathered lace
- ❑ Four black seed beads
- ❑ Craft or fabric glue or iron-on hem tape (optional)
- ❑ Sewing needle and white thread (optional)
- ❑ Six-strand embroidery floss; for amount see Color Key.

CUTTING INSTRUCTIONS:

NOTE: See Towel Cutting Diagram.

A: For Large Towel, cut one from cloth 4½" x 8½".
B: For Small Towel, cut one from cloth 3" x 4¾".
C: For Guest Towel, cut one from cloth 3" x 3½".
D: Cut lace into two 5" and two 4" lengths.

STITCHING INSTRUCTIONS:

1: Finish edges of A-C pieces as follows: turn under ¼" twice, then secure by using glue or iron-on hem tape, or press and then sew. With ends of lace folded under ½" to wrong side, using 5" lengths for Large Towel and 4" lengths for Small Towel, sew or glue one length of lace to wrong side on each end of Large and Small Towels.

NOTE: Separate floss into 1-, 2- or 3-ply strands as needed.

2: Centering motif (**NOTE:** Use arrows on motif graphs to locate center of motifs.) ½" from one end of Large Towel and ¼" from one end of Small Towel, using three strands floss for Large Towel and two strands for Small and Guest Towels in colors indicated, Cross Stitch, Straight Stitch and Backstitch, embroider pot and fern as indicated on corresponding motif graphs.

3: Using two strands black for Large Towel and one strand black for Small and Guest Towels, Backstitch and Straight Stitch and attaching seed beads or working French Knots as indicated, embroider hanger and hook on each piece as indicated.

Towel Cutting Diagram

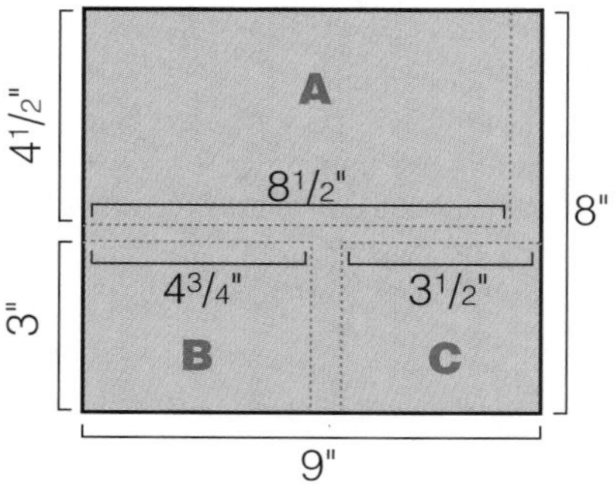

Small & Guest Towel Motif Graph

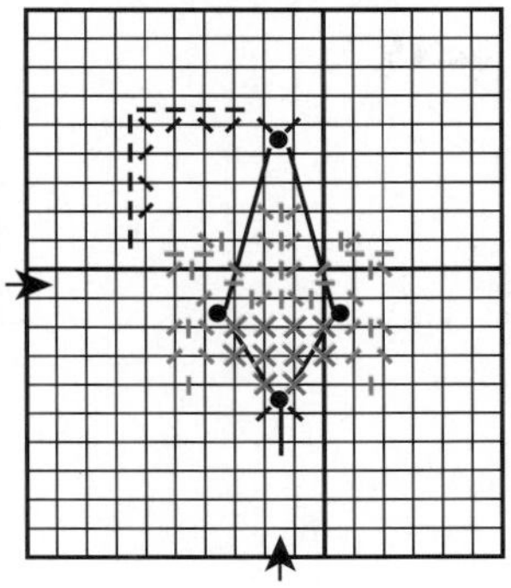

COLOR KEY: Towels
Embroidery floss
Avocado – 3 yds.
Brown – 3 yds.
Black – 1 yd.

STITCH KEY:
— Backstitch/Straight Stitch
● French Knot
✦ Bead Attachment

Large Towel Motif Graph

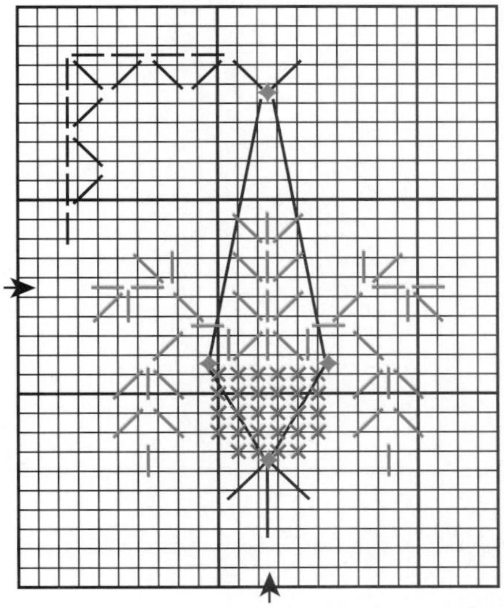

BARBIE® doll and friends pictured with permission of Mattel, Inc. ©1996 Mattel, Inc. All rights reserved.

BARBIE® doll and friends pictured with
permission of Mattel, Inc. ©1996 Mattel, Inc.
All rights reserved.

FASHION DOLL Camper

Designed by
Trudy Bath Smith
& Stephen J. Smith

NOTE: Optional pieces named in this pattern are found in Camper Accessories on page 134.
SIZE: 14¼" across x 32½" long x 14⅝" tall.
MATERIALS:

- ❑ 40 sheets of 7-count plastic canvas
- ❑ 14 sheets of lt. blue 7-count plastic canvas
- ❑ Four sheets of white 7-count plastic canvas
- ❑ 26 Darice® 3" plastic canvas radial circles
- ❑ Four ¼"-thick yardsticks
- ❑ 3½ feet ⅜" wooden dowel
- ❑ Four red 18-mm. foil-backed half-round acrylic stones
- ❑ Six ⅜" upholstery tacks
- ❑ Four black 8-mm. half-round acrylic stones
- ❑ Three silver 8-mm. pearl beads
- ❑ Seven 1" round acrylic mirrors
- ❑ 8¾" clear 4-mm. flexible plastic tubing
- ❑ 1¼ yds. white ½" scalloped edging
- ❑ ¼ yd. print cotton broadcloth
- ❑ ¼ yd. striped coordinating color cotton broadcloth
- ❑ Sewing needle and matching color thread
- ❑ Iron-on binding (optional)
- ❑ 10 Velcro® closure strips
- ❑ Craft glue or glue gun
- ❑ Fine metallic braid:
  - ❑ Silver – 1½ yds.
- ❑ Metallic cord:
  - ❑ White/Silver – 200 yds.
  - ❑ Red/Silver – ½ yd.
- ❑ Worsted-weight or plastic canvas yarn:

Nylon Plus™	Needloft™ yarn
❑ #02	#00 Black – 2½ oz.
❑ #11	#07 Pink – 9½ oz.
❑ #09	#32 Royal – 18 oz.
❑ #04	#35 Sail Blue – 6 oz.
❑ #40	#37 Silver – 2 oz.
❑ #01	#41 White – 7 oz.
❑ #54	#55 Watermelon – 5 oz.

CHASSIS & FLOOR

NOTE: Camper must be assembled in order written.

CUTTING INSTRUCTIONS:

NOTES: Graphs and diagrams on pages 96-99. Use clear canvas for all pieces.

A: For floor #1, cut two 70 x 88 holes.

B: For floor #2, cut two 68 x 88 holes.

C: For floor #3, cut two according to graph.

D: For front axle inner and outer pieces, cut eight inner pieces and four outer pieces according to graphs.

E: For rear axle inner and outer pieces, cut eight inner pieces and four outer pieces according to graphs.

F: For tire bottoms, cut seven 5 x 61 holes (no graph).

G: For mounted tire outer and inner sides, cut out centers of twenty-four 3" circles according to graph.

H: For spare tire outer and inner sides, use remaining 3" circles (no graph). Do not cut out centers.

STITCHING INSTRUCTIONS:

NOTE: D, E, twelve G and one H piece are unworked.

1: For floor, holding duplicate pieces together and working through both thicknesses as one, using colors and stitches indicated, work A-C pieces according to graphs, overlapping edges as indicated on graphs (see Floor Overlap Diagram); work through all thicknesses at overlap areas to continue established flooring pattern across uncoded areas (leave indicated areas unworked) to join pieces (see Floor Assembly Diagram). With Royal, Whipstitch outside edges of floor together.

2: For each front axle (make two), holding two outer D pieces together with four inner D pieces between at matching cutout edges, with Silver, Whipstitch outside edges together through all thicknesses according to Front Axle Assembly Diagram; Overcast edges of outer axle pieces. (Cutout edges are not finished.) For each rear axle (make four), repeat with E pieces as for front axle.

3: For tire bottoms (make seven), overlapping one hole at ends and working through both thicknesses at overlap area to join, using Black and Continental Stitch, work F pieces, forming rings.

4: For each mounted tire outer side (make six), holding two G pieces together and working through both thicknesses as one, using colors and stitches indicated, work according to graph; with cord, Whipstitch cutout edges of each side together.

5: For each mounted tire (make six), with Black, Whipstitch one tire outer side and one F together; holding two unworked G pieces together for tire inner side, Whipstitch to tire bottom through all thicknesses.

6: For spare tire (make one), work one H according to G graph, using cord and Cross Stitch to fill uncut circle center; using unworked H for tire inner side, assemble as for mounted tire in Step 5.

NOTE: Saw yardsticks into two 30" and four 10½" lengths and dowel into three 13½" lengths; smooth ends with sandpaper.

7: For chassis, glue yardstick pieces together according to Chassis Assembly Diagram. To assemble front tires and axles, insert one end of one dowel through cutout on one front axle, then through cutout on inner side of one tire. With end of dowel showing through cutout on outer side of tire, push one upholstery tack into end of dowel (**NOTE:** Tires should turn easily.) Repeat at opposite end of dowel with remaining front axle and one tire (see Axle/Tire Assembly Diagram).

8: Assemble rear axles and tires as in Step 7. Glue inner edges of each axle to chassis according to Axle/Tire Assembly Diagram.

9: Set spare tire aside; it will be attached later to rear cargo door. Set floor aside; it will be joined later to chassis.

A – Floor #1
(cut 2) 70 x 88 holes

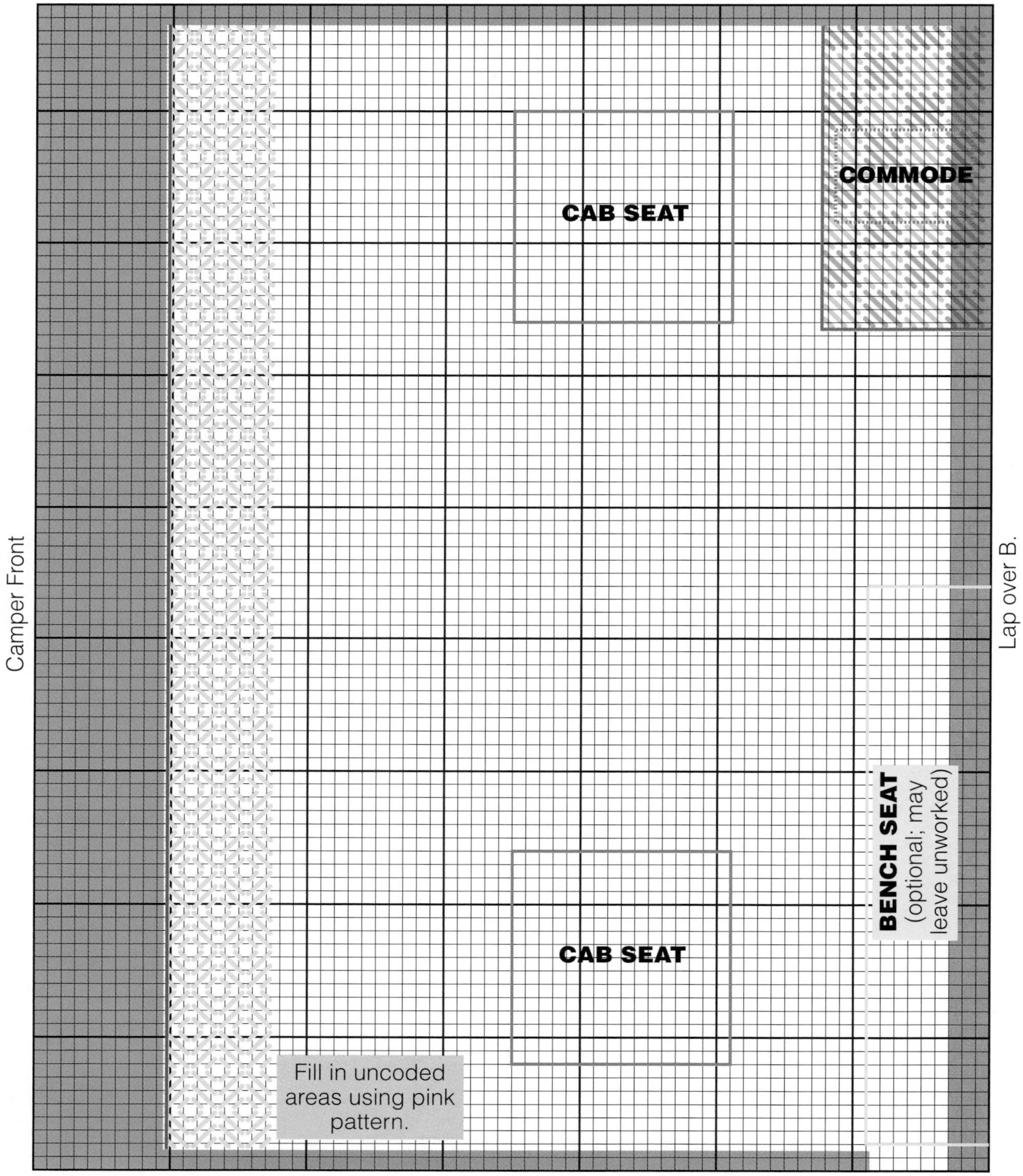

Floor Assembly Diagram

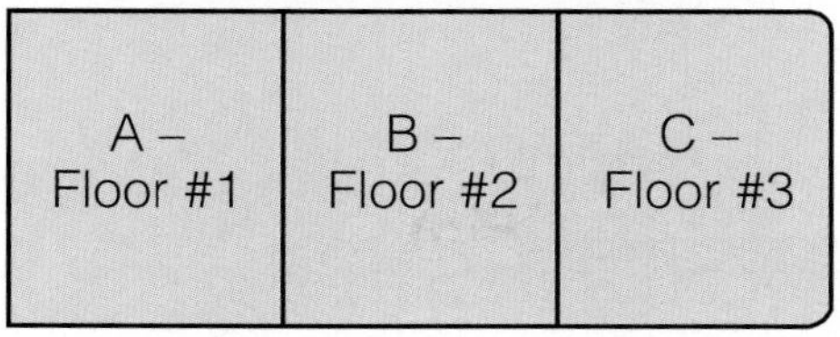

Floor Overlap Diagram

As worked area of floor #1 nears overlap area, alternate pieces with 3-hole overlap; work across area through all thicknesses.

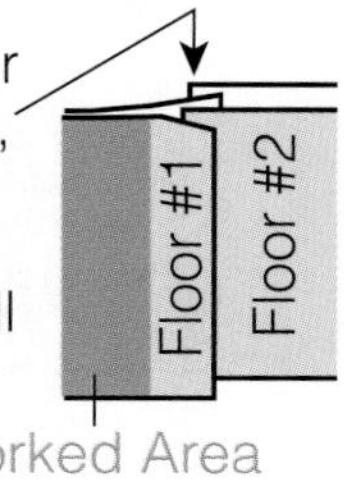

B – Floor #2
(cut 2) 68 x 88 holes

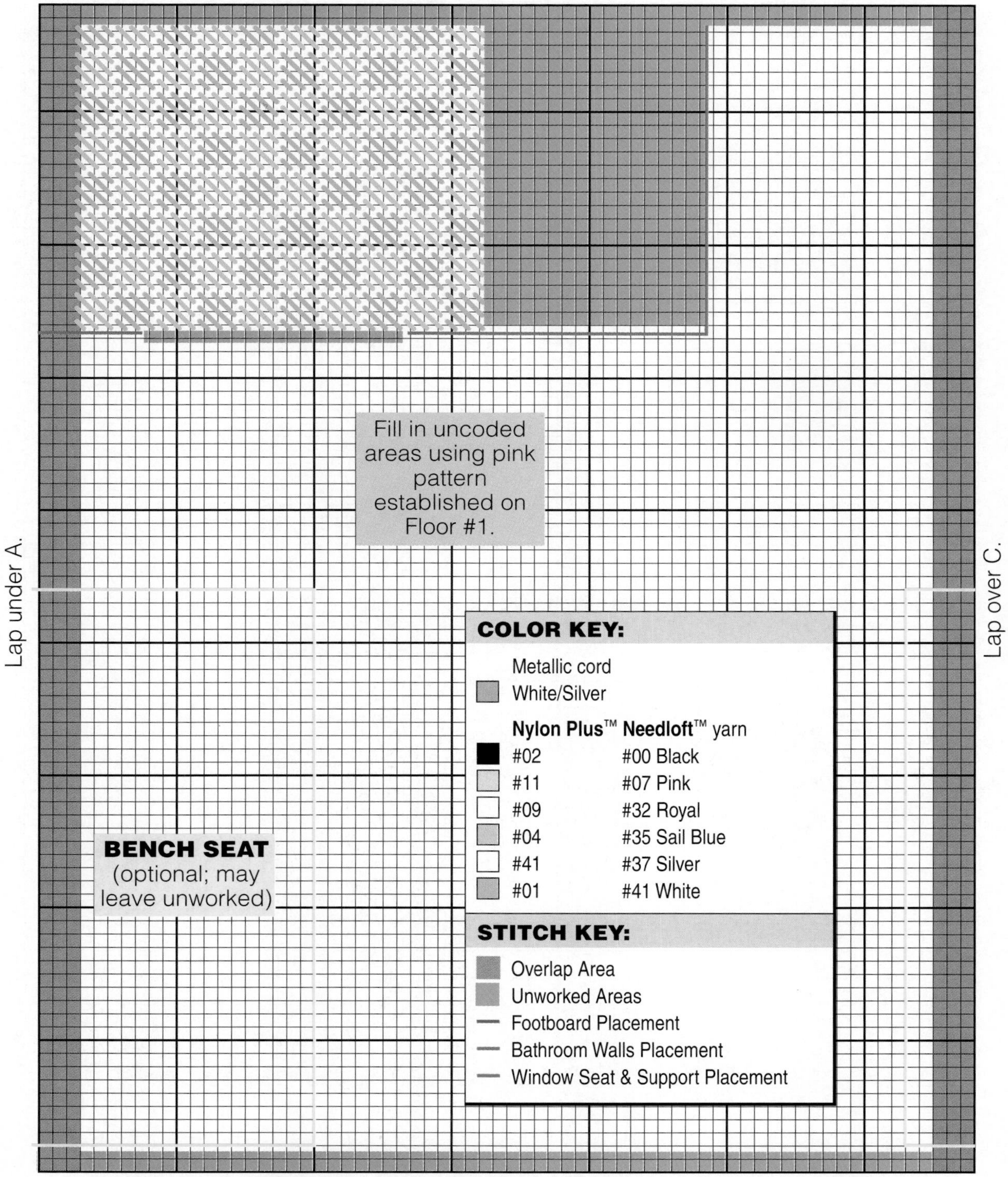

C – Floor #3

(cut 2) 68 x 88 holes

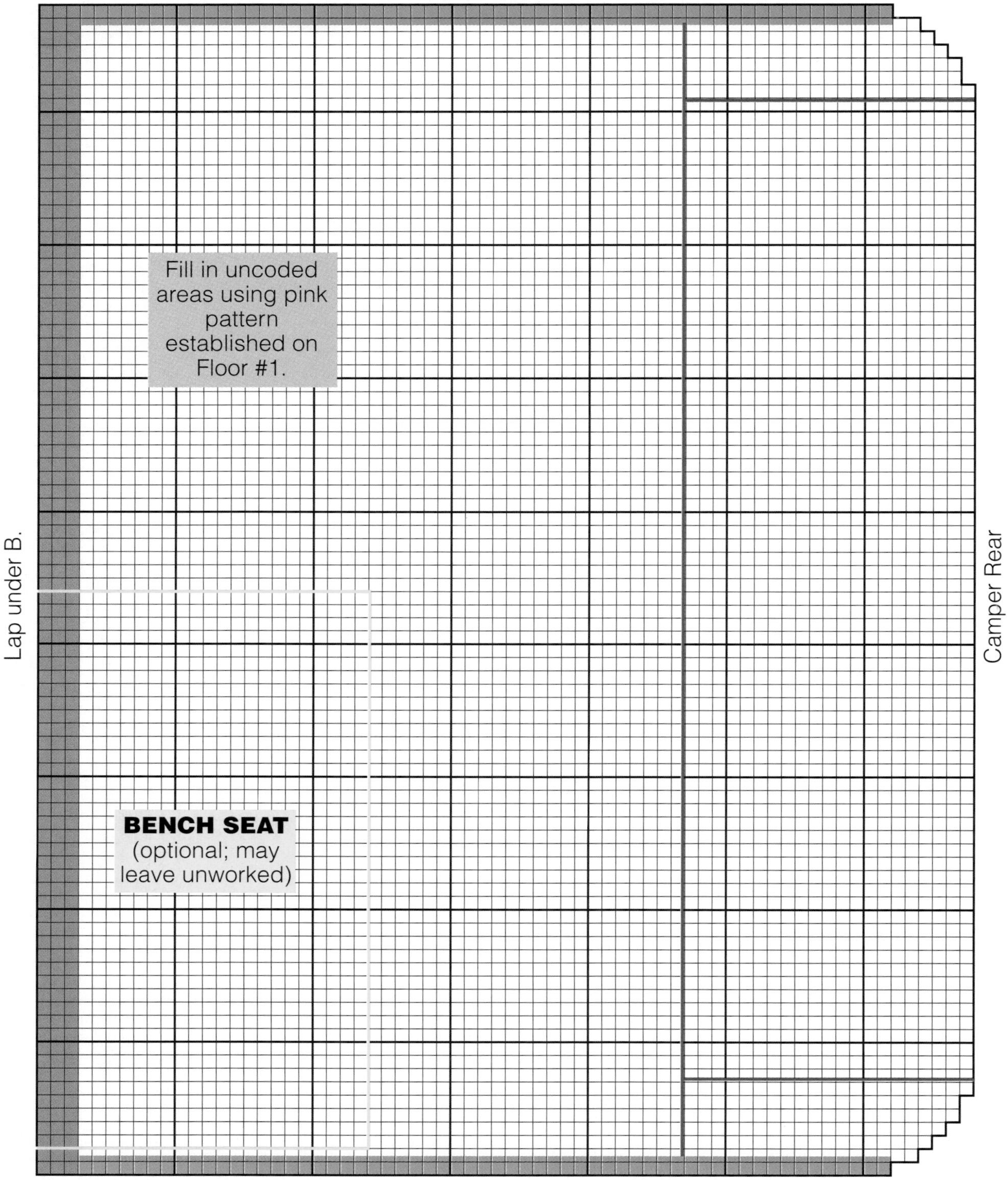

D – Outer Front Axle Piece
(cut 4) 15 x 18 holes

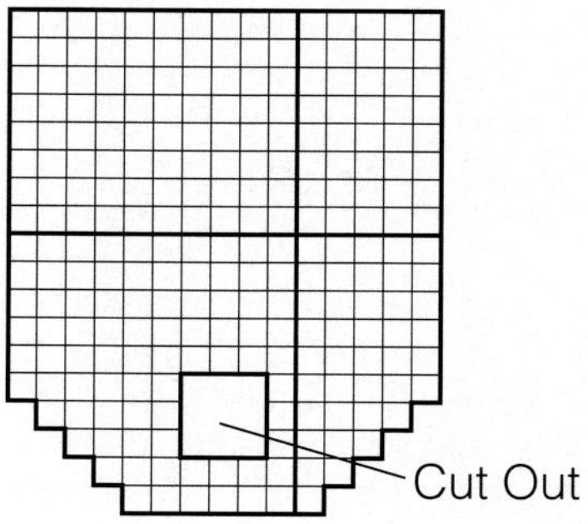

Front Axle Assembly Diagram

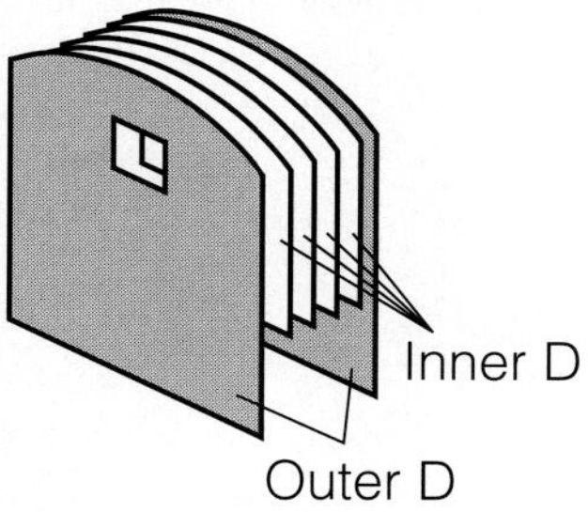

D – Inner Front Axle Piece
(cut 8) 11 x 15 holes

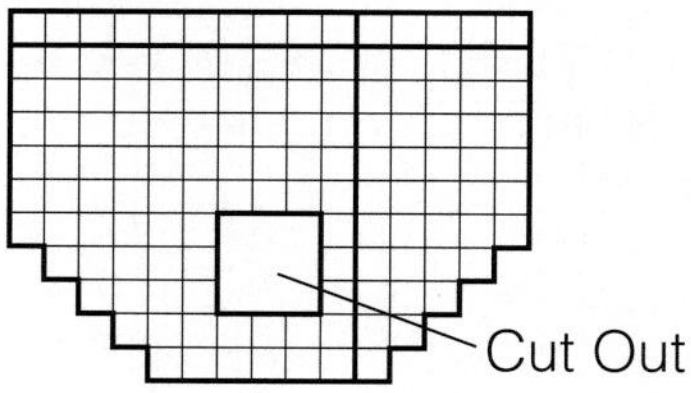

G – Tire Side
(cut 24 from 3" circles)
Cut out gray centers carefully.

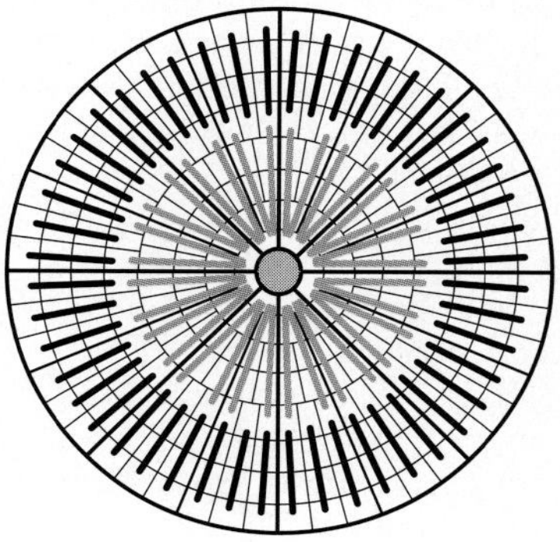

COLOR KEY:

Metallic cord
White/Silver

Nylon Plus™	Needloft™ yarn
#02	#00 Black
#11	#07 Pink
#09	#32 Royal
#04	#35 Sail Blue
#41	#37 Silver
#01	#41 White

STITCH KEY:

- Overlap Area
- Unworked Areas
- Footboard Placement
- Bathroom Walls Placement
- Window Seat & Support Placement

E – Outer Rear Axle Piece
(cut 4) 18 x 36 holes

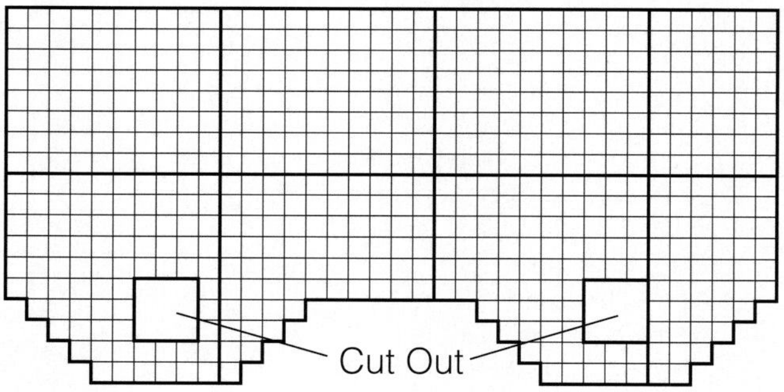

E – Inner Rear Axle Piece
(cut 8) 11 x 36 holes

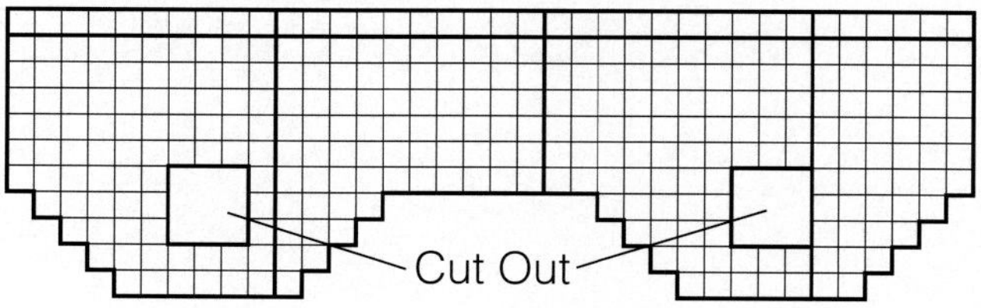

Chassis Assembly Diagram

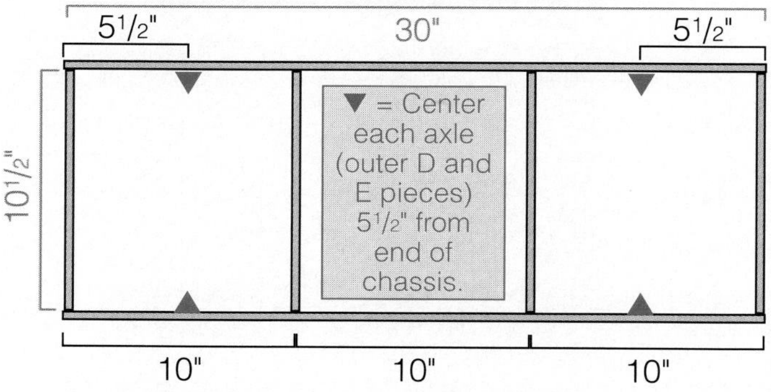

Axle/Tire Assembly Diagram
(underside view)

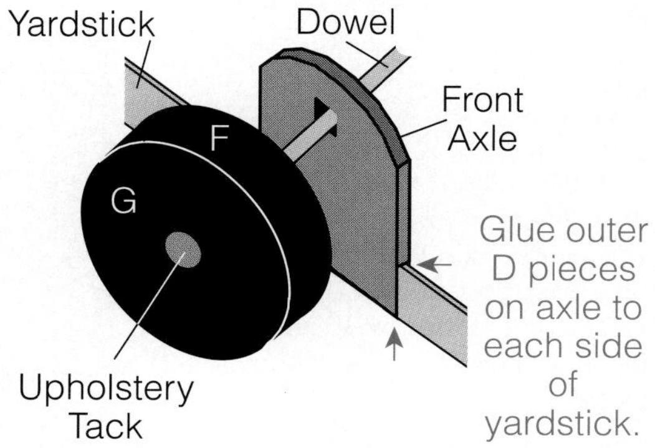

EXTERIOR WALLS

CUTTING INSTRUCTIONS:

NOTE: Diagrams and graphs continued on pages 102-109.

A: For cab passenger side wall and brace, cut two (one for wall and one for brace) from clear according to graph.

B: For bathroom wall and brace, cut two (one for wall and one for brace) from clear according to graph.

C: For kitchen wall and brace, cut two (one for wall and one for brace) from clear according to graph.

D: For back corner walls and braces, cut four (two for walls and two for braces) from clear 8 x 70 holes.

E: For back wall and brace, cut two (one for wall and one for brace) from clear according to graph.

F: For back door support wall and brace, cut two (one for wall and one for brace) from clear according to graph.

G: For large window support wall and brace, cut two (one for wall and one for brace) from clear according to graph.

H: For cab driver side wall and brace, cut two (one for wall and one for brace) from clear according to graph.

I: For windshield wall, cut one from clear according to graph.

J: For front hood wall, cut one from clear 13 x 88 holes (no graph).

K: For grille wall, cut one from clear according to graph.

L: For cab doors, linings and braces, cut six (two from blue for linings, two from clear for doors and two from clear for braces) according to graph.

M: For cab door hinges, cut two from clear 11 x 27 holes.

N: For back door, lining and brace, cut three (one from blue for lining, one from clear for door and one from clear for brace) according to graph.

O: For back door hinge, cut one from clear 13 x 58 holes.

P: For cargo door and brace, cut two (one for door and one for brace) from clear according to graph.

Q: For cargo door hinge, cut one from clear 11 x 60 holes.

R: For detachable large window interior and exterior wall and brace, cut three (one from blue for interior wall, one from clear for exterior wall and one from clear for brace) according to graph.

STITCHING INSTRUCTIONS:

NOTE: Braces and blue interior pieces are unworked.

1: Overlapping side walls as indicated and working through both thicknesses at overlap areas to join, using colors and stitches indicated, work one A (leave uncoded area unworked), one B and one C piece for passenger side walls according to graphs. (See Passenger Side Walls Assembly Diagram.)

2: Working as for passenger side walls (**NOTE:** Large window support wall and cab driver side wall do not overlap; they are joined with stitches indicated), work one F, one G and one H (leave uncoded area unworked) piece for driver side walls according to graphs. (See Driver Side Walls Assembly Diagram.)

3: Using colors and stitches indicated, work two D and one E piece according to graphs. Holding brace E to wrong side of worked piece, with matching colors, Whipstitch

B – Bathroom Exterior Wall & Brace
(cut 1 each) 49 x 70 holes

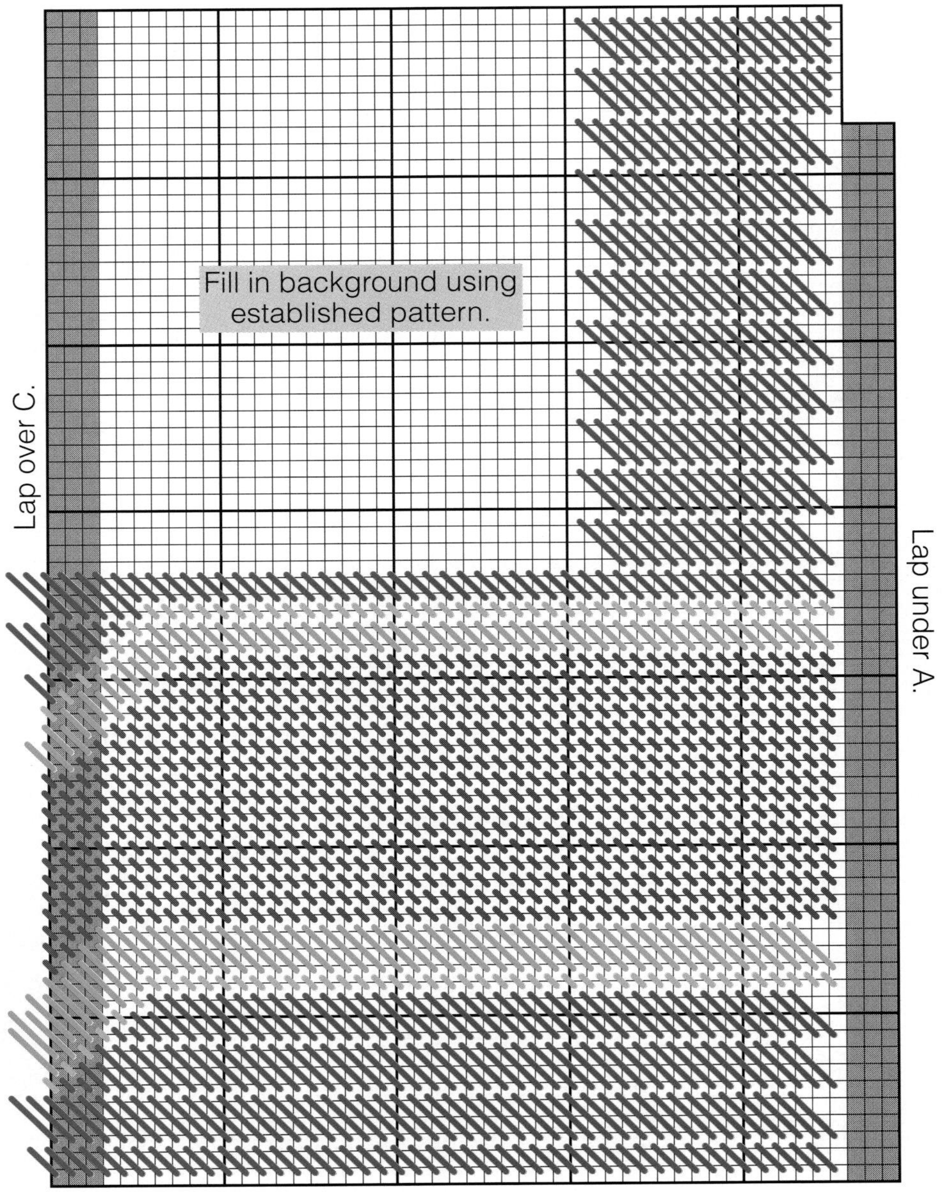

edges of cargo area cutout together.

4: Using colors and stitches indicated, work two clear L pieces on opposite side of canvas for cab doors, one clear N for back door, P (hold cargo door and brace together and work through both thicknesses as one) for cargo door and one clear R for exterior detachable large window wall according to graphs.

5: Using colors indicated and Continental Stitch, work M, O and Q pieces according to graphs (leave uncoded areas unworked); with matching colors, Overcast short edges of hinges as indicated.

6: To finish doors and removable wall, holding blue linings and detachable large window wall interior to wrong side of matching doors and exterior wall with braces between, with cord for window cutouts and with matching colors, Whipstitch edges of L, N and R pieces together. With Royal, Whipstitch unfinished edges of cargo door together.

7: To attach each door, holding unworked area of one hinge and indicated area (Primary Hinge Attachment, green outline) of corresponding exterior wall piece right sides together, with matching colors, work Continental Stitches through both thicknesses (see Step 1 of Hinge Assembly Diagram) and over long edge of hinge to cover uncoded areas. Bend unattached long edge of hinge up and slip through cutout on door (see Step 2 of diagram). Whipstitch unfinished edge of hinge to wall as indicated (Secondary Hinge Attachment) and according to diagram.

8: Using colors and stitches indicated, work I and K pieces according to graphs. With cord, Overcast cutout edges of grille. Using Royal and Slanted Gobelin Stitch over 3 bars (see Stitch Illustration on page 105), work J in horizontal rows across 88-hole length.

9: Glue one acrylic mirror to wrong side of each cutout on grille.

10: Set pieces aside.

A – Cab Passenger Side Exterior Wall & Brace

(cut 1 each) 63 x 70 holes

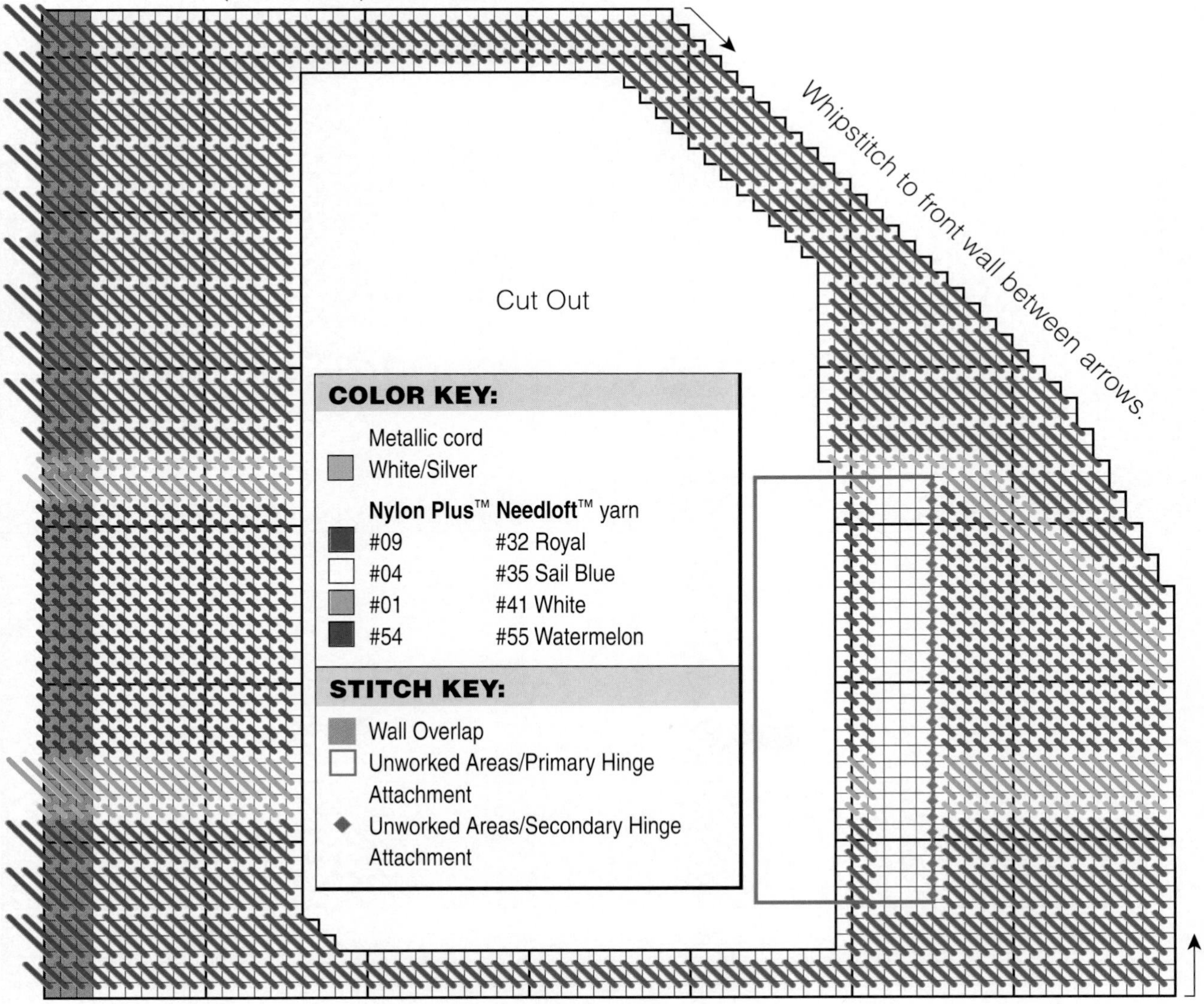

Cut Out
Whipstitch to front wall between arrows.
COLOR KEY:
Metallic cord
White/Silver
Nylon Plus™ Needloft™ yarn
#09 #32 Royal
#04 #35 Sail Blue
#01 #41 White
#54 #55 Watermelon
STITCH KEY:
Wall Overlap
Unworked Areas/Primary Hinge Attachment
Unworked Areas/Secondary Hinge Attachment

C – Kitchen Exterior Wall & Brace

(cut 1 each) 70 x 81 holes

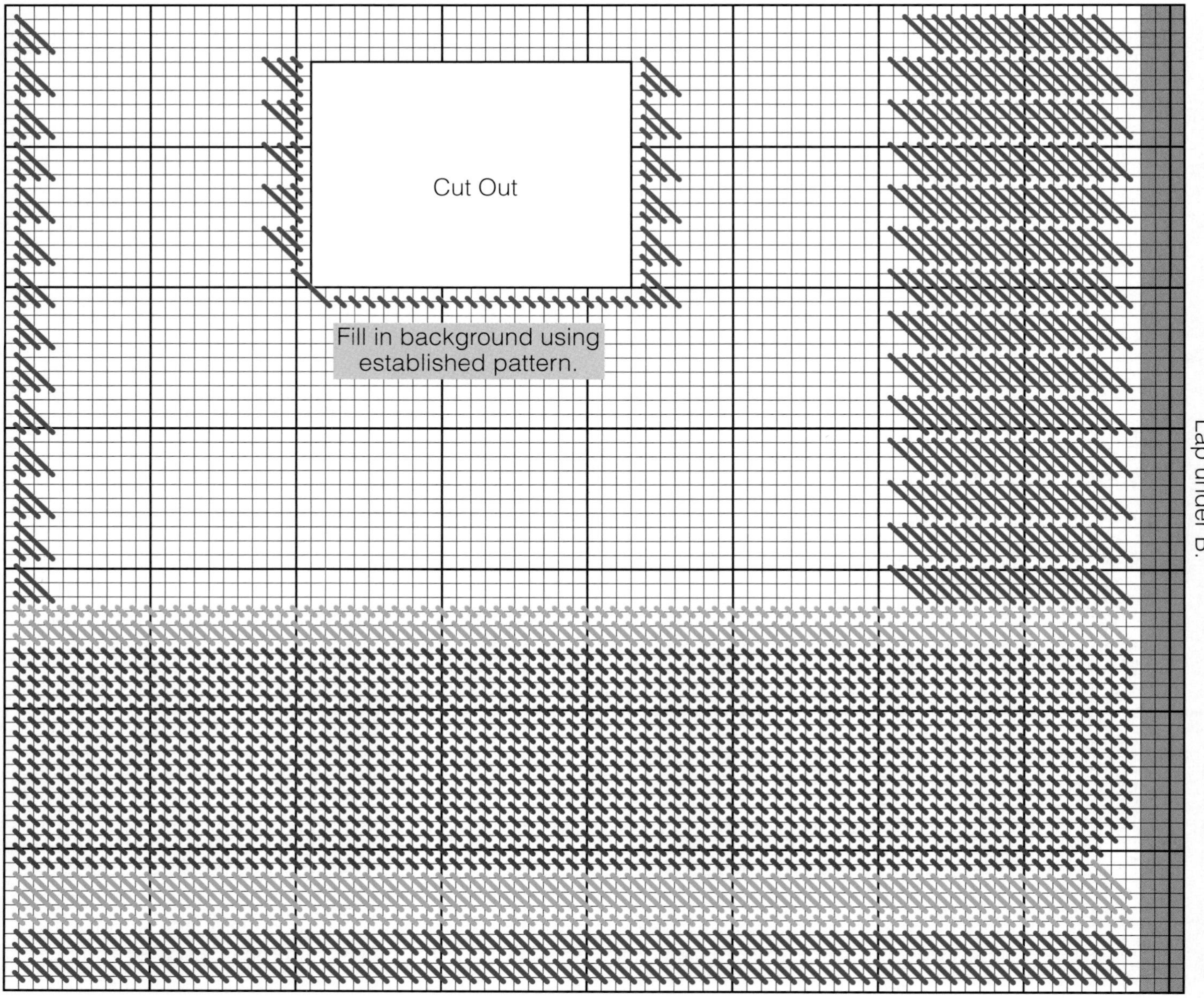

D – Back Corner Exterior Wall & Brace

(cut 2 each) 8 x 70 holes

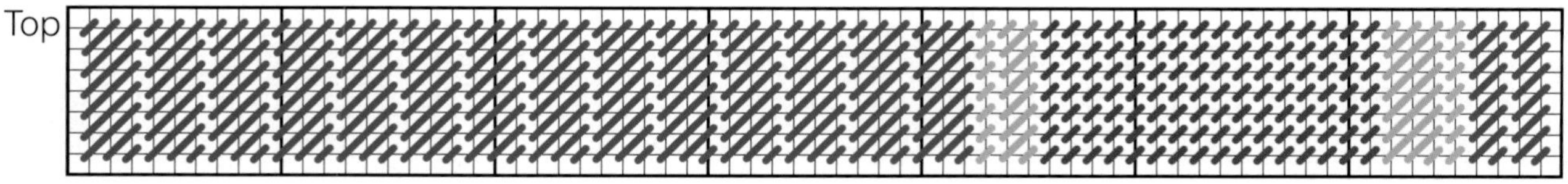

COLOR KEY:		STITCH KEY:
Metallic cord		Wall Overlap
White/Silver		Unworked Areas/Primary Hinge Attachment
Nylon Plus™ Needloft™ yarn		◆ Unworked Areas/Secondary Hinge Attachment
#09	#32 Royal	
#04	#35 Sail Blue	
#01	#41 White	
#54	#55 Watermelon	

E – Back Exterior Wall & Brace
(cut 1 each) 70 x 76 holes

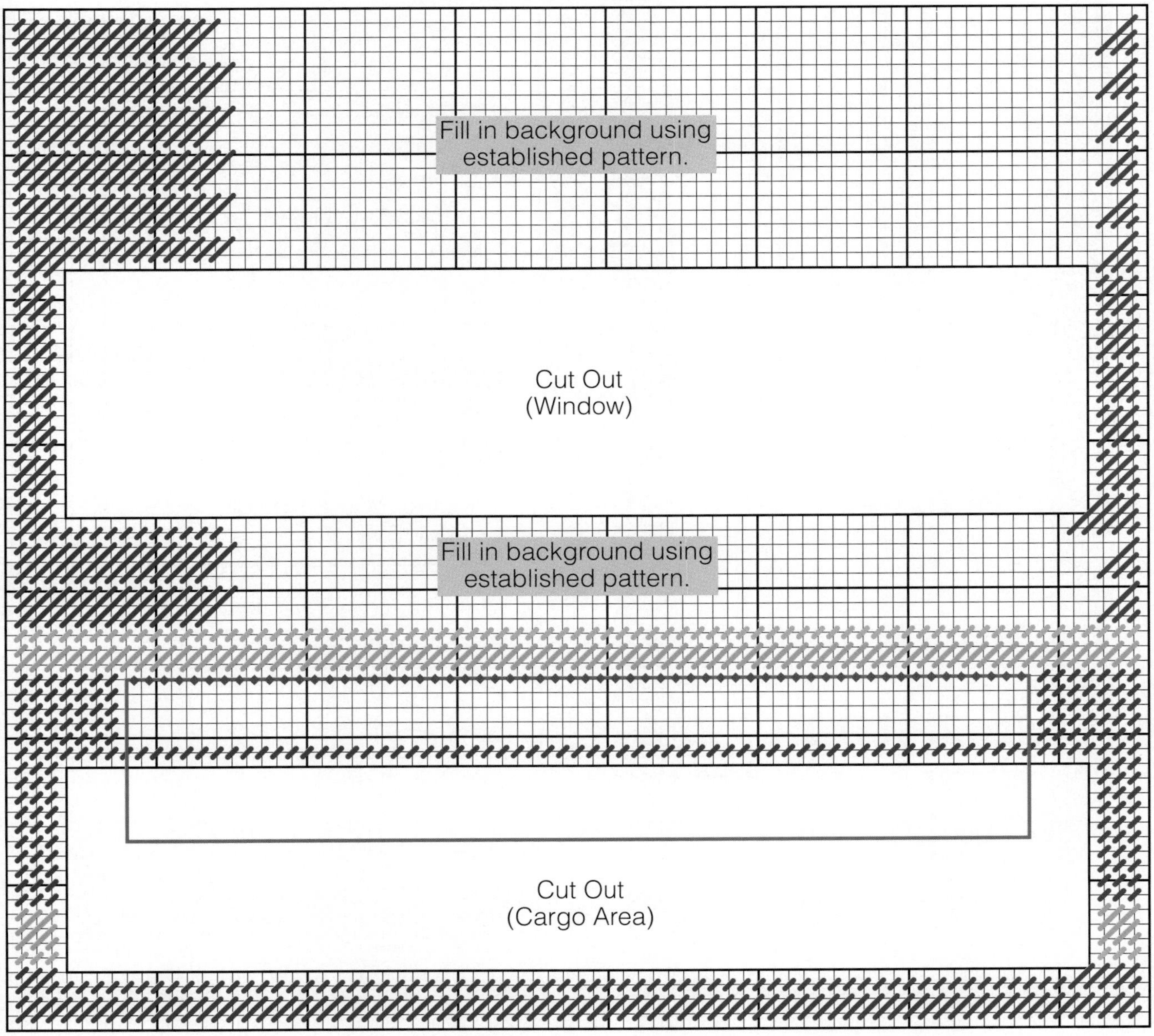

G – Large Window Exterior Support Wall & Brace

(cut 1 each) 70 x 90 holes

Lap under F.

Top

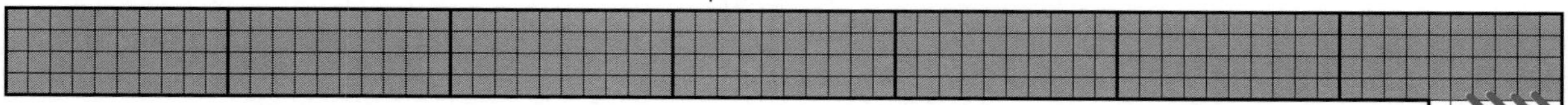

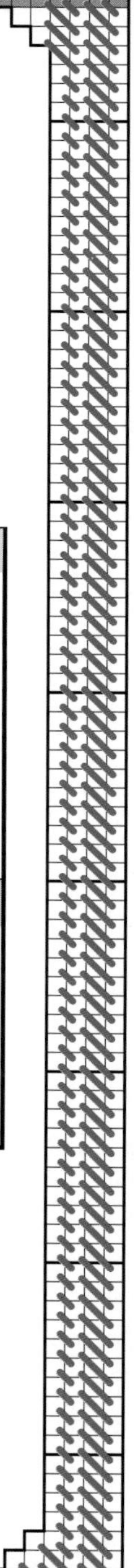

F – Back Door Exterior Support Wall & Brace

(cut 1 each) 38 x 70 holes

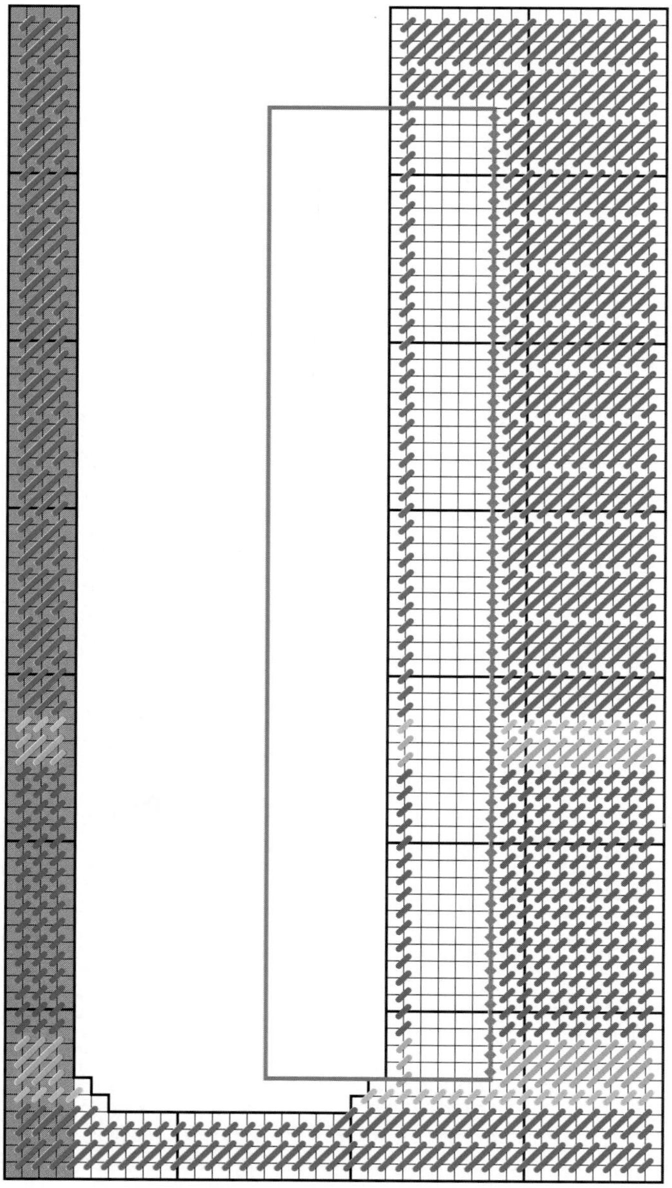

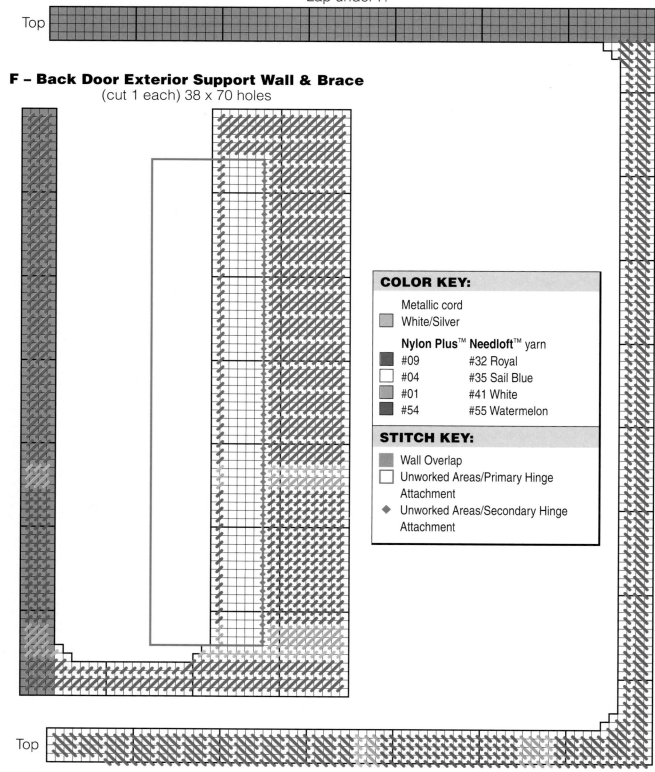

COLOR KEY:

Metallic cord
White/Silver

Nylon Plus™	**Needloft™** yarn
#09	#32 Royal
#04	#35 Sail Blue
#01	#41 White
#54	#55 Watermelon

STITCH KEY:

- Wall Overlap
- Unworked Areas/Primary Hinge Attachment
- ◆ Unworked Areas/Secondary Hinge Attachment

Top

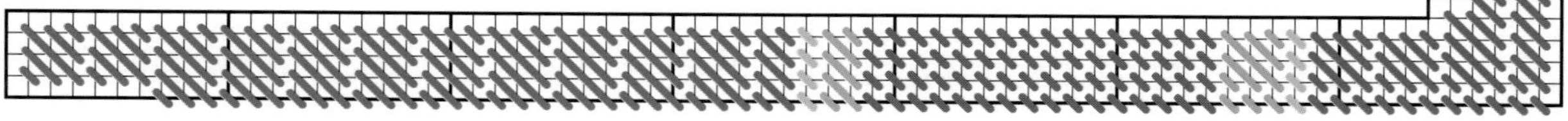

Hinge Assembly Diagram

(Back door shown for example.)

Step 1:
(Primary Hinge Attachment)
Attach hinge to wall by working through both thicknesses at matching unworked areas.

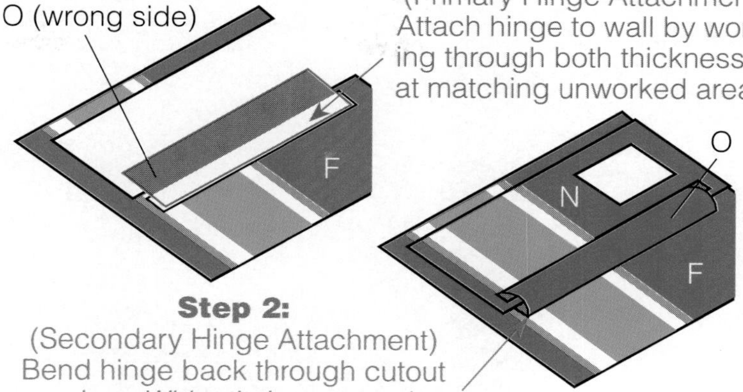

Step 2:
(Secondary Hinge Attachment)
Bend hinge back through cutout on door; Whipstitch to opposite edge.

Slanted Gobelin Stitch Illustration

(over 3 bars)

H – Cab Driver Side Side Exterior Wall & Brace

(cut 1 each) 63 x 70 holes

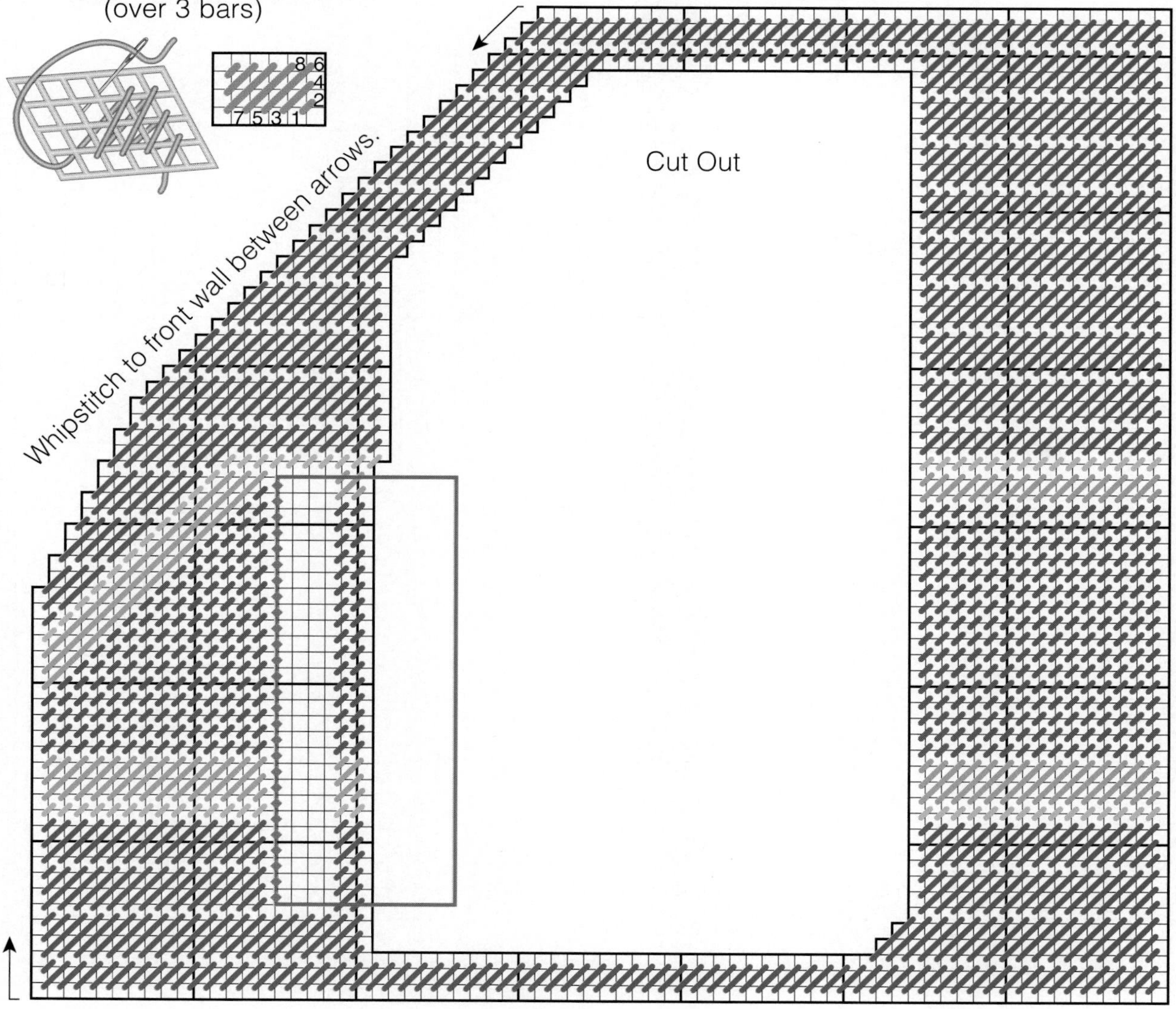

I – Windshield Exterior Wall
(cut 1) 35 x 88 holes

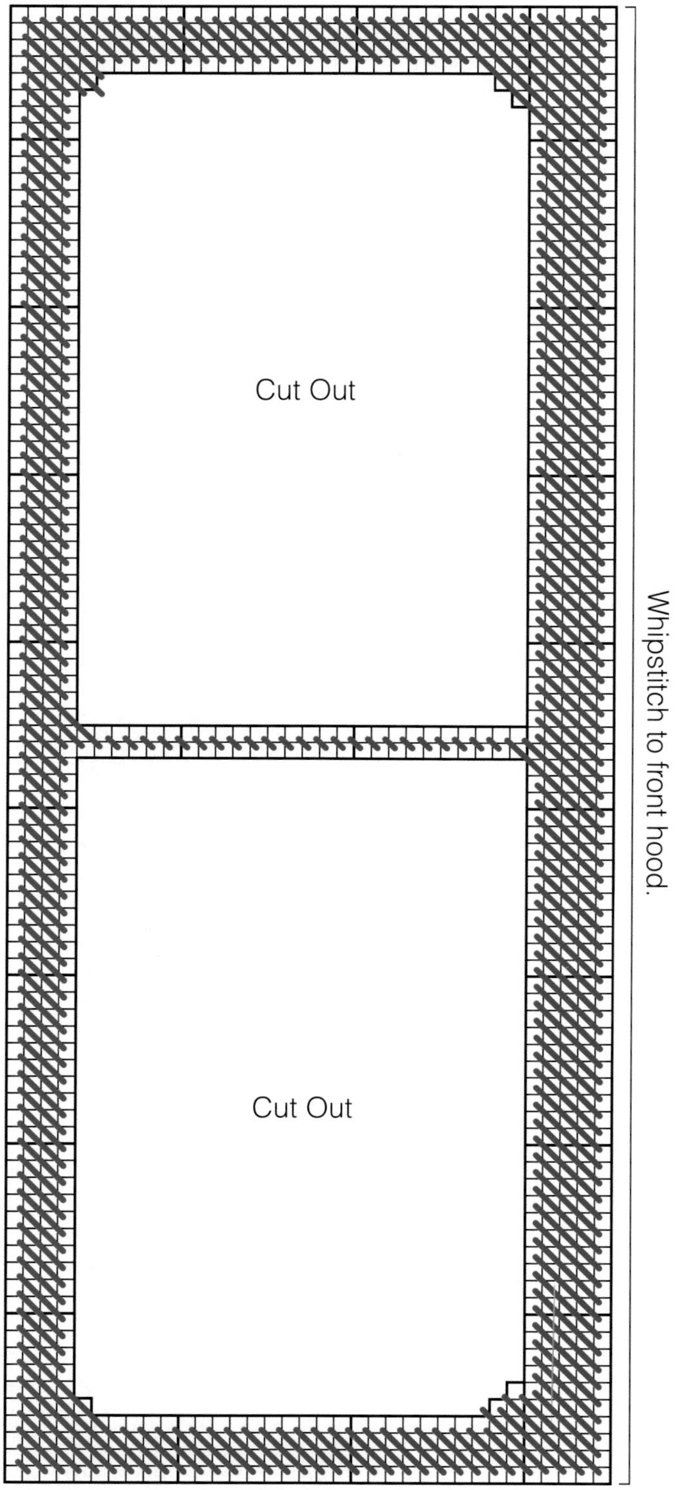

K – Grille Exterior Wall
(cut 1) 26 x 88 holes

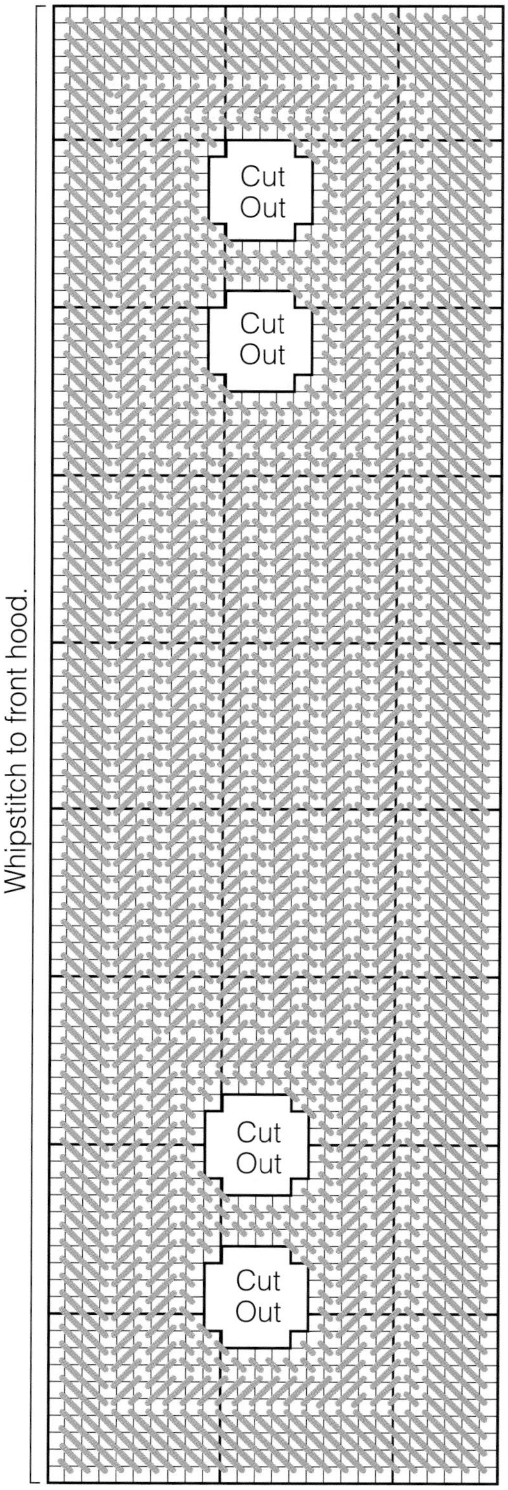

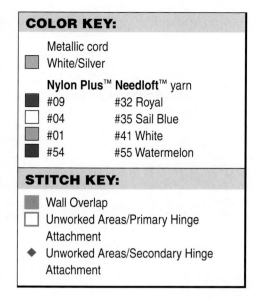

COLOR KEY:

Metallic cord
White/Silver

Nylon Plus™	Needloft™ yarn
#09	#32 Royal
#04	#35 Sail Blue
#01	#41 White
#54	#55 Watermelon

STITCH KEY:

- Wall Overlap
- Unworked Areas/Primary Hinge Attachment
- ◆ Unworked Areas/Secondary Hinge Attachment

L – Cab Door, Lining & Brace

(cut 2 from blue & 4 from clear) 42 x 61 holes

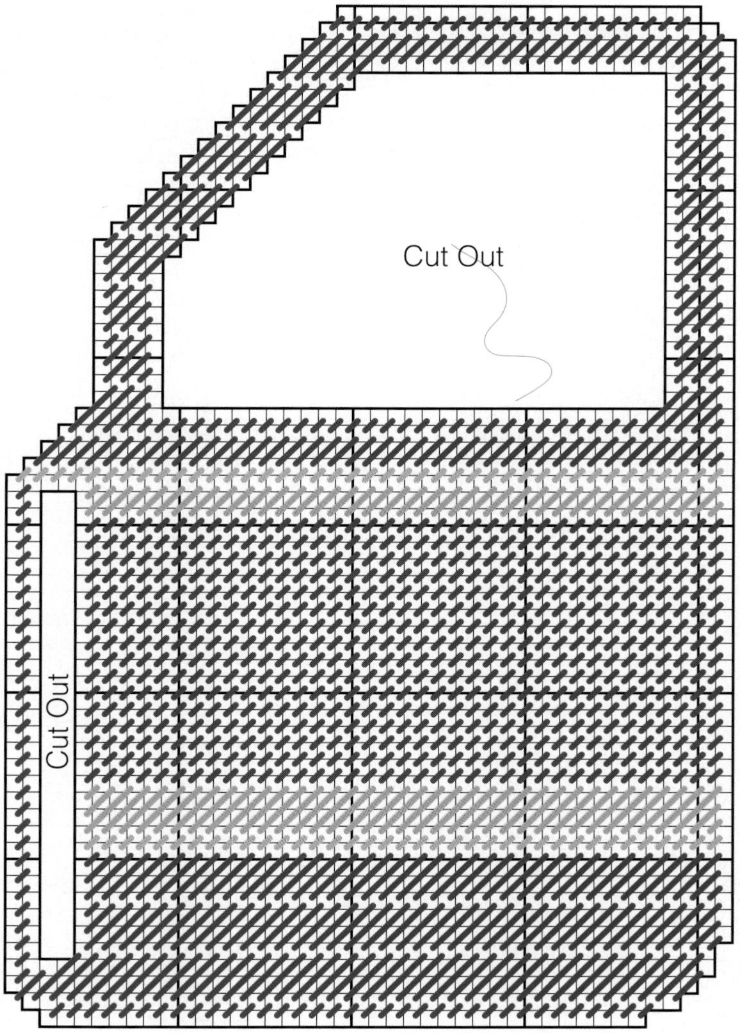

M – Cab Door Hinge

(cut 2) 11 x 27 holes

Overcast

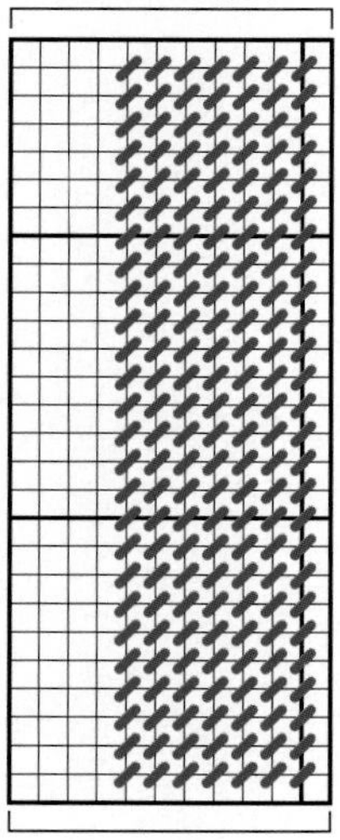

Overcast

N – Back Door, Lining & Brace

(cut 1 from blue & 2 from clear) 26 x 70 holes

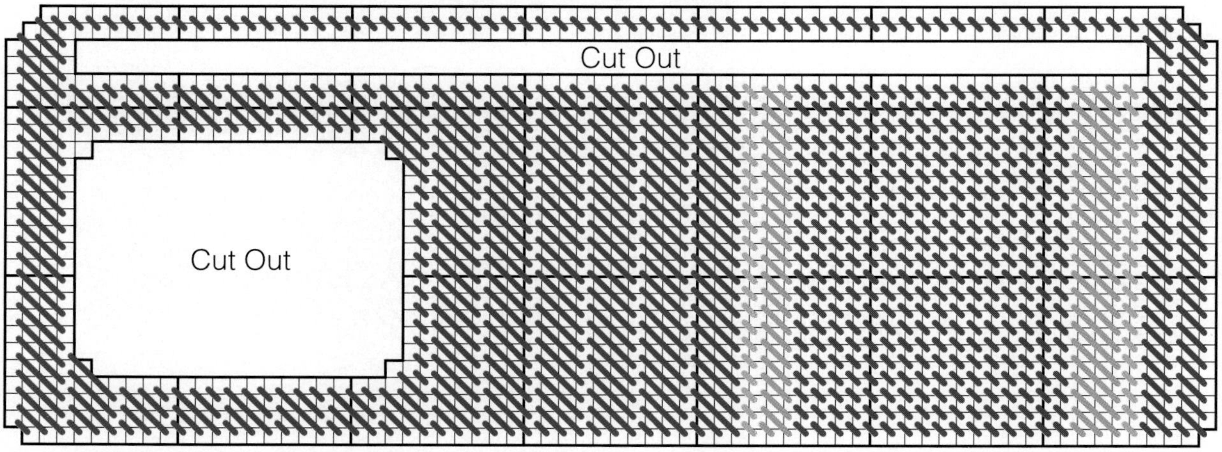

O – Back Door Hinge
(cut 1)
13 x 58 holes

Overcast

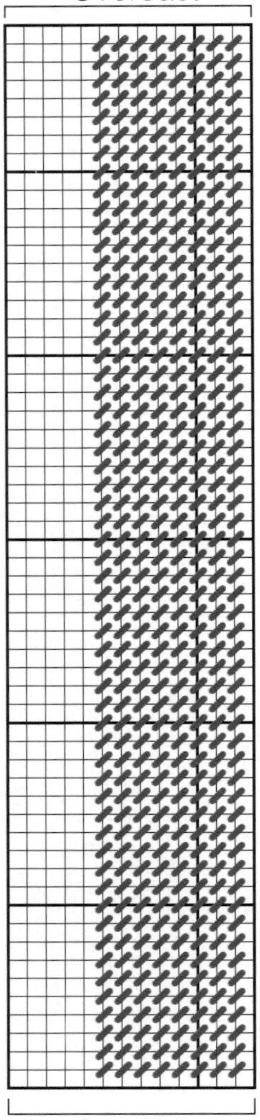

Overcast

Passenger Side Walls Assembly Diagram

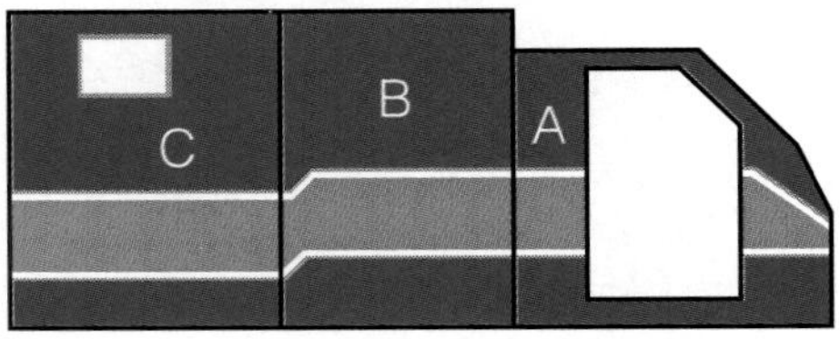

Driver Side Walls Assembly Diagram

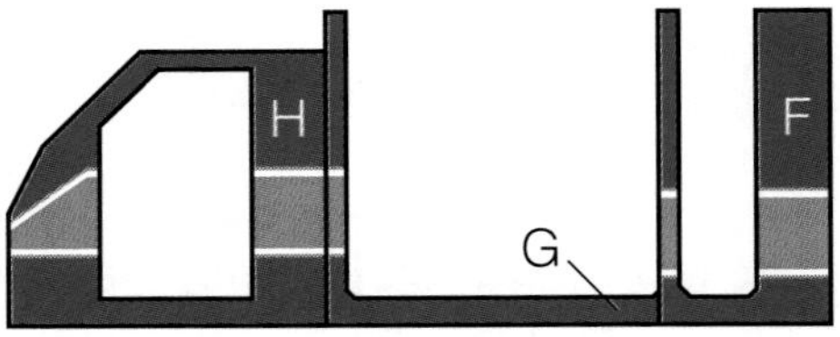

COLOR KEY:

Metallic cord
- White/Silver

Nylon Plus™ Needloft™ yarn

#09	#32 Royal
#04	#35 Sail Blue
#01	#41 White
#54	#55 Watermelon

STITCH KEY:

- Wall Overlap
- Unworked Areas/Primary Hinge Attachment
- ◆ Unworked Areas/Secondary Hinge Attachment

P – Cargo Door & Brace
(cut 1 each) 21 x 70 holes

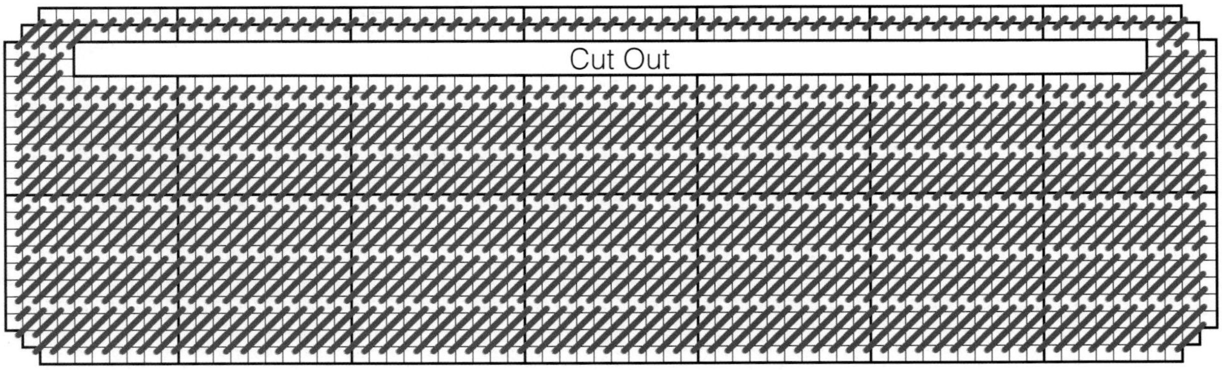

Q – Cargo Door Hinge
(cut 1) 11 x 60 holes

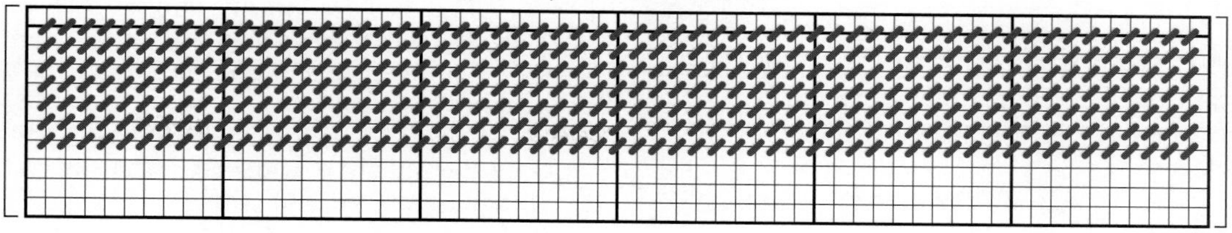

R – Detachable Large Window Interior & Exterior Wall & Brace
(cut 1 from blue & 2 from clear) 70 x 84 holes

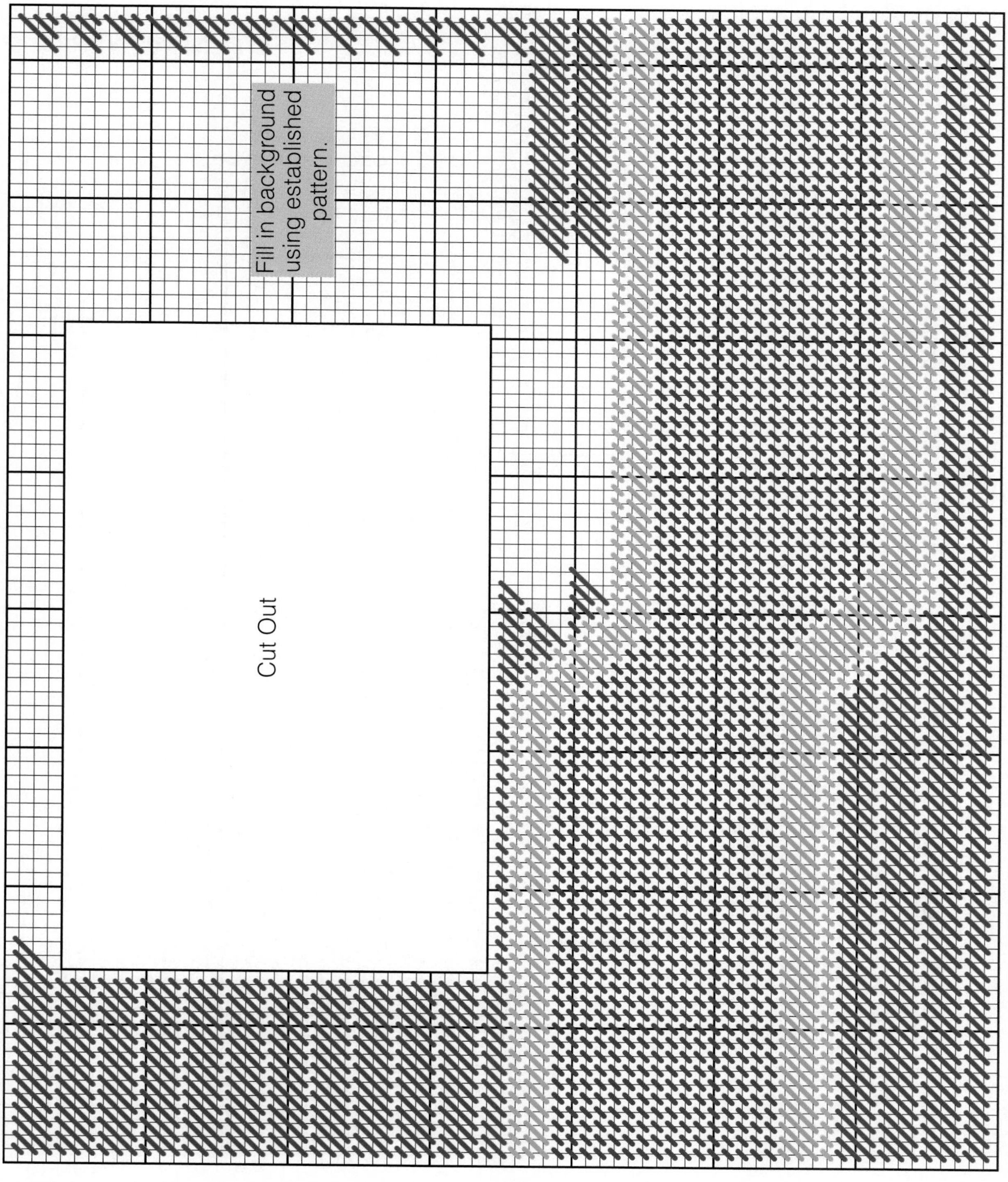

UNDERPINNING

CUTTING INSTRUCTIONS:

NOTE: Use clear canvas for all pieces.

A: For front underpinning piece, cut one 16 x 90 holes (no graph).

B: For front axle underpinning pieces, cut two according to graph.

C: For center underpinning pieces, cut two 16 x 57 holes (no graph).

D: For rear axle underpinning pieces, cut two according to graph.

E: For rear corner underpinning pieces, cut two 8 x 16 holes (no graph).

F: For rear underpinning piece, cut one 16 x 78 holes (no graph).

G: For door handles, cut three according to graph.

H: For rear view mirror fronts and backs, cut four (two for fronts and two for backs) according to graph.

I: For rear view mirror sides, cut two 1 x 6 holes (no graph).

J: For cargo door trim, cut two 2 x 37 holes (no graph).

STITCHING INSTRUCTIONS:

NOTE: One J piece is unworked.

1: Using colors and stitches indicated, work A, E and F pieces according to Front & Rear Underpinning Stitch Pattern Guide.

2: For driver side, working across indicated edges to join pieces, using Royal and Slanted Gobelin Stitch over 3 bars (see Stitch Illustration), work one of each B-D pieces. (See Underpinning Assembly Diagram.)

3: For passenger side, work remaining B-D pieces on opposite side of canvas as in Step 2. With matching colors, Whipstitch all underpinning pieces together according to diagram; Overcast unfinished edges.

4: Using cord and Continental Stitch, work G (one on opposite side of canvas), H (one front and one back on opposite side of canvas) and one J piece; Overcast G pieces.

5: For each rear view mirror, holding one of each H wrong sides together with one mirror between, Whipstitch together as indicated; holding one I between unfinished edges, Whipstitch together according to Rear View Mirror Assembly Diagram.

6: For cargo door trim, holding unworked J to wrong side of worked piece, with cord, Whipstitch together.

7: Set pieces aside.

COLOR KEY:

Metallic cord
White/Silver

Nylon Plus™ Needloft™ yarn

#09	#32 Royal
#04	#35 Sail Blue
#01	#41 White
#54	#55 Watermelon

STITCH KEY:

- Wall Overlap
- Unworked Areas/Primary Hinge Attachment
- ◆ Unworked Areas/Secondary Hinge Attachment

B - Front Axle Underpinning Piece
(cut 2)
16 x 65 holes

Join to C.

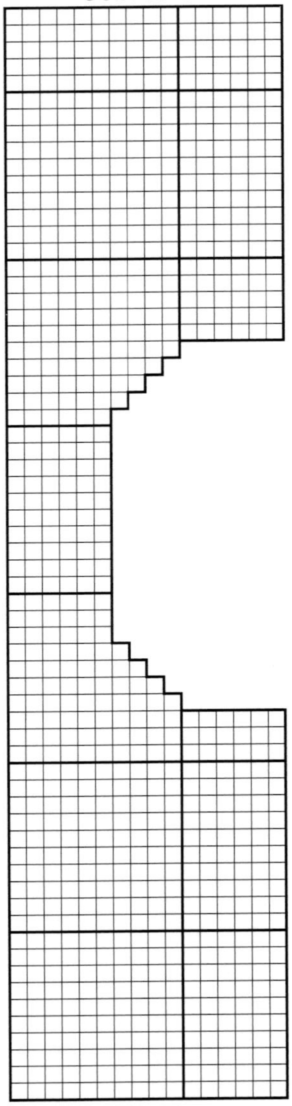

Front

D - Rear Axle Underpinning Piece
(cut 2)
16 x 73 holes

Rear

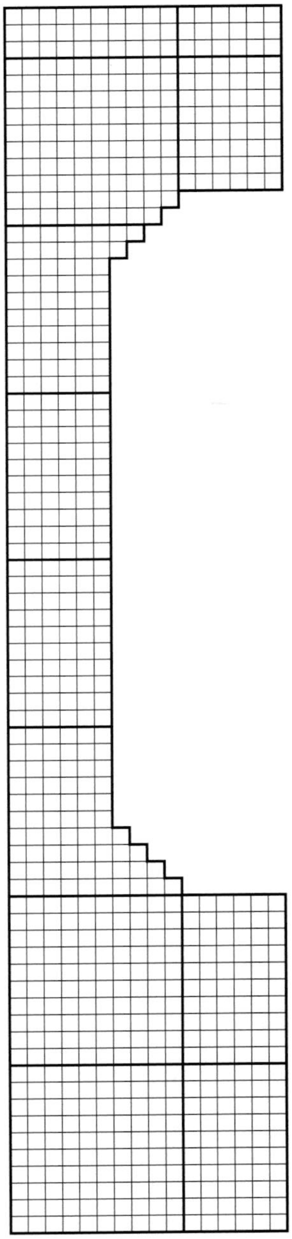

Join to C.

G – Door Handle
(cut 3)
2 x 6 holes

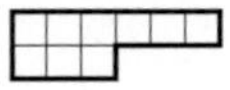

Rear View Mirror Assembly Diagram

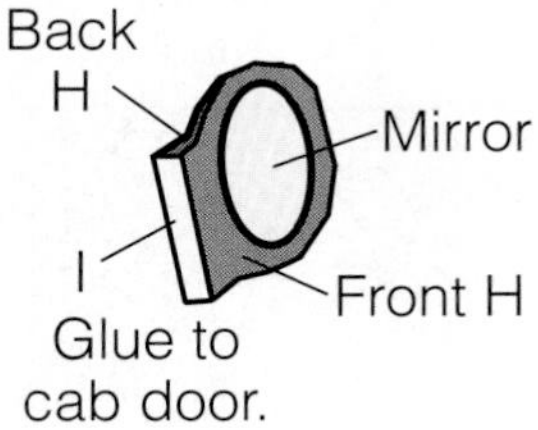

H – Rear View Mirror Front & Back
(cut 2 each)
8 x 8 holes

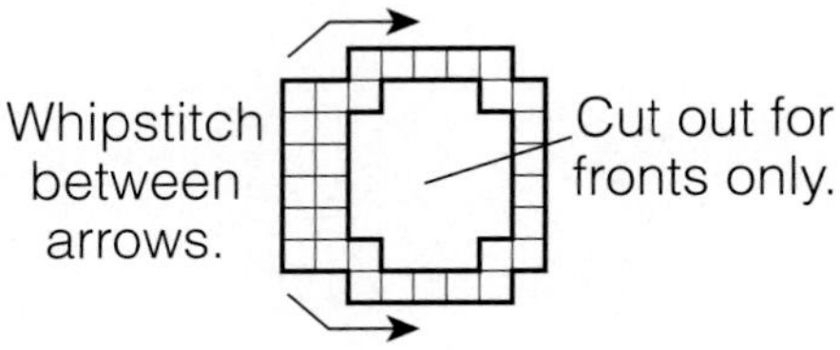

Underpinning Assembly Diagram
(top view)

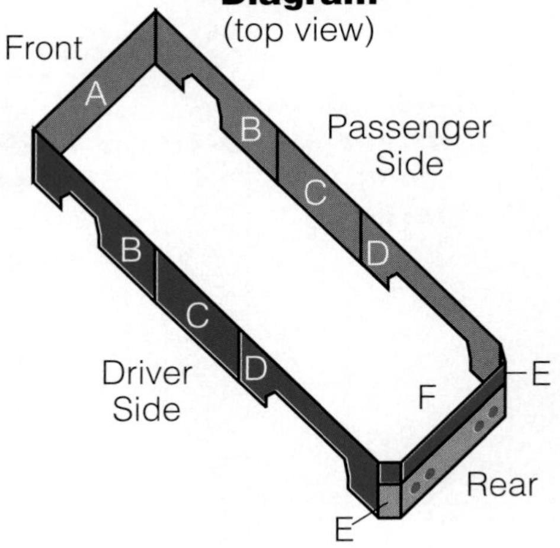

Slanted Gobelin Stitch Illustration
(over 3 bars)

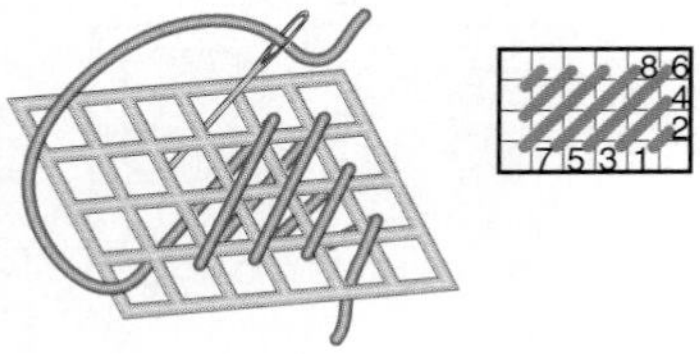

Front & Rear Underpinning Stitch Pattern Guide

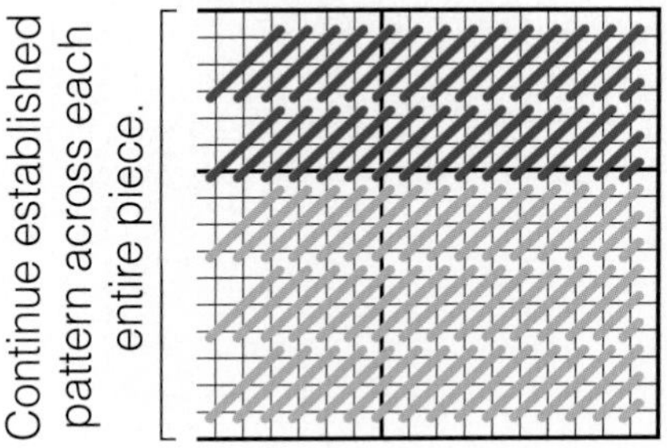

ROOF

Photo on page 121.

CUTTING INSTRUCTIONS:

NOTE: Graphs and diagrams on pages 112-114.

A: For sunroof top and lining, cut two (one from clear for top and one from blue for lining) according to graph.

B: For top extension and lining, cut two (one from clear for top extension and one from blue for lining) 7 x 90 holes (no graph).

C: For center top, cut one from clear 64 x 90 holes (no graph).

D: For center top lining, use one 70- x 90-hole sheet of blue canvas (no graph).

E: For rear top and lining, cut two (one from clear for top and one from blue for lining) according to graph.

F: For front overhang, cut two from clear 4 x 90 holes (no graph).

G: For front driver side overhang, cut two from clear according to graph.

H: For rear driver side overhang, cut two from clear according to graph.

I: For front passenger side overhang, cut two from clear according to graph.

J: For rear passenger side overhang, cut two from clear according to graph.

K: For back corner overhang, cut four from clear 8 x 10 holes (no graph).

L: For rear overhang, cut two from clear 10 x 78 holes (no graph).

STITCHING INSTRUCTIONS:

NOTE: Blue lining pieces are unworked.

1: Using Royal and stitches indicated, work A according to graph; using Slanted Gobelin Stitch over 3 bars (see Stitch Illustration), work B in horizontal rows across 90-hole length. Using pattern established on A, overlapping three holes and working through both thicknesses at overlap area to join, work C and E pieces. (See Top Assembly Diagram.)

2: Holding F pieces together, using Slanted Gobelin Stitch over narrow width, work F pieces through both thicknesses as one; holding matching pieces together and working through both thicknesses and over indicated edges to join pieces, work G-J pieces according to graphs.

3: Holding matching pieces together and working through both thicknesses as one, using Slanted Gobelin Stitch over 3 bars, work K (across 8-hole width) and L (across 78-hole length) pieces in horizontal rows.

4: Overlapping nine holes at one matching straight edge, with Sail Blue, Whipstitch D and lining E together.

5: Holding lining pieces to wrong side of matching top pieces (**NOTE**: Seams of joined top and joined lining pieces do not align.), with Royal, Whipstitch together through all thicknesses at seams according to Top Assembly Diagram. (**NOTE**: If desired, reinforce roof by inserting one or two thin plastic rulers between lining and top.)

6: With cord, Whipstitch cutout edges of sunroof together. With Royal, Whipstitch overhang pieces and top together according to Roof Assembly Diagram.

7: Set roof aside.

A – Sunroof Top & Lining

(cut 1 from blue & 1 from clear) 41 x 90 holes

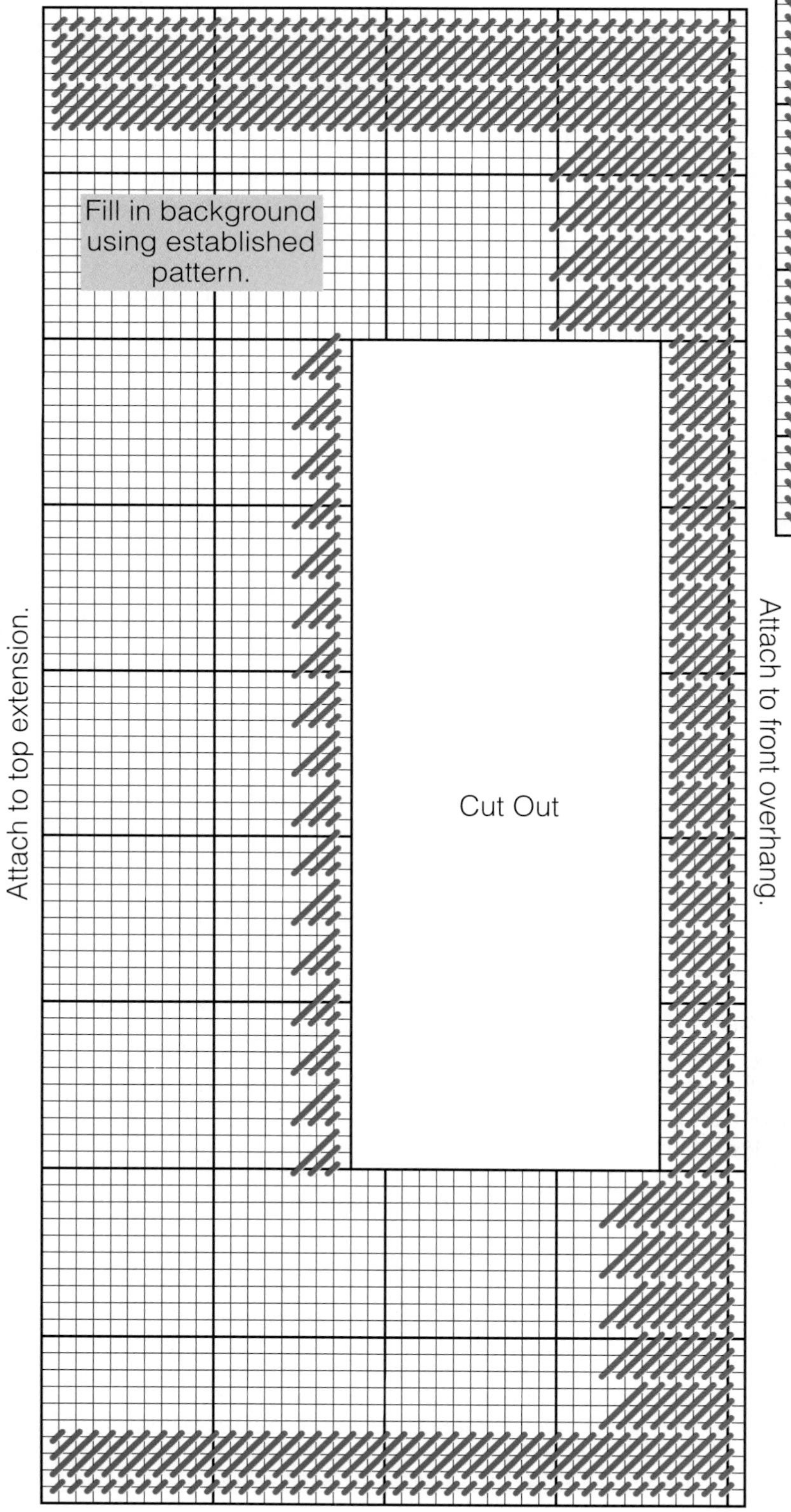

Work over to H to join.

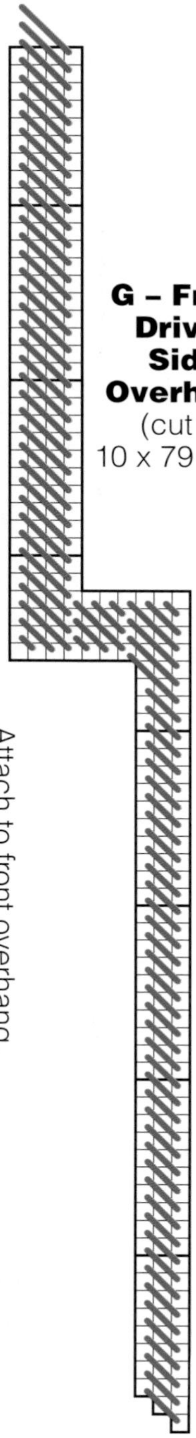

G – Front Driver Side Overhang

(cut 2)
10 x 79 holes

H – Rear Driver Side Overhang

(cut 2)
10 x 90 holes

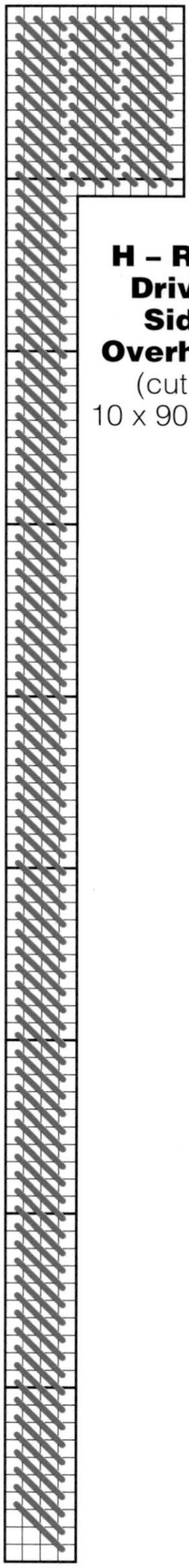

Work over from G to join.

E – Rear Top & Lining

(cut 1 from clear & 1 from blue) 70 x 90 holes

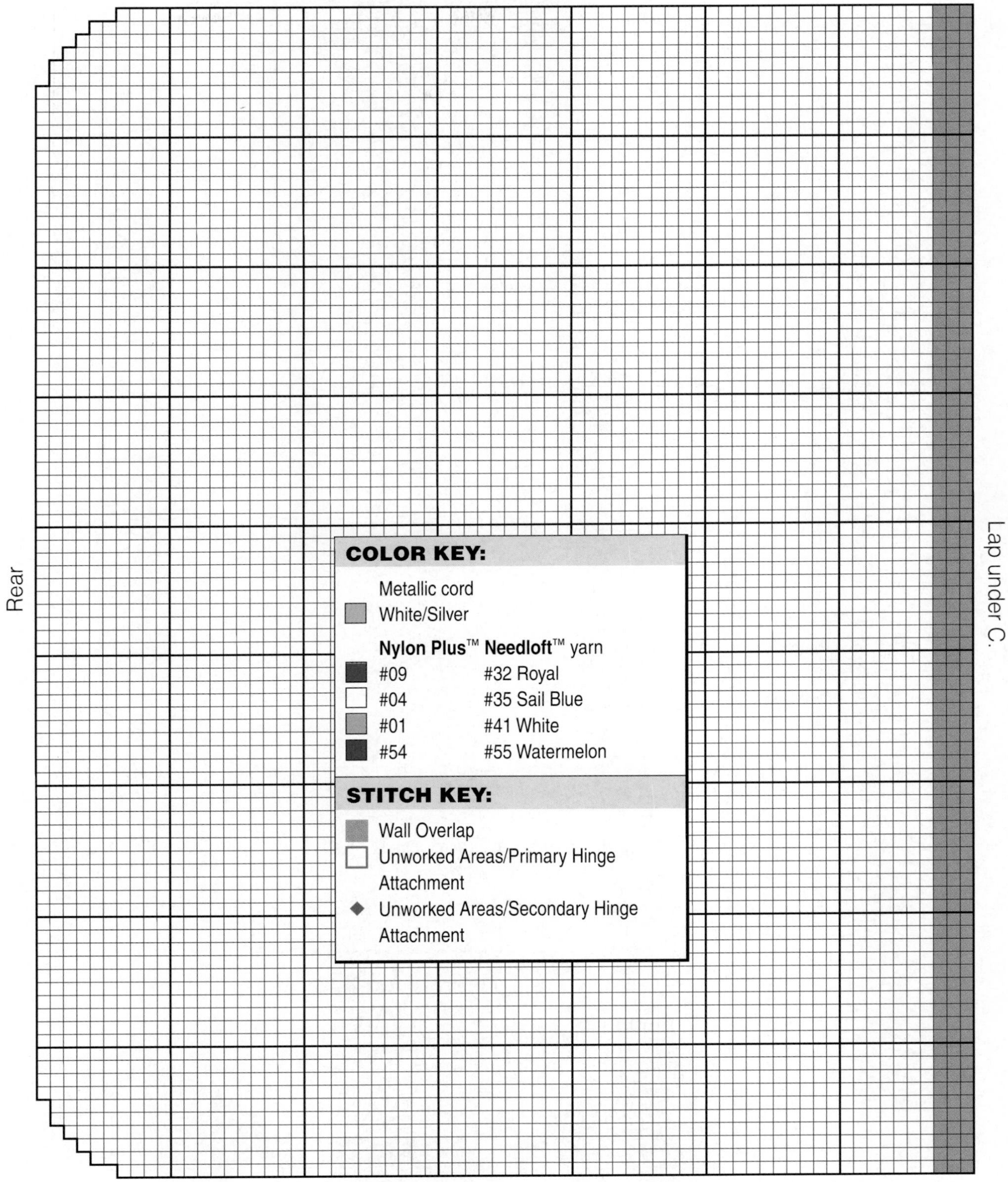

COLOR KEY:

Metallic cord
- White/Silver

Nylon Plus™ Needloft™ yarn

#09	#32 Royal
#04	#35 Sail Blue
#01	#41 White
#54	#55 Watermelon

STITCH KEY:

- Wall Overlap
- Unworked Areas/Primary Hinge Attachment
- ◆ Unworked Areas/Secondary Hinge Attachment

Work over from I to join.

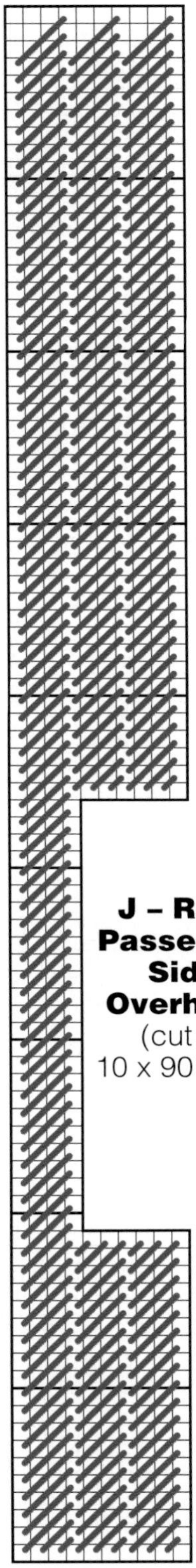

J – Rear Passenger Side Overhang
(cut 2)
10 x 90 holes

Top Assembly Diagram

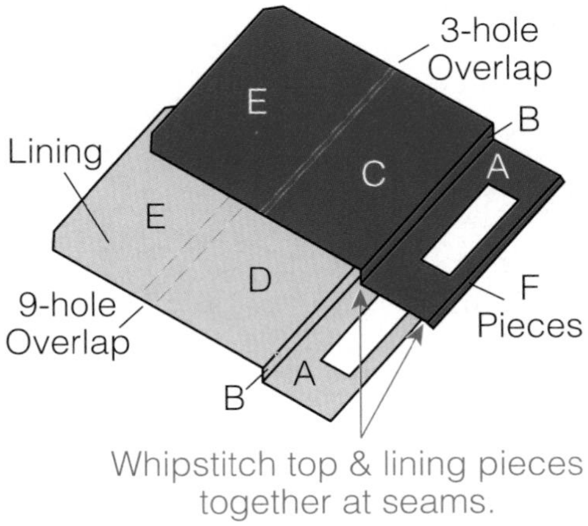

Slanted Gobelin Stitch Illustration
(over 3 bars)

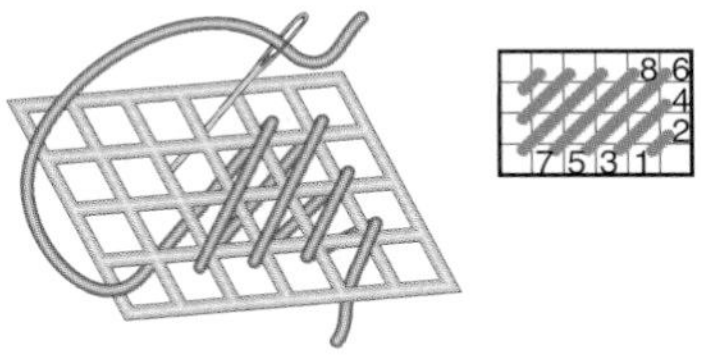

I – Front Passenger Side Overhang
(cut 2)
10 x 79 holes

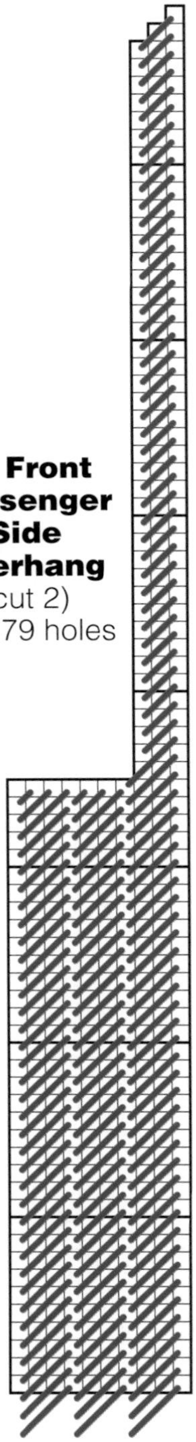

Work over to J to join.

COLOR KEY:

Metallic cord		
▩	White/Silver	
Nylon Plus™	**Needloft™** yarn	
▩	#09	#32 Royal
□	#04	#35 Sail Blue
▩	#01	#41 White
▩	#54	#55 Watermelon

STITCH KEY:

- ▩ Wall Overlap
- □ Unworked Areas/Primary Hinge Attachment
- ◆ Unworked Areas/Secondary Hinge Attachment

Roof Assembly Diagrams

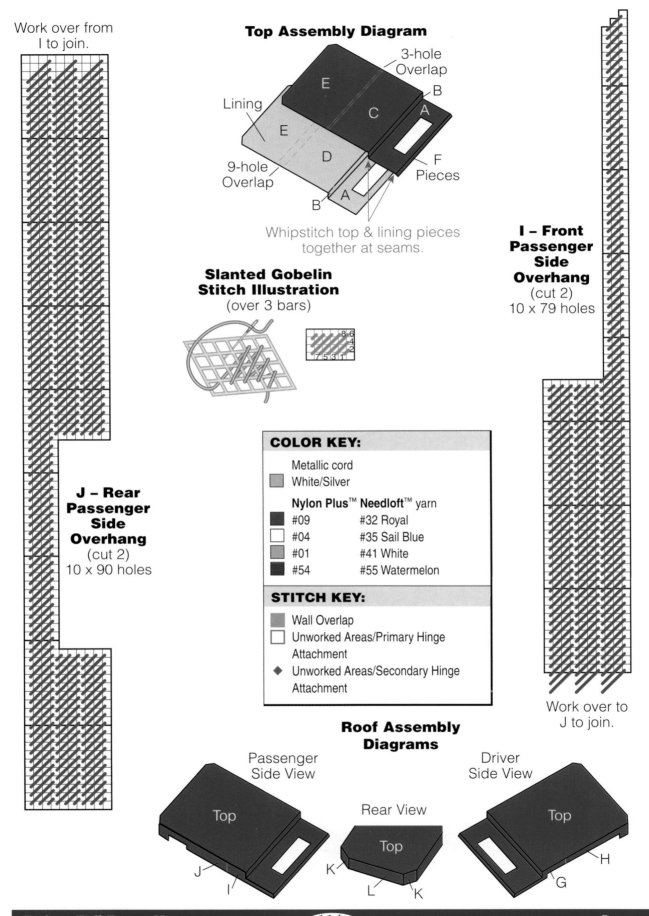

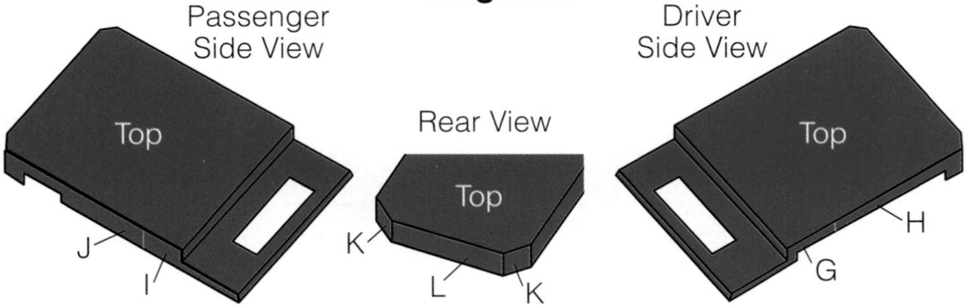

INTERIOR WALLS

CUTTING INSTRUCTIONS:

NOTE: Graphs continued on pages 116-119.

A: For cab passenger side wall, cut one from blue according to graph.

B: For bathroom wall, cut one from white according to graph.

C: For kitchen wall, cut one from blue according to graph.

D: For back corner walls, cut two from blue 8 x 70 holes (no graph).

E: For back wall, cut one from blue according to graph.

F: For back door support wall, cut one from blue according to graph.

G: For large window support wall, cut one from blue according to graph.

H: For cab driver side wall, cut one from blue according to graph.

I: For windshield wall, cut one from blue according to Windshield Exterior Wall I graph on page 106.

J: For front hood wall, cut one from blue 13 x 88 holes (no graph).

K: For grille wall, cut one from blue 26 x 88 holes (no graph).

STITCHING INSTRUCTIONS:

NOTE: A, D and F-K pieces are unworked.

1: Using colors and stitches indicated, work B, C and E pieces according to graphs, leaving uncoded areas unworked.

2: For passenger side wall, overlapping A-C pieces as indicated, using White and Running Stitch (see Stitch Illustration on page 116), stitch overlap areas together through both thicknesses according to graphs.

3: Set pieces aside.

COLOR KEY:

	Nylon Plus™	Needloft™ yarn
▢	#11	#07 Pink
▢	#04	#35 Sail Blue
▢	#01	#41 White

STITCH KEY:

- Running Stitch
- Wall Overlap
- Shower Wall Placement
- Towel Rack Placement

A – Cab Passenger Side Interior Wall

(cut 1 from blue) 55 x 63 holes

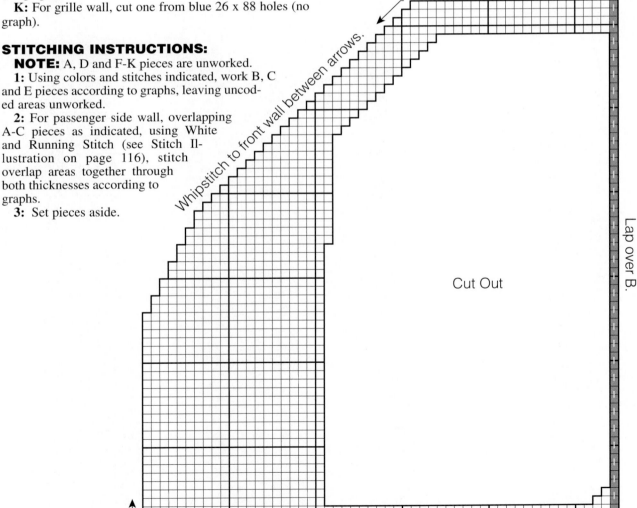

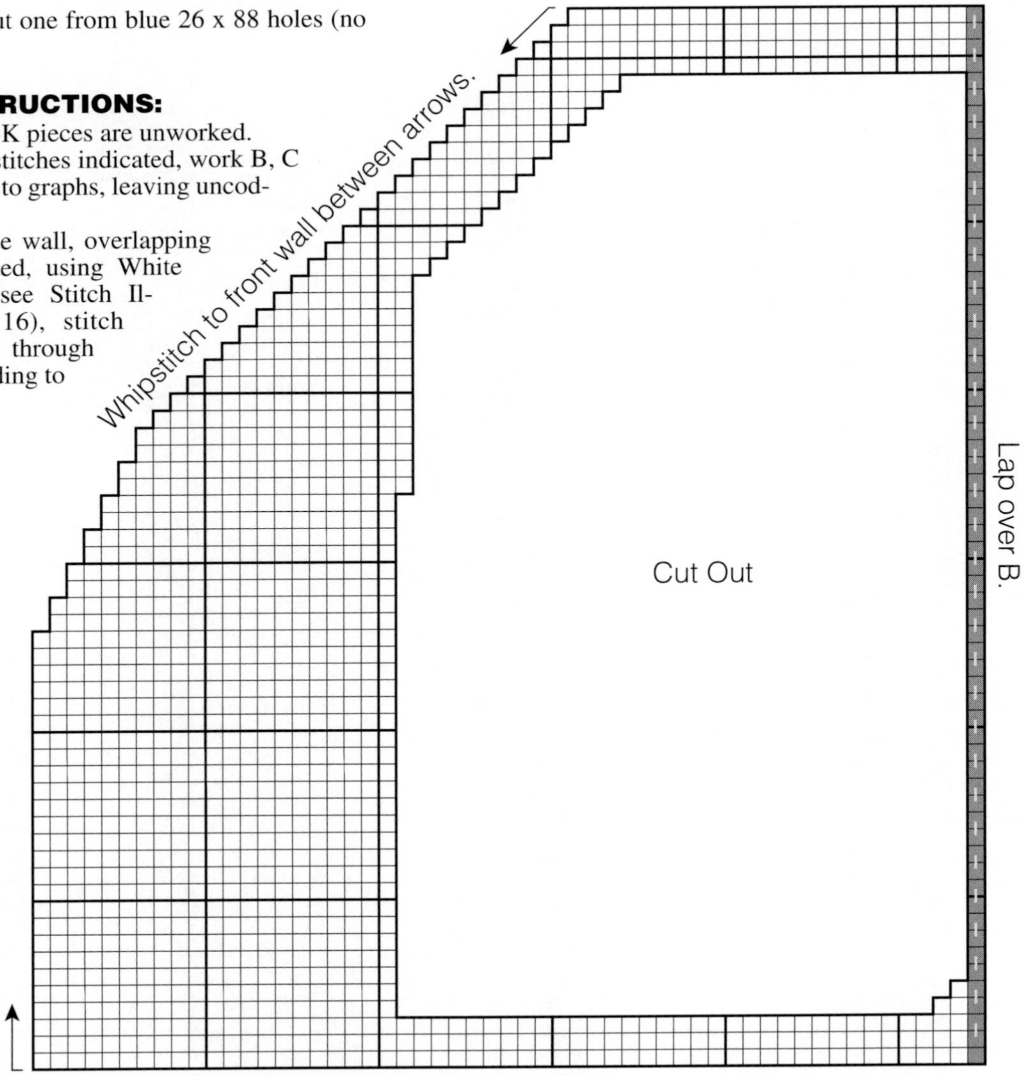

COLOR KEY:

	Nylon Plus™	Needloft™ yarn
▢	#11	#07 Pink
▢	#04	#35 Sail Blue
▢	#01	#41 White

STITCH KEY:

- — Running Stitch
- ▢ Wall Overlap
- — Shower Wall Placement
- O Towel Rack Placement

Running Stitch Illustration

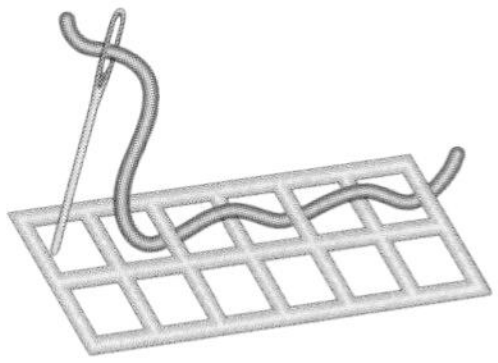

B – Interior Bathroom Wall
(cut 1 from white)
65 x 70 holes

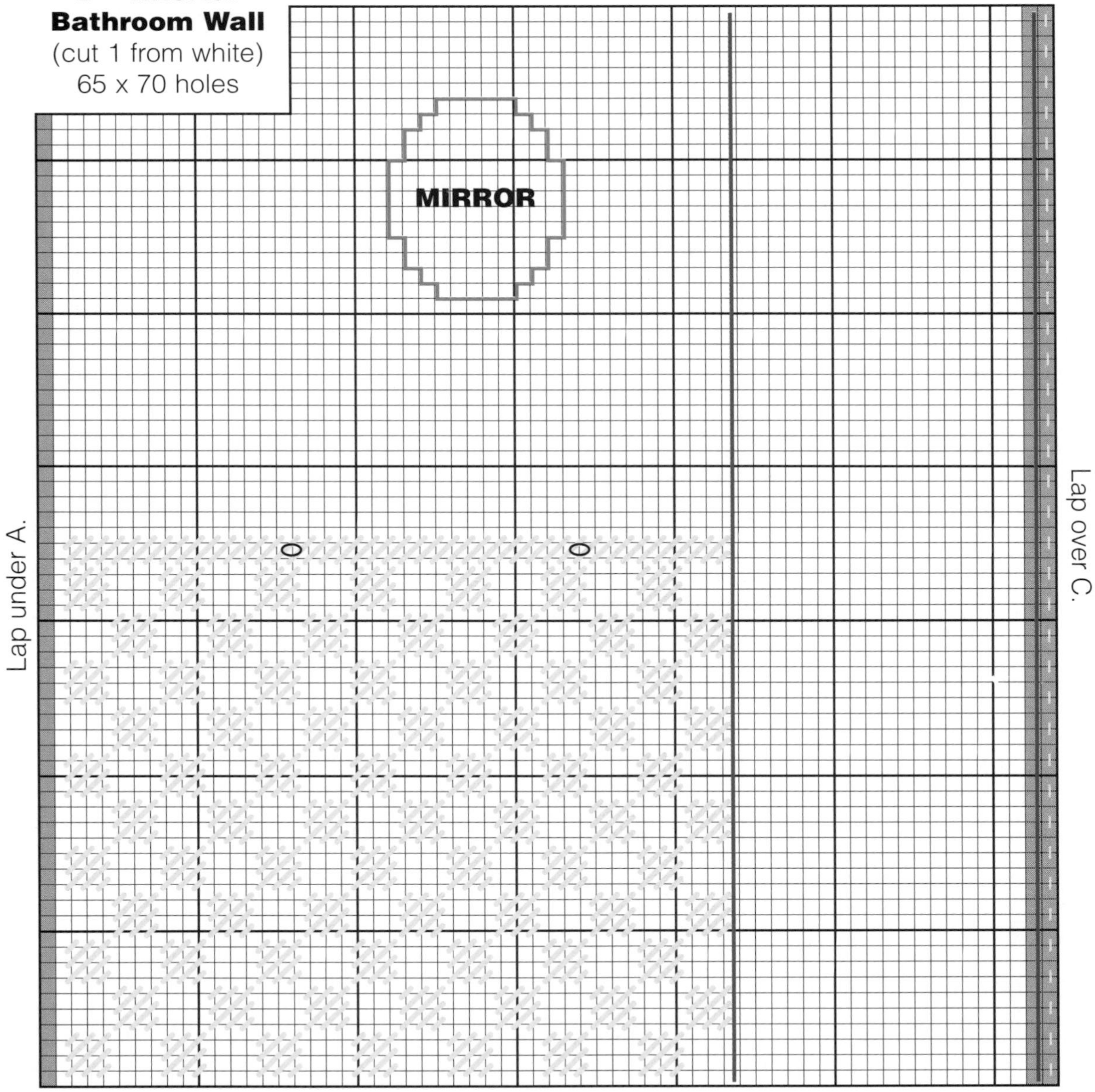

C – Interior Kitchen Wall

(cut 1 from blue) 70 x 78 holes

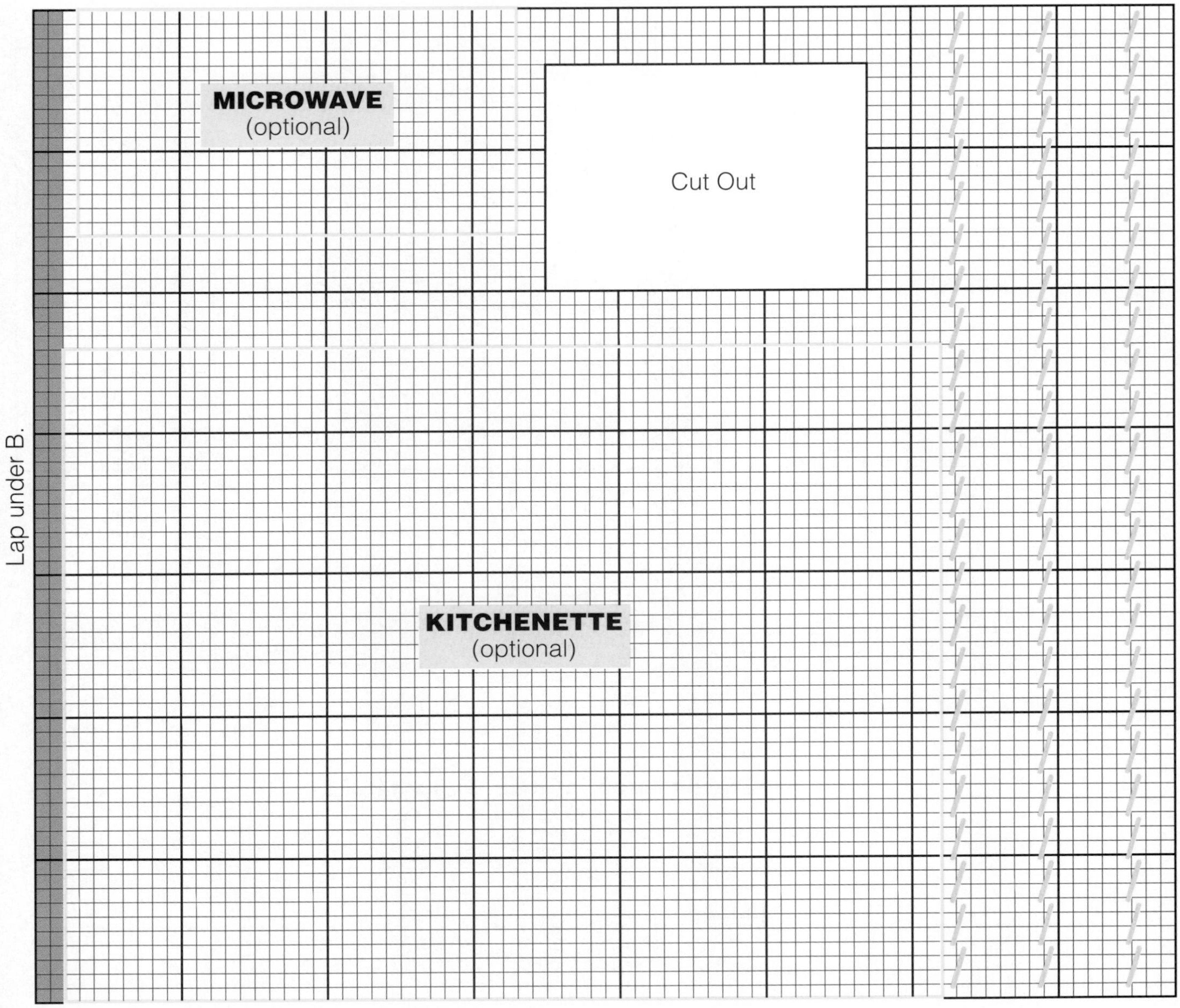

E – Interior Back Wall

(cut 1 from blue) 52 x 76 holes

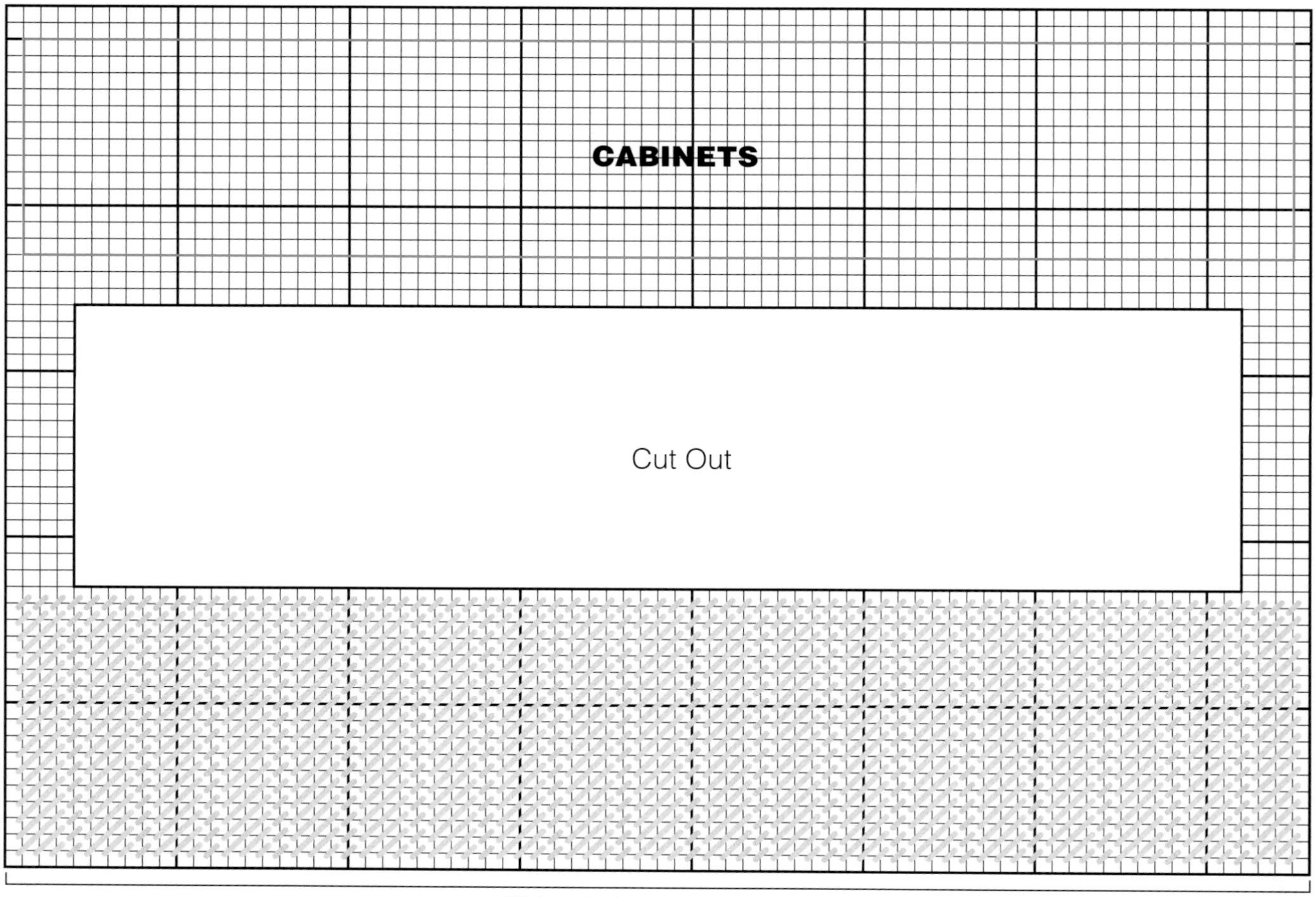

Whipstitch to window seat A.

F – Back Door Interior Support Wall

(cut 1 from blue)
38 x 70 holes

Lap over G.

Top

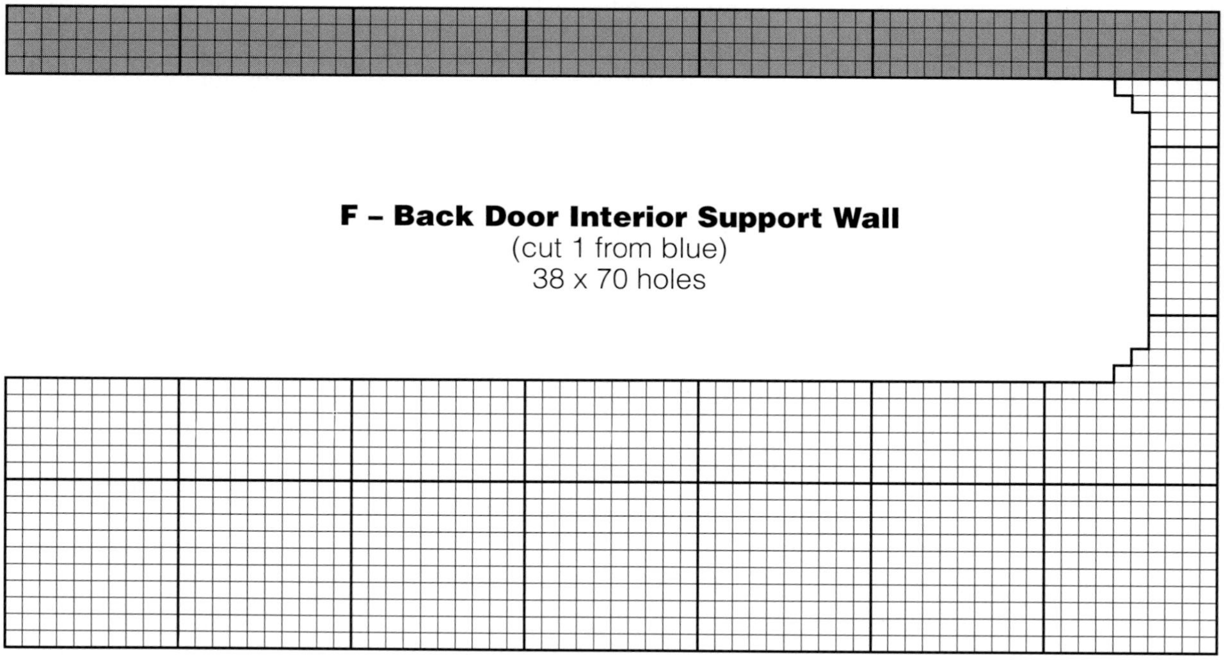

G – Large Window Interior Support Wall

(cut 1 from blue) 70 x 90 holes

H – Cab Driver Side Interior Wall

(cut 1 from blue) 70 x 74 holes

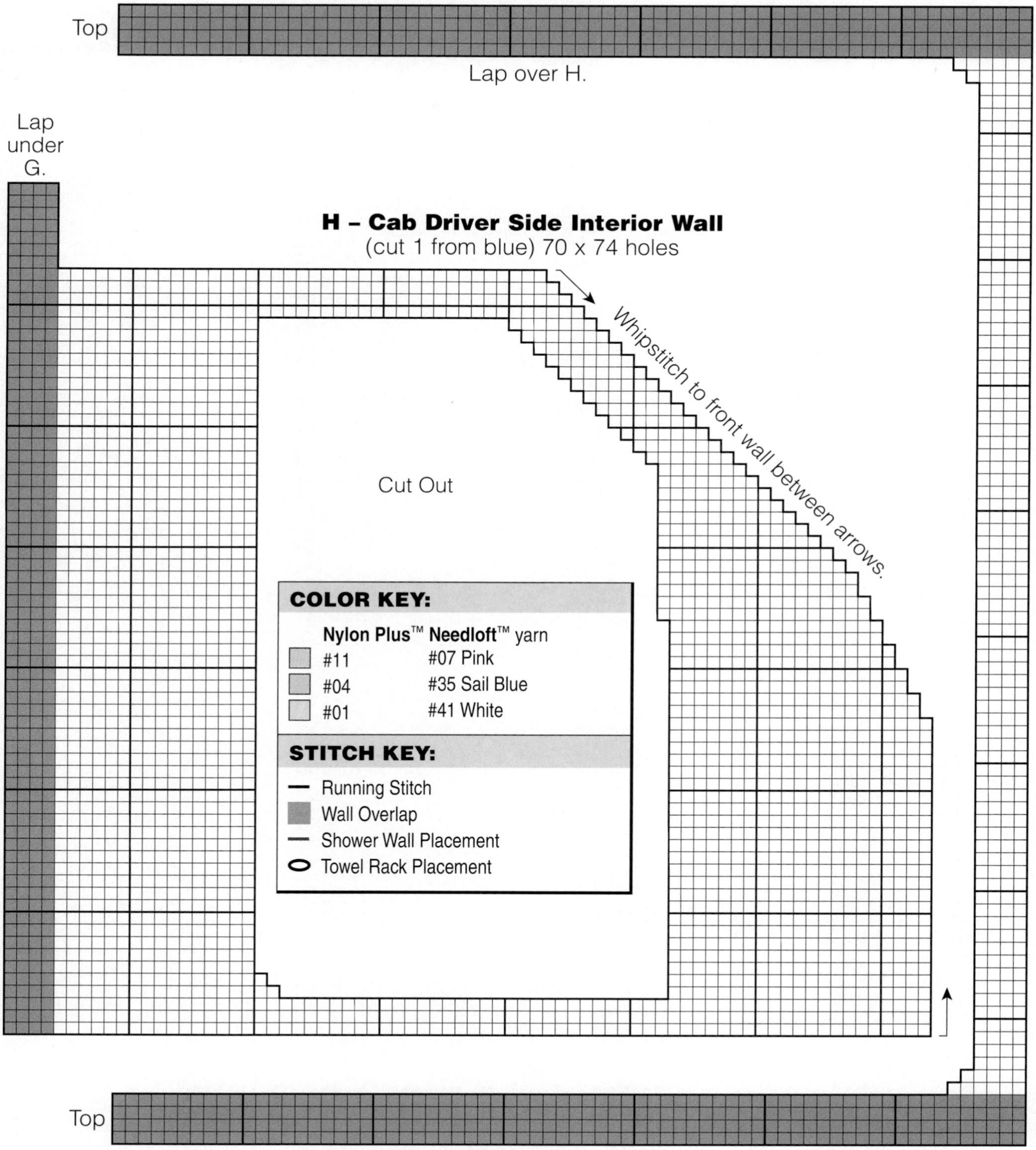

COLOR KEY:

	Nylon Plus™	**Needloft™** yarn
	#11	#07 Pink
	#04	#35 Sail Blue
	#01	#41 White

STITCH KEY:

- Running Stitch
- Wall Overlap
- Shower Wall Placement
- Towel Rack Placement

WINDOW SEAT

CUTTING INSTRUCTIONS:

NOTE: Use clear canvas for all pieces.

A: For seat, cut one according to graph.

B: For flap, cut one 4 x 86 holes (no graph).

C: For front, cut one 18 x 88.

D: For supports, cut two 18 x 20 holes (no graph).

STITCHING INSTRUCTIONS:

NOTE: D pieces are unworked.

1: Using colors and stitches indicated, work A according to graph; work B over narrow width according to pattern established on A. Using Sail Blue and stitches indicated, work C according to graph, leaving indicated areas unworked; Overcast unfinished edges.

2: Whipstitch A and B together at one matching straight edge; Overcast unfinished edges. Whipstitch one 18-hole edge of one D to each end of C as indicated.

3: Set pieces aside.

A – Window Seat
(cut 1) 21 x 86 holes

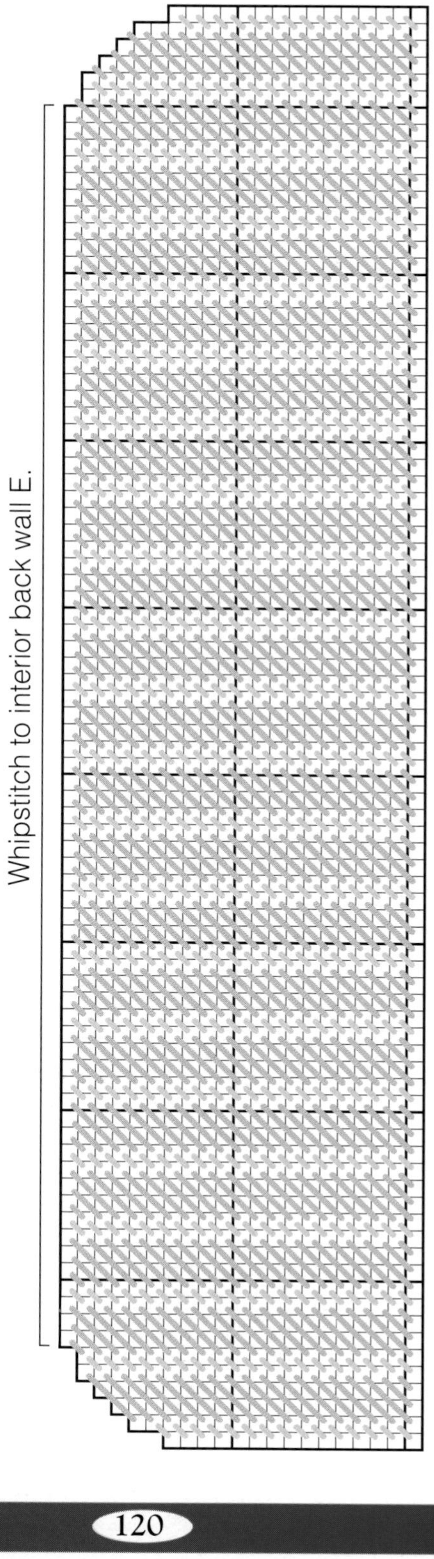

C – Window Seat Front
(cut 1) 18 x 88 holes

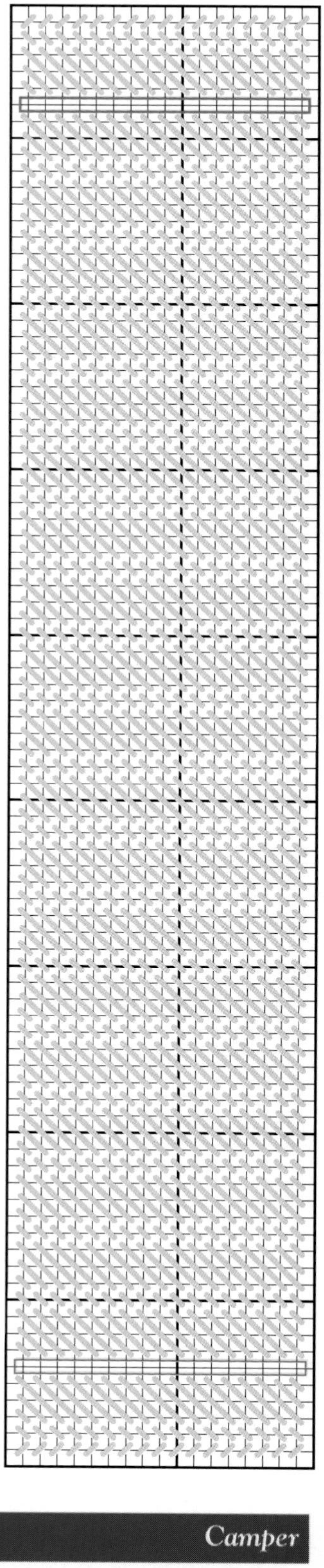

COLOR KEY:

Nylon Plus™	Needloft™ yarn
#04	#35 Sail Blue
#01	#41 White

STITCH KEY:

Unworked Areas

CABINETS

CUTTING INSTRUCTIONS:

NOTE: Graphs on page 122.

A: For cabinet front, cut one from clear according to graph.

B: For cabinet back, cut one from clear 15 x 74 holes (no graph).

C: For cabinet top and bottom, cut two (one for top and one for bottom) from clear 10 x 74 holes (no graph).

D: For cabinet ends, cut two from clear 10 x 15 holes (no graph).

E: For doors and linings, cut eight (four from clear for doors and four from white for linings) according to graph.

F: For hinges, cut four from clear 6 x 8 holes (no graph).

STITCHING INSTRUCTIONS:

NOTE: B and white E pieces are unworked.

1: Using Sail Blue and stitches indicated, work A and clear E (two on opposite side of canvas) pieces for doors

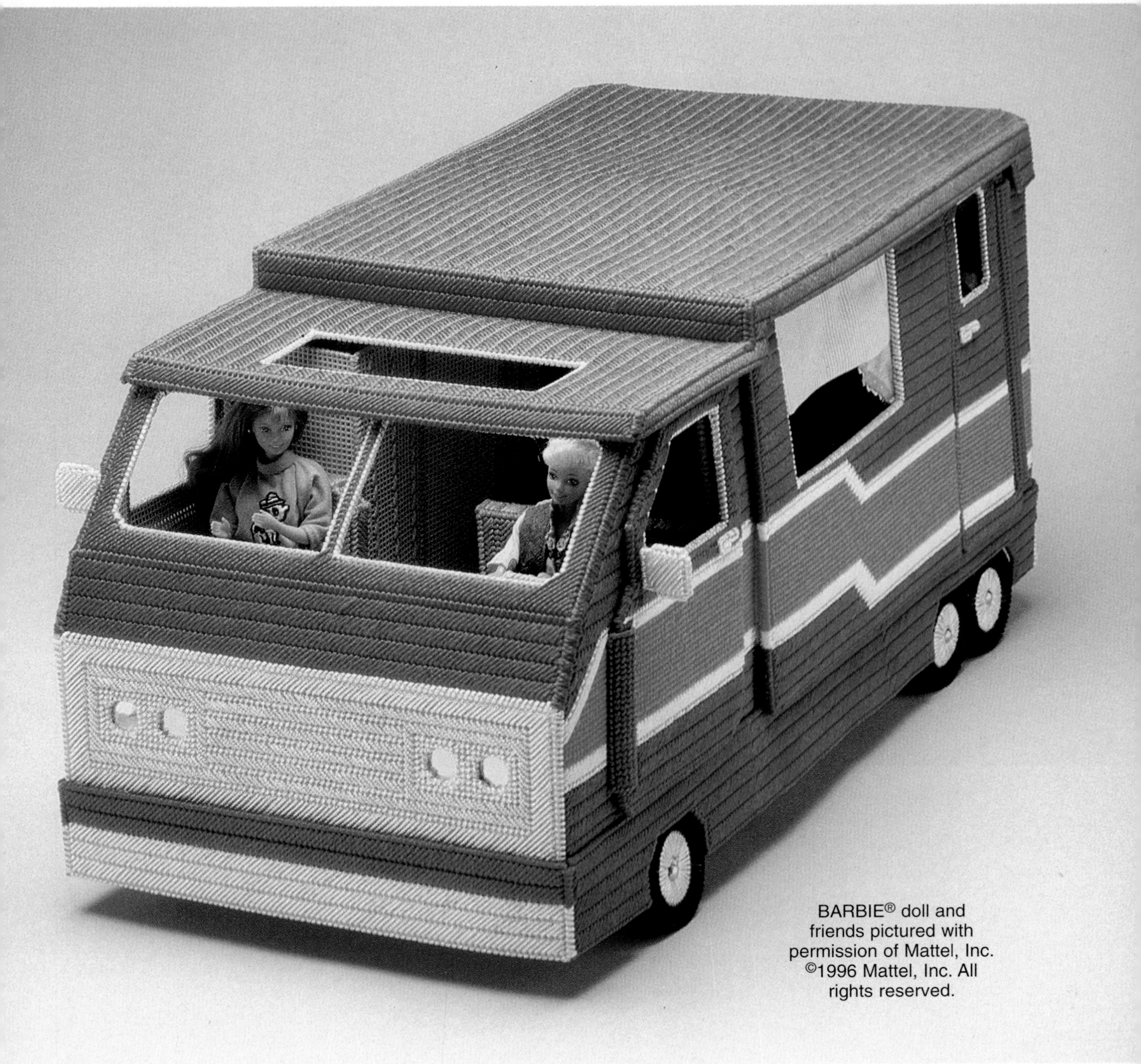

BARBIE® doll and friends pictured with permission of Mattel, Inc. ©1996 Mattel, Inc. All rights reserved.

according to graphs; using Slanted Gobelin Stitch over 3 bars, work C and D pieces across 10-hole width in vertical rows. Using Continental Stitch, work F pieces.

2: For each door, holding one lining E to wrong side of one door E, Whipstitch together. Overcast cutout edges of A and long edges of each F.

3: To attach each center door, Whipstitch one 6-hole edge of one F to A as indicated (Primary Hinge Attachment). Slip hinge through cutout on one door; Whipstitch opposite end to A as indicated (Secondary Hinge Attachment).

4: To attach each end door, working through all thicknesses to join D pieces as you work secondary hinge attachment, Whipstitch hinges to front as in Step 3. Whipstitch A-D pieces together, forming cabinet.

NOTE: Trim Velcro® closures to about ¼" x ½".

5: Glue closures to inside of each door and to corresponding areas on front. For door handles, glue one black 8-mm. stone to each door as indicated.

6: Whipstitch top edge of cabinet to interior back wall as indicated.

7: Set pieces aside.

COLOR KEY:

	Nylon Plus™	Needloft™ yarn
(light square)	#04	#35 Sail Blue
(dark square)	#01	#41 White

STITCH KEY:

- ▼ Primary Hinge Attachment
- ◆ Secondary Hinge Attachment
- O Stone Placement

A – Cabinet Front

(cut 1) 15 x 74 holes

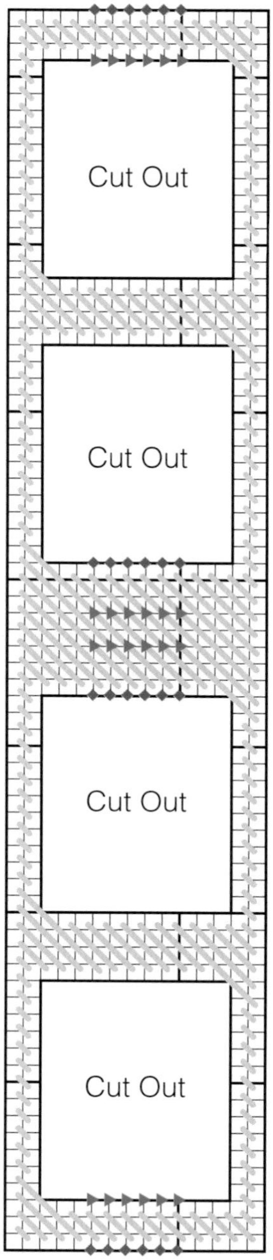

E – Door & Lining

(cut 4 from clear & 4 from white)
12 x 17 holes

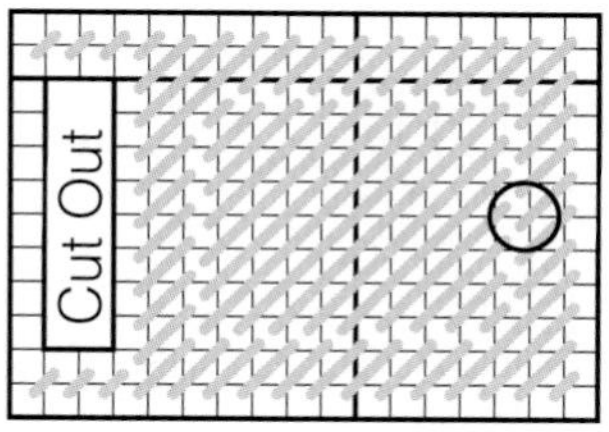

BATHROOM WALLS

CUTTING INSTRUCTIONS:

A: For front wall, cut two (one from white for inside wall and one from blue for outside wall) 24 x 62 holes (no graph).

B: For side wall, cut two (one from white for inside wall and one from blue for outside wall) 18 x 62 holes (no graph).

C: For bathroom door and lining, cut two (one from blue for door and one from white for lining) 21 x 62 holes (no graph).

D: For back and side shower walls, cut four (two from white for inside walls and two from blue for outside walls) 24 x 70 holes (no graph).

E: For shower door, cut two from white according to graph.

F: For shower floor, cut one from white 20 x 24 holes (no graph).

STITCHING INSTRUCTIONS:

NOTES: Blue A, white D and E pieces are unworked.

Stitch pattern guides and diagrams on page 124.

1: Using Sail Blue and stitches indicated, work white A and B pieces according to Bathroom Interior Wall Stitch Pattern Guide. Using Pink and stitches indicated, work blue B and blue D pieces according to Bathroom Exterior Wall Stitch Pattern Guide.

2: Holding blue A to wrong side of worked piece, B pieces wrong sides together and C pieces together with canvas colors matching walls, with Sail Blue, Whipstitch together through all thicknesses according to Front, Side & Door Assembly Diagram; Whipstitch outside edges together.

3: Using cord and stitches indicated, embroider knob through both thicknesses at center outside edge of door according to Knob Stitch Pattern; embroider drain at center of F according to Drain Stitch Pattern.

4: For shower door, holding E pieces together, with White, Whipstitch cutout edges together. Whipstitch one long edge of shower door, floor and white D pieces together according to Shower Interior Assembly Diagram; Whipstitch edges of shower door together.

5: Holding worked D pieces wrong sides together with shower interior walls, with Sail Blue, Whipstitch edges together according to Shower Exterior Assembly Diagram.

6: Set walls aside.

Drain Stitch Pattern

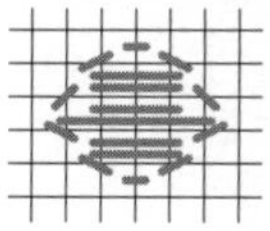

Knob Stitch Pattern

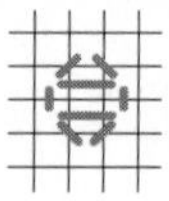

COLOR KEY:

Metallic cord		
■	White/Silver	
Nylon Plus™ Needloft™ yarn		
□	#11	#07 Pink
□	#04	#35 Sail Blue
□	#01	#41 White

E – Shower Door
(cut 2) 24 x 70 holes

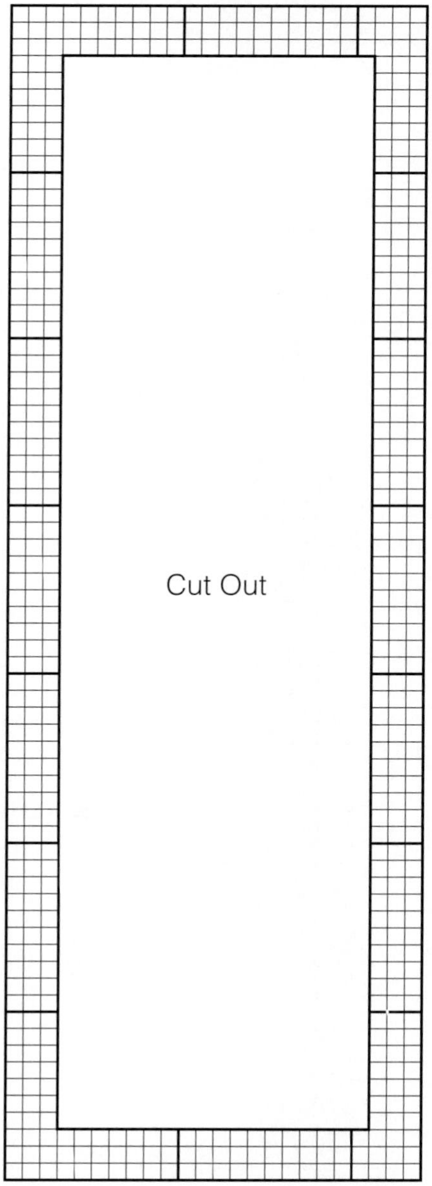

Front, Side & Door Assembly Diagram

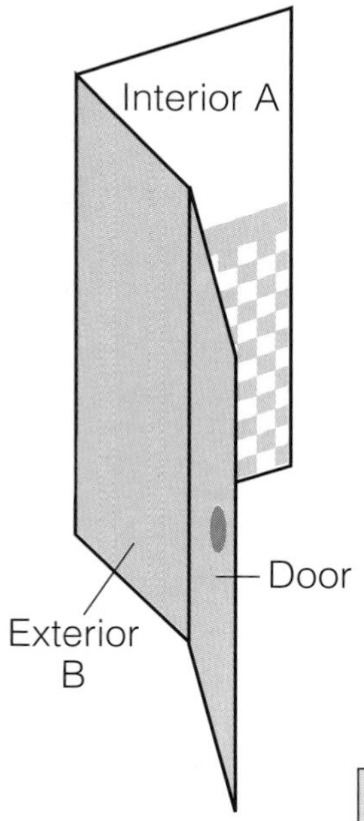

Bathroom Exterior Wall Stitch Pattern Guide

(Work blue canvas.)

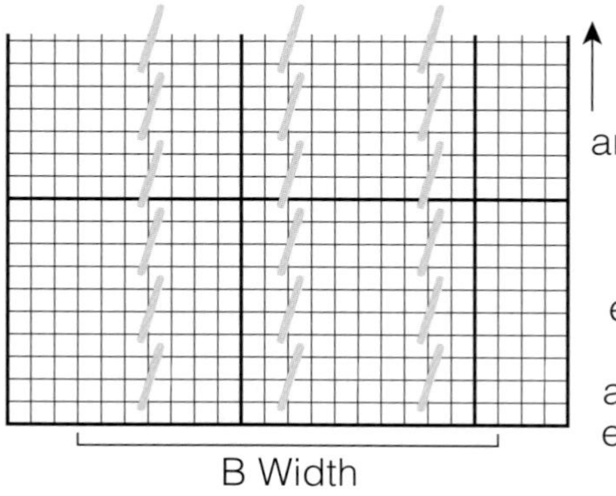

Leave uncoded areas of each piece unworked; continue established pattern across each entire piece.

Shower Interior Assembly Diagram

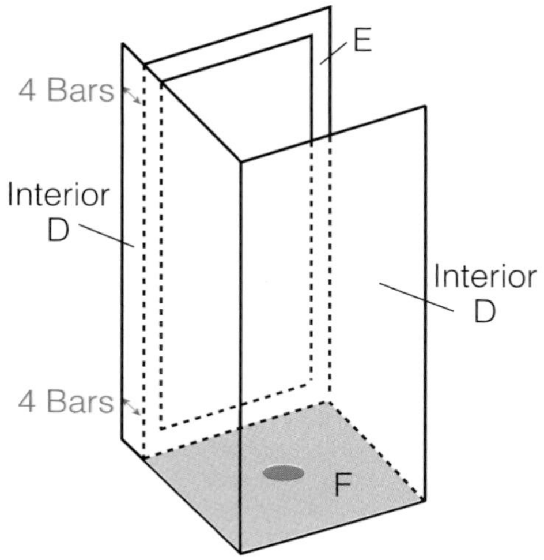

COLOR KEY:

	Metallic cord	
■	White/Silver	
	Nylon Plus™	**Needloft™** yarn
□	#11	#07 Pink
□	#04	#35 Sail Blue
□	#01	#41 White

Bathroom Interior Wall Stitch Pattern Guide

(Work white canvas.)

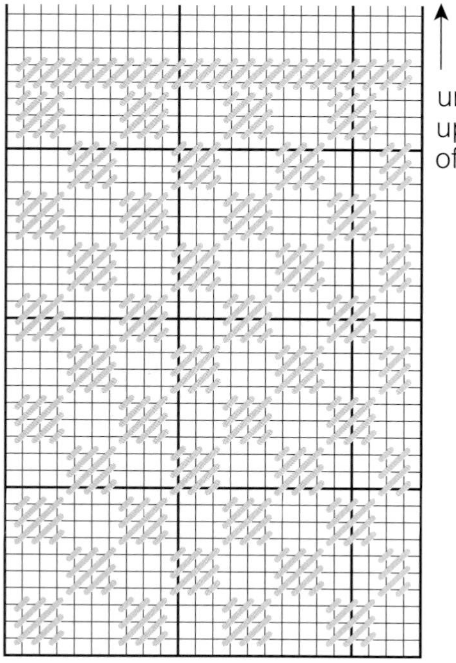

Leave uncoded and upper portion of each piece unworked.

Shower Exterior Assembly Diagram

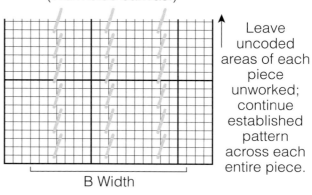

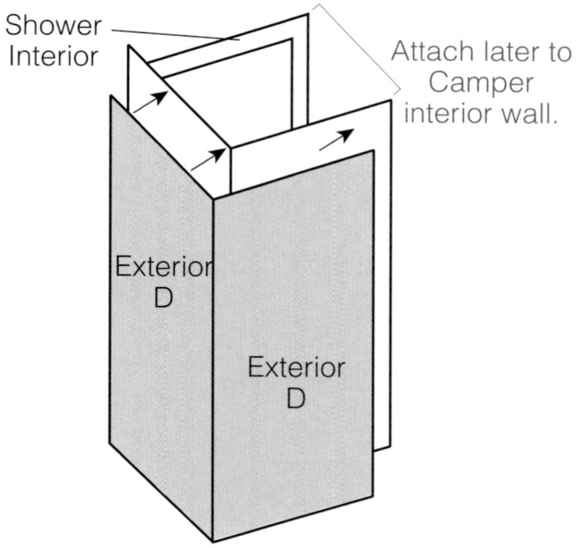

BATHROOM COMMODE

CUTTING INSTRUCTIONS:

NOTE: Use clear canvas for all pieces.

A: For bowl front, cut one according to graph.

B: For bowl back, cut one according to graph.

C: For seat, cut one according to graph.

D: For bowl bottom, cut one 7 x 9 holes (no graph).

E: For lid, cut one according to graph.

F: For tank front and back, cut two (one for front and one for back) 11 x 14 holes (no graph).

G: For tank sides, cut two 2 x 11 holes (no graph).

H: For tank top, cut one 3 x 16 holes (no graph).

I: For tank bottom, cut one 2 x 14 holes (no graph).

STITCHING INSTRUCTIONS:

NOTE: D and I pieces are unworked.

1: Using White and Continental Stitch, work A-C pieces; using Slanted Gobelin Stitch over narrow width, work F pieces according to graph and work E, G and H pieces. Overcast cutout edges of C and side and front edges of E as indicated on graph. Using cord and Straight Stitch, embroider handle on one F for tank front as indicated.

2: For bowl, Whipstitch X edges of A together as indicated; Whipstitch A-C pieces together according to Bowl Assembly Diagram. (**NOTE:** Seat is slightly larger than bowl top.) Whipstitch D to bottom of bowl.

3: Whipstitch unfinished edge of lid to back of bowl. Whipstitch F, G and I together; Overcast unfinished edges of tank and tank top. Glue tank top to tank and tank and bowl together according to Commode Assembly Diagram.

4: Set commode aside.

A – Commode Bowl Front
(cut 1) 12 x 31 holes

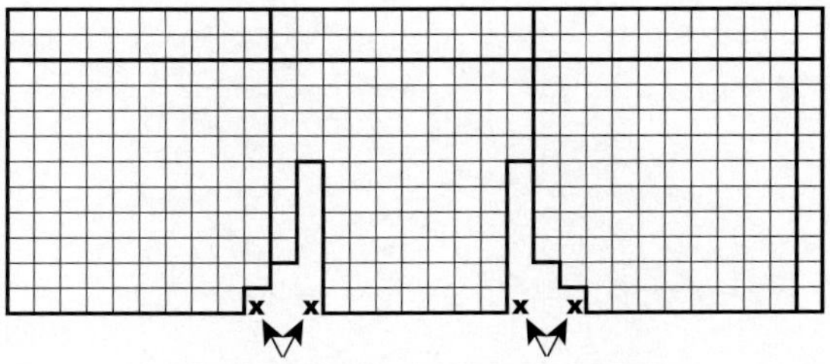

Whipstitch X edges together.

B – Commode Bowl Back
(cut 1)
9 x 12 holes

Top

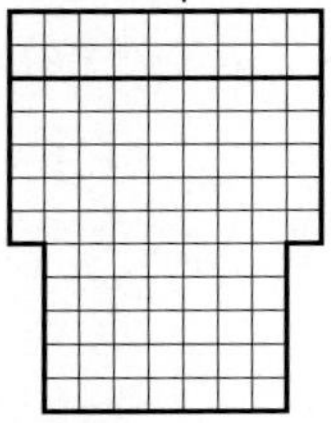

C – Commode Seat
(cut 1)
12 x 14 holes

Whipstitch to back of bowl.

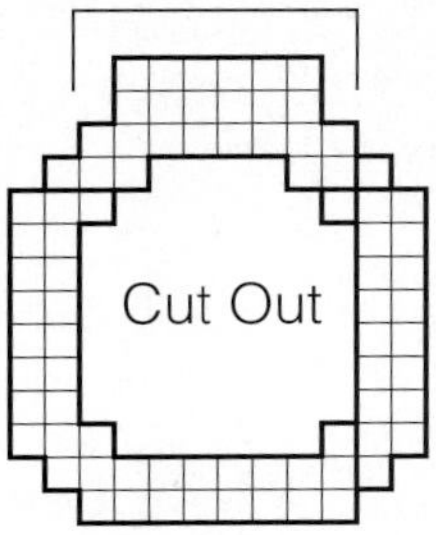

COLOR KEY:

Metallic cord
White/Silver

Nylon Plus™ Needloft™ yarn
#11 #07 Pink
#04 #35 Sail Blue
#01 #41 White

Bowl Assembly Diagram

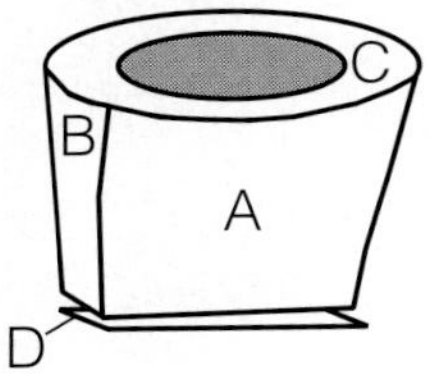

E – Commode Lid
(cut 1)
12 x 14 holes

Whipstitch to back of bowl.

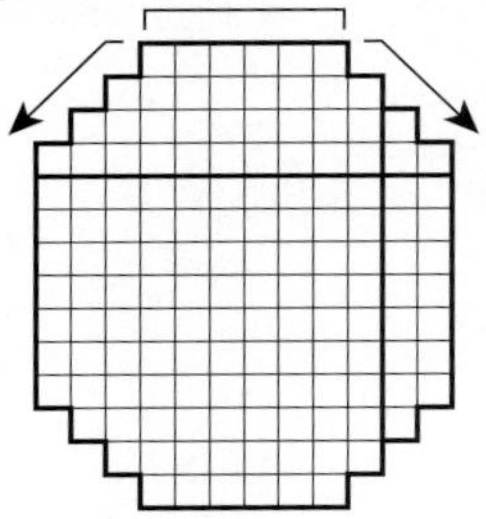

Overcast between arrows.

F – Commode Tank Front & Back
(cut 1 each)
11 x 14 holes

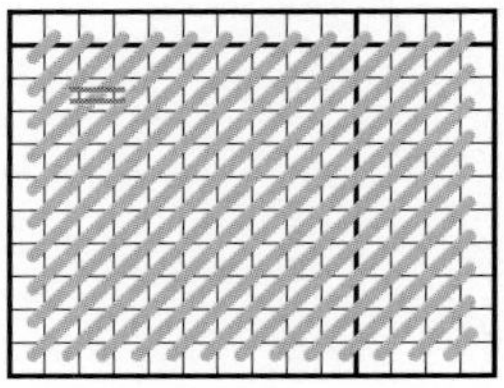

Commode Assembly Diagram

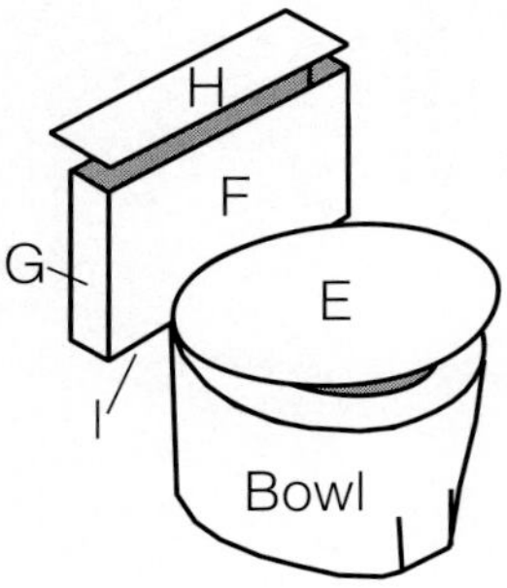

BATHROOM HARDWARE

CUTTING INSTRUCTIONS:

NOTE: Use clear canvas for all pieces.

A: For towel rack, cut one according to graph.

B: For mirror, cut one according to graph.

C: For shower head long and short sides, cut one each according to graph.

D: For shower head, cut one according to graph.

E: For shower hook, cut two according to graph.

STITCHING INSTRUCTIONS:

1: For towel rack, using cord and stitches indicated, work A according to graph; Overcast unfinished edges. For mirror, using Pink and stitches indicated, work B according to graph; Overcast edges. Glue one acrylic mirror to center of B.

2: For shower head, using White and Continental Stitch, work C pieces on opposite sides of canvas; holding pieces wrong sides together, Whipstitch together as indicated. Using cord and stitches indicated, work D

according to graph; Whipstitch to unfinished open edges of shower head sides.

3: For shower head hook, using Sail Blue and Continental Stitch, work E pieces on opposite sides of canvas; holding pieces wrong sides together, Whipstitch together.

4: Glue shower hook as indicated to upper area of wall opposite shower door. Glue one silver 8-mm. bead to wall below and on either side of hook (see Shower Hardware Assembly Diagram). Run a thin line of glue on unfinished bar of shower head; insert bar into one end of plastic tubing and glue opposite end to wall under hook. Place shower head over hook.

5: Set pieces aside.

A – Hardware Towel Rack
(cut 1)
4 x 19 holes

Shower Hardware Assembly Diagram

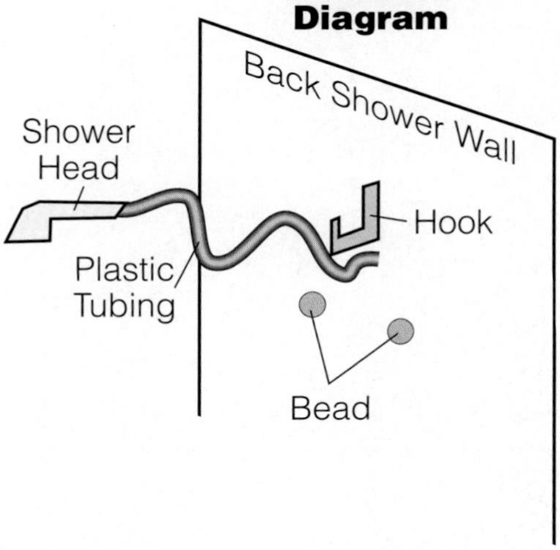

COLOR KEY:	
Metallic cord	
White/Silver	
Nylon Plus™	**Needloft™** yarn
#11	#07 Pink
#04	#35 Sail Blue
#01	#41 White

B – Hardware Mirror
(cut 1)
11 x 13 holes

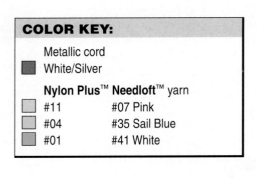

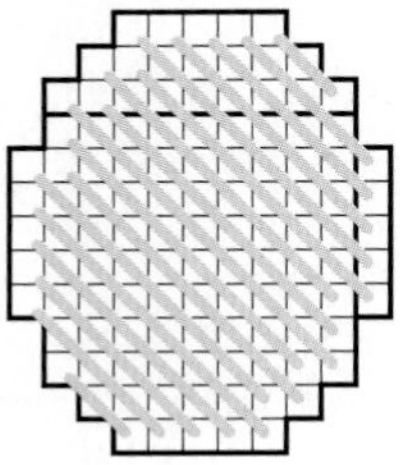

D – Hardware Shower Head
(cut 1)
3 x 3 holes

E – Hardware Shower Hook
(cut 2)
6 x 7 holes

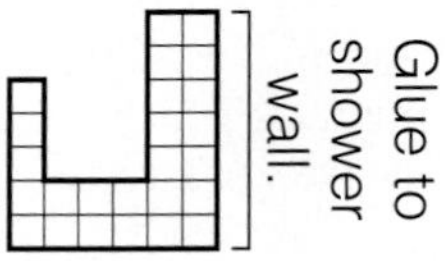

C – Hardware Shower Head Long & Short Side
(cut 1 each)
Long Side 4 x 18 holes
Short Side 4 x 13 holes

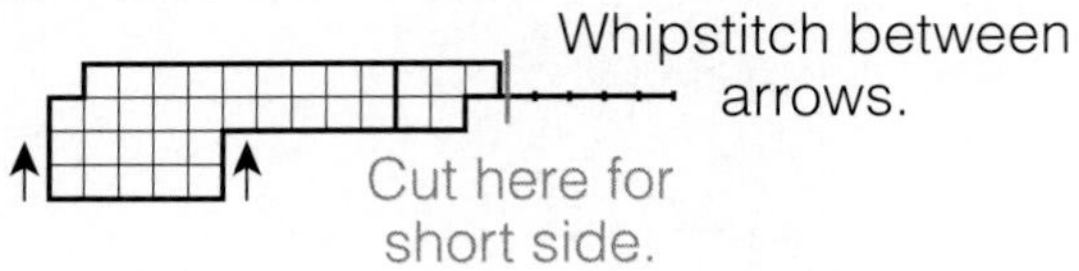

DASH & CONSOLE

CUTTING INSTRUCTIONS:

A: For dashboard front, cut two from clear according to graph.

B: For dashboard top, cut two from clear 13 x 86 holes (no graph).

C: For console top, cut one from clear according to graph.

D: For console sides, cut two from clear according to graph.

E: For console front pieces, cut two from clear 11 x 21 holes and one from clear 14 x 21 holes (no graphs).

F: For steering wheel, cut two from clear according to graph.

G: For steering column, cut one from clear according to graph.

H: For glove compartment door and lining, cut two (one from clear for door and one from white for lining) 11 x 24 holes.

I: For glove compartment interior pieces, cut two from white 10 x 24 holes, two from white 9 x 10 holes and one from white 9 x 24 holes (no graphs).

J: For footboard, cut two from clear 10 x 86 holes (no graph).

K: For pedals, cut two from clear 3 x 7 holes (no graph).

STITCHING INSTRUCTIONS:

NOTE: One B, one F, white H, I and one J pieces are unworked.

1: Using colors and stitches indicated, work one A (leave indicated and uncoded areas unworked), C, D (one on opposite side of canvas), one F and clear H according to graphs. Using metallic braid and cord in colors indicated, Backstitch and Straight Stitch, embroider A as indicated.

2: Using Silver for dashboard and Pink for footboard and Slanted Gobelin Stitch over 2 bars, work one B and one J piece in horizontal rows across length. Using Silver and Slanted Gobelin Stitch over 2 bars, work E pieces across narrow width in horizontal rows.

3: Using Silver for steering column, Black for pedals and Continental Stitch, work G and K pieces; with matching colors, Overcast edges. For dashboard, steering wheel and footboard, holding unworked pieces to wrong side of matching worked pieces, with matching colors, Whipstitch B, F and J pieces together.

4: For glove compartment, with Gray, Whipstitch I pieces together according to Glove Compartment Assembly Diagram. Holding unworked A to wrong side of worked piece, Whipstitch glove compartment assembly through all thicknesses to wrong side of cutout on dashboard front; Whipstitch remaining edges of A pieces together.

5: For glove compartment door, holding lining H to wrong side of door H, Whipstitch side and top edges together as indicated. Holding inside of door to right side of front, Whipstitch unfinished edges of door and front together as indicated.

6: For console, Whipstitch C-E pieces together according to Console Assembly Diagram; Overcast side and bottom edges. Whipstitch back edge of C to front as indicated. For steering mechanism, with right side of steering column facing up, Whipstitch G to front as indicated.

NOTE: Trim closure to about ¼" x 1".

7: Glue closure to inside of glove compartment door and corresponding area on front. For knob, glue one silver 8-mm. bead to door as indicated.

8: Set pieces aside.

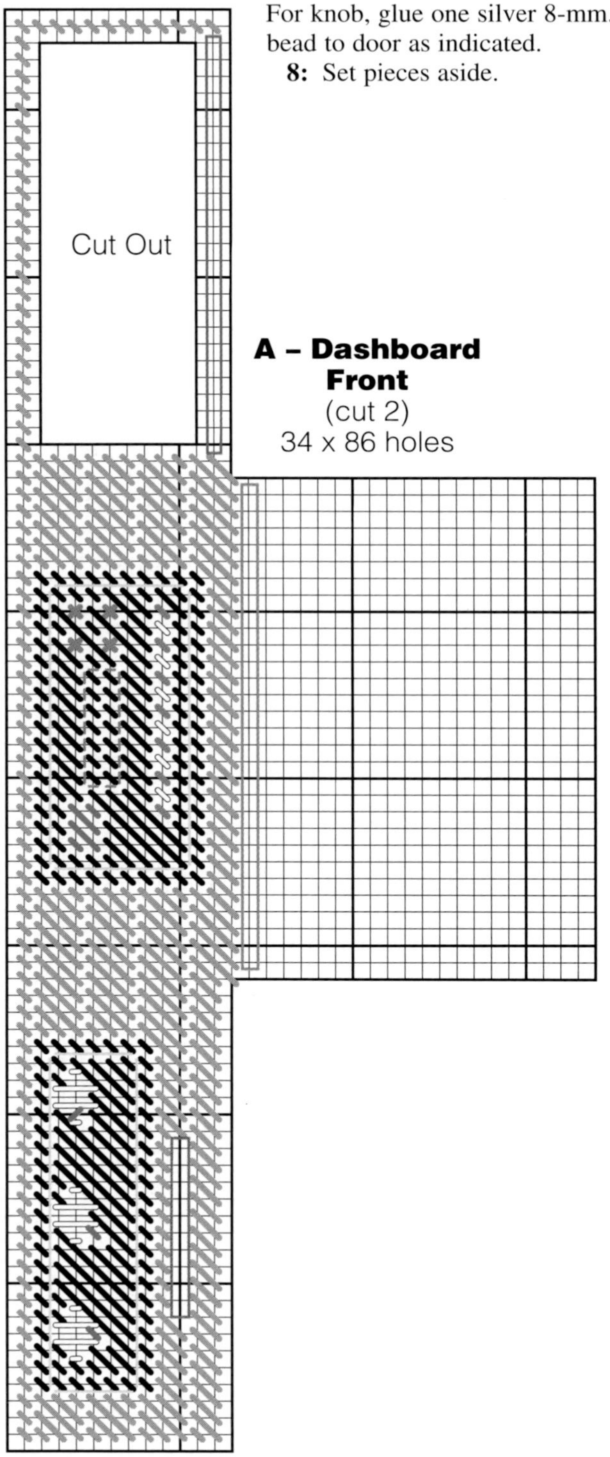

A – Dashboard Front
(cut 2)
34 x 86 holes

C – Console Top
(cut 1) 14 x 30 holes

Whipstitch to A.

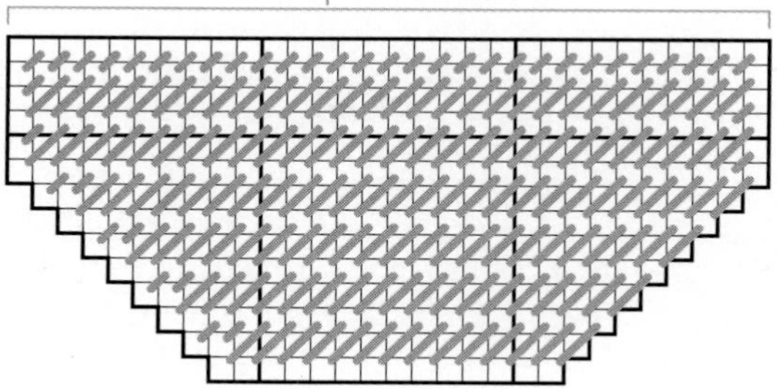

Glove Compartment Assembly Diagram

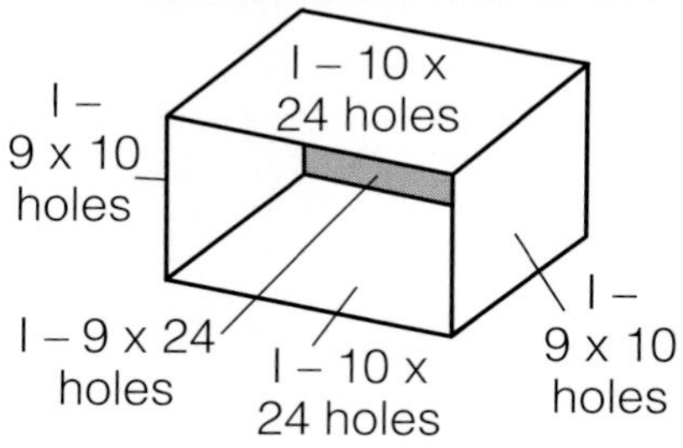

Console Assembly Diagram

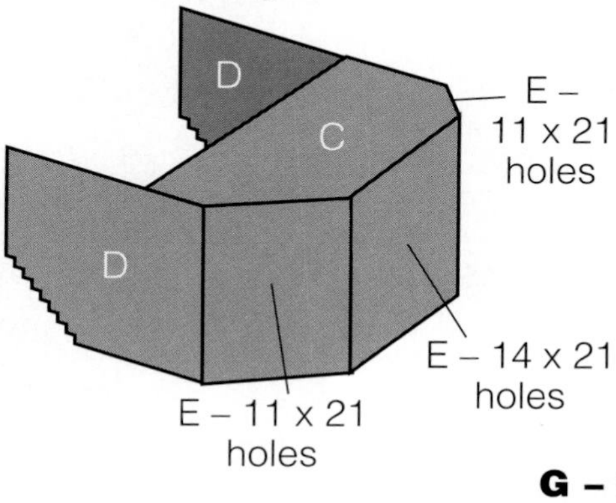

D – Console Side
(cut 2) 21 x 23 holes

Top

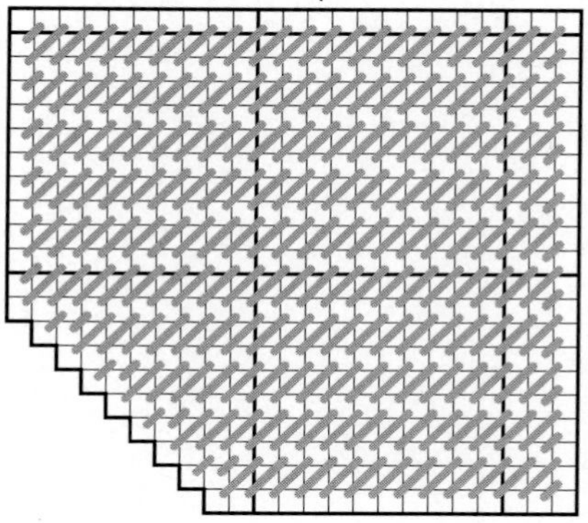

G – Steering Column
(cut 1) 8 x 11 holes

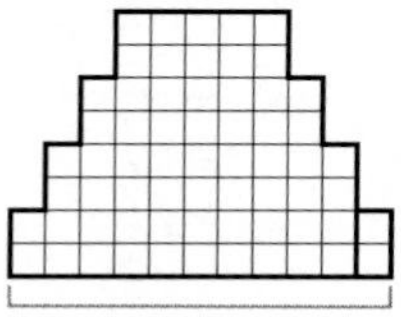

Whipstitch to A.

F – Steering Wheel
(cut 2) 17 x 17 holes

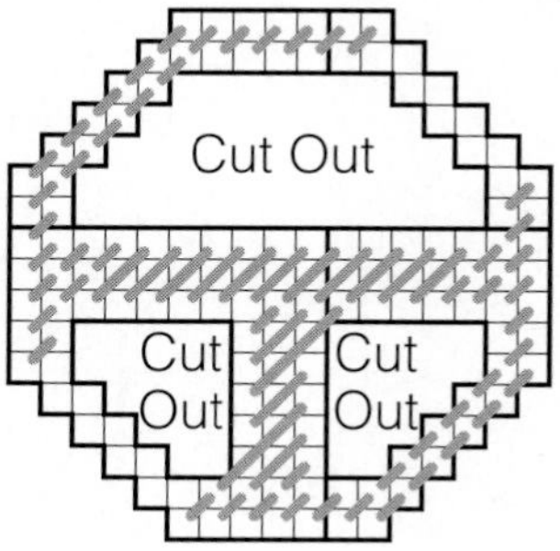

H – Glove Compartment Door
(cut 1 from clear & 1 from white)
11 x 24 holes

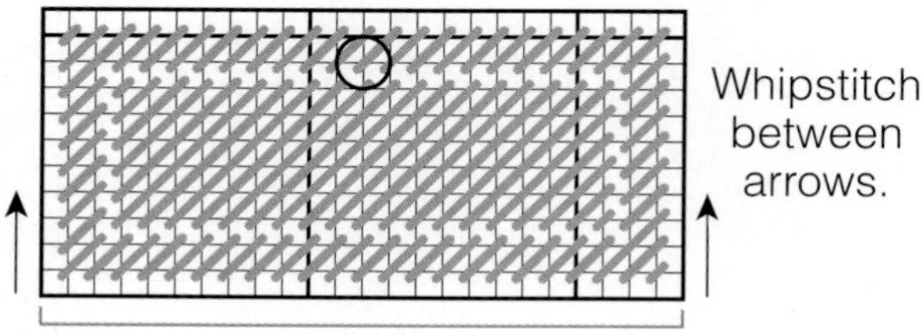

Whipstitch to A.

COLOR KEY:

Fine metallic braid		
Silver		
Metallic cord		
White/Silver		
Red/Silver		
Nylon Plus™	**Needloft™** yarn	
	#02	#00 Black
	#11	#07 Pink
	#40	#37 Silver
	#01	#41 White

STITCH KEY:

- Backstitch/Straight Stitch
- Unworked Area/Door Attachment
- Unworked Area/Console Attachment
- Unworked Area/Steering Column Attachment
- Knob Placement

CAB SEATS

CUTTING INSTRUCTIONS:

NOTE: Use clear canvas for all pieces.

A: For sides, cut four according to graph.

B: For seat backs, cut two according to graph.

C: For seats, cut two 16 x 20 holes.

D: For backs, cut two according to graph.

E: For top pieces, cut four 4 x 5 holes and two 4 x 12 holes (no graphs).

F: For fronts, cut two 4 x 20 holes (no graph).

G: For seat bottoms, cut two 20 x 20 holes (no graph).

H: For base sides, cut eight 11 x 16 holes (no graph).

I: For base bottom, cut two 16 x 16 holes (no graph).

STITCHING INSTRUCTIONS:

NOTE: G and I pieces are unworked.

1: Using colors and stitches indicated, work A (two on opposite side of canvas) and B-D pieces according to graphs; using Sail Blue and Slanted Gobelin Stitch over narrow width, work E, F and H pieces.

2: For each seat, with Sail Blue, Whipstitch A-G pieces together according to Step 1 of Cab Seat Assembly Diagram. Whipstitch H and I pieces together according to Step 2; Overcast unfinished edges of base. Glue base to center of seat bottom.

3: Set seats aside.

B – Seat Back
(cut 2) 20 x 24 holes

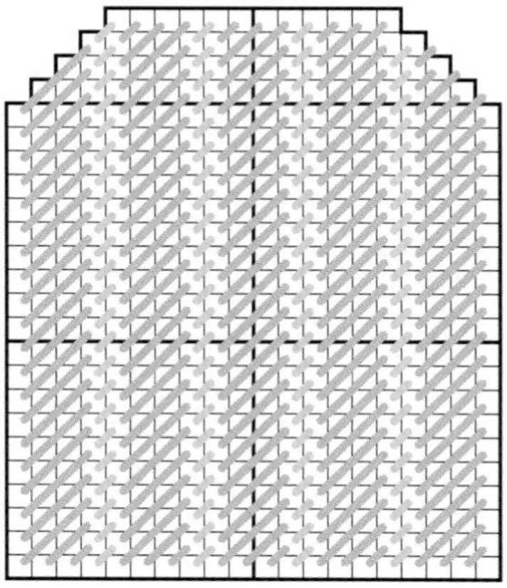

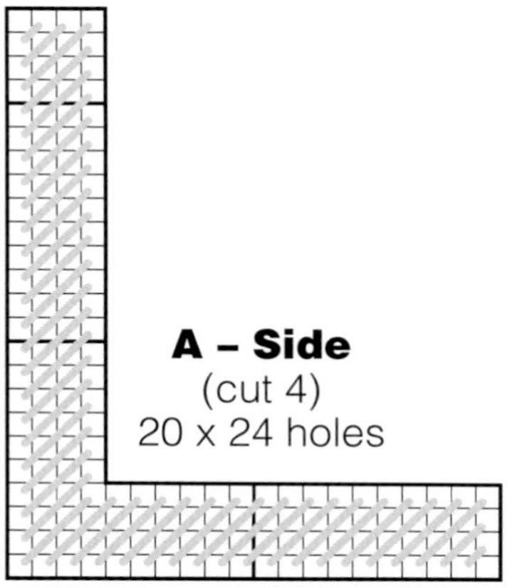

A – Side
(cut 4)
20 x 24 holes

C – Seat
(cut 2) 16 x 20 holes

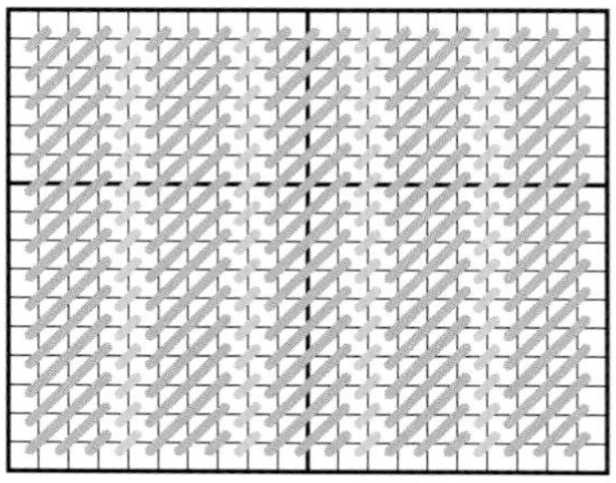

COLOR KEY:

	Nylon Plus™	Needloft™ yarn
(light)	#04	#35 Sail Blue
(dark)	#01	#41 White

D – Back
(cut 2) 20 x 28 holes

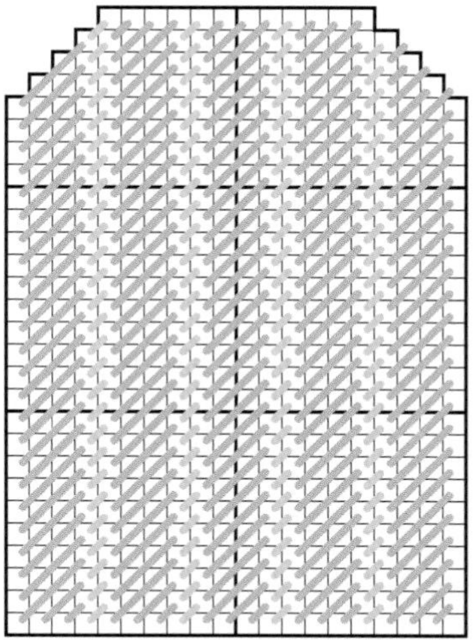

Cab Seat Assembly Diagram
Step 1

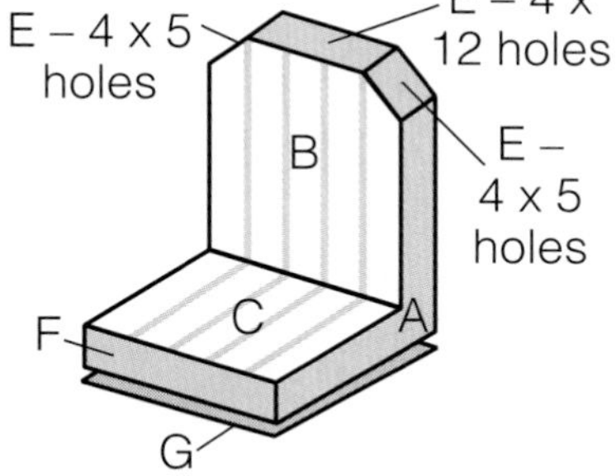

Step 2

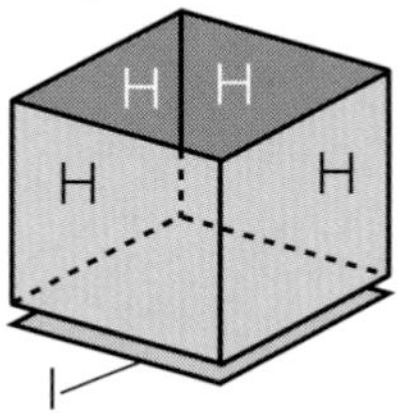

CURTAINS

CUTTING INSTRUCTIONS:

A: For kitchen window tapered curtains, cut two from print fabric according to Tapered Curtain Cutting Guide.

B: For detachable window wall tapered curtains, cut two from print fabric according to Tapered Curtain Cutting Guide.

C: For back window tapered curtains, cut two angled and one straight from print fabric according to Tapered Curtain Cutting Guide.

D: For kitchen window straight curtain, cut one from striped fabric according to Straight Curtain Cutting Guide.

E: For detachable window wall straight curtain, cut one from striped fabric according to Straight Curtain Cutting Guide.

F: For back wall straight curtain, cut one from striped fabric according to Straight Curtain Cutting Guide.

G: For kitchen window curtain trim, cut two 4" lengths of scalloped edging (no guide).

H: For detachable window wall curtain trim, cut two $7\frac{1}{2}$" lengths of scalloped edging (no guide).

I: For back wall straight curtain trim, cut one 16" length of scalloped edging (no guide).

J: For shower curtain ruffle, cut one according to Shower Curtain Cutting Guide.

K: For shower curtain, cut one according to Shower Curtain Cutting Guide.

L: For shower curtain ruffle trim, cut one 4" length of scalloped edging (no guide).

STITCHING INSTRUCTIONS:

1: Finish edges of A-F and J-K pieces by turning under twice $\frac{1}{8}$", then secure using iron-on binding, glue or press and then sew.

2: Run a line of stitches at top of each A, B, C, J and K piece as indicated by green dotted lines on cutting guides; pull thread to gather fabric and knot ends of thread on wrong side.

NOTE: Turn ends of edging under and secure on wrong side.

3: Glue or sew one G to angled edge of each A and and one H to angled edge of each B. Tack matching edges of C pieces together as shown in Back Wall Curtain Diagram. Glue or sew I to bottom edges of joined C pieces.

4: For shower curtain, glue L to bottom edge of ruffle.

5: Set curtains aside.

Tapered Curtain Cutting Guide

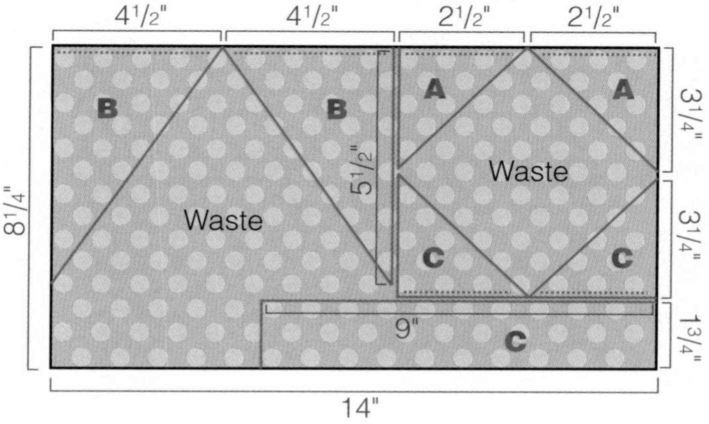

Back Wall Curtain Diagram

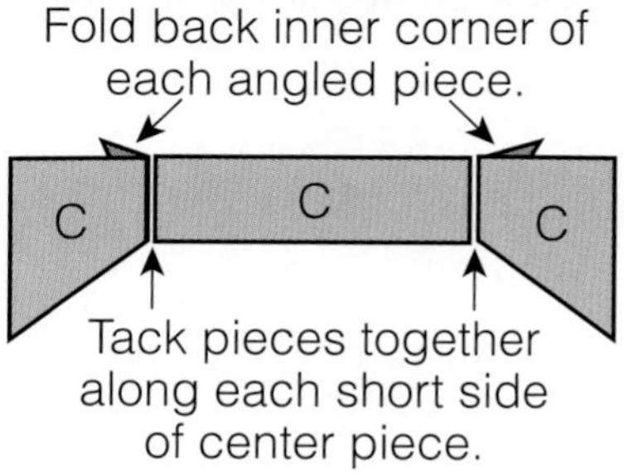

Straight Curtain/Shower Curtain Cutting Guide

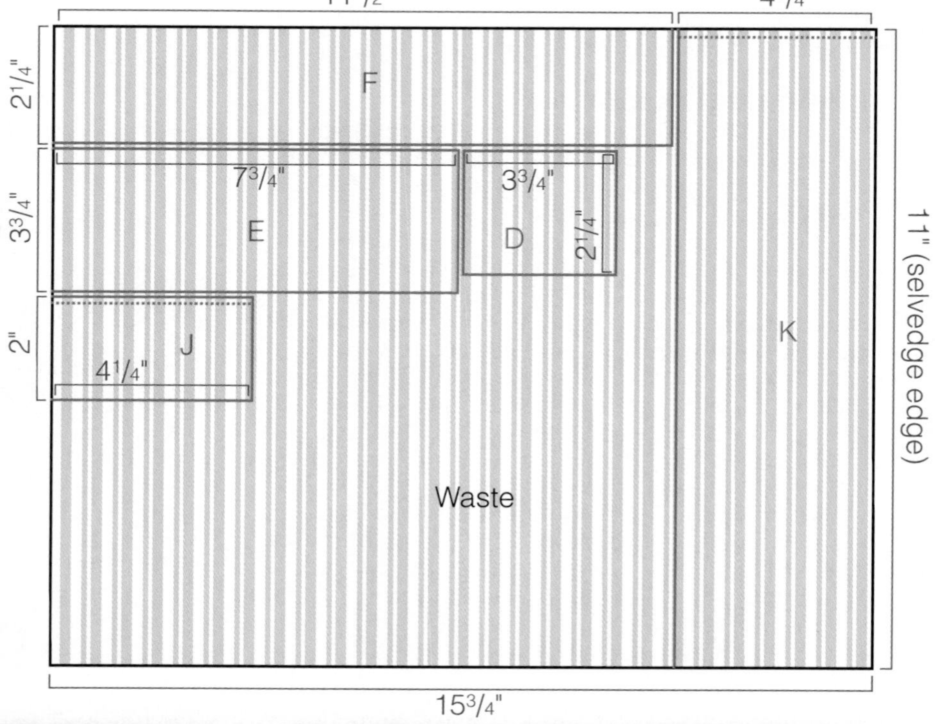

KEY:

— = **Cut Lines**
----- = **Gather Stitches**

ASSEMBLY

STITCHING INSTRUCTIONS:

NOTE: When joining walls, work as instructed holding corresponding interior and exterior pieces wrong sides together with braces between as shown in Wall Overlap Assembly Diagram.

1: Assemble back wall: Matching top edges, with cord, Whipstitch window cutout edges of exterior and interior E pieces together according to Back Wall Assembly Diagram; with matching colors, Whipstitch exterior and interior D pieces and back wall together.

2: Assemble front wall: With Royal for windshield seam and cord for grille seam, Whipstitch I-K pieces together according to Front Wall Assembly Diagram; with cord, Whipstitch cutout edges together.

3: Assemble passenger side wall and join to back wall: Holding interior and exterior passenger side walls together (**NOTE**: Overlap areas do not align), Whipstitch kitchen wall to back wall.

4: Assemble driver's side wall and join to back wall: Overlapping blue walls as indicated, with Royal, Whipstitch interior F-H pieces together. Holding interior and exterior walls together (overlap braces as indicated), Whipstitch back door support wall to back wall. With cord for windows and with matching colors, Whipstitch cutout edges together.

5: Join front and side walls: With cord for grille area and with Royal, Whipstitch front and side walls together as indicated. With matching colors, Whipstitch unfinished top edges of walls together.

6: Join walls and floor: Set floor on edge of table or work bench; matching front ends, set walls over floor. Slide assembly over the edge of the surface slightly to access stitching area. With Royal, Whipstitch bottom edges of walls to unworked bar inside outer edge of floor.

7: Assemble floor and chassis: With chassis setting on tires, run glue over each top surface of frame. Lift floor/wall assembly; with front edge over single-wheel axle end, set floor on chassis. Let glue dry.

FINISHING INSTRUCTIONS:

1: Join walls and underpinning: Slide underpinning assembly down over walls; glue inner top edge of underpinning to edges of floor. Let glue dry.

NOTE: Trim closures to about ¼" x 1".

2: Glue closures to inside of each door at handle area, bottom and side edges of detachable window wall and to corresponding areas on walls. Glue red 20-mm. stones to rear underpinning for tail lights as shown in photo. Glue side edge of one rear view mirror and one door handle to each cab door, remaining door handle to back door, cargo trim to cargo door and spare tire over trim as shown.

3: Glue bottom edge of window seat front and supports to floor as indicated. Run glue over top edges; glue to underside of window seat.

4: With two rows of holes on dashboard top hanging over front, glue wrong side of B to top of front (see Dashboard Assembly Diagram). Glue narrow end of steering column to wrong side center of steering wheel. Glue top of steering wheel to edge of dashboard top. Glue pedals to footboard and footboard to front wall and floor of Camper according to Footboard Assembly Diagram. Glue console and dashboard to front wall (see Dashboard Assembly Diagram).

5: Glue bathroom walls and cab seats to interior walls and floor as indicated. Holding wrong sides of curtains to interior wall windows, glue straight curtains to top and side edges of corresponding windows; pulling gather stitches tighter if needed to fit, glue corresponding angled curtains over straight curtains. Glue shower curtains over top edge of shower door as shown.

6: Glue kitchenette, microwave and bench seats (see Camper Accessories on page 134) to interior as indicated.

Wall Overlap Assembly Diagram

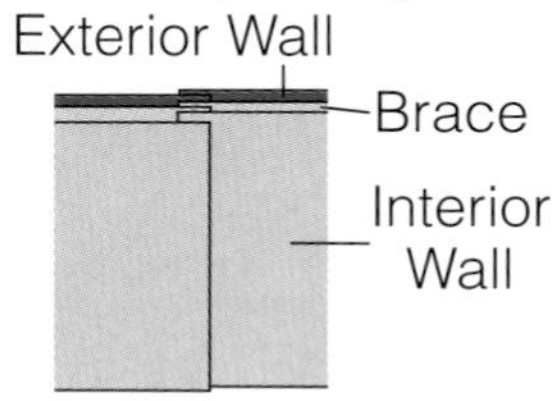

Front Wall Assembly Diagram

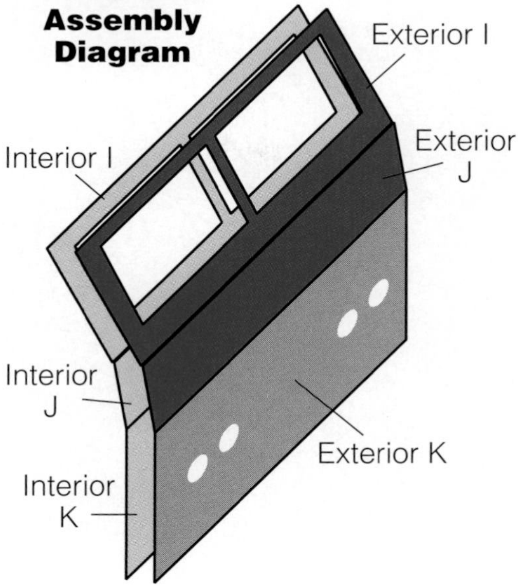

Back Wall Assembly Diagram

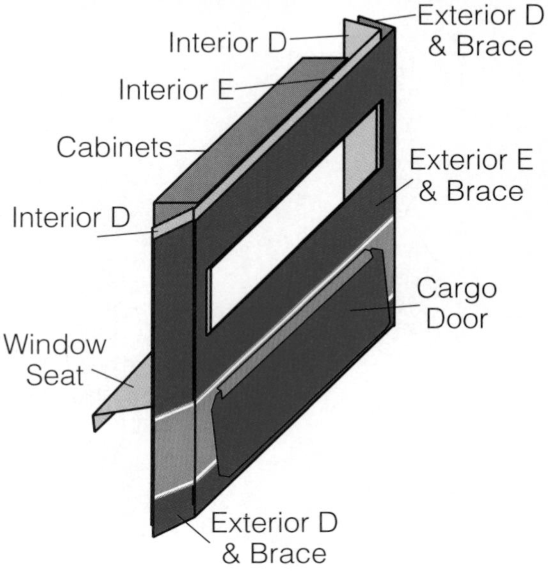

Footboard Assembly Diagram

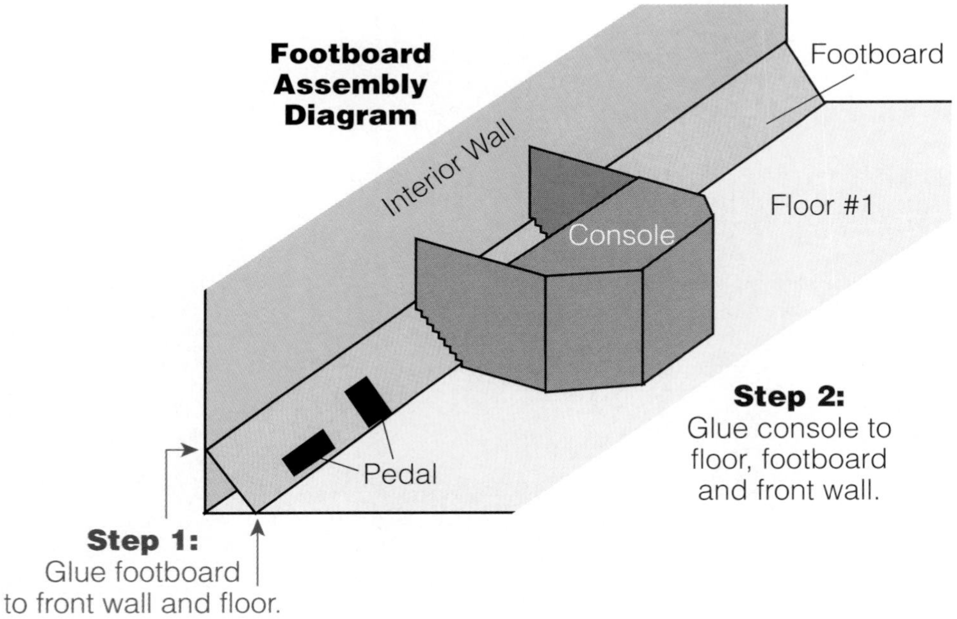

Dashboard Assembly Diagram

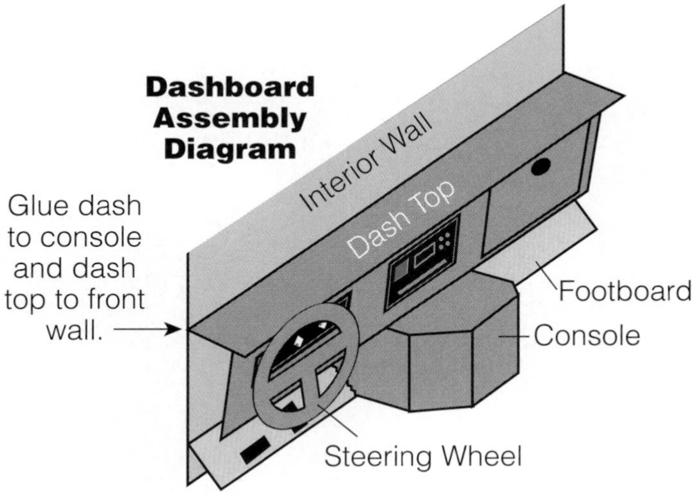

FASHION DOLL

Camper Accessories

Designed by
Trudy Bath Smith &
Stephen J. Smith

BARBIE® doll and friends pictured with permission of
Mattel, Inc. ©1996 Mattel, Inc. All rights reserved.

MATERIALS FOR ENTIRE SET:

- ❑ 12 sheets of 7-count plastic canvas
- ❑ 11 sheets of white 7-count plastic canvas
- ❑ One sheet of stoneware blue 7-count plastic canvas
- ❑ ½ sheet of black 7-count plastic canvas
- ❑ Scraps of neon blue and neon pink 7-count plastic canvas
- ❑ Clear plastic beverage bottle
- ❑ Five black 8-mm. half-round acrylic stones
- ❑ Two silver 8-mm. pearl beads
- ❑ ⅜" round acrylic mirror
- ❑ 13" wooden ¼" dowel
- ❑ Polyester fiberfill
- ❑ ½ yd. print or stripe coordinating color cotton broadcloth
- ❑ 9" x 12" square of coordinating color felt
- ❑ ⅔ yd. white ⅜" satin ribbon
- ❑ 1⅔ yds. white ½" scalloped lace edging
- ❑ 1⅓ yd. coordinating color ⅛" rattail cord
- ❑ Iron-on binding (optional)
- ❑ Sewing needle and matching color thread (optional)
- ❑ Five Velcro™ closure strips
- ❑ Craft glue or glue gun
- ❑ 8" silver heavy metallic braid
- ❑ Fine metallic braid:
  - ❑ Silver – 1 yd.
- ❑ Metallic cord:
  - ❑ White/Silver – 70 yds.
  - ❑ Red/Silver – ½ yd.
- ❑ Worsted-weight or plastic canvas yarn:

Nylon Plus™	Needloft™ yarn
❑ #02	#00 Black – 60 yds.
❑ #11	#07 Pink – 4½ yds.
❑ #09	#32 Royal – ½ yd.
❑ #04	#35 Sail Blue – 9½ oz.
❑ #40	#37 Silver – 3½ yds.
❑ #01	#41 White – 3 oz.
❑ #07	#48 Royal Dark – 23 yds.
❑ #54	#55 Watermelon – 2 oz.

For materials for individual items, see individual materials lists.

KITCHENETTE

SIZE: 3" x 9¼" x 7" tall.

MATERIALS:

- ❑ 2½ sheets of 7-count plastic canvas
- ❑ One sheet of white 7-count plastic canvas
- ❑ One sheet of stoneware blue 7-count plastic canvas
- ❑ Scraps of black 7-count plastic canvas
- ❑ Clear plastic beverage bottle
- ❑ Five black 8-mm. half-round acrylic stones
- ❑ Two silver 8-mm. pearl beads
- ❑ Two Velcro™ closures
- ❑ Craft glue or glue gun
- ❑ Metallic cord; for amount see Color Key on page 136.
- ❑ Worsted-weight or plastic canvas yarn; for amounts see Color Key.

OVEN

CUTTING INSTRUCTIONS:

NOTES: Use clear canvas for door front and handle pieces and stoneware blue canvas for remaining pieces. Graphs and diagrams on pages 136-139.

A: For oven interior walls, cut four (one for each side, top and bottom) 15 x 22 holes and one 22 x 22 holes for back (no top, bottom or back graphs).

B: For racks, cut two according to graph.

C: For rack supports, cut eight 2 x 14 holes (no graph).

D: For door inside and front pieces, cut one from stoneware blue for inside and one from clear for front according to graph.

E: For door handle, cut two 2 x 17 holes (no graph).

STITCHING INSTRUCTIONS:

1: For each rack support, using Black and Continental Stitch and working through all thicknesses, work two C pieces and one unworked 15 x 22-hole A piece together as indicated on A graphs. With Black, Whipstitch A pieces together according to Oven Assembly Diagram. Place racks on rack supports.

2: Using Sail Blue and Continental Stitch, work front D. Holding E pieces together, using metallic cord and Continental Stitch, work handle through both thicknesses; Whipstitch unfinished edges together. With cord, Overcast unfinished cutout edges of each D piece.

NOTE: Cut one 3" x 3½" piece from beverage bottle.

3: Holding unworked inside door piece to wrong side of door front with clear plastic between, with Sail Blue for bottom cutout edges and with cord, Whipstitch unfinished edges of door pieces together. Glue handle to center top of door front as indicated. (**NOTE:** Assemblies are attached in Cabinet instructions.)

Oven Assembly Diagram

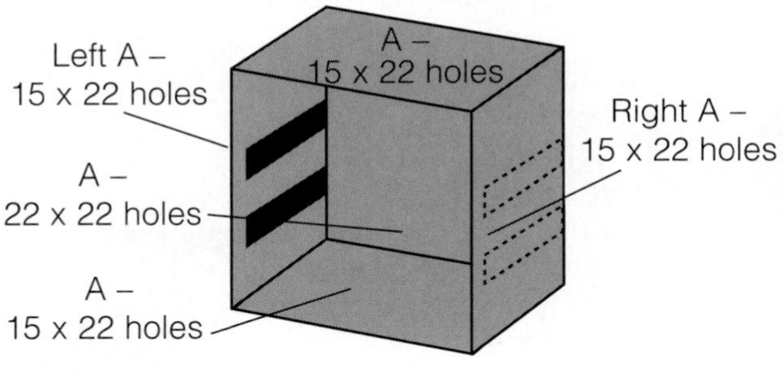

A – Oven Interior Left Side Wall
(cut 1 from blue)
15 x 22 holes

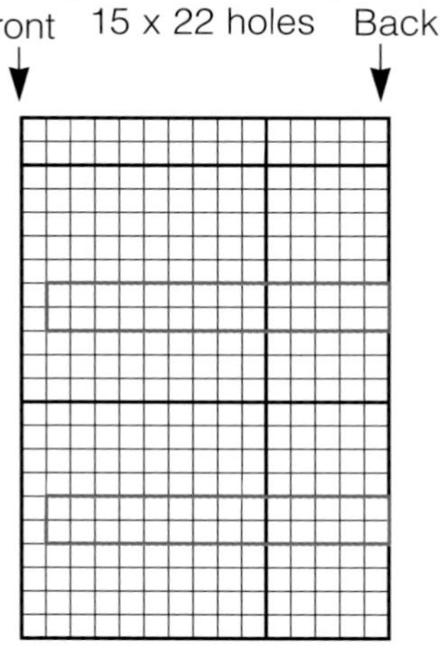

A – Oven Interior Right Side Wall
(cut 1 from blue)
15 x 22 holes

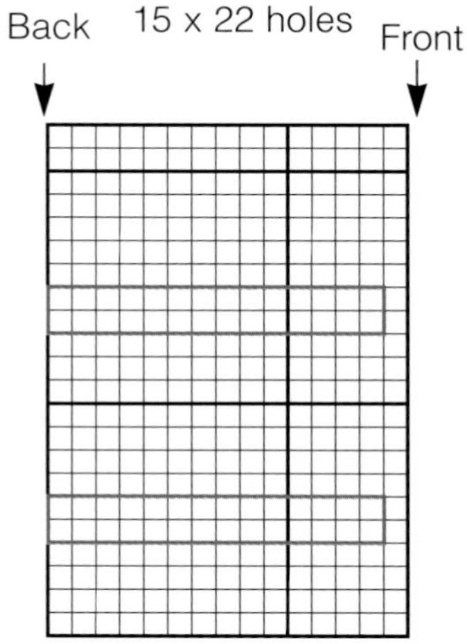

B – Oven Rack
(cut 2 from gray)
14 x 21 holes

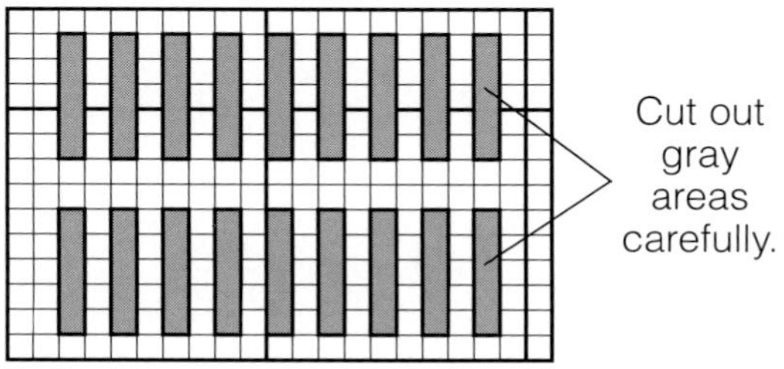

COLOR KEY:

Metallic cord
White/Silver – 30 yds.

Nylon Plus™	Needloft™ yarn
#02	#00 Black – 5 yds.
#04	#35 Sail Blue – 2½ oz.
#01	#41 White – 8 yds.

STITCH KEY:

Oven Rack Support Attachment
Handle Placement
Drawer Placement

D – Oven Door Inside & Front
(cut 1 from blue and 1 from clear)
26 x 26 holes

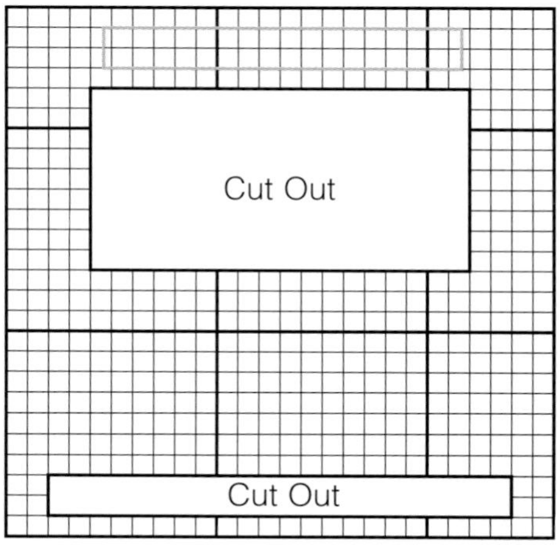

DRAWER CUTTING INSTRUCTIONS:

NOTE: Use clear canvas for drawer front and handle, white canvas for drawer support pieces and stoneware blue canvas for remaining pieces.

A: For drawer front, cut one 11 x 30 holes.

B: For handle, cut two 2 x 17 holes (no graph).

C: For drawer sides, cut two 9 x 17 holes (no graph).

D: For drawer back, cut one 9 x 26 holes (no graph).

E: For drawer bottom, cut one 17 x 26 holes (no graph).

F: For drawer support pieces, cut two 17 x 28 holes and two 11 x 17 holes (no graphs).

STITCHING INSTRUCTIONS:

1: Using Sail Blue and stitches indicated, work A according to graph; Overcast unfinished edges. Holding B pieces together, using metallic cord and Continental Stitch, work handle through both thicknesses; Whipstitch unfinished edges together.

2: With Black, Whipstitch unworked C-E pieces together according to Drawer Assembly Diagram. Glue handle to center of drawer front as shown in photo, and glue drawer to wrong side of front as indicated.

3: With White, Whipstitch unworked F pieces together according to Drawer Support Assembly Diagram. (**NOTE:** Assemblies are attached in Cabinet Instructions.)

A - Drawer Front
(cut 1 from clear)
11 x 30 holes

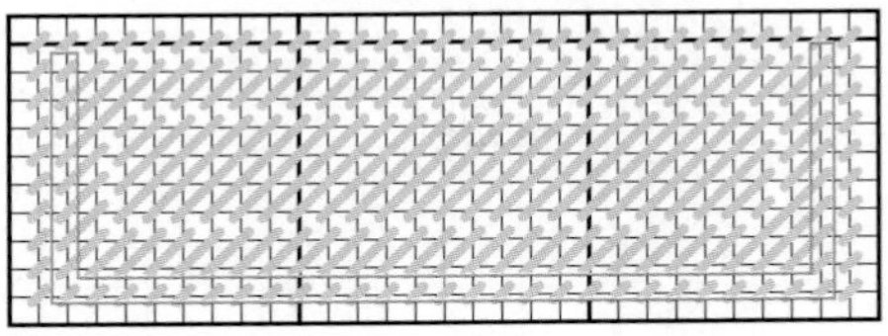

Drawer Support Assembly Diagram

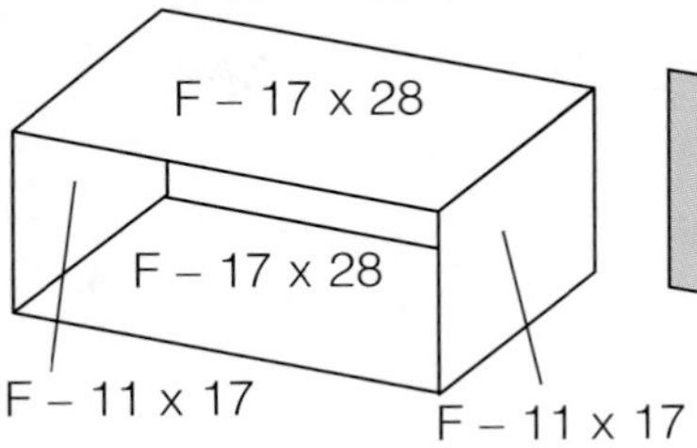

Drawer Assembly Diagram

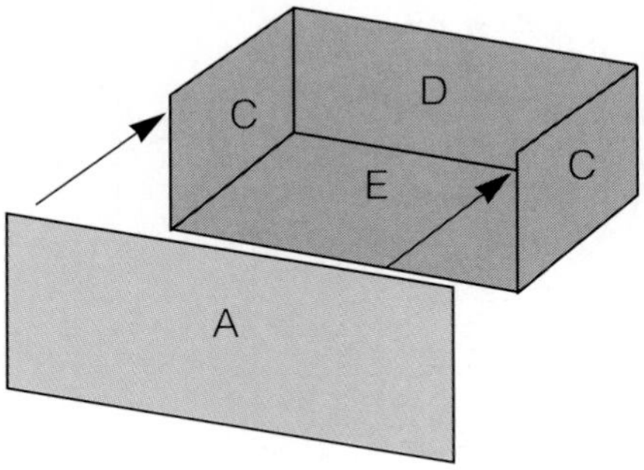

REFRIGERATOR CUTTING INSTRUCTIONS:

NOTES: Use clear canvas for door front and handle and white canvas for remaining pieces. Graphs continued on page 138.

A: For refrigerator interior walls, cut two 15 x 25 holes for sides, two 15 x 22 holes for top and bottom and one 22 x 25 holes for back (no top, bottom and back graphs).

B: For shelves, cut two 14 x 21 holes (no graph).

C: For shelf supports, cut four 2 x 12 holes (no graph).

D: For drawer front, cut two according to graph.

E: For drawer sides, cut two 5 x 14 holes (no graph).

F: For drawer back, cut one 5 x 19 holes (no graph).

G: For drawer bottom, cut one 14 x 19 holes (no graph).

H: For door shelf pieces, cut two 4 x 15 holes, two 3 x 15 holes and four 3 x 4 holes (no graphs).

I: For door inside and front pieces, cut one from white for inside and one from clear for front according to graph.

J: For handle, cut two from clear 2 x 19 holes (no graph).

STITCHING INSTRUCTIONS:

NOTE: Interior pieces are unworked.

1: For each top shelf support, using White and Continental Stitch and working through all thicknesses, work two C pieces and one 15- x 25-hole A piece together as indicated on A graphs. With White, Whipstitch A pieces together according to Refrigerator Assembly Diagram; Whipstitch one B for bottom shelf to sides as indicated and to corresponding area on back (see diagram).

2: With White, Whipstitch E-G pieces together according to Refrigerator Drawer Assembly Diagram; Whipstitch unfinished side and bottom edges of drawer to one D as indicated. Holding remaining D and attached D together, Whipstitch unfinished edges together.

3: For each door shelf, with White, Whipstitch one 4- x 15-hole, one 3- x 15-hole and two 3- x 4-hole H pieces together according to Refrigerator Door Shelf Assembly Diagram. Whipstitch unfinished side and bottom edges of each shelf to inside door piece as indicated on I graph.

4: Using Sail Blue and Continental Stitch, work front I on opposite side of canvas. Holding J pieces together, using metallic cord and Continental Stitch, work handle through both thicknesses; Whipstitch unfinished edges together. Holding I pieces wrong sides together, with Sail Blue for cutout edges and with cord, Whipstitch unfinished edges of door pieces together.

5: Slide drawer into refrigerator below bottom shelf and place remaining shelf on shelf supports. Glue handle to door front as shown in photo. (**NOTE:** Assemblies are joined in Cabinet Instructions.)

Refrigerator Assembly Diagram

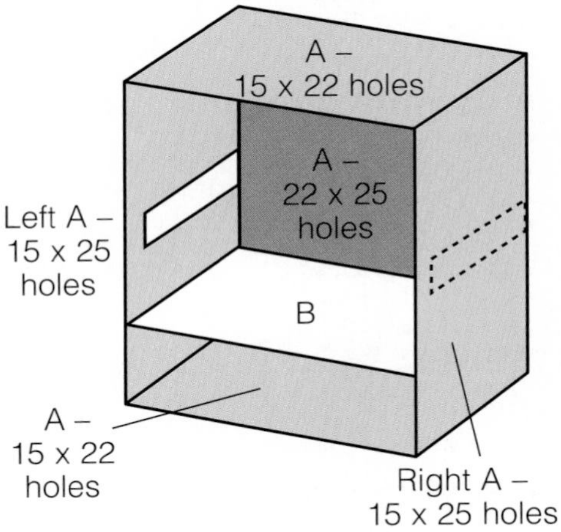

Refrigerator Door Shelf Assembly Diagram

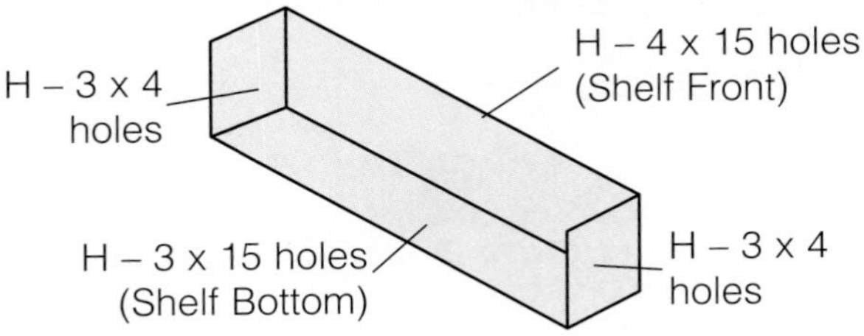

Refrigerator Drawer Assembly Diagram

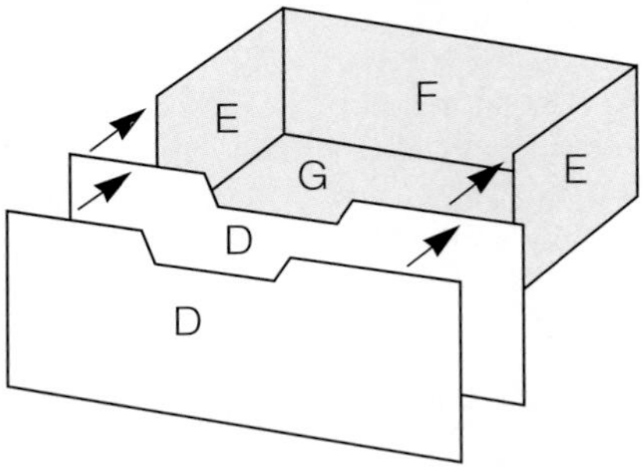

A – Refrigerator Interior Left Side Wall
(cut 1 from white)
15 x 25 holes

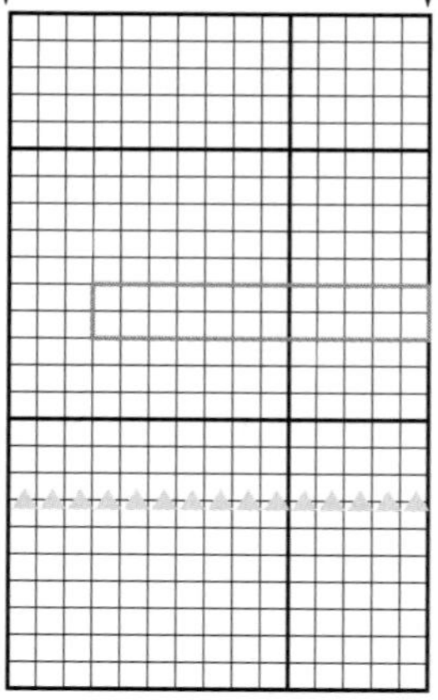

A – Refrigerator Interior Right Side Wall
(cut 1 from white)
15 x 25 holes

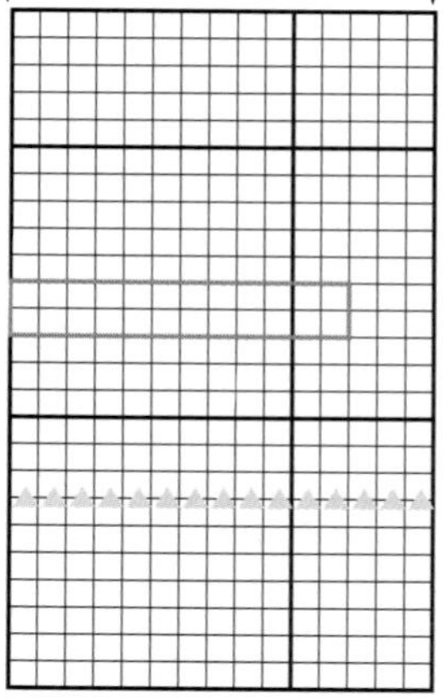

COLOR KEY:

Metallic cord
#12 White/Silver – 30 yds.

Nylon Plus™	Needloft™ yarn
#02	#00 Black – 5 yds.
#04	#35 Sail Blue – 2½ oz.
#01	#41 White – 8 yds.

STITCH KEY:

- Oven Rack Support Attachment
- Handle Placement
- Drawer Placement
- Refrigerator Top Shelf Attachment
- ▲ Refrigerator Bottom Shelf Attachment
- ▼ Refrigerator Drawer Attachment
- ♥ Refrigerator Door Shelf Attachment
- Unworked Areas/Primary Hinge Attachment
- Unworked Areas/Support Wall Attachment
- ◆ Unworked Areas/Secondary Hinge Attachment
- ○ Knob Placement

I – Refrigerator Door Inside & Front
(cut 1 from white & 1 from clear)
25 x 29 holes

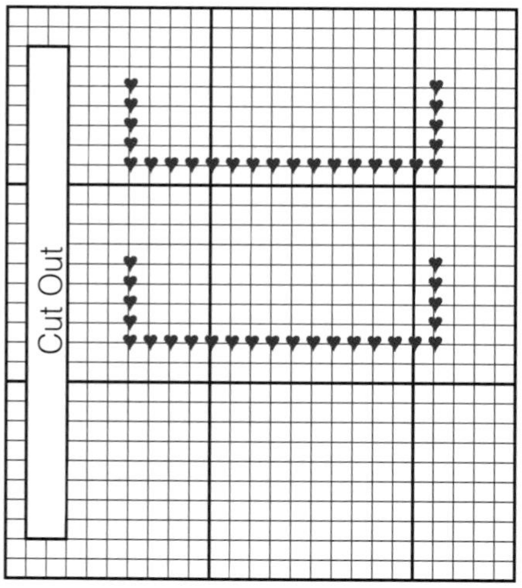

Slanted Gobelin Stitch Illustration
(over 4 bars)

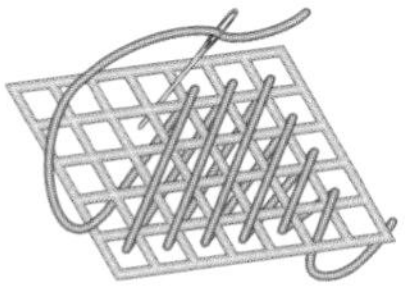

D – Refrigerator Drawer Front
(cut 2 from white)
6 x 21 holes

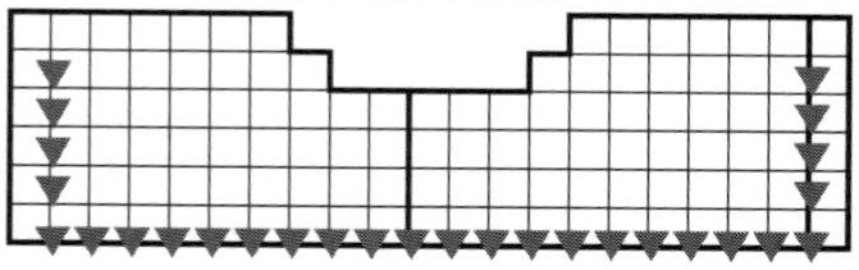

CABINET CUTTING INSTRUCTIONS:

NOTE: Use clear canvas for A-L pieces and black canvas for burners.

A: For front, cut one according to graph.
B: For back, cut one 45 x 60 holes (no graph).
C: For sides, cut two 18 x 45 holes (no graph).
D: For support wall, cut one 18 x 44 holes (no graph).
E: For top, cut one according to graph.
F: For bottom, cut one 18 x 60 holes (no graph).
G: For sink sides, cut two 5 x 47 holes (no graph).
H: For sink bottoms, cut two according to graph.
I: For faucet, cut one according to graph.
J: For faucet base, cut three 5 x 10 holes (no graph).
K: For oven door hinge, cut one 8 x 20 holes.
L: For refrigerator door hinge, cut one 8 x 23 holes (no graph).
M: For burners, cut four according to graph.

STITCHING INSTRUCTIONS:

NOTE: B, D, F, two J and M pieces are unworked.

1: Using yarn and cord colors and stitches indicated, work A and E pieces according to graphs, leaving indicated areas unworked. Using Sail Blue and Slanted Gobelin Stitch over 4 bars (see Stitch Illustration above), work C pieces in horizontal rows across width of each piece.

2: For each sink, using metallic cord and Slanted Gobelin Stitch, work one G according to graph, overlapping two holes at short ends as indicated on graph and working through both thicknesses at overlap area to join. Using cord and Continental Stitch, work H pieces. Holding right sides together and easing to fit, Whipstitch one side to each sink bottom. Whipstitch sink sides to wrong side of cutouts on E.

3: For faucet and base, work I according to graph; Overcast unfinished edges. Using Sail Blue and Slanted Gobelin Stitch over 4 bars, work one J piece. Holding one unworked J to wrong side of worked piece, Whipstitch one long and one short edge together. Holding remaining J to back of base at unfinished top edges, Whipstitch long edges together through all thicknesses.

4: Using Sail Blue and Continental Stitch, work K and L

pieces according to graphs, leaving uncoded areas unworked; Overcast unfinished short edges of hinges as indicated.

5: With Sail Blue, Whipstitch oven and refrigerator interiors and drawer support to wrong side of front. Holding unworked areas of K and front right sides together as indicated, work Continental Stitch through both thicknesses, Whipstitching unfinished edge of hinge to front as you work (primary hinge attachment). Bend hinge forward and slip through cutout on oven door. Whipstitch opposite long edge of hinge to front as indicated (secondary hinge attachment).

6: Holding unworked area of L and front right sides together as indicated, attach refrigerator door to front as for oven hinge above. Whipstitch top edge of A and E together as shown in photo. Whipstitch corresponding edges of D to indicated areas of front and top. Whipstitch assembly, B, C and F pieces together. (**NOTE:** Support wall is not joined to back or bottom of cabinet.) Slide drawer inside drawer support.

NOTE: Trim closure strips to about ¼" x 1".

7: Glue closure strips to oven and refrigerator doors and to corresponding areas on front (not shown in photo). Glue black 8-mm. stones to front for oven knobs as indicated. Glue one unworked burner to oven top over each silver area as shown.

8: Glue indicated area of faucet to center of base and one silver 8-mm. bead to base on either side of faucet as shown. Glue bottom edges of base to cabinet top and back between sinks as shown.

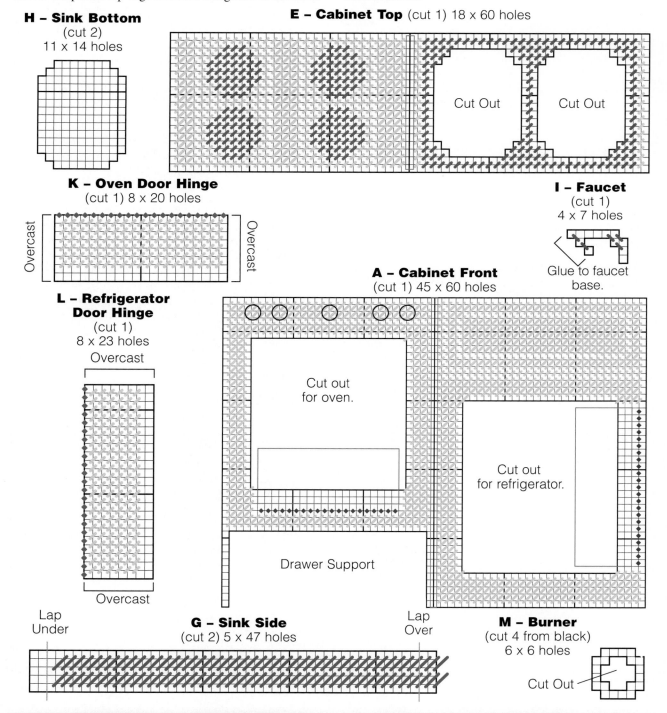

H – Sink Bottom
(cut 2)
11 x 14 holes

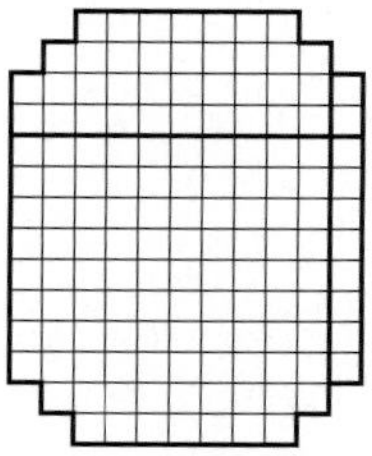

E – Cabinet Top (cut 1) 18 x 60 holes

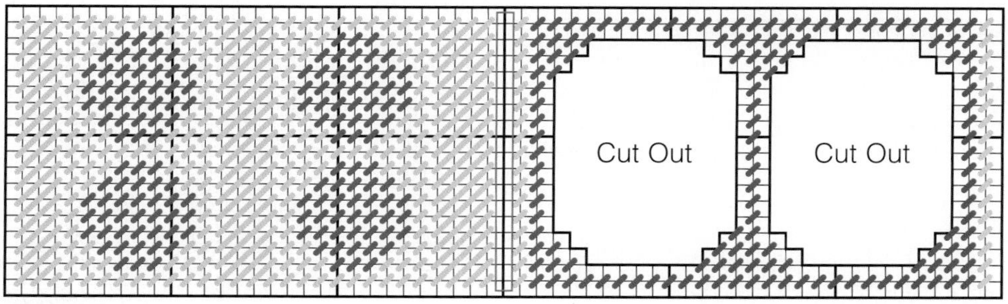

K – Oven Door Hinge
(cut 1) 8 x 20 holes

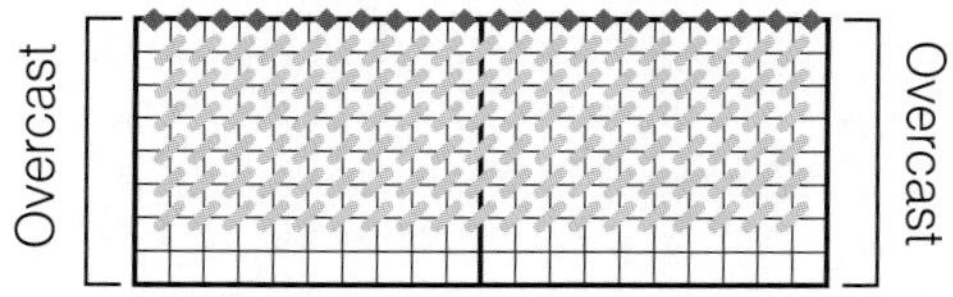

I – Faucet
(cut 1)
4 x 7 holes

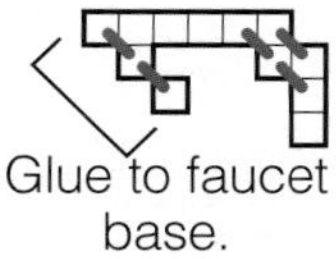

L – Refrigerator Door Hinge
(cut 1)
8 x 23 holes

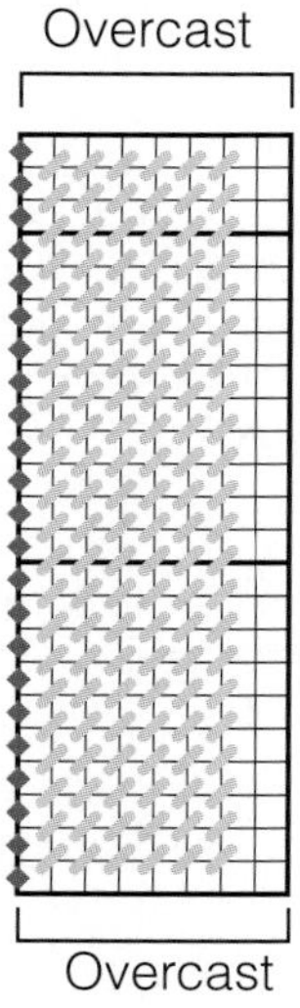

A – Cabinet Front
(cut 1) 45 x 60 holes

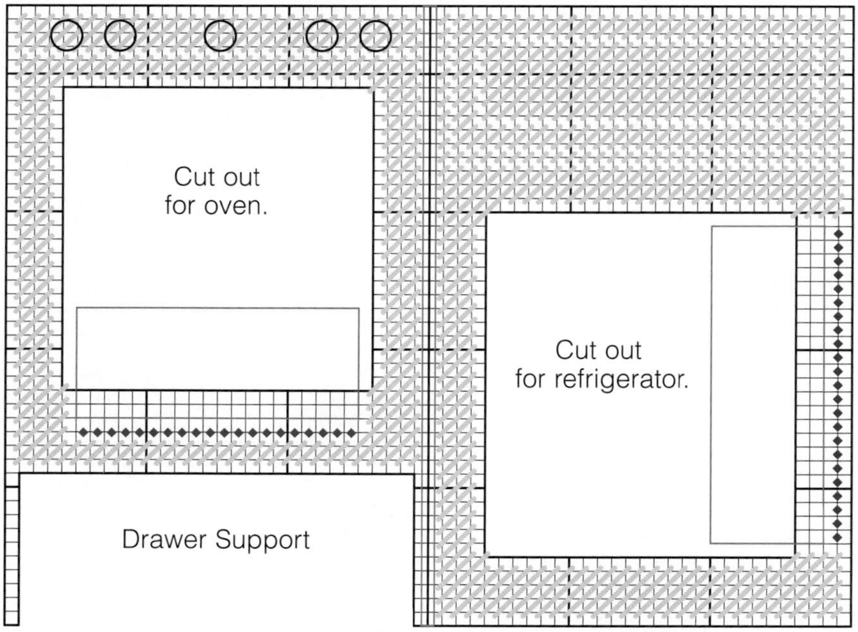

G – Sink Side
(cut 2) 5 x 47 holes

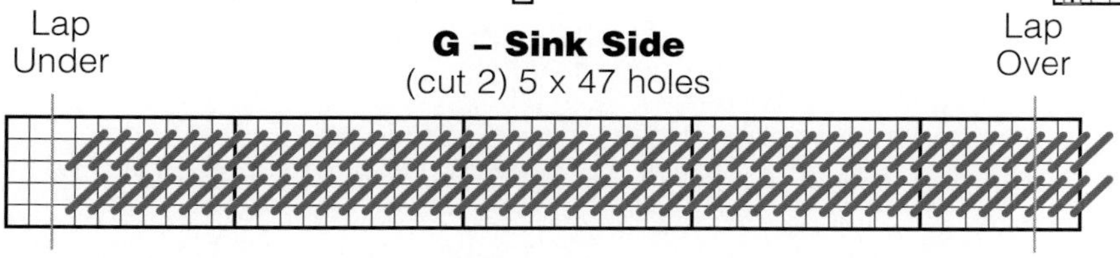

M – Burner
(cut 4 from black)
6 x 6 holes

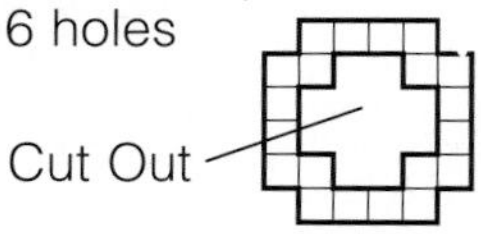

MICROWAVE

SIZE: 1⅝" x 2½" x 4⅝".

MATERIALS:

- ❏ One sheet of 7-count plastic canvas
- ❏ ¼ sheet of white 7-count plastic canvas
- ❏ Clear plastic beverage bottle
- ❏ One Velcro™ closure
- ❏ Craft glue or glue gun
- ❏ Metallic cord; for amounts see Color Key.
- ❏ Worsted-weight or plastic canvas yarn; for amounts see Color Key.

CUTTING INSTRUCTIONS:

NOTE: Use white canvas for oven interior pieces and inside door and clear canvas for remaining pieces.

A: For front, cut one according to graph.

B: For back, cut one from clear 16 x 30 holes (no graph).

C: For top and bottom, cut one each from clear 10 x 30 holes (no graph).

D: For sides, cut two from clear 10 x 16 holes (no graph).

E: For door inside and front pieces, cut one for inside and one for front according to graph.

F: For hinge, cut one 8 x 8 holes.

G: For door handle, cut two from clear 1 x 8 holes (no graph).

H: For oven interior pieces, from white, cut two 8 x 16 holes, two 8 x 10 holes and one 10 x 16 holes (no graphs).

STITCHING INSTRUCTIONS:

NOTE: B, inside E and H pieces are unworked.

1: Using yarn and metallic cord colors and stitches indicated, work A according to graph, leaving indicated areas unworked. Using Black and Straight Stitch, embroider buttons as indicated on graph.

2: Using Black and Slanted Gobelin Stitch over 3 bars (see Stitch Illustration), work C and D pieces in vertical rows across length of each piece. Using Black and Continental Stitch, work front E and F pieces according to graphs, leaving uncoded areas of F unworked. Overcast unfinished edges of F as indicated.

3: With cord, holding G pieces together, Whipstitch unfinished edges together. With cord, Overcast unfinished window cutout edges of front E. (**NOTE:** Window cutout on inside door is unfinished.)

NOTE: Cut one 1¾" x 2½" piece from beverage bottle.

4: Holding inside door piece to wrong side of door front with clear plastic between, with Black for hinge cutout edges and with cord, Whipstitch unfinished edges of door pieces together.

5: Holding unworked areas of F and A right sides together as indicated, work Continental Stitch through both thicknesses, Whipstitching unfinished edge of hinge to front as you work (primary hinge attachment). Bend hinge forward and slip through cutout on door. Whipstitch opposite long edge of hinge to front as indicated (secondary hinge attachment).

NOTE: Trim closure strip to about ¼" x 1".

6: With White, Whipstitch H pieces together according to Microwave Interior Assembly Diagram. Whipstitch interior to wrong side of cutout on A. With cord for front edges and with Black, Whipstitch A, unworked B, C and D pieces together. Glue closure to inside of door and corresponding area on front. Glue handle to door as shown in photo.

A – Front
(cut 1 from clear) 16 x 30 holes

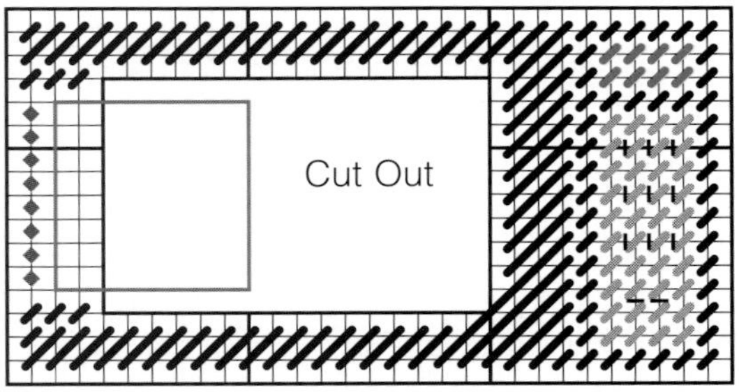

F – Hinge
(cut 1 from clear)
8 x 8 holes
Overcast

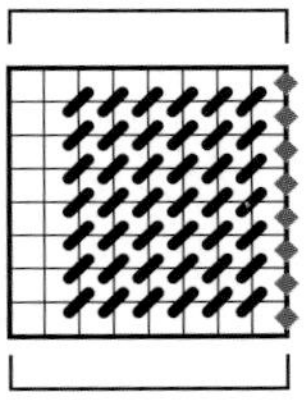

Overcast

E – Door Inside & Front
(cut 1 from white & 1 from clear)
14 x 22 holes

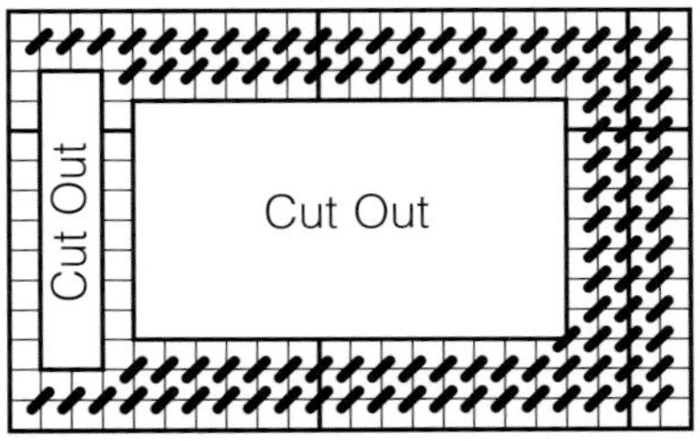

COLOR KEY:

Metallic cord
- ☐ White/Silver – 5 yds.
- ■ Red/Silver – ½ yd.

	Nylon Plus™	Needloft™ yarn
■	#02	#00 Black – 20 yds.
■	#40	#37 Silver – 1½ yds.
☐	#01	#41 White – 4 yds.

STITCH KEY:

- — Backstitch/Straight Stitch
- ☐ Unworked Areas/Primary Hinge Attachment
- ◆ Unworked Areas/Secondary Hinge Attachment

Microwave Interior Assembly Diagram

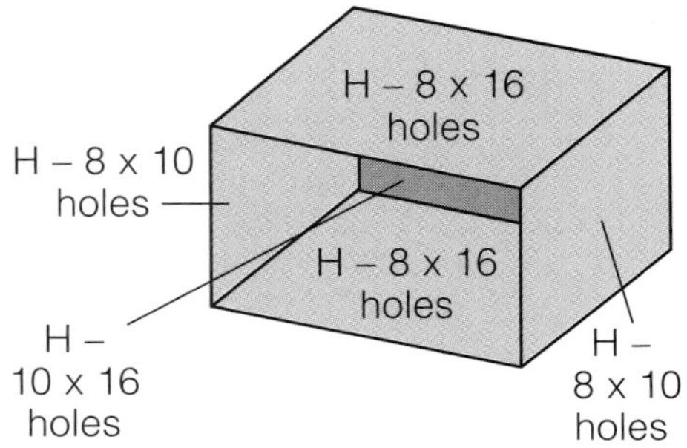

Slanted Gobelin Stitch Illustration
(over 3 bars)

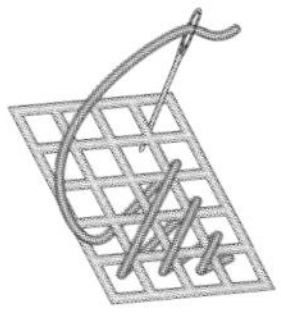

BENCH SEATS

SIZE: Each seat is 4" x 6½" x 5" tall.

MATERIALS:
- ❏ Three sheets of 7-count plastic canvas
- ❏ Worsted-weight or plastic canvas yarn; for amounts see Color Key.

CUTTING INSTRUCTIONS:

NOTE: Use clear canvas throughout.

A: For sides, cut four according to graph.
B: For fronts, cut two 18 x 42 holes (no graph).
C: For backs, cut two 33 x 42 holes (no graph).
D: For bottoms, cut two 25 x 42 holes (no graph).
E: For tops, cut two 4 x 42 holes (no graph).
F: For seat backs, cut two 15 x 42 holes (no graph).
G: For seats, cut two 22 x 42 holes (no graph).
H: For seat flaps, cut two 4 x 42 holes (no graph).

STITCHING INSTRUCTIONS:

NOTE: D pieces are unworked.

1: Using Sail Blue and stitches indicated, work A pieces (two on opposite side of canvas) according to graph; work B and C pieces according to Front & Back Stitch Pattern Guide. Using colors and stitches indicated, work E-H pieces according to Bench Seat Stitch Pattern Guide.

2: For each seat, with Sail Blue, Whipstitch E-H pieces together according to Step 1 of Bench Seat Assembly Diagram; Whipstitch assembly and remaining pieces together according to Step 2, leaving edges of seat and flap unjoined. Overcast unfinished edges.

Bench Seat Assembly Diagram

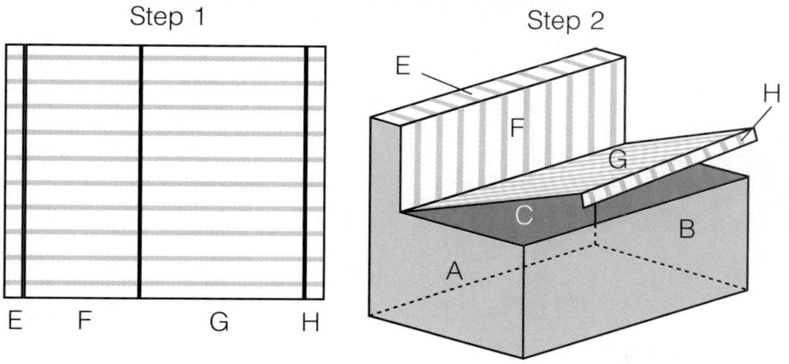

COLOR KEY:

	Nylon Plus™	Needloft™ yarn
▢	#04	#35 Sail Blue – 4 oz.
▢	#01	#41 White – 44 yds.

Bench Seat Stitch Pattern Guide

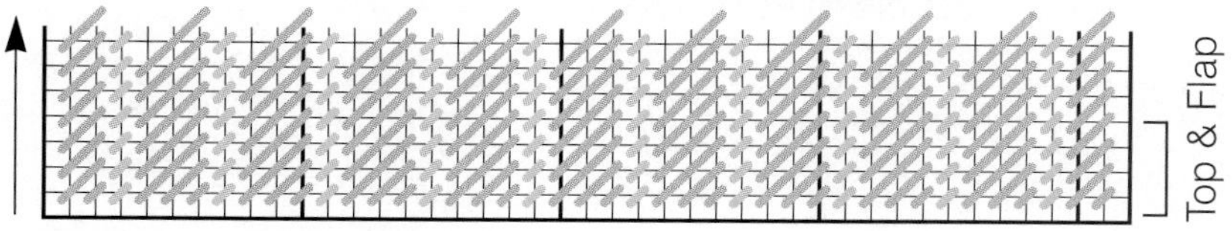

Continue established pattern across each entire piece.

A – Side
(cut 4) 25 x 33 holes

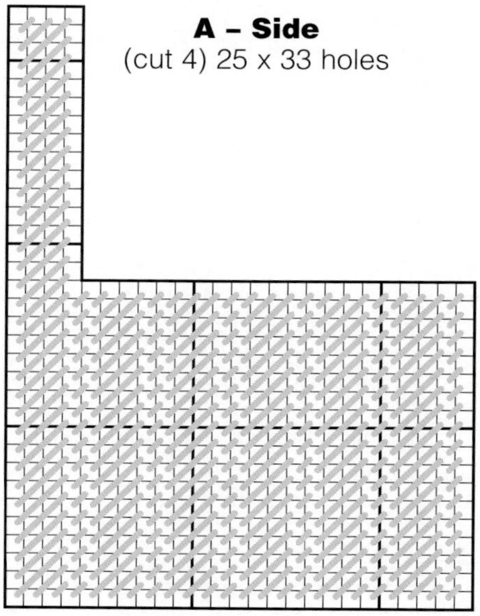

Front & Back Stitch Pattern Guide

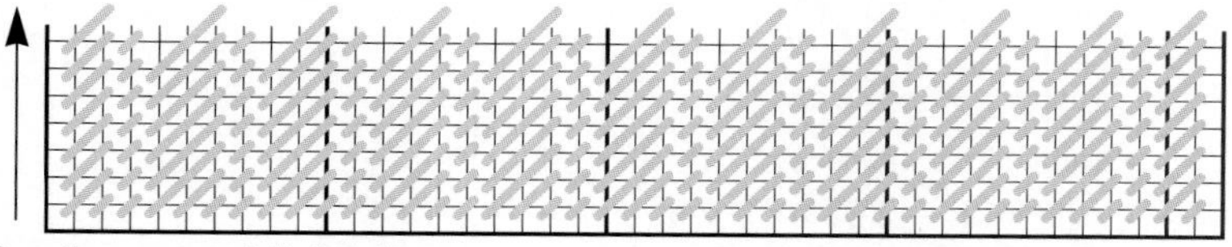

Continue established pattern across each entire piece.

FOLDING TABLE

SIZE: 6½" x 7⅞" x about 5" tall.

MATERIALS:

- ❑ Two sheets of 7-count plastic canvas
- ❑ Metallic cord; for amount see Color Key.
- ❑ Worsted-weight or plastic canvas yarn; for amounts see Color Key.

CUTTING INSTRUCTIONS:

A: For leg pieces, cut six according to graph.
B: For leg supports, cut twelve according to graph.
C: For table top, cut three according to graph.

STITCHING INSTRUCTIONS:

NOTE: Pieces are unworked.

1: For each leg, holding three A pieces together, with metallic cord, Whipstitch cutout edges together through all thicknesses. With White, Whipstitch outside edges together as indicated on graph.

2: For each leg support, holding three B pieces together, using White and stitches indicated, Whipstitch to one C piece through all thicknesses according to graph and as indicated on C graph.

3: Holding remaining C pieces to wrong side of worked piece, with cord, Whipstitch together.

4: To assemble table, slide leg slots together, forming stand. Place support openings firmly over each leg of stand.

C – Table Top
(cut 3) 43 x 52 holes

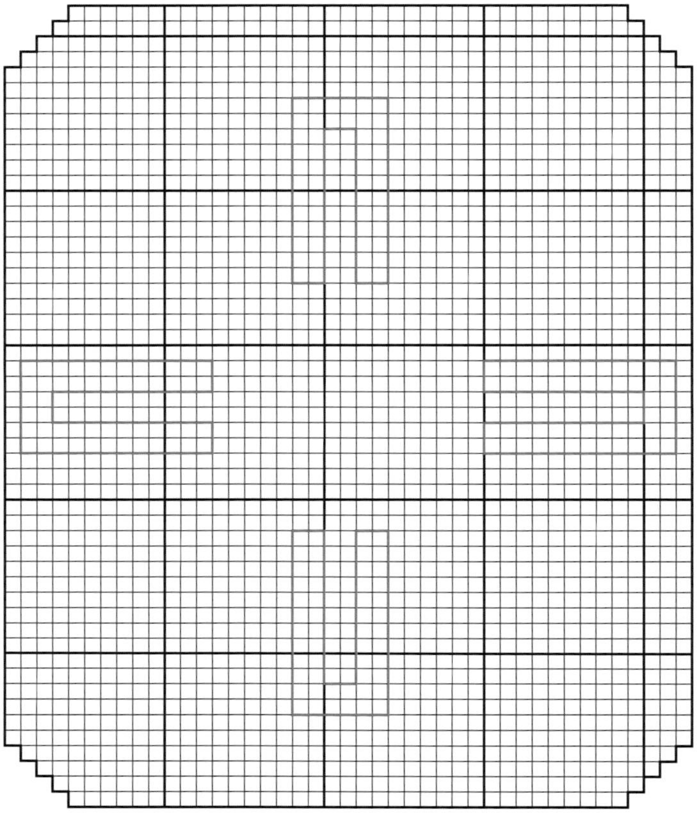

B – Leg Support
(cut 12)
6 x 12 holes

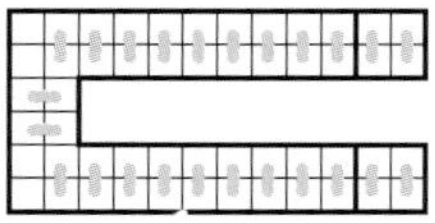

A – Leg Piece
(cut 6)
30 x 34 holes

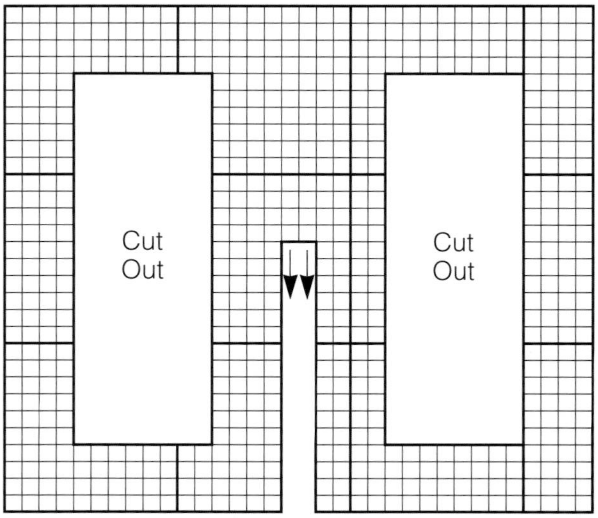

Whipstitch between arrows.

COLOR KEY:

Metallic cord
☐ White/Silver – 9 yds.

Nylon Plus™ #01 — Needloft™ yarn #41 White – 9 yds.

STITCH KEY:

☐ Leg Support Attachment

PICNIC TABLE

SIZE: About 11" across x 13" tall.

MATERIALS:
- ❑ One sheet of 7-count plastic canvas
- ❑ Six sheets of white 7-count plastic canvas
- ❑ 13" wooden ¼" dowel
- ❑ Worsted-weight or plastic canvas yarn; for amounts see Color Key.

CUTTING INSTRUCTIONS:

NOTES: Use clear canvas for umbrella pieces and white canvas for remaining pieces. Graphs continued on pages 144 and 145.

A: For umbrella top pieces, cut seven according to graph.

B: For umbrella overhang pieces, cut seven according to graph.

C: For table base, cut two according to graph.

D: For pole supports, cut ten according to graph.

E: For seat and table supports, cut sixteen according to graph.

F: For seat, cut three according to graph.

G: For table top, cut three according to graph.

STITCHING INSTRUCTIONS:

NOTE: Table and seat pieces are unworked.

1: Using Watermelon and stitches indicated, work A and B pieces according to graphs. Easing to fit, Whipstitch side edges of each A piece together, forming umbrella top. Whipstitch long straight edge of one B piece to matching edge of each top piece. Overcast unfinished edges of umbrella, leaving top point open for pole.

2: Holding eight D pieces together, with Sail Blue, Whipstitch pole supports to one C through all thicknesses as indicated on graph, forming table base top. For each seat and table support, holding two E pieces together, Whipstitch together as indicated.

3: With top edge of each seat and table support facing inside, Whipstitch indicated bottom edge of each support to base top as indicated on C graph. Whipstitch indicated center top edge of each support to one F piece as indicated, forming seat bottom.

4: Holding remaining C to wrong side of base top, Whipstitch together. Holding remaining F pieces to wrong side of seat bottom, Whipstitch inside and outside edges together.

5: Whipstitch indicated top edge of each support to one G piece as indicated, forming table bottom. Holding remaining G pieces to wrong side of table bottom, Whipstitch together.

6: Slip dowel through cutouts in table and attached pole supports on base. Slide cutouts of remaining pole supports on dowel, stopping about ¾" from top edge. Slide top point opening of umbrella on dowel.

COLOR KEY:

	Nylon Plus™	Needloft™ yarn
■	#04	#35 Sail Blue – 40 yds.
■	#54	#55 Watermelon – 55 yds.

STITCH KEY:

- ☐ Pole Support Attachment
- ☐ Support Attachment/Base
- ☐ Support Attachment/Seat
- ☐ Support Attachment/Table

B – Umbrella Overhang Piece
(cut 7 from clear) 4 x 27 holes

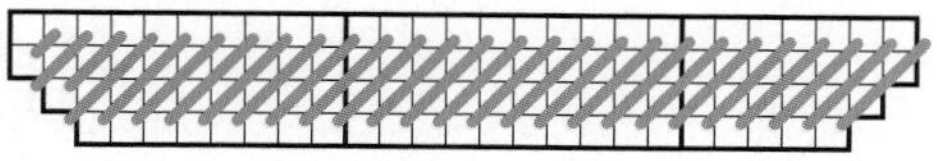

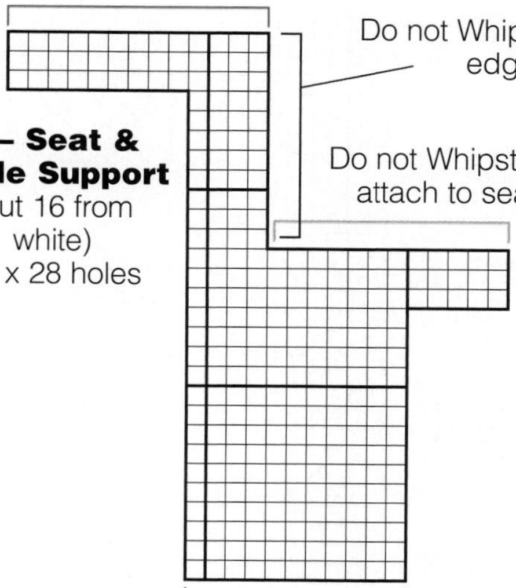

E – Seat & Table Support
(cut 16 from white)
25 x 28 holes

A – Umbrella Top Piece
(cut 7 from clear) 27 x 31 holes

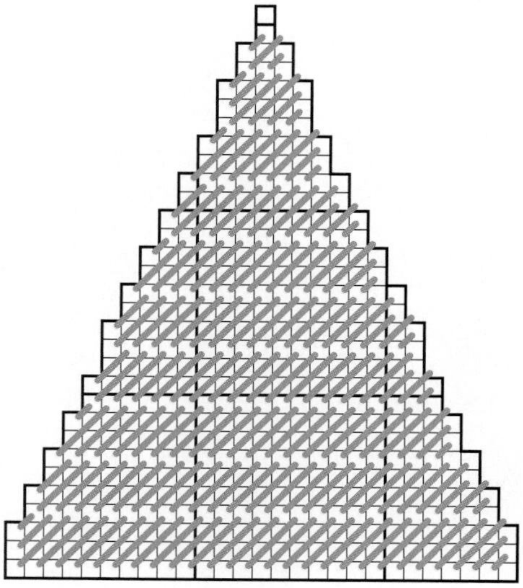

C – Table Base
(cut 2 from white) 58 x 58 holes

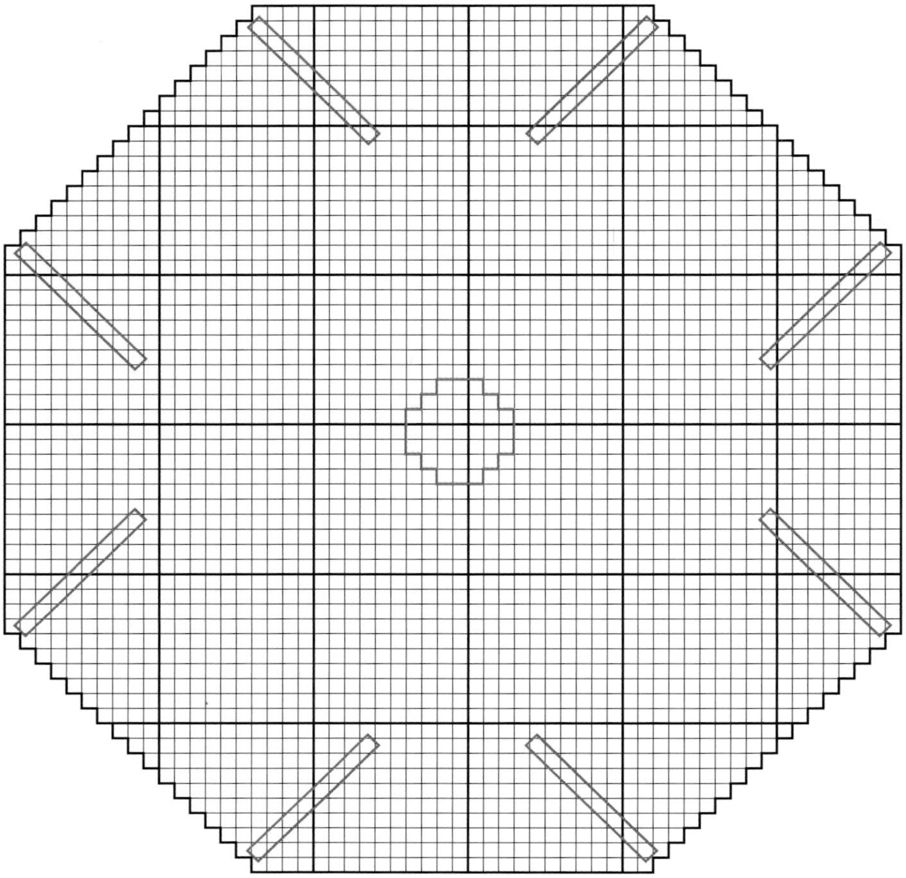

D – Pole Support
(cut 10 from white)
7 x 7 holes

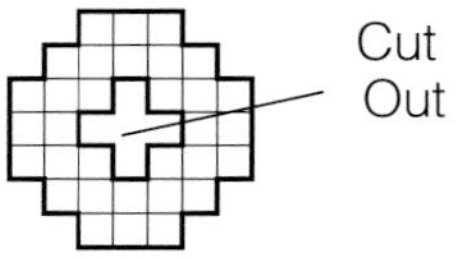

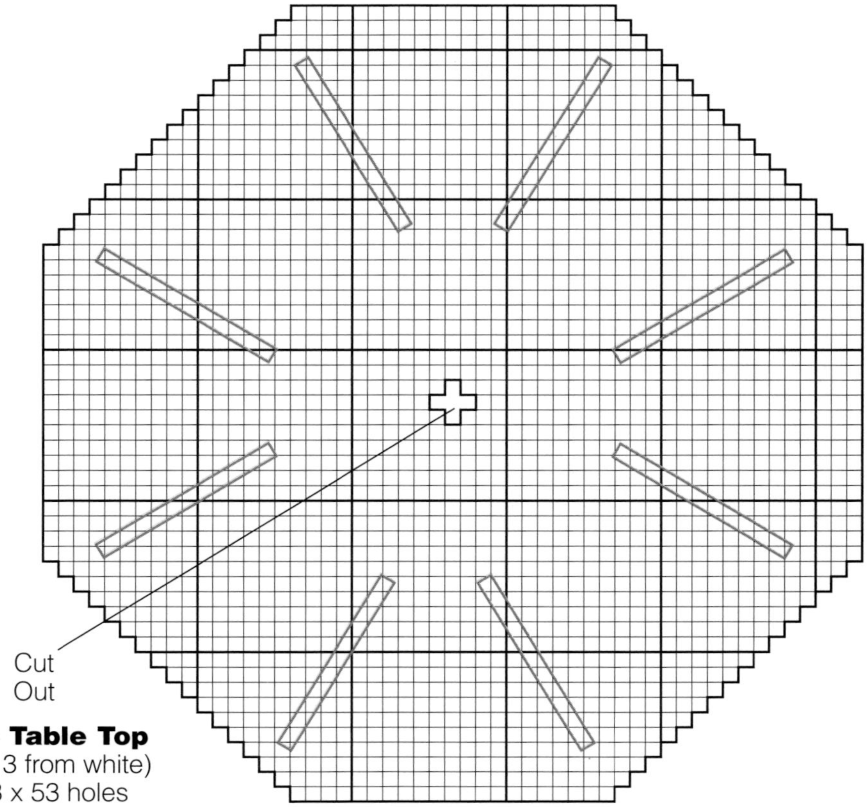

G – Table Top
(cut 3 from white)
53 x 53 holes

F – Seat
(cut 3 from white) 69 x 69 holes

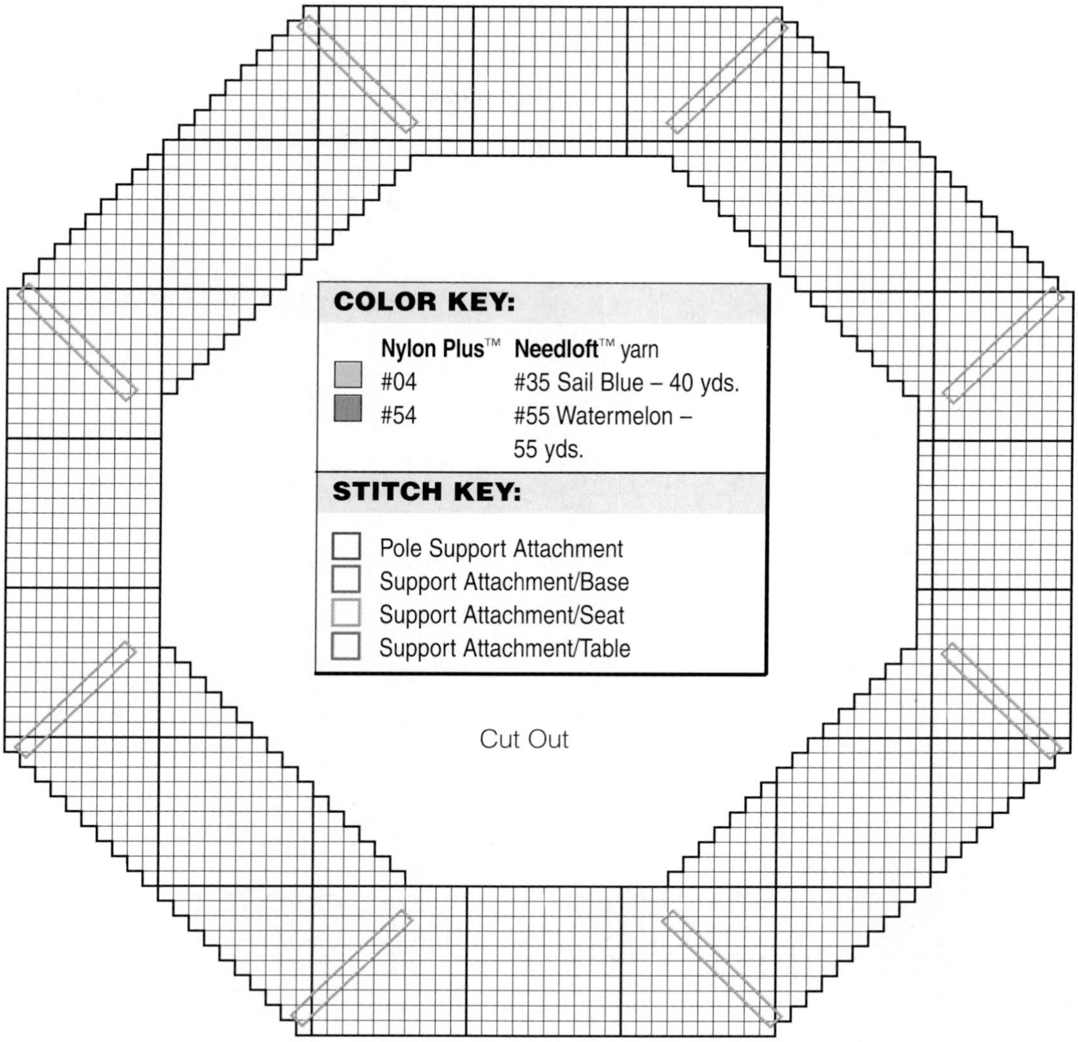
COLOR KEY:
Nylon Plus™ Needloft™ yarn
#04 #35 Sail Blue – 40 yds.
#54 #55 Watermelon – 55 yds.
STITCH KEY:
Pole Support Attachment
Support Attachment/Base
Support Attachment/Seat
Support Attachment/Table
Cut Out

BARBECUE PIT

SIZE: 3" x 4" x 6 ⅜" tall.

MATERIALS:
- ❑ ¾ sheet of 7-count plastic canvas
- ❑ ¼ sheet of black 7-count plastic canvas
- ❑ Craft glue or glue gun
- ❑ Worsted-weight or plastic canvas yarn; for amounts see Color Key on page 146.

CUTTING INSTRUCTIONS:

NOTES: Use black canvas for grill and lining pieces and clear canvas for remaining pieces. Graphs on page 146.

A: For barbecue front and lining, cut one from clear for front and one for lining according to graph.

B: For barbecue back and lining, cut one from clear for back and one from black for lining 7 x 25 holes (no graph).

C: For barbecue sides and linings, cut two from clear for sides and two from black for linings 7 x 13 holes.

D: For barbecue bottom and lining, cut one from clear for bottom and one from black for lining 13 x 25 holes (no graph).

E: For grill supports, cut four from black canvas 2 x 11 holes (no graph).

F: For grill, cut one according to graph.

G: For stand sides, cut four from clear 7 x 31 holes (no graph).

H: For base, cut two 13 x 25 holes.

STITCHING INSTRUCTIONS:

NOTE: D, F, one H and lining pieces are unworked.

1: Using Sail Blue and stitches indicated, work clear A and one H (leave indicated area unworked) according to graphs; work B, C and G pieces according to Barbecue Stitch Pattern Guide. For each grill support, holding two E pieces together with one lining C and working through all thicknesses, using Black and Continental Stitch, work according to Side/Lining Graph.

2: Holding lining pieces to wrong side of corresponding worked pieces, with Sail Blue, Whipstitch A-D pieces together, forming barbecue; Whipstitch unfinished edges together.

3: Holding G pieces wrong sides together, Whipstitch together, forming stand. Whipstitch one end of stand to worked H as indicated on graph. Holding unworked H to wrong side of worked piece, Whipstitch together. Glue bottom of barbecue to top of base. Set grill on supports.

A – Barbecue Front & Lining
(cut 1 from clear & 1 from black)
7 x 25 holes

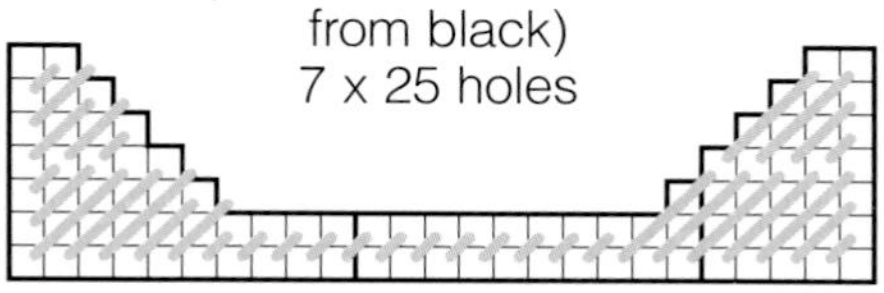

COLOR KEY:

	Nylon Plus™	Needloft™ yarn
■	#02	#00 Black – 2 yds.
□ (grey)	#04	#35 Sail Blue – 50 yds.

STITCH KEY:

- □ Unworked Area/Stand Attachment
- □ Grill Support Attachment

Barbecue Stitch Pattern Guide

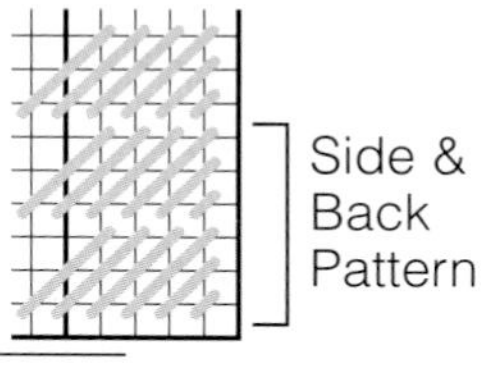

Continue established pattern across each entire piece.

F – Grill
(cut 1 from black)
18 x 24 holes

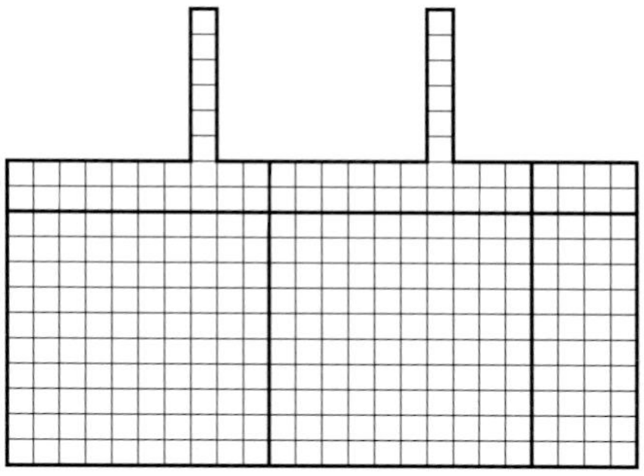

H – Base
(cut 2 from clear)
13 x 25 holes

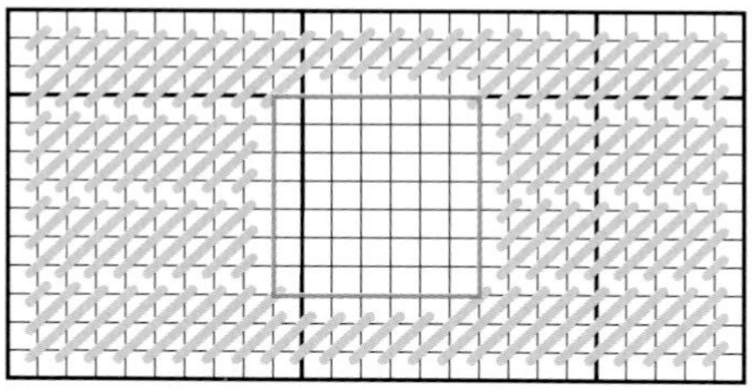

Side/Lining Graph

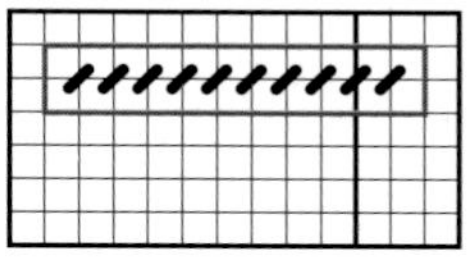

ENTERTAINMENT CENTER

SIZE: 1¼" x 2¾" x 6¼" (with speakers attached), not including handle.

MATERIALS:

- ❑ ½ sheet of 7-count plastic canvas
- ❑ Scraps of stoneware blue and black 7-count plastic canvas
- ❑ Two Velcro™ closure strips
- ❑ Craft glue or glue gun
- ❑ Fine metallic braid; for amount see Color Key.
- ❑ Metallic cord; for amount see Color Key.
- ❑ Worsted-weight or plastic canvas yarn; for amounts see Color Key.

CUTTING INSTRUCTIONS:

NOTE: Use stoneware blue canvas for speaker box fronts, black canvas for speakers and clear canvas for remaining pieces.

A: For component box front and back, cut two (one for front and one for back) from clear 17 x 18 holes.

B: For component box top and bottom, cut two (one for top and one for bottom) from clear 8 x 18 holes (no graph).

C: For component box sides, cut two from clear 8 x 17 holes (no graph).

D: For handle, cut two from clear according to graph.

E: For speaker box fronts and backs, cut four (two from blue for fronts and two from clear for backs) 9 x 17 holes (no graph).

F: For speaker box tops and bottoms, cut four (two for tops and two for bottoms) from clear 8 x 9 holes (no graph).

G: For speaker box sides, cut four from clear 8 x 17 holes (no graph).

H: For speakers, cut two large and two small according to graphs.

STITCHING INSTRUCTIONS:

NOTE: Front E and H pieces are unworked.

1: Using colors and stitches indicated, work one A for front according to graph. Using yarn and braid colors indicated and Straight Stitch, embroider trim as indicated on graph.

2: Using Black and Slanted Gobelin Stitch over width of each piece, work back A, B, C, clear E, F and G pieces. Using metallic cord and Continental Stitch, work D pieces. Holding D pieces wrong sides together, Whipstitch together. Whipstitch short ends of handle to center top of one B.

3: With cord for front edges and with Black, Whipstitch A-C pieces together, forming component box.

NOTE: Cut one 18" length of Black.

4: Thread 18" strand of Black from back to front through one back E, then component box and from front to back through remaining back E according to Speaker Box Attachment Diagram; knot ends.

5: For each speaker box, with cord for front edges and

with Black, Whipstitch one of each E, two F and two G pieces together. Glue one closure to each side of component box and corresponding speaker box side. Glue H pieces to speaker box fronts as shown in photo.

A – Component Box Front & Back
(cut 1 each) 17 x 18 holes

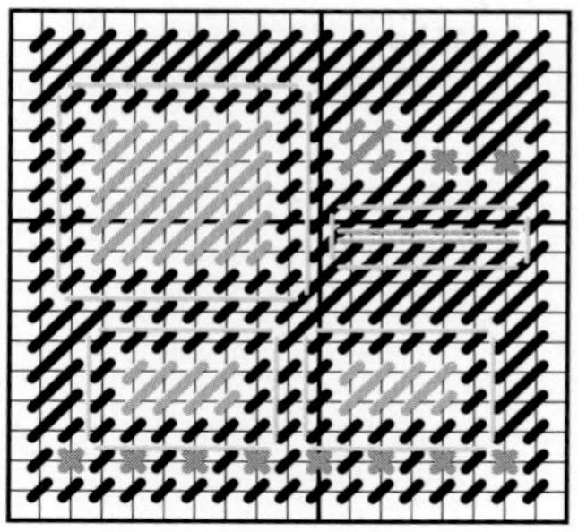

D – Handle
(cut 2)
7 x 14 holes

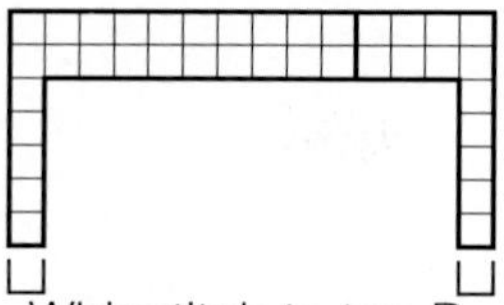

H – Large Speaker
(cut 2 from black)
7 x 7 holes

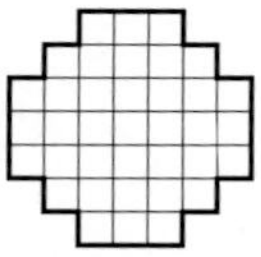

H – Small Speaker
(cut 2 from black)
5 x 5 holes

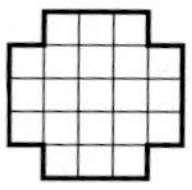

COLOR KEY:

	Fine metallic braid	
☐	Silver – 1 yd.	
	Metallic cord	
■	White/Silver – 5 yds.	
	Nylon Plus™	**Needloft**™ yarn
■	#02	#00 Black – 30 yds.
■	#40	#37 Silver – 2 yds.

STITCH KEY:

— Backstitch/Straight Stitch

Speaker Box Attachment Diagram
(back view)

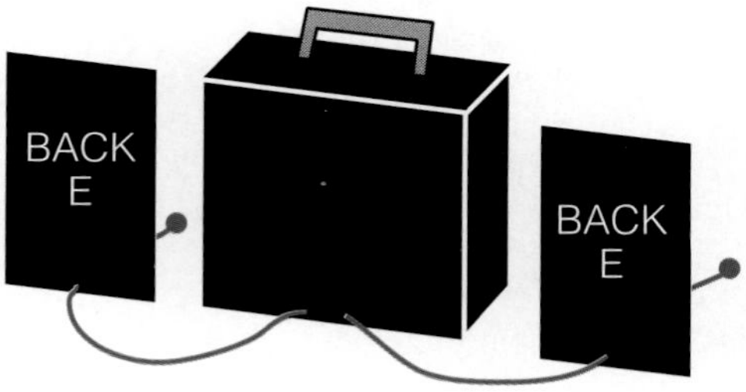

ICE CHEST

SIZE: 2¼" x 3½".

MATERIALS:
- ❑ ½ sheet each of clear and white 7-count plastic canvas
- ❑ Worsted-weight or plastic canvas yarn; for amounts see Color Key.

CUTTING INSTRUCTIONS:

NOTE: Use white canvas for lining pieces.

A: For chest sides, cut two 11 x 20 holes.

B: For chest ends, cut two 11 x 11 holes.

C: For chest side linings, cut two 13 x 20 holes (no graph).

D: For chest end linings, cut two 11 x 13 holes (no graph).

E: For chest bottom and lining, cut one from each color 11 x 20 holes (no graph).

F: For lid top and lining, cut one from each color 13 x 22 holes (no graph).

G: For lid sides and linings, cut two from each color 3 x 22 holes (no graph).

H: For lid ends and linings, cut two from each color 3 x 13 holes (no graph).

STITCHING INSTRUCTIONS:

NOTE: Lining pieces and bottom are unworked.

1: Using Royal Dark and Slanted Gobelin Stitch, work A and B pieces according to graphs. Using White and Continental Stitch for lid top and Slanted Gobelin Stitch over narrow width for lid sides and ends, work F, G and H pieces.

2: Holding lining pieces to wrong side of corresponding worked pieces and working through all thicknesses, with White, Whipstitch F-H pieces together, forming lid. Whipstitch unfinished edges of lid together.

3: Holding lining pieces to wrong side of corresponding worked pieces and working through all thicknesses (**NOTE:** Top edges of lining pieces will extend two holes over edge of top.), with Royal Dark, Whipstitch A-E pieces together, forming chest. Whipstitch top edges of A and B pieces to corresponding bars on C and D pieces; do not Overcast unfinished top edge of lining.

NOTE: Cut two 9" lengths of White.

4: For each handle, thread one 9" strand of White from back to front (through both thicknesses) of chest side at one ◆ hole as indicated on B graph, then back down through neighboring ◆ hole, leaving about ⅝" loop of yarn on outside. Knot; trim ends. Place a drop of glue on each knot to secure.

A – Chest Side
(cut 2 from clear) 11 x 20 holes

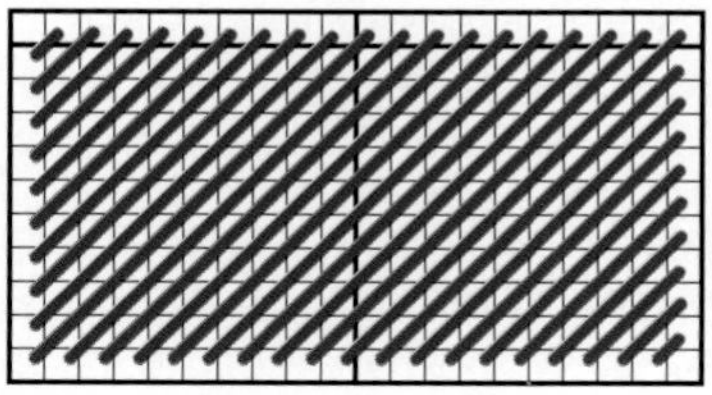

B – Chest End
(cut 2 from clear)
11 x 11 holes

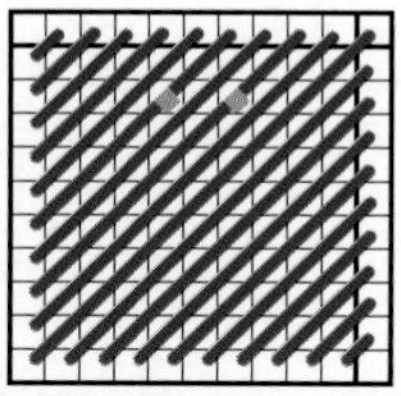

COLOR KEY:

	Nylon Plus™	**Needloft**™ yarn
☐	#01	#41 White – 13 yds.
■	#07	#48 Royal Dark – 15 yds.

STITCH KEY:

◆ Handle Attachment

CAMERA & BEACH BAG

SIZE: Camera is ¾" x 1⅛", not including strap; Beach Bag is 1⅝" x 1¾" x 2" tall, not including strap.

MATERIALS:
- ❏ Scraps of clear, neon blue, neon pink and white 7-count plastic canvas
- ❏ ⅜" round acrylic mirror
- ❏ Craft glue or glue gun
- ❏ 8" silver heavy metallic braid
- ❏ Worsted-weight or plastic canvas yarn; for amounts see Color Key.

CUTTING INSTRUCTIONS:

A: For camera front and back, cut two (one for front and one for back) from clear according to graph.

B: For beach bag side, cut one from blue 12 x 32 holes.

C: For beach bag bottom, cut one from pink according to graph.

D: For sail motif, cut one from white according to graph.

E: For hull motif, cut one from pink according to graph.

STITCHING INSTRUCTIONS:

NOTE: C-E pieces are unworked.

1: For Camera, using Black and Continental Stitch, work A pieces. Holding A pieces wrong sides together and omitting shutter button on front, Whipstitch together. For strap, thread metallic cord from back to front at one top outside corner of camera, then from front to back at opposite outside corner. Trim to desired length, knot ends. Glue acrylic mirror to center of front.

2: For Beach Bag, overlapping two holes at short ends to join as indicated, with White, Whipstitch ends of B together. Leaving about 12" of yarn hanging, using a 32" strand of White and Running Stitch (see Stitch Illustration), work one side of B according to graph; loop twice through top hole.

3: Leaving about 3" of yarn between coded areas for strap, loop twice through top hole on opposite side of B, then work Running Stitch down side according to graph. Using remaining ends of White and easing to fit, Whipstitch C to bottom edge of B. Glue motifs to side of bag as shown in photo.

Lap Under **B – Beach Bag Side** (cut 1 from blue) 12 x 32 holes Lap Over

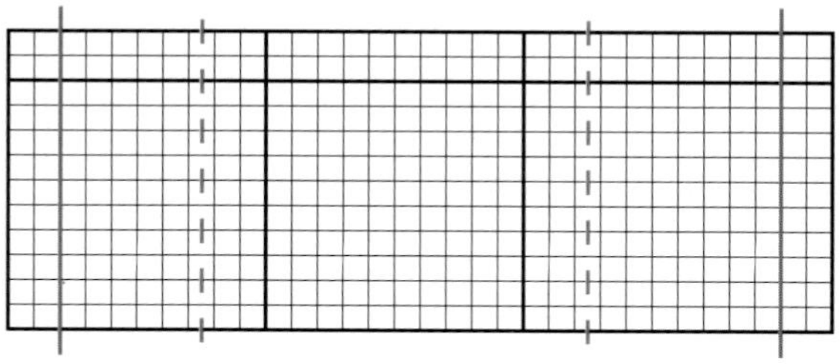

A – Camera Front
(cut 1 from clear)
5 x 7 holes

A – Camera Back
(cut 1 from clear)

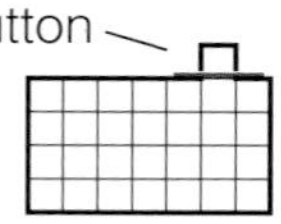

C – Beach Bag Bottom
(cut 1 from pink)
7 x 11 holes

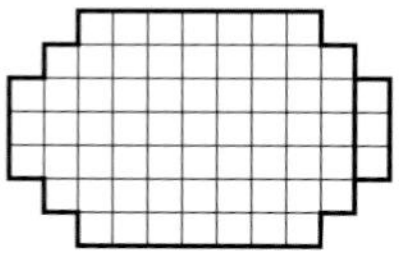

E – Hull Motif
(cut 1 from pink)
2 x 6 holes

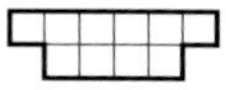

Running Stitch Illustration

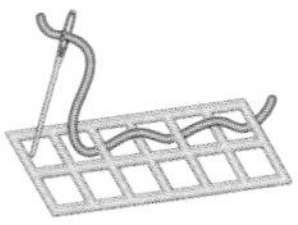

D – Sail Motif
(cut 1 from white)
4 x 4 holes

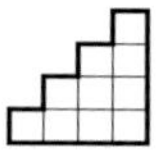

COLOR KEY:

	Nylon Plus™	Needloft™ yarn
☐	#02	#00 Black – 2 yds.
■	#01	#41 White – 1½ yds.

STITCH KEY:

— Running Stitch

LAWN CHAIRS

LOUNGER

SIZE: 2⅝" x about 12" long.

MATERIALS:
- ❏ One sheet of 7-count plastic canvas
- ❏ Metallic cord; for amount see Color Key on page 149.
- ❏ Worsted-weight or plastic canvas yarn; for amounts see Color Key.

CUTTING INSTRUCTIONS:

A: For Lounger seat, cut two 17 x 33 holes.

B: For Lounger seat back, cut two 17 x 31 holes.

C: For Lounger foot rest, cut two 15 x 17 holes.

D: For Lounger seat support sides, cut four according to graph.

E: For Lounger seat support ends, cut four 3 x 15 holes.

F: For Lounger foot rest support, cut two according to graph.

G: For Lounger back braces, cut four according to graph.

STITCHING INSTRUCTIONS:

NOTE: One of each A-C is unworked.

1: Using colors and stitches indicated, work one A, one B, one C, D, E, F and G (two on opposite side of canvas) pieces according to graphs. For each seat support side, end and back brace, hold two like pieces wrong sides together. With metallic cord, Whipstitch D and E pieces together according to Step 1 of Lounger Seat Support Assembly Diagrams.

2: With Watermelon, Whipstitch seat support to

unworked A according to Step 2. Whipstitch back braces to unworked B as indicated and according to Step 3. Holding F pieces wrong sides together, Whipstitch foot rest support to unworked C according to Step 4. With cord, Whipstitch unfinished edges of seat support, back braces and foot rest support together.

3: Holding matching A, B and C pieces wrong sides together (back support end of back joins seat), with Watermelon, Whipstitch together through all thicknesses as indicated; Whipstitch unfinished edges together.

D – Lounger Seat Support Side

(cut 4) 6 x 32 holes

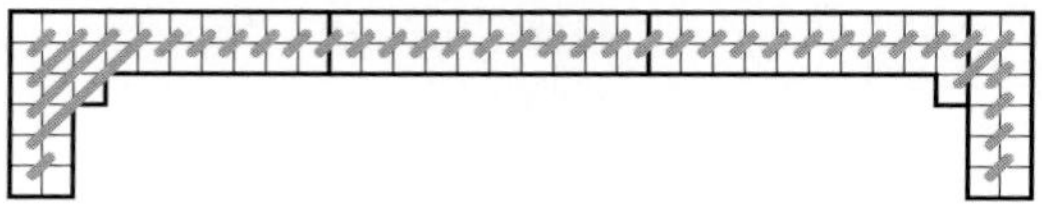

C – Lounger Foot Rest

(cut 2) 15 x 17 holes

Attach to seat.

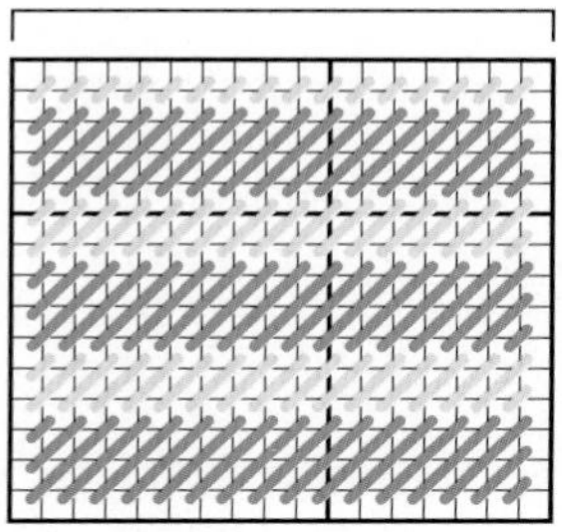

A – Lounger Seat

(cut 2) 17 x 33 holes

Attach to seat back.

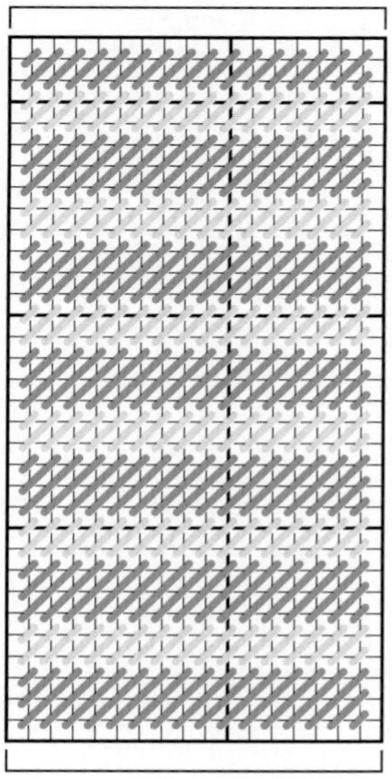

Attach to foot rest.

E – Lounger Seat Support End

(cut 4) 3 x 15 holes

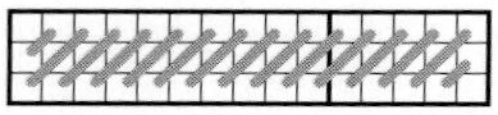

COLOR KEY:

Metallic cord		
White/Silver – 12 yds.		
Nylon Plus™	**Needloft™** yarn	
#01	#41 White – 10 yds.	
#54	#55 Watermelon – 22 yds.	

G – Lounger Back Brace

(cut 4) 7 x 12 holes

Whipstitch to seat back.

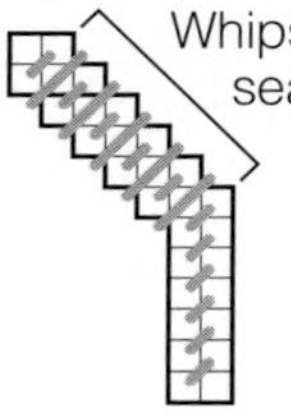

F – Lounger Foot Rest Support

(cut 2) 6 x 15 holes

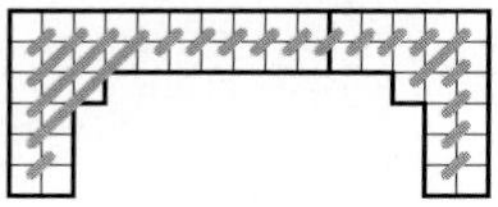

B – Lounger Seat Back

(cut 2) 17 x 31 holes

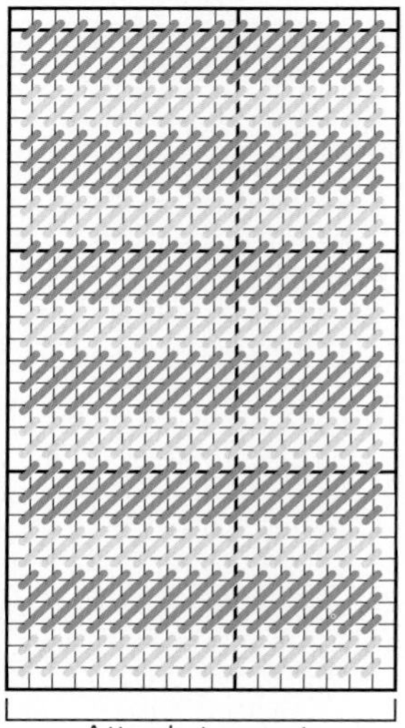

Attach to seat.

Lounger Seat Support Assembly Diagrams

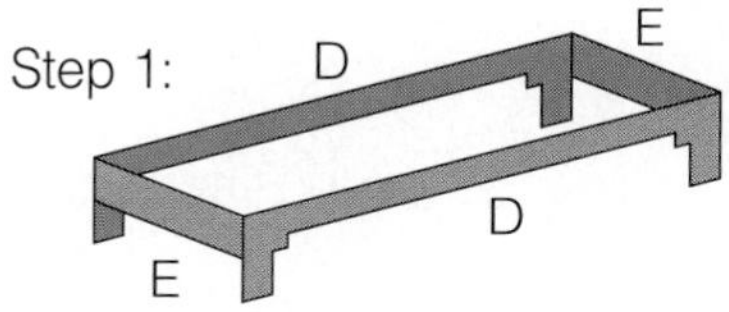

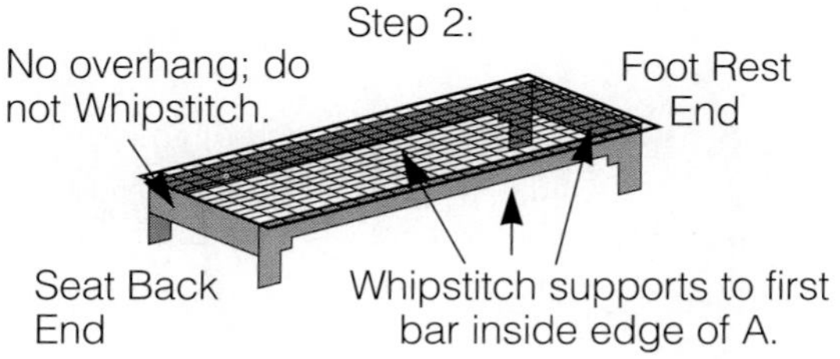

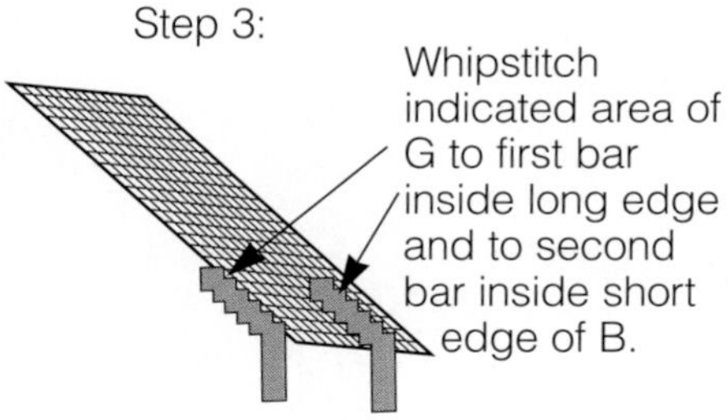

Step 3:
Whipstitch indicated area of G to first bar inside long edge and to second bar inside short edge of B.

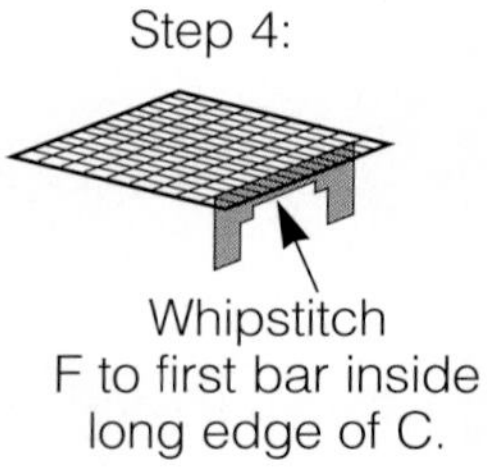

Step 4:
Whipstitch F to first bar inside long edge of C.

CHAIR

SIZE: 2⅝" x about 6½" long.

MATERIALS:

- ❑ ½ sheet of 7-count plastic canvas
- ❑ Metallic cord; for amount see Color Key.
- ❑ Worsted-weight or plastic canvas yarn; for amounts see Color Key.

CUTTING INSTRUCTIONS:

A: For Chair seat and seat back, cut four (two for seat and two for seat back) 17 x 21 holes.

B: For Chair seat support sides, cut four 2 x 19 holes (no graph).

C: For Chair seat support ends, cut four according to graph.

D: For Chair back brace pieces, cut two 2 x 7 holes and one 2 x 13 holes (no graph).

STITCHING INSTRUCTIONS:

1: Using colors and stitches indicated, work two A and C pieces according to graphs. Using metallic cord and Continental Stitch, work B and D pieces.

2: For each seat support side and end, hold two matching pieces wrong sides together. With cord, Whipstitch B and C pieces together through all thicknesses according to Step 1 of Chair Seat Support Assembly Diagrams. Whipstitch to one unworked A according to Step 2.

3: Whipstitch D pieces together according to Step 3; Whipstitch back brace to remaining unworked A according to Step 4. Whipstitch unfinished edges of seat support and back brace together.

4: Holding one support A wrong sides together with each worked piece, with Royal Dark, Whipstitch together (back support end joins seat) through both thicknesses; Whipstitch unfinished edges together. With cord, tack bottom corners of back support to seat support legs.

COLOR KEY:

	Metallic cord	
▩	White/Silver – 7 yds.	
	Nylon Plus™	**Needloft™** yarn
▢	#01	#41 White – 5 yds.
■	#07	#48 Royal Dark – 8 yds.

C – Seat Support End

(cut 4) 6 x 15 holes

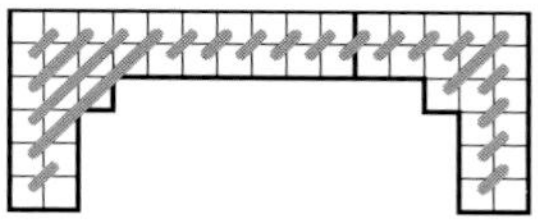

A – Chair Seat & Seat Back

(cut 2 each) 17 x 21 holes

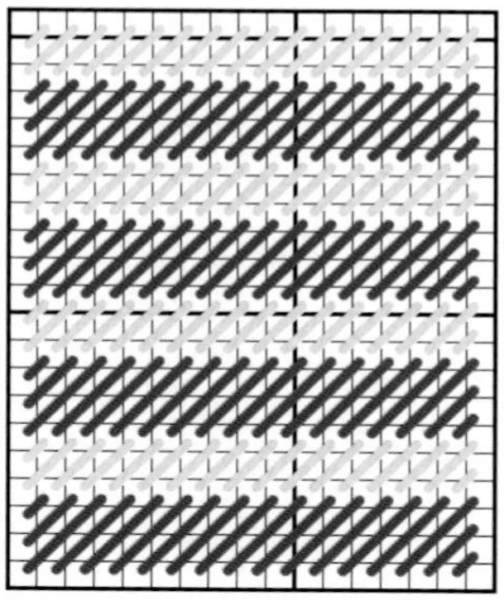

Chair Seat Support Assembly Diagrams

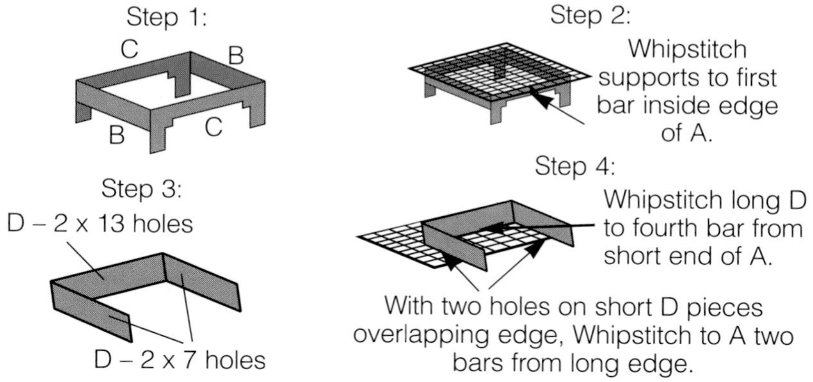
Step 1:
C
B
B
C
Step 2:
Whipstitch supports to first bar inside edge of A.
Step 3:
D – 2 x 13 holes
D – 2 x 7 holes
Step 4:
Whipstitch long D to fourth bar from short end of A.
With two holes on short D pieces overlapping edge, Whipstitch to A two bars from long edge.

PILLOWS

SIZE: Square pillow is 1¾" x 1¾"; each round pillow is 1⅞" across.

MATERIALS:

- ❑ Scraps of 7-count plastic canvas
- ❑ Small amount of polyester fiberfill
- ❑ Worsted-weight or plastic canvas yarn; for amounts see Color Key.

CUTTING INSTRUCTIONS:

A: For square pillow, cut two 11 x 11 holes.

B: For gingham print pillow, cut two according to graph.

C: For flower motif pillow, cut two according to graph.

STITCHING INSTRUCTIONS:

1: Using colors and stitches indicated, work A and B pieces according to graphs. Using White and Continental Stitch, work C pieces.

2: Using Pink and French Knot, embroider flowers on A pieces and one C as indicated on graphs. Using Royal and Lazy Daisy Stitch, embroider leaves on C as indicated.

3: Holding matching pieces wrong sides together, with Pink for square and flower motif pillows and with White for gingham print pillow, Whipstitch each pillow together, stuffing with fiberfill before closing.

COLOR KEY:		
	Nylon Plus™	Needloft™ yarn
■	#11	#07 Pink – 4½ yds.
■	#09	#32 Royal – ½ yd.
■	#01	#41 White – 13 yds.

STITCH KEY:

● French Knot

⬭ Lazy Daisy Stitch

A – Square Pillow
(cut 2) 11 x 11 holes

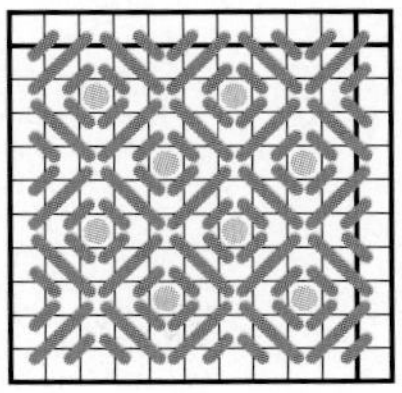

C – Flower Motif Pillow
(cut 2) 11 x 11 holes

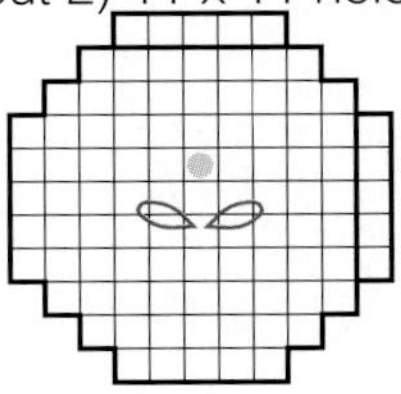

B – Gingham Print Pillow
(cut 2) 11 x 11 holes

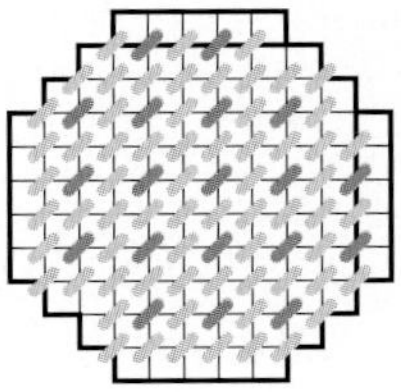

LINENS

BED SHEET & PILLOWS

SIZE: Sheet is 9⅛" x 12⅜"; each Pillow is 2¼" x 3½".

MATERIALS FOR ONE SHEET AND TWO PILLOWS:

- ❑ ½ yd. print or stripe coordinating color cotton broad cloth
- ❑ ⅔ yd. white ½" scalloped edging
- ❑ ⅔ yd. coordinating color ⅛" rattail cord
- ❑ Small amount of polyester fiberfill
- ❑ Iron-on binding or sewing needle and matching color thread
- ❑ Craft glue or glue gun (optional)

CUTTING INSTRUCTIONS:

A: For sheet, from fabric, cut one 10½" x 12½" and one 2⅛" x 10½".

B: For pillows, from fabric, cut two 4⅛" x 5¾" and two 1¾" x 5¾".

C: For trim, cut edging and rattail cord each into one 10" and two 4¾" lengths.

STITCHING INSTRUCTIONS:

NOTES: Finish outside edges by turning under twice ⅜", then secure using iron-on binding, glue, or press and then sew. Finish inner edges by turning under once ⅜", then secure as above.

1: For sheet, finish one short and long edges of large A. Finish one long and short edges of small A.

2: Holding unfinished edges of A pieces together with right sides showing, finish remaining edge of small A to cover raw edge of large A.

3: Place straight edge of 10" length of edging across large A just under inner finished edge of small A. Glue or sew thicknesses together, turning ends of edging to wrong side to finish. Glue or sew 10" length of rattail cord about ⅛" above scalloped edge.

4: For each pillow, finish one long and two short edges of one large B. Finish one long and two short edges of one small B. Join B pieces as in Step 2 above.

5: Fold in half wrong sides together. Use iron-on binding, glue or sew finished side and bottom edges together. Using one remaining length of edging and rattail cord, finish pillow as in Step 3 above, joining matching ends of trim at seam. Stuff lightly with fiberfill, then glue or sew pillow together under cord to close.

BLANKET

SIZE: 8½" x 11½".

MATERIALS FOR ONE:

- ❑ 9" x 12" square of coordinating color felt
- ❑ ⅔ yd. white ⅜" satin ribbon
- ❑ ⅔ yd. coordinating color ⅛" rattail cord
- ❑ Iron-on binding or glue

CUTTING INSTRUCTIONS:

A: For blanket, cut one 8½" x 11½" from felt.

B: Cut ribbon in half.

STITCHING INSTRUCTIONS:

1: Matching edges, with iron-on binding or glue, secure one length of ribbon across one short end of A; turn ends under and secure on wrong side. Secure remaining length of ribbon on back side, covering ends of front-side ribbon. Clip ends even with blanket edges.

2: Secure rattail cord over inner edge of ribbon, and finish as above.

THROW PILLOWS

SIZE: Each is 2¼" x 2¼".

MATERIALS FOR FOUR:

- ❑ Scraps of print or stripe coordinating color cotton broadcloth
- ❑ ⅔ yd. white ½" scalloped lace edging
- ❑ Small amount of polyester fiberfill
- ❑ Iron-on binding or sewing needle and matching color thread
- ❑ Craft glue or glue gun

CUTTING INSTRUCTIONS:

A: For pillows, from fabric, cut eight 2⅞" x 2⅞".

B: For trim, cut edging into four 8" lengths.

STITCHING INSTRUCTIONS:

NOTE: Finish edges by turning under ⅜" using iron-on binding, or press and then sew.

1: For each pillow, finish edges on two A pieces. Holding A pieces wrong sides together and stuffing lightly with fiberfill before closing, sew or bind edges together. Glue one length of lace edging around outside of pillow.

TO MAKE UP BED:

Place table top of folding table between bench seats; cover with linens.

BARBIE® doll and friends pictured with permission of
Mattel, Inc. ©1996 Mattel, Inc. All rights reserved.

FASHION DOLL

Patio

Designed by Carolyn Christmas

SIZE: Sofa is 2½" x 6⅜" x 5⅜" tall; each Chair is 2½" x 2¾" x 5⅜" tall; Coffee Table is 2¾" x 5½" x 2" tall; End Table is 2⅞" square x 2⅝" tall; Pillows are about 1½" square.

MATERIALS:
- ❏ Three sheets of white 7-count plastic canvas
- ❏ Craft glue or glue gun
- ❏ Worsted-weight or plastic canvas yarn; for amounts see Color Key on page 155.

FURNITURE

NOTE: Graphs on pages 154 and 155.

SOFA & CHAIRS

CUTTING INSTRUCTIONS:

A: For Sofa front and back, cut one each according to graphs.

B: For Sofa seat, cut one 16 x 41 holes (no graph).

C: For Sofa and Arm Chair ends, cut four (two for Sofa ends and two for Arm Chair ends) according to graph.

D: For Chair and Arm Chair fronts and backs, cut two (one for each chair front and one for each chair back) according to each graph.

E: For Chair and Arm Chair seats, cut two (one for each chair seat) 16 x 17 holes (no graph).

F: For Chair ends, cut two according to graph.

STITCHING INSTRUCTIONS:

NOTE: Front and end pieces are unworked.

1: Using White and stitches indicated, work back A and back D pieces according to graphs, and work B and E pieces according to Seat Stitch Pattern Guide, leaving uncoded areas unworked.

2: For Sofa, Whipstitch A and B pieces together as indicated on graphs. Whipstitch assembly and two C pieces together as indicated; Overcast unfinished top edges of back and arms.

3: For Arm Chair, using remaining C pieces, one of each D and one E, assemble as for Sofa in Step 2. For Chair, using remaining D, E and F pieces, Whipstitch together as indicated.

TABLES

CUTTING INSTRUCTIONS:

A: For Coffee Table sides, cut two according to graph.

B: For Coffee Table ends, cut two according to graph.

C: For Coffee Table top base, cut one 16 x 34 holes (no graph).

D: For Coffee Table top, cut one 18 x 36 holes.

E: For End Table sides, cut four according to graph.

F: For End Table top base, cut one 16 x 16 holes (no graph).

G: For End Table top, cut one 18 x 18 holes.

STITCHING INSTRUCTIONS:

NOTE: Side, end and top base pieces are unworked.

1: Using White and stitches indicated, work D and G pieces according to graphs; Overcast unfinished edges.

2: For Coffee Table, Whipstitch A-C pieces together. For End Table, Whipstitch E and F pieces together.

3: Glue D to Coffee Table base and G to End Table base.

CUSHIONS & PILLOWS

CUTTING INSTRUCTIONS:

A: For Sofa cushion top and bottom, cut two (one for top and one for bottom) 16 x 40 holes (no graph).

B: For Sofa cushion side and end pieces, cut two 1 x 40 holes for sides and two 1 x 16 holes for ends (no graphs).

C: For Chair cushion tops and bottoms, cut four (two for tops and two for bottoms) 16 x 16 holes (no graph).

D: For Chair cushion side pieces, cut eight 1 x 16 holes (no graph).

E: For Throw Pillows, cut six 10 x 10 holes.

STITCHING INSTRUCTIONS:

NOTE: Cushion bottom, side and end pieces are unworked.

1: Using Lilac and Continental Stitch, work one A and two C pieces according to Seat Cushion Stitch Pattern Guide, leaving uncoded areas unworked. Using colors and stitches indicated, work E pieces according to graph.

2: For Sofa cushion, with Lilac, Whipstitch A and B pieces together. For each Chair cushion, using C and D pieces, repeat as for Sofa cushion.

3: For each Throw Pillow, holding two E pieces wrong sides together, with Lilac, Whipstitch together, stuffing with yarn scraps before closing.

D – Chair & Arm Chair Front (cut 1 each) 14 x 17 holes

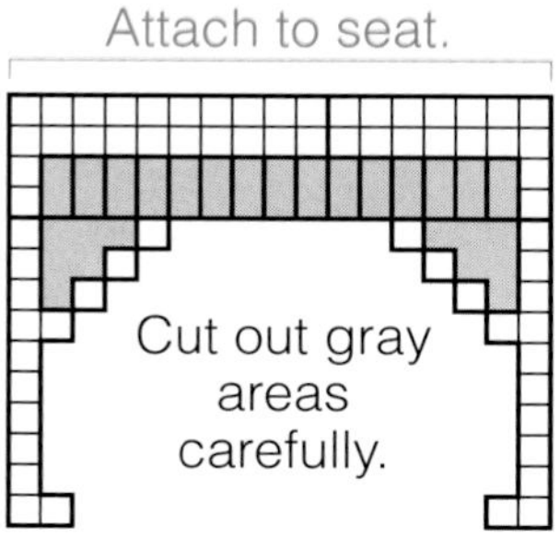

A – Sofa Back (cut 1) 35 x 41 holes

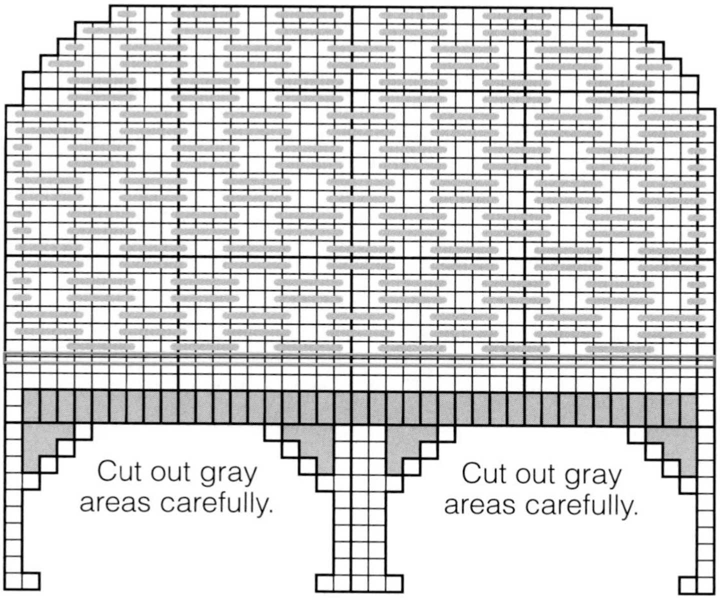

F – Chair End (cut 2) 14 x 16 holes

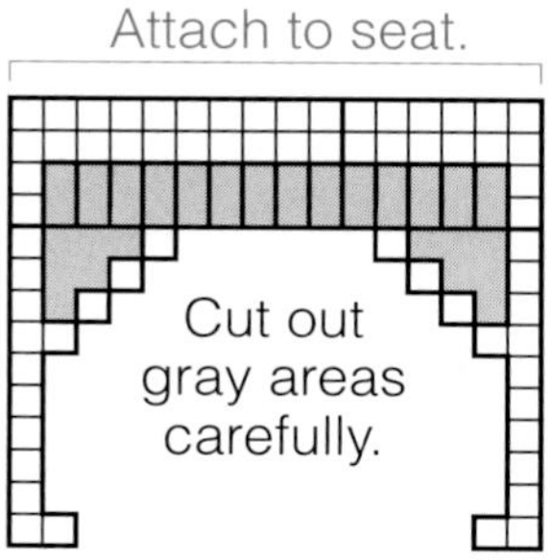

Seat Cushion Stitch Pattern Guide

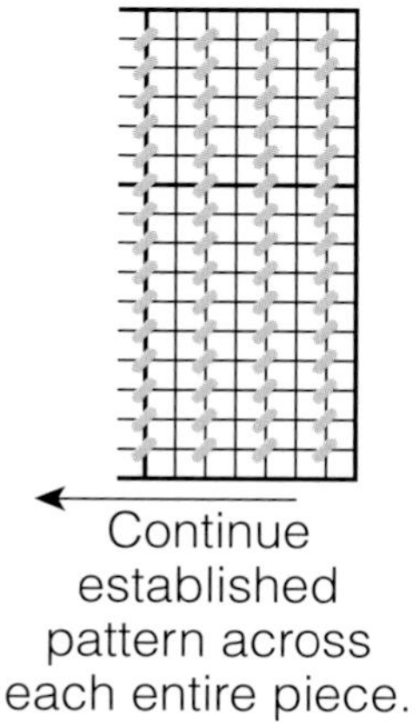

A – Sofa Front (cut 1) 14 x 41 holes

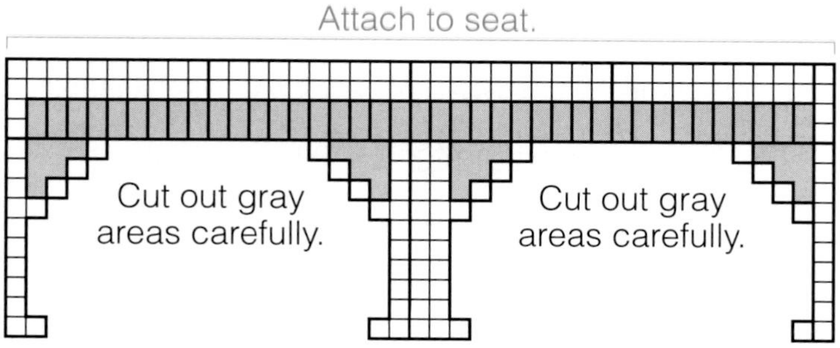

Seat Stitch Pattern Guide

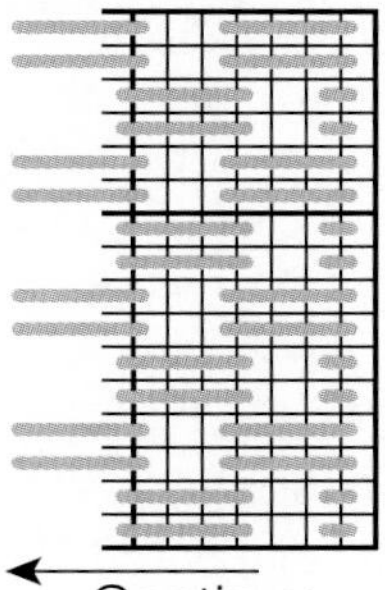

Continue established pattern across each entire piece.

C – Sofa & Arm Chair End
(cut 2 each)
16 x 22 holes

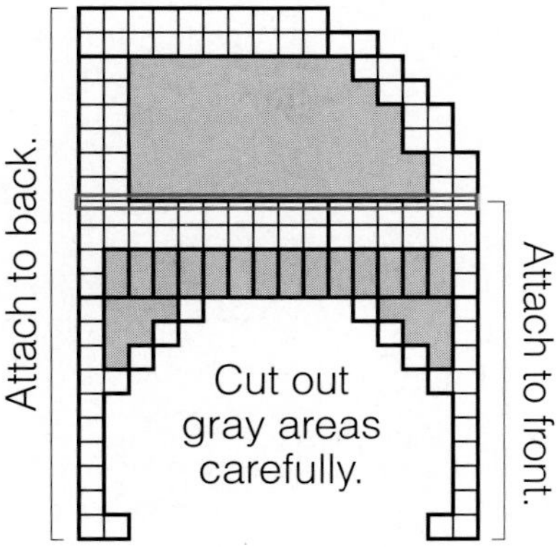

D – Chair & Arm Chair Back
(cut 1 each)
17 x 35 holes

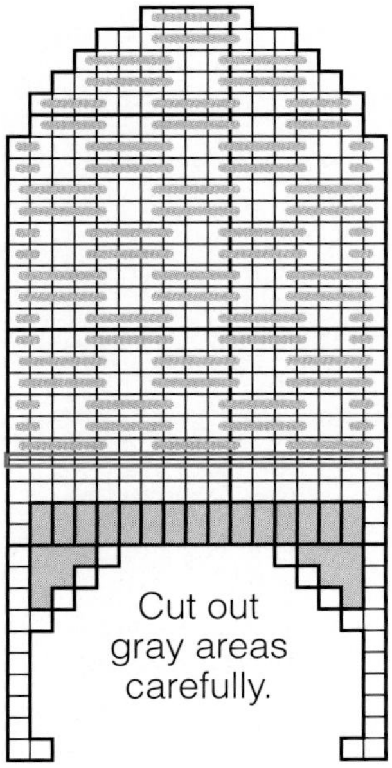

COLOR KEY:

Nylon Plus™ Needloft™ yarn

#01	#41 White – 43 yds.
#22	#45 Lilac – 22 yds.

STITCH KEY:

- Seat/Front & Back Attachment
- Seat/End Attachment

E – Throw Pillow
(cut 6)
10 x 10 holes

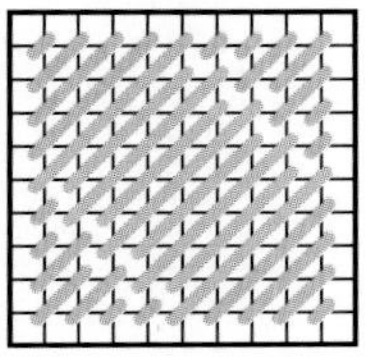

G – End Table Top
(cut 1) 18 x 18 holes

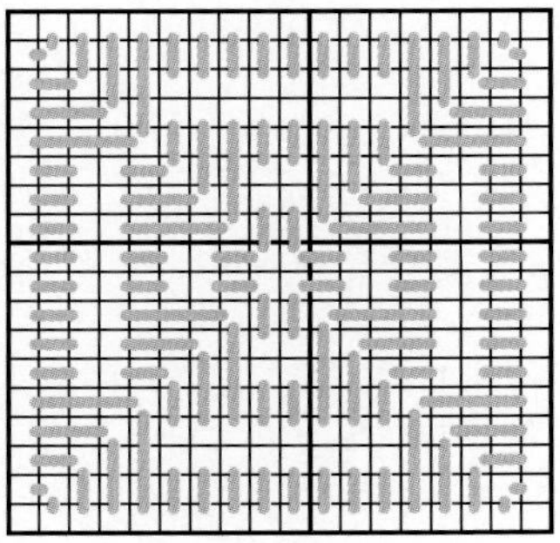

E – End Table Side
(cut 4) 16 x 16 holes

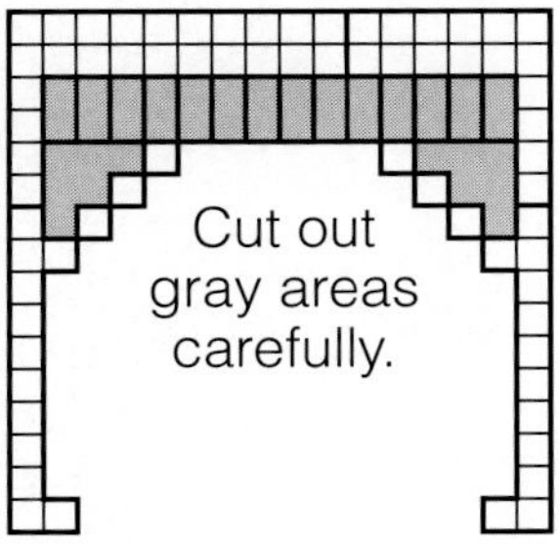

B – Coffee Table End
(cut 2) 12 x 16 holes

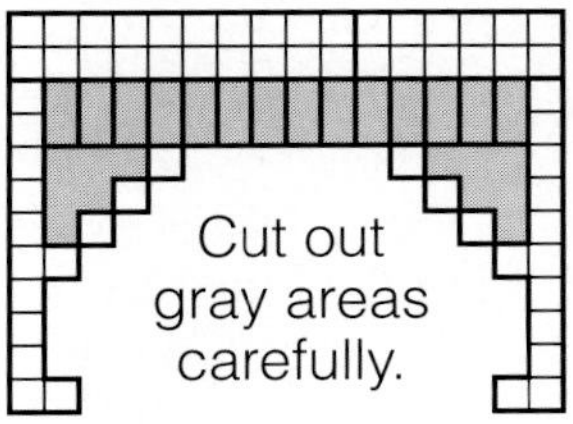

D – Coffee Table Top (cut 1) 18 x 36 holes

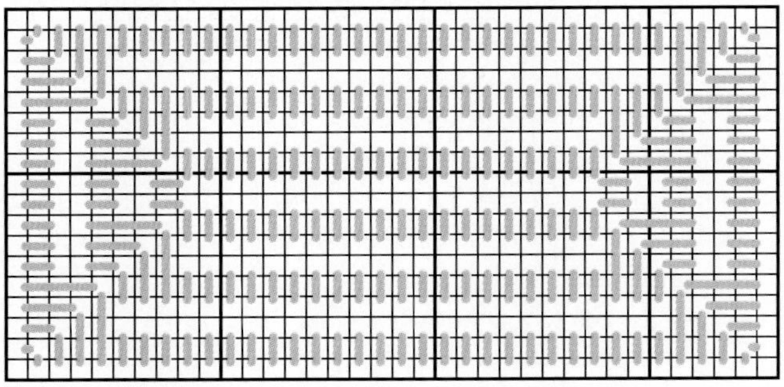

A – Coffee Table Side (cut 2) 12 x 34 holes

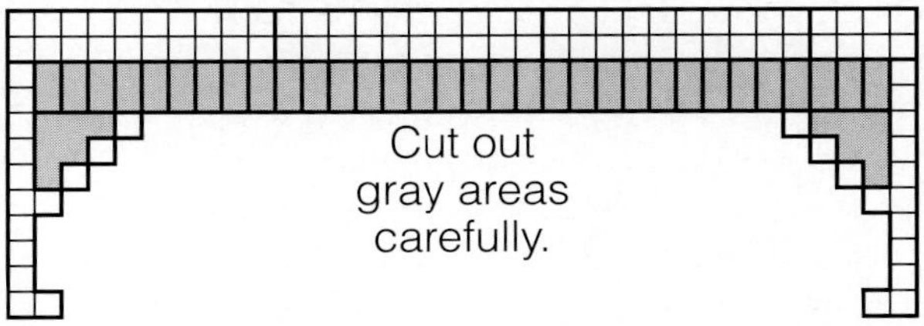

Ready, Set, Stitch!

BASIC INSTRUCTIONS TO GET YOU STARTED

Most plastic canvas stitchers love getting their projects organized before they even step out the door in search of supplies. A few moments of careful planning can make the creation of your project even more fun.

First of all, prepare your work area. You will need a flat surface for cutting and assembly, and you will need a place to store your materials. Good lighting is essential, and a comfortable chair will make your stitching time even more enjoyable.

Do you plan to make one project, or will you be making several of the same item? A materials list appears at the beginning of each pattern. If you plan to make several of the same item, multiply your materials accordingly. Your shopping list is ready.

SUPPLIES

Yarn, canvas, needles, cutters and most other supplies needed to complete the projects in this book are available through craft and needlework stores and mail order catalogs. Other supplies are available at fabric, hardware and discount stores. For mail order information, see page 159.

• Needles & Other Stitching Tools

Blunt-end tapestry needles are used for stitching plastic canvas. Choose a No. 16 needle for stitching 7-count, a No. 18 for stitching 10-count and a No. 24 or 26 for stitching on Aida cloth. A small pair of embroidery scissors for snipping yarn is handy. Try using needle-nosed jewelry pliers for pulling the needle through several thicknesses of canvas and out of tight spots too small for your hand.

• Canvas

Most projects can be made using standard-size sheets of canvas. Standard-size sheets of 7-count (7 holes per inch) are always 70 x 90 holes and are about 10½" x 13½". For larger projects, 7-count canvas also comes in 12" x 18" (80 x 120 holes) and 13½" x 22½" (90 x 150 holes) sheets. Other shapes are available in 7-count, including circles, diamonds, purse forms and ovals.

10-count canvas (10 holes per inch) comes only in standard-size sheets, which vary slightly depending on brand. They are 10½" x 13½" (106 x 136 holes) or 11" x 14" (108 x 138 holes).

Some canvas is soft and pliable, while other canvas is stiffer and more rigid. To prevent canvas from cracking during or after stitching, you'll want to choose pliable canvas for projects that require shaping, like round baskets with curved handles. For easier shaping, warm canvas pieces with a blow-dry hair dryer to soften; dip in cool water to set. If your project is a box or an item that will stand alone, stiffer canvas is more suitable.

Both 7- and 10-count canvas are available in a rainbow of colors. Most designs can be stitched on colored as well as clear canvas. When a pattern does not specify color in the materials list, you can assume clear canvas was used in the photographed model. If you'd like to stitch only a portion of the design, leaving a portion unstitched, use colored canvas to coordinate with yarn colors.

Buy the same brand of canvas for each entire project. Different brands of canvas may differ slightly in the distance between each bar.

• Marking and Counting Tools

To avoid wasting canvas, careful cutting of each piece is important. For some pieces with square corners, you might be comfortable cutting the canvas without marking it beforehand. But for pieces with lots of angles and cutouts, you may want to mark your canvas before cutting.

Always count before you mark and cut. To count holes on the graphs, look for the bolder lines showing each ten holes. These ten-count lines begin in the lower left-hand corner of each graph and are on the graph to make counting easier. To count holes on the canvas, you may use your tapestry needle, a toothpick or a plastic hair roller

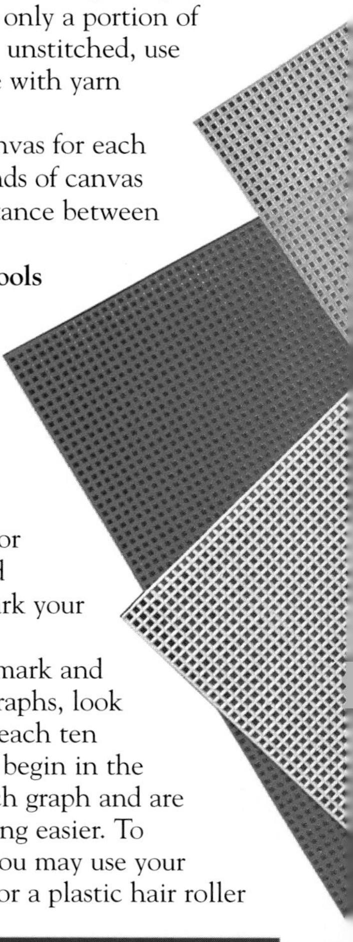

pick. Insert the needle or pick slightly in each hole as you count.

Most stitchers have tried a variety of marking tools and have settled on a favorite, which may be crayon, permanent marker, grease pencil or ball point pen. One of the best marking tools is a fine-point overhead projection marker, available at office supply stores. The ink is dark and easy to see and washes off completely with water. After cutting and before stitching, it's important to remove all marks so they won't stain yarn as you stitch or show through stitches later. Cloth and paper toweling removes grease pencil and crayon marks, as do fabric softener sheets that have already been used in your dryer.

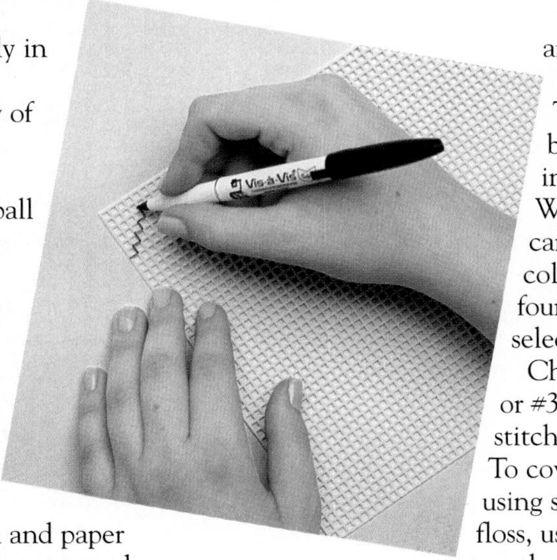

• Cutting Tools

You may find it helpful to have several tools on hand for cutting canvas. When cutting long, straight sections, scissors, craft cutters or kitchen shears are the fastest and easiest to use. For cutting out detailed areas and trimming nubs, you may like using manicure scissors or nail clippers. Many stitchers love using Ultimate Plastic Canvas Cutters, available only from The Needlecraft Shop catalog. If you prefer laying your canvas flat when cutting, try a craft knife and cutting surface – self-healing mats designed for sewing and kitchen cutting boards work well.

• Yarn and Other Stitching Materials

You may choose two-ply nylon plastic canvas yarn (the color numbers of two popular brands are found in the general materials lists and Color Keys) or four-ply worsted-weight yarn for stitching on 7-count canvas. There are about 42 yards per ounce of plastic canvas yarn and 50 yards per ounce of worsted-weight yarn.

Worsted-weight yarn is widely available and comes in wool, acrylic, cotton and blends. If you decide to use worsted-weight yarn, choose 100% acrylic for best coverage. Select worsted-weight yarn by color instead of the color names or numbers found in the Color Keys. Projects stitched with worsted-weight yarn often "fuzz" after use. "Fuzz" can be removed by shaving with a fabric shaver to make your project look new again.

Plastic canvas yarn comes in more than 60 colors and is a favorite of many plastic canvas designers. These yarns "wear" well both while stitching and in the finished product. When buying plastic canvas yarn, shop using the color names or numbers found in the Color Keys, or select colors of your choice.

Choose sport-weight yarn or #3 pearl cotton for stitching on 10-count canvas. To cover 10-count canvas using six-strand embroidery floss, use 12 strands held together. Single and double plies of yarn will also cover 10-count and can be used for embroidery or accent stitching worked over needlepoint stitches – simply separate worsted-weight yarn into 2-ply or plastic canvas yarn into 1-ply. Nylon plastic canvas yarn does not perform as well as knitting worsted when separated and can be frustrating to use, but it is possible. Just use short lengths, separate into single plies and twist each ply slightly.

Embroidery floss or #5 pearl cotton can be used for embroidery, and each can be used for cross stitching on cloth.

Metallic cord is a tightly-woven cord that comes in dozens of glittering colors. Some are solid-color metallics, including gold and silver, and some have colors interwoven with gold or silver threads. If your metallic cord has a white core, the core may be removed for super-easy stitching. To do so, cut a length of cord; grasp center core fibers with tweezers or fingertips and pull. Core slips out easily. Though the sparkly look of metallics will add much to your project, you may substitute contrasting colors of yarn.

Natural and synthetic raffia straw will cover 7-count canvas if flattened before stitching. Use short lengths to prevent splitting, and glue ends to prevent unraveling.

CUTTING CANVAS

Follow all Cutting Instructions, Notes and labels above graphs to cut canvas. Each piece is labeled with a letter of the alphabet. Square-sided pieces are cut according to hole count, and some may not have a graph.

Unlike sewing patterns, graphs are not designed to be used as actual patterns but rather as counting, cutting and stitching guides. Therefore, graphs may not be actual size. Count the holes on the graph (see Marking & Counting Tools on page 156), mark your canvas to match, then cut. The old carpenters' adage – "Measure twice, cut once" – is good advice. Trim off the nubs close to the bar, and trim all corners diagonally.

For large projects, as you cut each piece, it is a good idea to label it with its letter and name. Use sticky labels, or fasten scrap paper notes through the canvas with a twist tie or a quick stitch with a scrap of yarn. To stay organized, you many want to store corresponding pieces together in zip-close bags.

If you want to make several of a favorite design to give as gifts or sell at bazaars, make cutting canvas easier and faster by making a master pattern. From colored canvas, cut out one of each piece required. For duplicates, place the colored canvas on top of clear canvas and cut out. If needed, secure the canvas pieces together with paper fasteners, twist ties or yarn. By using this method, you only have to count from the graphs once.

If you accidentally cut or tear a bar or two on your canvas, don't worry! Boo-boos can usually be repaired in one of several ways: heat the tip of a metal skewer and melt the canvas back together; glue torn bars with a tiny drop of craft glue, super glue or hot glue; or reinforce the torn section with a separate piece of canvas placed at the back of your work. When reinforcing with extra canvas, stitch through both thicknesses.

STITCHING THE CANVAS

Stitching Instructions for each section are found after the Cutting Instructions. First, refer to the illustrations of basic stitches found on page 160 to familiarize yourself with the stitches used. Illustrations will be found near the graphs for pieces worked using special stitches. Follow the numbers on the tiny graph beside the illustration to make each stitch – bring your needle up from the back of the work on odd numbers and down through the front of the work on the even numbers.

Before beginning, read the Stitching Instructions to get an overview of what you'll be doing. You'll find that some pieces are stitched using colors and stitches indicated on graphs, and for other pieces you will be given a color and stitch to use to cover the entire piece.

Cut yarn lengths no longer than 18" to prevent fraying. Thread needle; do not tie a knot in the end. Bring your needle up through the canvas from the back, leaving a short length of yarn on the wrong side of the canvas. As you begin to stitch, work over this short length of yarn. If you are beginning with Continental Stitches, leave a 1" length, but if you are working longer stitches, leave a longer length.

In order for graph colors to contrast well, graph colors may not match yarn colors. For instance, a light yellow may be selected to represent the metallic cord color gold, or a light blue may represent white yarn.

When following a graph showing several colors, you may want to work all the stitches of one color at the same time. Some stitchers prefer to work with several colors at once by threading each on a separate needle and letting the yarn not being used hang on the wrong side of the work. Either way, remember that strands of yarn run across the wrong side of the work may show through the stitches from the front.

As you stitch, try to maintain an even tension on the yarn. Loose stitches will look uneven, and tight stitches will let the canvas show through. If your yarn twists as you work, you may want to let your needle and yarn hang and untwist occasionally.

When you end a section of stitching or finish a thread, weave the yarn through the back side of your last few stitches, then trim it off.

CONSTRUCTION & ASSEMBLY

After all pieces of an item needing assembly are stitched, you will find the order of assembly is listed in the Stitching Instructions and sometimes illustrated in diagrams found with the graphs. For best results, join pieces in the order written. Refer to the Stitch Key and to the directives near the graphs for precise attachments.

FINISHING TIPS

To combat glue strings when using a hot glue gun, practice a swirling motion as you work. After placing the drop of glue on your work, lift the gun slightly and swirl to break the stream of glue, as if you were making an ice cream cone. Have a cup of water handy when gluing. For those times that you'll need to touch the glue, first dip your finger into the water just enough to dampen it. This will minimize the glue sticking to your finger, and it will cool and set the glue more quickly.

To attach beads, use a bit more glue to form a cup around the bead. If too much shows after drying, use a craft knife to trim off excess glue.

Scotchguard® or other fabric protectors may be used on your finished projects. However, avoid using a permanent marker if you plan to use a fabric protector, and be sure to remove all other markings before stitching. Fabric protectors can cause markings to bleed, staining yarn.

PROBLEMS

Sometimes even the most experienced needlecrafters can find themselves having trouble following instructions. If you have difficulty completing your project, write to:

Fashion Doll Dream Home Editors
The Needlecraft Shop
23 Old Pecan Road
Big Sandy, Texas 75755

For supplies, first shop your local craft and needlework stores. If you are unable to find the supplies you need, write to the address below for a free catalog. The Needlecraft Shop *carries plastic canvas in a variety of shapes, sizes and colors, 65 colors of plastic canvas yarn and a large selection of pattern books.*

the Needlecraft Shop™

23 Old Pecan Road
Big Sandy, Texas 75755
(903) 636-4000

Stitches

BACKSTITCH
is usually used as an embroidery stitch to outline or add detail. Stitches can be any length and go in any direction.

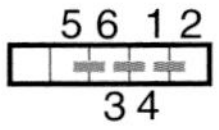

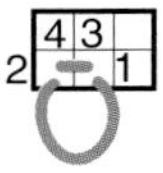

CONTINENTAL STITCH
can be used to stitch designs or fill in background areas.

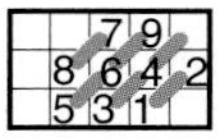

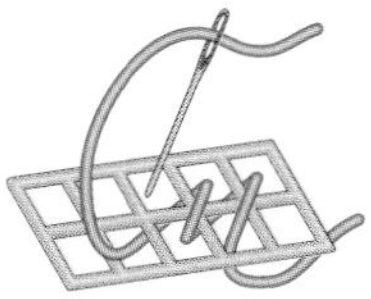

CROSS STITCH
can be used as a needlepoint stitch or as an embroidery stitch stitched over background stitches with contrasting yarn or floss.

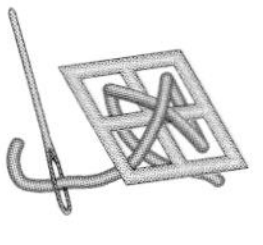

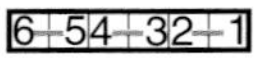

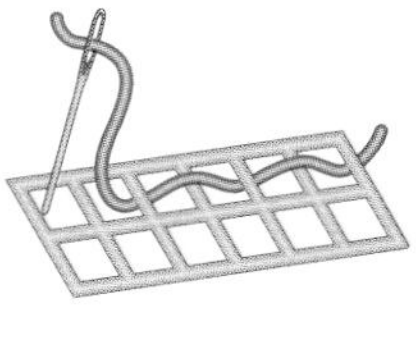

FRENCH KNOT
is usually used as an embroidery stitch to add detail. Can be made in one hole or over a bar. If dot on graph is in hole as shown, come up and go down with needle in same hole. If dot is across a bar, come up in one hole and go down one hole over.

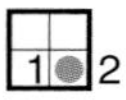

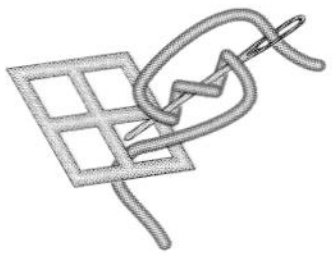

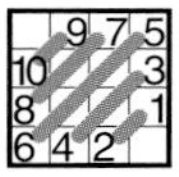

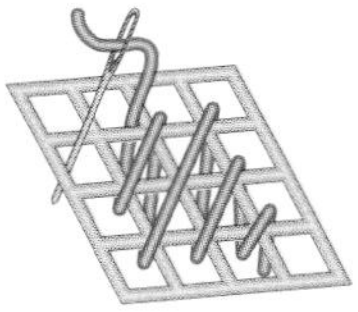

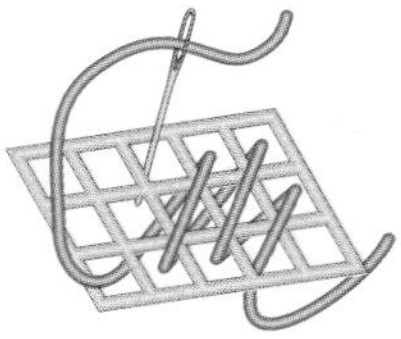

LAZY DAISY STITCH
is usually used as an embroidery stitch to add detail. Can be any length and go in any direction. Come up and go down in same hole, leaving loop. Come up in another hole for top of stitch, put needle through loop and go down in same hole.

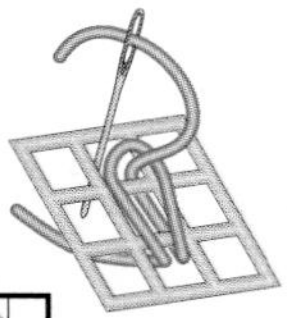

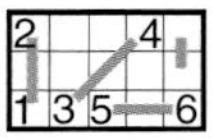

LONG STITCH
is a horizontal or vertical stitch used to stitch designs or fill in background areas. Can be stitched over two or more bars.

MODIFIED TURKEY WORK STITCH
is used to fill in background areas or as an embroidery stitch to add a loopy or fringed texture. Stitch over one bar leaving a loop, then stitch over the same bar to anchor the loop.

OVERCAST
is used to finish edges. Stitch two or three times in corners for complete coverage.

RUNNING STITCH
is used as a straight line stitch to add detail. Stitches can be any length and go in any direction.

SCOTCH STITCH
is used to fill in background areas. Stitches cover a square area over three or more bars.

SLANTED GOBELIN STITCH
can be used to stitch designs or fill in background areas. Can be stitched over two or more bars in vertical or horizontal rows.

STRAIGHT STITCH
is usually used as an embroidery stitch to add detail. Stitches can be any length and can go in any direction. Looks like Backstitch except stitches do not touch.

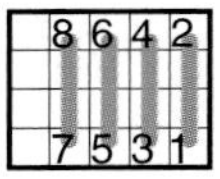

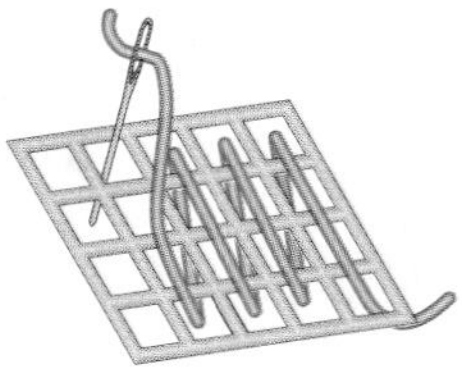

WHIPSTITCH
is used to join two or more pieces together.

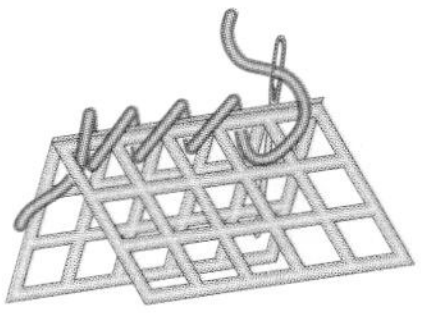